JUDY THOMPSON

How Do You Say?
The Sound is in the Color

DICTIONARY
Expressions • Pronunciation • Spelling
FOR ENGLISH FLUENCY

*Never doubt that a small group of thoughtful,
committed citizens can change the world.
Indeed it's the only thing that ever has.*

MARGARET MEAD

Copyright © 2021 Judy Thompson

ALSO BY JUDY THOMPSON

English is Stupid, Students are Not©

English Phonetic Alphabet Workbook©

Speaking Made Simple© Course Curriculum

Backpacker's Guide to Teaching English© Series

ONLINE COURSES

The Effective Communicator

Opinions Matter

on WizTango.com

JUDY THOMPSON

How Do You Say?

suite · meet · toe · know · more · door · head · said · city · pretty · turn · learn · suit · boot

The Sound is in the Color

DICTIONARY

Expressions · Pronunciation · Spelling
FOR ENGLISH FLUENCY

All rights reserved. This work is the intellectual property of the author. This book contains material protected under International and Federal Copyright Laws and Treaties. Any unauthorized reprint or use of this material is prohibited. No part of this publication may be reproduced, distributed, or transmitted in any form or by any means, including photocopying, recording, or other electronic or mechanical methods, without the prior written permission of the author, except in the case of brief quotations embodied in critical reviews and certain other noncommercial uses permitted by copyright law.

Thompson Language Center
Niagara Falls, Canada

Copyright © 2012, 2013, 2018, 2021 by Judy Thompson
Copyright © 2001 original idea by Judy Thompson
(English is Stupid is a registered trademark.)

Originally published as **Grass is Black – Pronunciation Dictionary**
Published by Thompson Language Center, 2013

Developed in Canada

Fourth Edition

ISBN: 978-0-9812058-3-0

CIP available upon request.

Every effort has been made to trace ownership of all copyrighted material and to secure permission from copyright holders. In the event of any question arising as to the use of any material, we would be pleased to make the necessary corrections in future printings.

Edited by: Noreen Brigden
Text design by: Noreen Brigden
Cover design by: McCorkindale Advertising & Design
Layout and Production by: McCorkindale Advertising & Design

Printed in USA (subject to change)

Acknowledgments

For their help creating this dictionary, many thanks to:

First draft team, initial definitions:
David Lee, Mississauga; Sybil Jones, Toronto; Carol Adams, Ottawa;
Des and Pat Hall, Ottawa; Rana Helmy, Oakville; Shari White, London;
Catherine Savard, Ottawa; Geraldine and Sofia Albanez, Hamilton;
Karen Lee, Mississauga; Marlene Tash, Mississauga; Mary Wuergler, Barrie;
Morgan Cooper, Port Colborne; Mike Clancy, Hamilton;
Edward J. Richard, Mississauga

Second draft, format and flesh-out at Benmiller Inn in Goderich:
Valeeta Blancher-Bennett, London; Teresa Kinney, London;
Marjorie Schoemaker, Stratford; Jane Eligh-Feryn, Stratford;
Shari White, London; Catherine Savard, Ottawa; Carol Adams, Ottawa;
Morgan Cooper, Port Colborne; Jennifer Jones, London;
Tammie McIntosh, London; Karen Lee, Mississauga;
Sharon Lam, London; Lindsay Doyle, Caledon; Ayden Young, Ottawa

Third draft team:
Carol Adams, Ottawa; Jane Eligh-Feryn, Stratford;
Morgan Cooper, Port Colborne; Ayden Young, Ottawa

First edit of the entire dictionary:
Beth Ellis, Brampton

Final edit team:
Carol Adams, Ottawa; Valeeta Blancher-Bennett, London;
Teresa Kinney, London; Marjorie Schoemaker, Stratford;
Jane Eligh-Feryn, Stratford; Monica Long, Caledon; Ayden Young, Ottawa

Standardized format: Morgan Cooper, Port Colborne

Design: Noreen Brigden

John Denison, Angela Larsen, Jennifer MacAulay, Kim Saniga,
Judith Lott, Gillian Stead, Sue Breen and Chris McCorkindale
And to:
The Ryans, Coopers,
Brennan, Ayden and Rick ...just because

Table of Contents

Introduction 8
About This Book... 10
Important Notes 11
Thompson Vowel Chart 12
How This Book Works 13
Abbreviations 14
Legend 15
Index 16
Chapter 1: /ay/ is Gray 27
Chapter 2: /a/ is Black 53
Chapter 3: /ɛy/ is Green 73
Chapter 4: /e/ is Red 95
Chapter 5: /ɪy/ is White 117
Chapter 6: /i/ is Pink 135
Chapter 7: /ow/ is Gold 155
Chapter 8: /o/ is Olive 171
Chapter 9: /uw/ is Blue 191
Chapter 10: /u/ is Mustard 205
Chapter 11: /^/ is Wood 225
Chapter 12: /oy/ is Turquoise 233
Chapter 13: /aw/ is Brown 239
R Vowels
Chapter 14: /ɛr/ is Purple 249
Chapter 15: /ar/ is Charcoal 263
Chapter 16: /or/ is Orange 273
Thompson Language Center Product List............. 288

Introduction

For all the teachers who have embraced the
English Phonetic Alphabet (EPA)
and especially for those who haven't

I started teaching ESL at a small school on the second floor of a community center in Brampton, Ontario. As a brand new teacher, I revered my seasoned co-workers who were creative, capable and compassionate. I felt lucky to work every day with people like Lydia Aiello, Monica Long and Beth Ellis. Although I soon developed my own ideas about how pronunciation should be taught and my career took me away from that cozy school in Brampton, I stayed in touch with those remarkable teachers who taught me so much.

After *English is Stupid, Students are Not* © was released in 2009, I came to know a wider community of extraordinary English Language teachers. In 2010, the educators who had embraced *English is Stupid* asked me to write a workbook of classroom exercises. I said yes, and then quickly realized I had bitten off more than I could chew. Sitting at my computer, overwhelmed with the task ahead, I picked up the phone and asked Lydia, Monica and Beth for help. Although I hadn't taught with them for years, they showed up and sat around my kitchen table drinking coffee, talking, laughing and banging off *Mystery Match* word puzzles like there was no tomorrow. More than the exercises they'd generated, their moral support carried me over a hump, and the **English Phonetic Alphabet Workbook** was completed on time for the 2011 Teachers of English as a Second Language (TESL) Ontario Conference.

The **How Do You Say?** Sound Dictionary was a pet project I'd had on the back burner for over a decade. No one (except Samuel Johnson) can write a dictionary by themselves. I began to enroll my new community of ESL teachers for help. This is how I came to be sitting in a boardroom at the beautiful Benmiller Inn in Goderich, Ontario,

Ontario, on July 28, 2012, with a room full of strangers creating a ground-breaking dictionary from a pile of downloaded word lists. These volunteers had travelled from across the province to support a project they believed in. They worked diligently until 6:00 pm on Saturday, and I thought they were done for the day. I was wrong. The teachers returned to the boardroom after dinner toting chocolate, and they continued to work. Sometime after 11:00 that night, I realized these women weren't strangers at all and that I had always known them. They were every ESL teacher I had ever met.

My name is on the cover, but **How Do You Say?** would not exist without the tireless support of the teachers who helped create it. I respectfully dedicate the world's first sound dictionary to English teachers everywhere and lovingly acknowledge the difference they make.

Teacher Judy

About this Book

The gulf between written and spoken English is wide. Native English-speaking children have difficulty learning to read, and non-native English learners can often read well but don't speak English confidently. The problem is the alphabet. There simply isn't enough information in the crazy alphabet to spell English from hearing it or speak English from reading it. Until now!

English is Stupid, Students are Not was released in 2009 as a guide for all levels of English as a Second Language (ESL) students. *English is Stupid* showcases a simple account of how speaking works differently than writing and provides a six-step program to train people to converse confidently. *How Do You Say?* does more. Based on the *Thompson Vowel Chart* from *English is Stupid*, students can easily determine the color associated with words they hear and therefore the **pronunciation**. *How Do You Say?* is also a writing resource to look up the **spelling** of words according to how they sound. Last but not least *How Do You Say?* is a dictionary of **expressions**. English is abstract. Red chair, red sweater and red chair are things colored red. Red tape, red eye and red letter are something else entirely (bureaucracy, overnight flight and good news). *How Do You Say?* contains thousands of expressions sourced by the color of their main words.

In 2009, the 2,000 most common English words were divided into categories by main vowel sound, and the resulting word lists were arranged alphabetically. With the help of a team of ESL teachers from across Ontario, simple definitions were generated for each entry. In 2012, a group of volunteers (some new and some veterans) gathered at the Benmiller Inn in Ontario to standardize the look of each chapter, add homonyms, and flesh out the text with expressions. More volunteers were added to the team as editors, and the world's first Sound Dictionary was finished and printed as *Grass is Black* in October 2012. Only the title was changed to **How Do You Say?** in 2018.

The concept of organizing an English dictionary by sound and color is simple, effective and revolutionary.

Important Notes:

Overriding Pronunciation Rules

Words can begin with vowel sounds, but all interior syllables begin with consonants sounds – regardless of spelling. This is physiologically how human beings speak. For more information on this phenomenon, see *English is Stupid, Students are Not*, Chapter Two on *Word Stress* and Chapter Four on *Linking*.

General American (GA) Accent

Due to the wide range of English accents, good pronunciation teachers qualify exactly which accent they are teaching. This dictionary was created by Canadians from Southern Ontario whose accent is known as the General American (GA) accent. GA is the neutral North American accent sought for Hollywood movies, sitcoms and news broadcasts... Foreign actors trained to speak in the performing arts in North America study the accent featured in this dictionary.

This text may contain typos and omissions.
Please contact Thompson Language Center
with observations and suggestions for the next edition.
It is our intention to generate a living digital
document, and we welcome your input.

Thompson Vowel Chart

Color Word	Color	EPA	Phonetic Spelling	Example	Phonetic with 'f'
gray		/Ay/	/grAy/	made	face
black		/a/	/blak/	mad	fat
green		/Ey/	/grEyn/	Pete	feel
red		/e/	/red/	pet	fell
white		/Iy/	/wIyt/	bite	file
pink		/i/	/piNgk/	bit	fill
gold		/Ow/	/gOwld/	note	fold
olive		/o/	/oliv/	not	fall
blue		/Uw/	/blUw/	cute	food
mustard		/u/	/mustErd/	cut	fun
wood		/^/	/w^d/	good	full
turquoise		/Oy/	/tErkOyz/	boy	foil
brown		/Aw/	/brAwn/	cow	found
purple		/Er/	/pErpul/	girl	first
charcoal		/Ar/	/chArkOwl/	car	far
orange		/Or/	/Orenj/	door	four

© English is Stupid, Students are Not — Exercise Manual

How This Book Works

There are over a million words in English, and each one belongs to one of sixteen families based on their main vowel sound. For more information, see *English is Stupid, Students are Not* – the complete guide to spoken English.

There are sixteen vowel sounds in General American English, and each of these vowel sounds is featured in the names of sixteen ordinary colors. Students no longer have to rely on crazy English spelling to try to figure out how to pronounce English because they remember the sounds of words by color. For example, *head*, *said*, *friend* and *guess* are all **Red** words, regardless of spelling because they share the same main vowel sound Short e or /e/.

Long-held rules like *i before e except after c* and *when two vowels go walking...* simply aren't true. English spelling doesn't make sense. Stay calm. It's all fixed. Learners ***hear the main vowel sound*** and when they know the colors, can look up the spelling in the color chapter. The same /e/ sound is in *head*, *said*, *friend*, and *guess* above. Their spelling is found in the **Red** section of ***How Do You Say?***. The spelling of the 2,000 most common words in English are found in the pages of ***How Do You Say?*** by using the main vowel sound in each word.

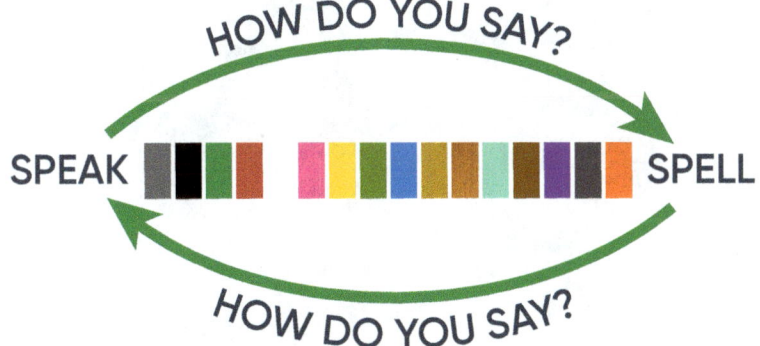

Abbreviations

abbr	abbreviation
adj	adjective
adv	adverb
cont	contraction
interj	interjection
noun	noun
pr	proper
prep	preposition
pron	pronoun
proverb	proverb
verb	verb
CAN	Canada
NA	North America
UK	United Kingdom
USA	United States of America

Legend

1. entry
2. homonym
3. phonetic spelling
4. inflections
5. function
6. definitions
7. numbers for multiple meanings of a single entry
8. sample sentence
9. change function is a circle bullet •
10. collocations/expressions
11. explanation
12. bold stressed syllable
13. schwa

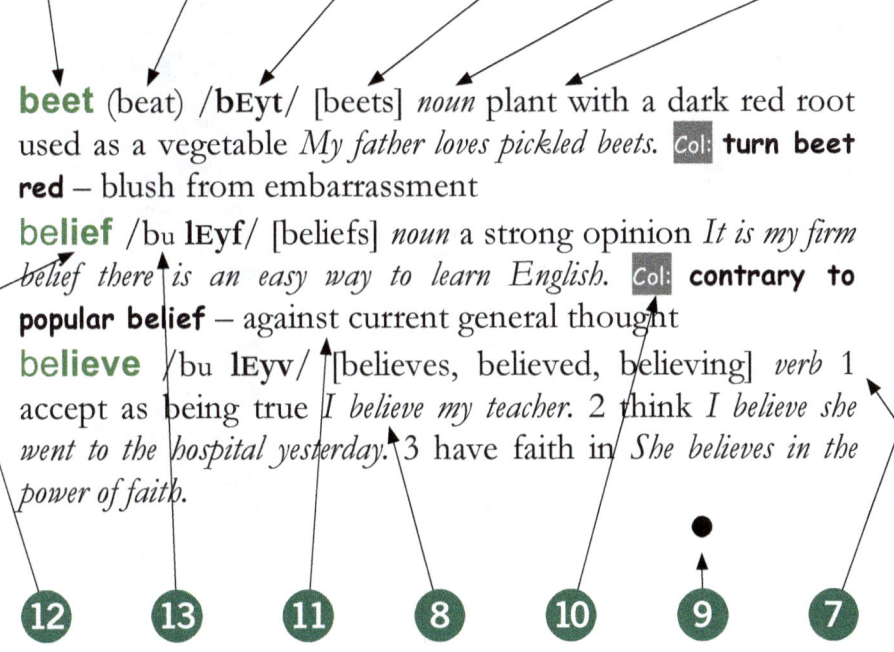

beet (beat) /bEyt/ [beets] *noun* plant with a dark red root used as a vegetable *My father loves pickled beets.* Col: **turn beet red** – blush from embarrassment

belief /bu lEyf/ [beliefs] *noun* a strong opinion *It is my firm belief there is an easy way to learn English.* Col: **contrary to popular belief** – against current general thought

believe /bu lEyv/ [believes, believed, believing] *verb* 1 accept as being true *I believe my teacher.* 2 think *I believe she went to the hospital yesterday.* 3 have faith in *She believes in the power of faith.*

Index

a /a/
A, a (eh) /**Ay**/
A.M. /**Ay** em/
abdomen /**ab** du mun/
about /u b**Aw**t/
above /u **buv**/
account /u k**Aw**nt/
ace /**Ays**/
ache /**Ayk**/
achieve /u Ch**Eyv**/
acid /**a** sud/
acquire /u kw**I** y**Er**/
across /u **kros**/
act /**akt**/
addition /u **di** Shun/
ade (aid, aide) /**Ayd**/
adjustment /u **jus** munt/
adult /**a** dult/
adult /u **dult**/
adulterant /u **dul** tu runt/
advertise /ad v**Er** t**I**yz/
advertisement /ad v**Er** tuz munt/
Africa /**a** fru ku/
after /**af** d**Er**/
again /u g**Ayn**/
against /u g**Aynst**/
age /**Ayj**/
agree /u gr**Ey**/
aid (aide, ade) /**Ayd**/
aide (aid, aid) /**Ayd**/
AIDS /**Aydz**/
ain't /**Aynt**/
air (ere, heir) /**Ayr**/
aisle (I'll, isle) /**Iyl**/
alert /u l**Ert**/
all (awl) /**ol**/
allergic /u l**Er** jik/
allow /u l**Aw**/
alphabet /**al** fu bet/
although /**al** Thow/
aluminum /u l**Uw** mu num/
always /**ol** wuz/
am /**am**/
America /u **me** ri ku/
among /u **muNg**/
amount /u m**Awnt**/
amuse /u my**Uwz**/
an /**an**/
and /**and**/
angle /**aN** gul/
angry /**aN** gr**Ey**/
animal /**a** nu mul/
announce /u n**Awns**/
announcement /u n**Awns** munt/
answer /**an** s**Er**/
ant (aunt) /**ant**/
any /**e** n**Ey**/
apartment /u p**Art** munt/
apostrophe /u **po** stru f**Ey**/

appeal /u p**Eyl**/
appear /u p**Eyr**/
apple /**a** pul/
apply /u pl**Iy**/
appreciate /u pr**Ey** ShE y**Ayt**/
approve /u pr**Uwv**/
apricot /**a** pru kot/
April /**Ay** prul/
arc /**Ark**/
arch /**ArCh**/
architect /**Ar** ku tekt/
Arctic /**Ar** dik/
are (R) /**Ar**/
argue /**Ar** gy**Uw**/
arm /**Arm**/
army /**Ar** m**Ey**/
around /u r**Awnd**/
art /**Art**/
artery /**Ar** du r**Ey**/
as /**az**/
Asia /**Ay** Zhu/
ask /**ask**/
ass /**as**/
asthma /**az** mu/
at /**at**/
ate (eight) /**Ayt**/
attack /u **tak**/
attention /u **ten** Shun/
attraction /u **trak** Shun/
audio /**o** d**Ey** y**Ow**/
August /**o** gust/
aunt (ant) /**ant**/
author /**o** Th**Er**/
authority /u **THOr** u d**Ey**/
auto /**o** d**Ow**/
automatic /**o** du **ma** dik/
awake /u w**Ayk**/
away /u w**Ay**/
awl (all) /**ol**/
aye (eye, I) /**Iy**/

B (be, bee) /**bEy**/
baby /**bAy** b**Ey**/
back /**bak**/
bacon /**bAy** kun/
bad /**bad**/
bag /**bag**/
balance /**ba** luns/
ball /**bol**/
balloon /bu l**Uwn**/
baloney (bologna) /bu l**Ow** n**Ey**/
banana /bu **na** nu/
band /**band**/
bar /**bAr**/
barbecue /**bAr** bu ky**Uw**/
barber /**bAr** b**Er**/
bark /**bArk**/
barn /**bArn**/

base (bass) /**bAys**/
basket /**bas** get/
bath /**baTH**/
bazaar (bizarre) /bu **zAr**/
be (B, bee) /**bEy**/
bean, (been) /**bEyn**/
beat, (beet) /**bEyt**/
beautiful /**bEyUw** du ful/
because /b**Ey** kuz/
bed /**bed**/
bee (B, be) /**bEy**/
beef /**bEyf**/
been (bean) /**bEyn**/
been /**bin**/
beet (beat) /**bEyt**/
before /bu **fOr**/
behavior /b**Ey** h**Ay** vy**Er**/
belief /bu l**Eyf**/
believe /bu l**Eyv**/
bell /**bel**/
below /bu **low**/
bent /**bent**/
berry /**be** r**Ey**/
berth (birth) /**bErTH**/
best /**best**/
better /**be** d**Er**/
between /bu tw**Eyn**/
big /**big**/
bike /**bIyk**/
bird /**bErd**/
birth (berth) /**bErTH**/
birthday /**bErTH** d**Ay**/
bit /**bit**/
bitch /**biCh**/
bite (byte) /**bIyt**/
bitter /**bi** d**Er**/
bizarre (bazaar) /bu **zAr**/
black /**blak**/
bladder /**bla** d**Er**/
blade /**blAyd**/
blanket /**blaNg** kut/
blister /**bli** sd**Er**/
blood /**blud**/
blouse /**blAwz**/or /**blAws**/
blue /**blUw**/
blush /**bluSh**/
boar (bore) /**bOr**/
board (bored) /**bOrd**/
boat /**bowt**/
body /**bo** d**Ey**/
boil /**bO** yul/
boiler /**bOy** l**Er**/
boisterous /**bOy** strus/
bologna (baloney) /bu **lOw** n**Ey**/
bone /**bOwn**/
book /**b^k**/
boot /**bUwt**/
border /**bOr** d**Er**/
bored (board) /**bOrd**/

INDEX

boring /bO riNg/
born /bOrn/
borrow /bO rOw/
both /bOwTH/
bottle /bo dul/
bough (bow) /bAw/
bought /bot/
bounce /bAwns/
boundary /bAwn drEy/
bow (bough) /bAw/
bow /bOw/
box /boks/
boy (buoy) /bOy/
brain /brAyn/
brake (break) /brAyk/
branch /branCh/
brass /bras/
bread /bred/
break (brake) /brAyk/
breath /breTH/
breathe /brEyTH/
brick /brik/
bridge /brij/
bright /brIyt/
bring /briNg/
broccoli /bro ku lEy/
broil /brO yul/
broiler /brOy lEr/
broke /brOwk/
broken /brOw kun/
broom /brUwm/
brother /bruThEr/
brown /brAwn/
bruise /brUwz/
brush /bruSh/
bucket /bu kut/
buddy /bu dEy/
buffalo /bu fu lOw/
buffet /bu fAy/
build /bild/
bulb /bulb/
bull /b^l/
buoy (boy) /bOy/
burglar /bEr glEr/
burn /bErn/
burst /bErst/
bus /bus/
business /biz nus/
busy /bi zEy/
but (butt) /but/
butt (but) /but/
butter /bu dEr/
button /bu tun/
buy (by, bye) /bIy/
by (buy, bye) /bIy/
bye (buy, by) /bIy/
byte (bite) /bIyt/

C (sea, see) /sEy/

cabbage /ka buj/
café /kafAy/
cake /kAyk/
calf /kaf/
calendar /ka lu dEr/
call /kol/
came /kAym/
camera /kam ru/
can /kan/
Canada /ka nu du/
candidate /kan du dAyt/
cantaloupe /kan tu lOwp/
canvas /kan vus/
capote /ku pOw dEy/
car /kAr/
card /kArd/
care /kAyr/
carnival /kAr nu vul/
carpenter /kAr pen tEr/
carriage /ke rij/
carry /ke rEy/
cart /kArt/
carton /kAr tun/
cartoon /kAr tUwn/
cartridge /kAr truj/
cash /kaSh/
cat /kat/
caught (cot) /kot/
cauliflower /ko lEy flA wEr/
celery /sel rEy/
cent (scent, sent) /sent/
center, center /sen tEr/
certain /sEr tun/
certainly /sEr tun lEy/
certify /sEr du fIy/
cha /Chu/
chalk /Chok/
chance /Chans/
change /ChAynj/
chaos /kA yos/
charcoal /ChAr kOwl/
chauffeur /ShOw fEr/
cheap /ChEyp/
check /Chek/
cheek /ChEyk/
cheese /ChEyz/
chemical /ke mu kul/
cher /ChEr/
cherry /Che rEy/
chest /Chest/
chief /ChEyf/
child /ChIyld/
children /Chil drun/
chili (chilly) /Chi lEy/
chilly (chili) /Chi lEy/
chin /Chin/
China /ChIy nu/
choir /kwI yEr/
choose /ChUwz/

chord (cord) /kOrd/
chorus /kO rus/
chose /ChOwz/
church /ChErCh/
circle /sEr kul/
circus /sEr kus/
city /si dEy/
clear /klEyr/
clock /klok/
close /klOwz/ /klOws/
cloth /kloTH/
clothes (close) /klOwz/
cloud /klAwd/
clown /klAwn/
club /klub/
clue /klUw/
coal /kOwl/
coarse (course) /kOrs/
coast /kOwst/
coat /kOwt/
cocoa /kOw kOw/
coconut /kOw ku nut/
coffee /kofEy/
coil /kO yul/
coin /kOyn/
coke /kOwk/
cold /kOwld/
college /ko luj/
collocation /ko lu kAy Shun/
cologne /ku lOwn/
colon /kOw lun/
colonel (kernel) /kEr nul/
color /ku lEr/
column /ko lum/
comb /kOwm/
come /kum/
comedy /ko mu dEy/
comfort /kum fErt/
comma /ko mu/
committee /ku mi dEy/
common /ko mun/
company /kum pu nEy/
competition /com pu ti Shun/
complete /kum plEyt/
computer /kum pyUw dEr/
concern /kun sErn/
condition /kun di Shun/
connection /ku nek Shun/
conscious /kon Shus/
construction /kun struk Shun/
contest /kon test/
contest /kun test/
contiguous /kun tig yU wus/
continent /kon tu nunt/
control /kun trOwl/
convert /kun vErt/
cook /k^k/
cookie /k^ kEy/
cool /kUwl/

copy /ko pEy/
cord (chord) /kOrd/
cork /kOrk/
corn /kOrn/
corner /kOr nEr/
cost /kost/
cot (caught) /kot/
cotton /ko tun/
cough /kof/
could /k^d/
coulda /k^ du/
count /kAwnt/
countable /kAw tu bul/
counter /kAw tEr/
country /kun trEy/
coupon /kUw pon/
course (coarse) /kOrs/
court /kOrt/
cousin /ku zun/
cover /ku vEr/
cow /kAw/
crab /krab/
crack /krak/
cream /krEym/
credit /kre dut/
crime /krIym/
cruel /krUwl/
crush /kruSh/
cry /krIy/
Cuba /kyUw bu/
cube /kyUwb/
cucumber /kyUw kum bEr/
cue (Q, queue) /kyUw/
culture /kul ChEr/
cup /kup/
curl /kErl/
current /kE runt/
curse /kErs/
cursor /kEr sEr/
curtain /kEr tun/
curve /kErv/
curvy /kEr vEy/
cushion /k^ Shun/
cut /kut/
cute /kyUwt/

D /dEy/
Dad /dad/
dam (damn) /dam/
damage /da muj/
damn (dam) /dam/
danger /dAyn jEr/
dark /dArk/
darling /dAr liNg/
darn /dArn/
date /dAyt/
daughter /do dEr/
day /dAy/

dead /ded/
dear (deer) /dEyr/
death /deTH/
debt /det/
December /du sem bEr/
decision /du si Zhun/
deck /dek/
deep /dEyp/
deer (dear) /dEyr/
degree /du grEy/
delete /du lEyt/
delicate /de lu kut/
deodorant /dEy Ow du runt/
depend /du pend/
deposit /du po zit/
desert (dessert) /du zErt/
desert /de sErt/
deserter /du zEr dEr/
design /du zIyn/
desire /du zI yEr/
desk /desk/
dessert /du zErt/
destroy /du strOy/
destruction /du struk Shun/
detail /dEy tAyl/
detergent /du tEr junt/
develop /du ve lup/
devote /du vOwt/
dew (due, do) /dUw/
dictionary /dik Shu ne rEy/
did /did/
different /dif runt/
digestion /du jes jun/
dime /dIym/
direction /dur ek Shun/
dirt /dErt/
dirty /dErd Ey/
discovery /du sku vE rEy/
discussion /du sgu Shun/
disease /du zEyz/
disgust /du sgust/
distance /dis duns/
divide /du vIyd/
division /du vi Zhun/
divorce /du vOrs/
do (dew, due) /dUw/
doctor /dok dEr/
does /duz/
dog /dog/
dollar /do lEr/
dome /dOwm/
don't /dOwnt/
done /dun/
donno /du nOw/
donut (doughnut) /dOw nut/
door /dOr/
double /du bul/
doubt /dAwt/
dougnut (donut) /dOw nut/

down /dAwn/
draw /dro/
drawer /drOr/
dream /drEym/
dress /dres/
drink /driNgk/
drive /drIyv/
drop /drop/
drowsy /drAw zEy/
drought /drAwt/
drown /drAwn/
drum /drum/
dry /drIy/
duck /duk/
due (dew, do) /dUw/
duel /dU wul/
dust /dust/

E /Ey/
early /Er lEy/
earn (urn) /Ern/
earth /ErTH/
east /Eyst/
eat /Eyt/
echo /e kOw/
ecology /Ey ko lu gEy/
economy /Ey ko nu mEy/
edge /ej/
education /e ju kAy Shun/
effect /u fekt/
egg /eg/
eh (A) /Ay/
eight (ate) /Ayt/
elastic /Ey la stik/
electric /u lek trik/
elephant /e lu funt/
eleven /u le vun/
embark /em bArk/
emotion /Ey mOw Shun/
emotional /Ey mOw Shu nul/
employ /em plOy/
employment /em plOy munt/
end /end/
engine /en jun/
engineer /en jun Eyr/
English /iNg lish/
enjoy /en jOy/
enough /u nuf/
equal /Ey kwul/
eraser /Ey rAy sEr/
err (air, heir) /Ayr/
error /e rEr/
essay /e sAy/
Europe /yE rup/
even /Ey vun/
event /u vent/
ever /e vEr/
every /ev rEy/

INDEX

ewe (U, you) /yUw/
ex (X) /eks/
example /eg zam pul/
exchange /eks ChAynj/
excite /ek sIyt/
existence /eg zi stuns/
exit /ek sut/ or /eg zit/
expansion /eks pan Shun/
expert /eks pErt/
expire /ek spI yEr/
export /eks pOrt/
eye (aye, I) /Iy/

F /ef/
face /fAys/
fair (fare) /fAyr/
fall /fol/
false /fols/
family /fam lEy/
far /fAr/
fare (fiair) /fAyr/
farm /fArm/
farmer /fAr mEr/
fart /fArt/
fast /fast/
fat /fat/
father /fo ThEr/
fear /fEyr/
feather /fe ThEr/
February /fe byU we rEy/
feeble /fEy bul/
feed /fEyd/
feel /Eyl/
feet /fEyt/
female /fEy mAyl/
fertile /fEr dul/
few /fyUw/
fiction /fik Shun/
field /fEyld/
fight /flyt/
fill /fil/
fine /flyn/
finger /fiN gEr/
fire /fI yEr/
first /fErst/
fish /fiSh/
five /flyv/
fix /fiks/
flag /flag/
flame /flAym/
flamingo /flu miN gOw/
flat /flat/
flew (flu, flue) /flUw/
flight /fIIyt/
flipper /fli pEr/
floor /flOr/
florist /flO rust/
floss /flos/

flour (flowers) /flA wEr/
flower (flour) /flA wEr/
flu (flew, flue) /flUw/
flue (flew, flu) /flUw/
focus /fOw kus/
foil /fO yul/
fold /fOwld/
follow /fo low/
food /fUwd/
fool /fUwl/
foot /f^t/
football /f^t bol/
footing /f^ diNg/
for (fore , four) /fOr/
force /fOrs/
fore (for, four) /fOr/
foreign /fO run/
fork /fOrk/
form /fOrm/
former /fOr mEr/
formula /fOrm yu lu/
fortune /fOr Chun/
forward /fOr wErd/
foul (fowl) /fAwl/
found /fAwnd/
fountain /fAwn tun/
four (for, fore) /fOr/
fowl (foul) /fAwl/
fox /foks/
fragile /fra jul/
free /frEy/
freeze /frEyz/
frequent /frEy kwunt/
Friday /frIy dAy/
friend /frend/
from /frum/
front /frunt/
frost /frost/
frown /frAwn/
froze /frOwz/
frozen /frOw zun/
fruit /frUwt/
fry /frIy/
fuck /fuk/
fudge /fuj/
fuel /fyU wul/
full /f^l/
fun /fun/
funny /fu nEy/
furniture /fEr nu ChEr/
further /fEr ThEr/
fuse /fyUwz/
future /fyUw ChEr/

G (gee) /jEy/
game /gAym/
garbage /gAr buj/
garden /gAr dun/

garlic /gAr luk/
gas /gas/
gave /gAyv/
gee (G) /jEy/
general /je nu rul/
genre /jon ru/
get /get/
ghost /gOwst/
giant /jI yunt/
gift /gift/
gimme /gi mEy/
girl /gErl/
give /giv/
glass /glas/
glasses /gla siz/
globe /glOwb/
glue /glUw/
go /gOw/
goat /gOwt/
God /god/
gold /gOwld/
golden /gOwl dun/
golf /golf/
gonna /g^ nu/
good /g^d/
goose /gUws/
goosebumps /gUws bumps/
gorgeous /gOr jus/
got /got/
gotta /go du/
government /gu vEr munt/
gown /gAwn/
grain /grAyn/
grandma /gra mu/
grape /grAyp/
grass /grass/
grate (great) /grAyt/
gravel /gra vul/
gray (grey) /grAy/
great,(grate) /grAyt/
green /grEyn/
grip /grip/
groin /grOyn/
ground /grAwnd/
group /grUwp/
growth /grOwTH/
guage /gAyj/
guard /gArd/
guess /ges/
guest /gest/
guide /gIyd/
guitar /gu tAr/
gum /gum/
gun /gun/
gym (Jim) /jim/

h /AyCh/
had /had/

HOW DO YOU SAY? PRONUNCIATION DICTIONARY

hafta /haf tu/
hair (hare) /hAyr/
half /haf/
ham /ham/
hammer /ha mEr/
hand /hand/
hang /haNg/
happen /ha pun/
happy /ha pEy/
harbor /hAr bEr/
hard /hArd/
hardware /hArd wAyr/
hare (hair) /hAyr/
harm /hArm/
harmony /hAr mu nEy/
harvest /hAr vust/
has /has/
hasta /ha stu/
haste /hAyst/
hat /hat/
have /hav/
hay (hey) /hAy/
head /hed/
health /helTH/
hear (here) /hEyr/
heard (herd) /hErd/
heart /hArt/
heat /hEyt/
height /hIyt/
heir (air, err) /Ayr/
hell /hel/
hello /hu lOw/
help /help/
her /hEr/
here (hear) /hEyr/
herd (heard) /hErd/
hey (hay) /hAy/
hi (high) /hIy/
hiccough/**hic**cup /hi kup/
high (hi) /hIy/
him (hymn) /him/
hip /hip/
his /hiz/
history /hi strEy/
hoarse (horse) /hOrs/
hobby /ho bEy/
hoist /hOyst/
hold /hOwld/
hole (whole) /hOwl/
home /hOwm/
honest /o nest/
honey /hu nEy/
hood /h^d/
hoof /h^f/
hoof /hUwf/
hook /h^k/
hooker /h^ kEr/
hope /hOwp/
horn /hOrn/
horror /hO rEr/

horse (hoarse) /hOrs/
hospital /ho spu dul/
hot /hot/
hour (our) /AwEr/
house /hAws/
housing /hAw ziNg/
how /hAw/
humor /hyUw mEr/
hundred /hun drud/
hurt /hErt/
hymn (him) /him/
hypocrite /hi pu krit/
hypothesis /hIy po THu sus/

I (aye, eye) /Iy/
I'll (aisle, isle) /Iyl/
ice /Iys/
idea /Iy dE yu/
if /if/
ill /il/
im**por**tant /im pOr tunt/
impulse /im puls/
in (inn) /in/
increase /in krEys/
in**crease** /in krEys/
industry /in du strEy/
ink /ink/
inn (in) /in/
insect /in sekt/
in**sert** /in sErt/
instrument /in stru munt/
in**sur**ance /in ShE runs/
in**tel**ligence /in te lu junz/
interest /in trust/
in**tim**idation /in ti mu dAy Shun/
into /in tUw/
in**ven**tion /in ven Shun/
iron /I yErn/
is /iz/
island /Iy land/
isle (aisle, I'll) /Iyl/
it /it/

j (jay) /jAy/
ja /ju/
jade /jAyd/
jam /jam/
January /jan yUw e rEy/
jar /jAr/
jaw /jo/
jeans /jEynz/
jello /je lOw/
jelly /je lEy/
jer /jEr/
jerk /jErk/
jewelry /jUwl rEy/
job /job/

jog /jog/
join /jOyn/
joint /jOynt/
journey /jEr nEy/
joy /jOy/
judge /juj/
Judy /jUw dEy/
juggle /ju gul/
juice /jUws/
July /ju lIy/
jump /jump/
June /jUwn/
jungle /juN gul/
jury /jEry/
just /just/
justice /jus dus/

k (Kay) /kAy/
kangaroo /kaNg gu rUw/
keep /kEyp/
kernel (colonel) /kEr nul/
kettle /ke dul/
key /kEy/
kick /kik/
kid /kid/
kind /kIynd/
kiss /kis/
knee /nEy/
knife /nIyf/
knight (night) /nIyt/
knot (not) /not/
know (no) /nOw/
knowledge /no luj/
koala /ku wo lu/

L /el/
lamb /lam/
land /land/
language /laN gwuj/
lard /lArd/
large /lArj/
lark /lArk/
last /last/
late /lAyt/
laugh /laf/
laundry /lon drEy/
law /lo/
lawyer /lO yEr/
lead (led) /led/
lead /lEyd/
leaf /lEyf/
lean /lEyn/
learn /lErn/
leather /le ThEr/
led (lead) /led/
left /left/
leg /leg/

20

INDEX

lemon /le mun/
let /let/
letter /le dEr/
lettuce /le dus/
level /le vul/
library /lIy bre rEy/
lieu /lUw/
lieutenant / lUw te nunt/
lift /lift/
light (lite) /lIyt/
like /lIyk/
lime /lIym/
limit /li mit/
line /lIyn/
linen /li nun/
lion /lI yun/
lip /lip/
liquid /li kwud/
list /list/
listen /li sun/
little /li dul/
live /liv/
live /lIyv/
liver /li vEr/
load /lOw/
loan (lone) /lOwn/
lock /lok/
loin /lOyn/
loiter /lOy dEr/
lone (loan) /lOwn/
lonely (lOwn lEy)
long /loNg/
look /l^k/
loony /lUw nEy/
loose /lUws/
loss /los/
lost /lost/
lotion /lOw Shun/
loud /lAwd/
love /luv/
low /lOw/
loyal /lO yul/
luck /luk/
lunch /lunCh/
lung /luNg/

M /em/
machine /mu ShEyn/
mad /mad/
made (maid) /mAyd/
maid (made) /mAyd/
mail (male) /mAyl/
make /mAyk/
male (mail) /mAyl/
man /man/
manager /ma nu jEr/
manual /man yU wul/
many /me nEy/

map /map/
March /mArCh/
margarine /mAr ju run/
mark /mArk/
marker /mAr kEr/
market /mAr kut/
marry (merry) /me rEy/
martial arts /mAr Shul Arts/
mass /mas/
match /maCh/
math /maTH/
may (May) /mAy/
measure /me ZhEr/
meat (meet) /mEyt/
medium /mEy dE yum/
meet (meat) /mEyt/
men /men/
merry (marry) /me rEy/
middle /mi dul/
military /mi lu te rEy/
milk /milk/
mind /mIynd/
mine /mIyn/
minute /mi nut/
mistake /mu stAyk/
mix /miks/
moist /mOyst/
moisture /mOys jEr/
Monday /mun dAy/
money /mu nEy/
monitor /mo nu dEr/
monkey /muNg kEy/
month /munTH/
moon /mUwn/
moose /mUws/
more /mOr/
morning (mourning) /mOr niNg/
mortgage /mOr guj/
mother /muThEr/
motion /mOw Shun/
motor /mOw dEr/
mountain /mAw tun/
mourning (morning) /mOr niNg/
mouse /mAws/
mouth /mAwTH/
move /mUwv/
much /muCh/
multiply /mul tu plIy/
murder /mEr dEr/
muscle /mu sul/
museum /myUw zE yum/
music /myUw zik/
must /must/
mustard /mus dErd/
my /mIy/
myself /mIy self/
mystery /mi strEy/

N /en/
nachos /no ChOwz/
nail /nAyl/
naïve /nI yEyv/
name /nAym/
nation /nAy Shun/
natural /na Chu rul/
near /nEyr/
neck /nek/
need /nEyd/
needle /nEy dul/
neighbor /nAy bEr/
nephew /ne fyUw/
nerve /nErv/
nervous /nEr vus/
never /ne vEr/
new /nUw/
news /nUwz/
next /nekst/
nice /nIys/
nickel /ni kul/
niece /nEys/
night (knight) /nIyt/
nine /nIyn/
no (know) /nOw/
noise /nOyz/
noisy /nOy zEy/
nook /n^k/
noon /nUwn/
normal /nOr mul/
north /nOrTH/
nose (knows) /nOwz/
not (knot) /not/
note /nOwt/
notebook /nOwt b^k/
nothing /nu THiNg/
noun /nAwn/
November /nOw vem bEr/
now /nAw/
number /num bEr/
nurse /nErs/
nut /nut/

O (oh, owe) /Ow/
oar (or) /Or/
observation /ob zEr vAy Shun/
occupation /ok yUw pAy Shun/
ocean /OwShun/
October /oktOwbEr/
of /uv/
off /of/
offer /o fEr/
office /o fis/
officer /o fi sEr/
oh (O, owe) /Ow/
ohms /Owmz/
oil /O yul/
oily /Oy lEy/

21

HOW DO YOU SAY? PRONUNCIATION DICTIONARY

ointment /Oynt munt/
old /Owld/
olive /o luv/
on /on/
once /wuns/
one (won) /wun/
only /Own lEy/
open /Ow pun/
opera /o pru/
operation /o pE rAy Shun/
opinion /u pin yun/
opposite /o pu sit/
optometrist /op to mu trust/
or (oar) /Or/
orange /O runj/
orchard /Or ChErd/
orchestra /Or ku stru/
order /Or dEr/
ordinary /Or du ne rEy/
organ /Or gun/
organization /Or gu nIy zAy Shun/
organize /Or gu nIyz/
orient /O rE yunt/
original /u ri ju nul/
ornament /Or nu munt/
other /u ThEr/
ounce /Awns/
our (hour) /AwEr/
out /Awt/
outer /Aw dEr/
outlet /Awt lut/
oven /u vun/
over /Ow vEr/
owe (O, oh) /Ow/
owl /A wul/
own /Own/
owner /Ow nEr/
oxygen /ok su jun/
oyster /Oys dEr/

P (pea, pee) /pEy/
pad /pad/
page /pAyj/
pain (pane) /pAyn/
paint /pAynt/
palm /pom/
pancreas /pan krE yus/
pane (pain) /pAyn/
papaya /pu pI yu/
paper /pAy pEr/
parcel /pAr sul/
pardon /pAr dun/
parent /pe runt/
park /pArk/
parka /pAr ku/
part /pArt/
partner /pArt nEr/
party /pAr dEy/

passed (past) /past/
past (passed) /past/
pasta /pa stu/
paste /pAyst/
paw /po/
payment /pAy munt/
pea, (P, pee) /pEy/
peace (piece) /pEys/
peach /pEyCh/
pearl /pErl/
pee (P, pea) /pEy/
pen /pen/
pencil /pen sul/
penny /pe nEy/
people /pEy pul/
perfume /pEr fyUwm/
perfume /pEr fyUwm/
period /pEy rE yud//
person /pEr sun/
Peru /pu rUw/
phone /fOwn/
photo /fOw dOw/
physical /fi zu kul/
pi (pie) /pIy/
piano /pE ya nOw/
pick /pik/
picture /pik ChEr/
pie (pi) /pIy/
piece (peace) /pEys/
pig /pig/
pin /pin/
pineapple /pIy na pul
pink /piNgk/
pipe /pIyp/
pizza /pEyt zu/
place /plAys/
plaid /plad/
plain (plane) /pAyn/
plane (plain) /pAyn/
planet /pla nut/
plant /plant/
plate /plAyt/
play /plAyt/
please /plEyz/
pleasure /ple zhEr/
plough /plAw/
plus /plus/
pneumonia /nu mOwn yu/
pocket /po kut/
point /pOynt/
poise /pOyz/
poison /pOy sun/
police /pu lEys/
polish /po liSh/
Polish /pOw liSh/
political /pu li du kul/
pool /pUwl/
poor /pUwr/
pork /pOrk/

porter /pOr dEr/
portion /pOr Shun/
position /pu zi Shun/
positive /po zu div/
possible /po su bul/
post /pOwst/
poster /pOw sdEr/
posting /pOw sdiNg/
pot /pot/
potato /pu tAy du/
pound /pAwnd/
pour /pOr/
pout /pAwt/
poverty /po vEr dEy/
powder /pAw dEr/
power /pA wEr/
present /pre zunt/
pretty /pri dEy/
pretzel /pre tzul/
price /prIys/
print /print/
prison /pri zun/
private /prIy vut/
prize /prIyz/
probably /pro bu blEy/
profit /pro fut/
program /prOw gram/
pronounce /pru nAwns/
property /pro pEr dEy/
pros (prose) /prOwz/
prose (pros) /prOwz/
protest /prOw test/
proverb /pro vErb/
prune /prUwn/
public /pub lik/
pudding /p^ diNg/
pull /p^l/
pump /pump/
punishment /pu nuSh munt/
pure /pyUwr/
purple /pEr pul/
purpose /pEr pus/
purse /pErs/
push /p^Sh/
put /p^t/

Q (cue, queue) /kyUw/
quarter /kwOr dEr/
quay (key) /kEy/
question /kwes jun/
queue (cue, Q) /kyUw/
quick /kwik/
quiet /kwI yut/
quite /kwIyt/

R (are) /Ar/
raccoon /ra kUwn/

INDEX

radish /**ra** du**Sh**/
rail /**rAy**l/
rain (reign, rein) /**rAy**n/
ran /**ran**/
range /**rAy**nj/
raspberry /**ras** be r**Ey**/
rat /**rat**/
rate /**rAy**t/
raw /**rO**/
ray /**rAy**/
reach /**rEyCh**/
reaction /r**E yak Sh**un/
read (red) /**red**/
read (reed) /**rEy**d/
ready /**re** d**Ey**/
reason /**rEy** zun/
receipt /ru **sEy**t/
record /**re** k**E**rd/
record /ru **kOr**d/
red (read) /**red**/
reed (read) /**rEy**d/
refer /ru **fE**r/
reference /**ref** runs/
reform /ru **fOr**m/
regret /ru **gret**/
regular /**reg** yu l**E**r/
reign (rain, rein) /**rAy**n/
rein (rain, reign) /**rAy**n/
rejoice /ru **jOy**s/
relation /ru **lAy Sh**un/
religion /ru **li** jun/
rent /**rent**/
reporter /ru **pOr** d**E**r/
represent /re pru **zent**/
resort /ru **zOr**t/
respect /ru **spekt**/
responsible /ru **spon** su bul/
rest /**rest**/
resume /**re** zu **mAy**/
return /ru **tEr**n/
rhyme /**rIy**m/
rhythm /**ri Th**um/
rib /**rib**/
rice /**rIy**s/
ride /**rIy**d/
right (write) /**rIy**t/
righteous /**rIy Ch**us/
ring /**ri**N**g**/
ripe /**rIy**p/
river /**ri** v**E**r/
road (rode, rowed) /**rOw**d/
roar /**rOr**/
roast /**rOw**st/
rod /**rod**/
rode /**rOw**d/
romance /**rOw** mans/
roof /**rUw**f/
room /**rUw**m/
roommate /**rUw** m**Ay**t/

rooster /**rUws** d**E**r/
root (route) /**rUw**t/
rope /**rOw**p/
rose /**rOw**z/
rotten /**ro** tun/
rough /**ruf**/
round /**rAw**nd/
route (root) /**rUw**t/
row /**rOw**/
royal /**rO** yul/
rub /**rub**/
rule /**rUw**l/
ruler /**rUw** l**E**r/
run /**run**/
rye /**rIy**/

S /es/
sad /**sad**/
safe /**sAy**f/
said /**sed**/
sail (sale) /**sAy**l/
salad /**sa** lud/
salami /su lo **mEy**/
sale (sail) /**sAy**l/
salmon /**sa** mun/
same /**sAy**m/
sand /**sand**/
sandwich /**sam** wij/
Saturday /**sa** d**E**r d**Ay**/
saucer /**so** s**E**r/
sausage /**so** suj/
saw /**so**/
say /**sAy**/
scale /**skAy**l/
scene (seen) /**sEy**n/
scent (cent, sent) /**sent**/
schedule /**She** j**U** wul/, /**ske** j**U** wul/
school /**skUw**l/
schwa /**Shw**o/
science /**sI** yuns/
scissors /**si** z**Er**z/
score /**skOr**/
screw /**skrUw**/
scrub /**skrub**/
sea (C, see) /**sEy**/
seam /**sEy**m/
season /**sEy** zun/
seat /**sEy**t/
second /**se** kund/
secret /**sEy** krut/
see (C, sea) /**sEy**/
seed /**sEy**d/
seem (seam) /**sEy**m/
seen (scene) /**sEy**n/
selection /su **lek Sh**un/
self /**self**/
send /**send**/

sense /**sens**/
sent (cent, scent) /**sent**/
sentence /**sen** tuns/
separate /**se** pu r**Ay**t/
September /sup **tem** b**E**r/
serendipity /**se** run **di** pu d**Ey**/
sergeant /**sAr** junt/
serious /**sEy** r**E** yus/
servant /**sEr** vunt/
serve /**sEr**v/
seven /**se** vun/
sew (so, sow) /**sOw**/
sewer /**sU** w**E**r/
sex /**seks**/
shade /**ShAy**d/
shake /**ShAy**k/
shall /**Shal**/
shame /**ShAy**m/
shampoo /**Sham pUw**/
sharpener /**ShAr** pu n**E**r/
sheep /**ShEy**p/
sheet /**ShEy**t/
shelf /**Shelf**/
shift /**Shift**/
ship /**Ship**/
shirt /**ShEr**t/
shit /**Shit**/
shock /**Shok**/
shoe /**ShUw**/
shook /**Sh^k**/
shop /**Shop**/
short /**ShOr**t/
shorts /**ShOr**ts/
should /**Sh^d**/
shoulda /**Sh^** du/
shoulder /**ShOw**l d**E**r/
shout /**ShAw**t/
show /**ShOw**/
shower /**ShA** w**E**r/
shut /**Shut**/
sick /**sik**/
side /**sIy**d/
sign /**sIy**n/
silly /**si** l**Ey**/
silver /**sil** v**E**r/
simple /**sim** pul/
sing /**si**N**g**/
single /**si**N gul/
Sioux /**sUw**/
sir /**sEr**/
sister /**sis** d**E**r/
sit /**sit**/
six /**siks**/
size /**sIy**z/
ski /**skEy**/
skin /**skin**/
skirt /**skEr**t/
skull /**skul**/
skunk /**skuNg**k/

23

HOW DO YOU SAY? PRONUNCIATION DICTIONARY

slay (sleigh) /slAy/
sleep /slEyp/
sleigh (slay) /slAy/
slope /slOwp/
slow /slOw/
slur /slEr/
small /smol/
smash /smaSh/
smell /smel/
smile /smIyl/
smoke /smOwk/
smooth /smUwTh/
snake /snAyk/
sneeze /snEyz/
snow /snOw/
so (sew, sow) /sOw/
soap /sOwp/
society /su sI yu dEy/
sock /sok/
soda /sOw du/
soft /soft/
soil /sO yul/
soiree /swo rAy/
soldier /sOwl jEr/
solid /so lud/
some (sum) /sum/
son (sun) /sun/
song /soNg/
soon /sUwn/
sore /sOr/
sort /sOrt/
sound /sAwnd/
soup /sUwp/
south /sAwTH/
sow (sew, so)
space /spAys/
spade /spAyd/
special /spe Shul/
spice /spIys/
spiral /spIy rul/
splash /splaSh/
splint /splint/
sponge /spunj/
spoon /spUwn/
sport /spOrt/
spring /spriNg/
square /skwAyr/
squirrel /skwErl/
stage /stAyj/
stake (steak) /stAyk/
stamp /stamp/
star /stAr/
start /stArt/
state /stAyt/
statement /stAyt munt/
station /stAy Shun/
steak (stake) /stAyk/
steal (steel) /stEyl/
steam /stEym/

steel (steal) /stEyl/
stem /stem/
step /step/
stern /stErn/
stew /stUw/
sticky /sti kEy/
still /stil/
stomach /stu muk/
stone /stOwn/
stood /st^d/
stop /stop/
storage /stO ruj/
store /stOr/
storm /stOrm/
story /stO rEy/
straight (strait) /strAyt/
strait (straight) /strAyt/
strange /strAynj/
stranger /strAyn jEr/
strawberry /stro be rEy/
street /strEyt/
stretch /strech/
strong /stroNg/
structure /struk ChEr/
student /stUw dunt/
style /stIyl/
substance /sub stuns/
subway /sub wAy/
such /such/
sudden /su dun/
sue /sUw/
suede (swayed) /swAyd/
sugar /Sh^ gEr/
suggest /su jest/
suit /sUwt/
suite (sweet) /sWEyt/
sum (some) /sum/
summer /su mEr/
sun (son) /sun/
sundae (Sunday) /sun dAy/
Sunday (sundae) /sun dAy/
support /su pOrt/
sure /ShEr/
surf /sErf/
surfer /sEr fEr/
surgery /sEr ju rEy/
surprise /su prIyz/
swayed (suede) /swAyd/
sweatshirt /swet ShErt/
sweet (suite) /sWEyt/
swim /swim/
sword /sOrd/
system /sis dum/

T (tea, tee) /tEy/
table /tAy bul/
tack /tak/
taco /to kOw/

tail (tale) /tAyl/
take /tAyk/
tale (tail) /tAyl/
talk /tok/
talker /to kEr/
tar /tAr/
target /tAr gut/
tart /tArt/
taste /tAyst/
taught (taut, tot) /tot/
taut (taught, tot) /tot/
tax (tacks) /taks/
tea (T, tee) /tEy/
teach /tEyCh/
tee (T, tea) /tEy/
teen /tEyn/
teeth /tEyTh/
tell /tel/
ten /ten/
tenant /te nunt/
test /test/
than /Than/
that /That/
the /Thu/
their (there, they're) /ThAyr/
them /Them/
then /Then/
there (their, they're) /ThAyr/
thermometer /THEr mo mu dEr/
these /ThEyz/
they /ThAy/
they're (their, there) /ThAyr/
thick /THik/
thigh /THIy/
thin /THin/
thing /THiNg/
think /THiNgk/
third /THErd/
thirsty /THErs dEy/
thirty /THEr dEy/
this /This/
those /ThOwz/
though /Thow/
thought /THot/
thousand /ThAw zund/
thread /THred/
three /THrEy/
threw (through) /THrUw/
throat /THrOwt/
through (threw) /THrUw/
throw /THrOw/
thumb /THum/
thunder /THun dEr/
Thursday /THErz dAy/
thyme (time) /tIym/
ticket /ti kut/
tie /tIy/
tiger /tIy gEr/
tight /tIyt/

INDEX

time (thyme) /tIym/
tin /tin/
tip /tip/
tire /tI yEr/
to (too, two) /tUw/
toast /tOwst/
today /tu dAy/
toe (tow) /tOw/
together /tu ge ThEr/
toilet /tOy lut/
tomato /tu mAy du/
tongue /tuNg/
too (to, two) /tuw/
took /t^k/
tool /tUwl/
tooth /tUwTH/
toothbrush /tUwTH bruSh/
top /top/
torn /tOrn/
torture /tOr ChEr/
tot (taught, taut) /tot/
touch /tuCh/
tour /tUwr/
tow (toe) /tOw/
towel /tA wul/
town /tAwn/
toy /tOy/
trade /trAyd/
traffic /tra fik/
train /trAyn/
transport /trans pOrt/
tray /trAy/
tree /trEy/
triangle /trI yaN gul/
trick /trik/
trouble /tru bul/
trout /trAwt/
truck /truk/
true /trUw/
trust /trust/
try /trIy/
tub /tub/
Tuesday /tUwz dAy/
tuna /tUw nu/
tune /tUwn/
turkey /tEr kEy/
turn /tErn/
turnip /tEr nup/
turquoise /tEr kOyz/
turtle /tEr dul/
twelve /twelv/
twist /twist/
two (to, too) /tUw/

U /yUw/
U (ewe, you) /yUw/
ugly /ug lEy/
umbrella /um bre lu/
uncle /uNg kul/

under /un dEr/
unicorn /yUw nu kOrn/
uniform /yUw nu fOrm/
union /yUw nyun/
unit /yUw nut/
until /un til/
unwilling /un wi liNg/
up /up/
upon /u pon/
urgent /Er junt/
urn (earn) /Ern/
us /us/
USA /yUw es Ay/
use /yUwz/

V /vEy/
vacuum /va kyUwm/
vain (vane, vein) /vAyn/
value /val yUw/
vane (vain, vane) /vAyn/
vein (vain, vane) /vAyn/
verse /vErs/
very /ve rEy/
vest /vest/
view /vyUw/
viewpoint /vyUw pOynt/
vine /vIyn/
violent /vIy lunt/
virtue /vEr ChUw/
VISA /vEy zu/
vote /vOwt/
vowel /vA wul/

w /dU bul yUw/
W /du bul yUw/
waist (waste) /wAyst/
wait (weight) /wAyt/
walk /wok/
wall /wol/
wallet /wo lut/
wanna /wo nu/
want /wont/
war (wore) /wOr/
warm /wOrm/
wart /wOrt/
was /wuz/
wash /woSh/
waste (waist) /wAyst/
watch /woCh/
water /wo dEr/
wax (whacks) /waks/
way (weigh) /wAy/
we (wee) /wEy/
we'll (wheel) /wEyl/
weak (week) /wEyk/
wear (where) /wAyr/
weather (whether) /we ThEr/

Wednesday /wenz dAy/
wee (we) /wEy/
week (weak) /wEyk/
weigh (way) /wAy/
weight (wait) /wAyt/
welcome /wel kum/
well /wel/
went /went/
were /wEr/
west /west/
wet /wet/
whacks (wax) /waks/
wharf /wOrf/
what /wut/
wheel (we'll) /wEyl/
when /wen/
where (wear) /wAyr/
whether (weather) /we ThEr/
which /wiCh/
while /wIyl/
whine (wine) /wIyn/
whistle /wi sul/
white /wIyt/
whiteboard /whIyt bOrd/
who /hUw/
who's (whose) /hUwz/
whole (hole) /hOwl/
whose (who's) /hUwz/
why (Y) /wIy/
wide /wIyd/
wife /wIyf/
wild /wIyld/
will /wil/
wind /wind/
wind /wIynd/
windbreaker /win brAy kEr/
window /win dOw/
wine (whine) /wIyn/
wing /wiNg/
winter /win tEr/
wire /wI yEr/
wise /wIyz/
wish /wiSh/
witch /wiCh/
with /wiTh/
wolf /w^lf/
woman /w^ mun/
women /wi mun/
won (one) /wun/
wonder /wun dEr/
wont /wOwnt/
wood (would) /w^d/
wooded /w^ dud/
wooden /w^ dun/
woodpecker /w^d pekEr/
woodwinds /w^d winz/
woof /w^f/
wool /w^l/
word /wErd/

25

HOW DO YOU SAY? PRONUNCIATION DICTIONARY

wore (war) /wOr/
work /wErk/
world /wErld/
worm /wErm/
worst /wErst/
worth /wErTH/
would (wood) /w^d/
woulda /w^ du/
wound /wAwnd/
wound /wUwnd/
wow /wAw/
wreath /rEyTH/
wrist /rist/
write (right) /rIyt/
wrong /roNg/
wrote /rOwt/

X (ex) /eks/

Y (why) /wIy/
yacht /yot/
yam /yam/
yard /yArd/
yarn /yArn/
year /yEyr/
yellow /ye lOw/
yes /yes/
yesterday /yes dEr dAy/
yogurt /yOw gErt/
you (ewe, U) /yUw/
young /yuNg/
your /yEr/
your /yOr/
yuk /yuk/

Z /zed/ CAN
Z /zEy/ USA
zipper /zi pEr/
zoo /zUw/
zoom /zUwm/
zucchini /zUw kEy nEy/

Chapter 1
/Ay/ is Gray

Chapter 1
/Ay/ is Gray

A, a (eh) /Ay/
A.M. /Ay em/
ace /Ays/
ache /Ayk/
ade (aid, aide) /Ayd/
again /u gAyn/
against /u gAynst/
age /Ayj/
aid (aide, ade) /Ayd/
aide (ade, aid) /Ayd/
AIDS /Aydz/
ain' t /Aynt/
air (err, heir) /Ayr/
Asia /Ay Zhu/
April /Ay prul/
ate (eight) /Ayt/
Australia /o srAyl yu/
awake /u wAyk/
away /uwAy/

baby /bAy bEy/
bacon /bAy kun/
base (bass) /bAys/
bass (base) /bAys/
basin) /bAy sun/
behavior /bEy hAyv yEr/
blade /blAyd/
brain /brAyn/
brake (break) /brAyk/
break (brake) /brAyk/
buffet /bu fAy/

café /ka fAy/
cake /kAyk/
came /kAym/
care /kAyr/
change /ChAynj/
chaos /kA yos/
collocation /ko lu kAy Shun/

danger /dAyn jEr/
date /dAyt/
day /dAy/

education /e ju kAy Shun/
eh (A) /Ay/
eight (ate) /Ayt/
eraser /Ey rAy sEr/
err (air, heir) /Ayr/
exchange /eks ChAynj/

face /fAys/
fair (fare) /fAyr/
fare (fair) /fAyr/
flame /flAym/

game /gAym/
gave /gAyv/
grain /grAyn/
grape /grAyp/
grate (great) /grAyt/
gray (grey) /grAy/
great (grate) /grAyt/
guage /gAyj/

H /AyCh/
hair (hare) /hAyr/
hare (hair) /hAyr/
haste /hAyst/
hay (hey) /hAy/
heir (air, err) /Ayr/
hey (hay) /hAy/

intimidation /in ti mu dAy shun/

J /jAy/
jade /jAyd/

K /kAy/

late /lAyt/

/ Ay / is Gray

made (maid) /mAyd/
maid (made) /mAyd/
mail (male) /mAyl/
make /mAyk/
male (mail) /mAyl/
may (May) /mAy/
mistake /mu stAyk/

nail /nAyl/
name /nAym/
nation /nAy Shun/
neighbor /nAy bEr/

observation /ob zEr vAy Shun/
occupation /ok yUw pAy Shun/
operation /o pE rAy Shun/
organization /Or gu nIy zAy Shun/

page /pAyj/
pain (pane) /pAyn/
paint /pAynt/
pane (pain) /pAyn/
paper /pAy pEr/
paste /pAyst/
payment /pAy munt/
place /plAys/
plain (plane) /pAyn/
plane (plain) /pAyn/
plate /plAyt/
play /plAy/
potato /pu tAy du/

rail /rAyl/
rain (reign, rein) /rAyn/
range /rAynj/
rate /rAyt/
ray /rAyt/
reign (rain, rein) /rAyn/
rein (rain, reign) /rAyn/
relation /ru lAy Shun/

safe /sAyf/
sail (sale) /sAyl/
sale (sail) /sAyl/
same /sAym/
say /sAy/
scale /skAyl/
shade /ShAyd/
shake /ShAyk/
shame /ShAym/
slay (sleigh) /slAy/
sleigh (slay) /slAy/
snake /snAyk/
soiree /swo rAy/
space /spAys/
spade /spAyd/
square /skwAyr/
stage /stAyj/
stake (steak) /stAyk/
state /stAyt/
statement /stAyt munt/
station /stAy Shun/
steak (stake) /stAyk/
straight (strait) /strAyt/
strait (straight) /strAyt/
strange /strAynj/
stranger /strAyn jEr/
suede (swayed) /swAyd/
swayed (suede) /swAyd/

table /tAy bul/
tail (tale) /tAyl/
take /tAyk/
tale (tail) /tAyl/
taste /tAyst/
their (there, they're) /ThAyr/
there (their, they're) /ThAyr/
they /ThAy/
they're (their, there) /ThAyr/
today /tu dAy/
tomato /tu mAy du/
trade /trAyd/
train /trAyn/
tray /trAy/

29

vain (vane, vein) /**vAyn**/
vane (vain, vein) /**vAyn**/
vein (vain, vane) /**vAyn**/

waist (waste) /**wAyst**/
wait (weight) /**wAyt**/
waste (waist) /**wAyst**/
way (weigh) /**wAy**/
wear (where) /**wAyr**/
weigh (way) /**wAy**/
weight (wait) /**wAyt**/
where (wear) /**wAyr**/

A, a /**Ay**/ [A's] *noun* 1 the first letter of the Latin alphabet *Apple starts with an A.* 2 the highest grade for schoolwork *I got an A on my test.* **AA** – short form for *Alcoholics Anonymous*, a twelve-step program for people with alcohol addiction   **AAA** – short form for *American Auto Association*, car/travel club `Col:` **ABC's** – refers to the Latin alphabet   **A-frame** – style of a building with no separate sides as the roof goes right to the ground   **A-list** – first choice or highest paid people   **A-one** – excellent, first rate   **A-plus or A+** – top marks   **A-team** – group of highly competent specialists   **A type** – an intense, highly motivated personality, often a first-born   **get an A** – top mark in school   **Grade A** – government-inspected top quality stamped on the food   **straight A's** – a grade or final mark of A in every subject

a.m. /**Ay em**/ *abbr* ante meridiem, Latin for before noon *I get up at 6:00 a.m. every day.*

ace /**Ays**/ [aces, aced, acing] *noun* 1 a single spot on a playing card *I have the ace of hearts.* 2 a serve that one's tennis opponent does not return *That serve was another ace for Borg.* 3 expert *He was a WWII flying ace.* • *verb* perform extremely well *She aced her final exams.* `Col:` **ace in the hole** – a powerful asset that may be held back   **ace up one's sleeve** – a secret, maybe dishonest, advantage

ache /**Ayk**/ [aches, ached, aching] *noun* 1 steady pain *I have a toothache from too much candy.* 2 desire *She ached to hold her new grandchild.* • *verb* dull, steady pain *My back aches after I work in the garden.* `Col:` **aches and pains** – a variety of minor, annoying physical suffering   **earache, backache, headache, stomach ache, toothache** – common specific ailments

ade (aid, aide) /**Ayd**/ [ades] *noun* drink from citrus fruit *Lemonade is refreshing in summer.*

again /u **gAyn**/ *adv* 1 once more *I didn't like tennis the first time I tried it but I want to try it again.* `Col:` **again and again** – repeat   **Play it again, Sam.** – misquote from the movie *Casablanca*

against /u **gAynst**/ *prep* 1 in opposite direction *Rowing against the current is hard work.* 2 in contact with *He leaned the ladder against the side of the house to fix the eaves trough.* `Col:` **against all odds** – small chance   **against my better judgment** – proceed with a bad idea   **against popular opinion** – opposite to what most people think or do   **against the law** – illegal   **running against the wind** – chose a difficult route   **you and me against the world** – alone together, a special bond

age /**Ayj**/ [ages, aged, aging] *noun* 1 length of time of life *He was 23 years of age when he graduated.* 2 period of time *It was very cold for a long time during the Ice Age.* 3 ripen *Wine and women get better with age.* • *verb* grow older *She aged gracefully.* `Col:` **age of majority** – legal age to vote and drink alcohol, about 18 years in North America   **age old** – been around a long time   **at an awkward age** – clumsy, uncomfortable teen years, half child/half adult   **come of age or of age** – grown up, mature, become an adult   **golden age** – nostalgic times in America from 1920-1960   **information age** – computer age   **ice age** – long period of cold temperatures   **legal age** – age of legal responsibility, age of majority   **old age** – senior citizens 65 + years collecting a pension   **with age** – because of time passed   **Rock of Ages** – Christian hymn   **Stone Age** – 2.9 million years ago   **under age** – can't legally vote or drink alcohol **years of age** – lifetime so far

aid (ade, aide) /**Ayd**/ [aids, aided, aiding] *noun* **1** help *There was a global request for aid after the earthquake.* • *verb* help *The fireman aided the accident victims.* [Col:] **aid and abet** – help a criminal **band aid** – small sticky bandage **financial aid** – help by giving money to a person or country **first aid kit** – small case with common medical supplies **first aid** – basic medical care **legal aid** – legal service provided to represent poor people **presidential aide** – assistant

aide (ade, aid) /**Ayd**/ [aides] *noun* assistant *The teachers' aide helped with the gifted children.*

AIDS /**Aydz**/ *noun* short form for Auto Immune Deficiency Syndrome *He got AIDS from his partner who got it from a dirty needle.*

ain' t /**Aynt**/ *verb* negative form of *isn't* used by uneducated people *That ain't right.* [Col:] **ain't gonna rain no more** – happy times are here (from an old song)

air (heir, err) /**Ayr**/ [airs, aired, airing] *noun* oxygen to breathe *Fresh air is good for you.* [Col:] **a breath of fresh air** – warm, pleasant, enthusiastic personality **air filter** – special mesh designed to clean dirt from the air **air fresheners** – products to mask odors and make things smell nice **air head** – stupid person **air of authority** – natural leadership qualities **air out** – allow fresh air to stale area or expose grievances **clear the air** – clear up a misunderstanding or tension, sometimes as an argument **fresh air** – unpolluted **putting on airs** – pretending to be better than others

Asia /**Ay** Zhu/ *prop noun* the largest continent *Russia, China and India are all in Asia.*

April /**Ay** prul/ [Apr., Aprils] *prop noun* **1** the fourth month of the year *My birthday is in April.* [Col:] **April Fool's Day** – First day of April, a day for jokes and fun **April Showers bring May flowers** – *proverb*, after annoying (bad) rain flowers (good) come

ate (eight) /**Ayt**/ *verb* past tense of *eat* swallow *I already ate my lunch.*

Australia /o **srAy**l yu/ *pr noun* the smallest continent *Australia is between the Indian and Pacific Oceans.*

awake /u **wAyk**/ [awakes, awoke, awaking] *verb* not sleep *I like to lay awake at night and read.* • *adj* not sleeping *Is she still awake?* [Col:] **wide awake** – thinking clearly

away /u **wAy**/ *adv* distance in space or time *We live five minutes away from the children's school.* • *adj* **1** absent *He has been away for two years.* **2** distant *My birthday is still 2 months away.* [Col:] **a heartbeat away** – very close **away from one's desk** – unavailable **break away** – separate from the whole or suddenly lead the pack **far-away look** – not thinking of the present **far and away** – by large margin **far away** – not near **give away** – free, for no money or compensation **go away** – leave **move away** – relocate **throw away** – discard **up, up and away** – start and rise quickly like a balloon

baby /**bAy** bEy/ [babies, babied, babying] *noun* a very young child or animal *The baby was born in June.* • *verb* show love by fussing over someone or something special *He babies that old car.* [Col:] **baby boomer** – an increase in population after WW II, people born between 1946 – 1964 **baby blues** – depression as result of having a baby **baby doll** – term of endearment **baby face** – youthful looking **baby food** – specially prepared food easy for babies to digest **cry baby** – cries too easily **like taking candy from a baby** – easy, often dishonest activity **sleep like a baby** – deep sleep **soft as a baby's bottom** – very, very soft and smooth throw the baby out with the bathwater – not separating and keeping the good part

bacon /b**Ay** kun/ *noun* smoked, salted stripe of pork *Bacon and eggs with toast is a popular breakfast.* Col: bring home the bacon – the income earner

base (bass) /b**Ays**/ [bases, based, basing] *noun* 1 bottom or foundation – *The base of the lamp was made from an old wine bottle.* 2 center of operations *There is an old army base near the airport.* 3 low class – *He tells rude jokes and has a base sense of humor.* • *verb* foundation for a decision or belief *What sources of information are you basing your opinion on?* Col: base of operation – headquarters   get to first base – kiss   home base – center of operations   off base – be wrong about something, off track   steal a base – a baseball term to take a base unnoticed   touch base – to connect

bass (base) /b**Ays**/ [basses] *noun* low tone instruments *He sings bass.* • *adj* low tone *She plays the bass guitar.*

basin /b**Ay** sun/ [basins] *noun* sink *Go wash your hands in the basin.*

beha**v**ior /b**Ey** h**Ayv** y**E**r/ [behaviors] *noun* the way a person acts *His bad behavior got him kicked out of school.* Col: best behavior – polite, mannerly

blade /bl**Ayd**/ [blades, bladed, blading] *noun* 1 the cutting part of a knife *The blade is sharp.* 2 one piece of grass *She made a musical noise by blowing air along a blade of grass.* • *verb* travel by in-line skates *My son blades in the roller park every day after school.*

brain /br**Ayn**/ [brains] *noun* 1 the organ inside the head used for thinking *The human brain weighs about six pounds.* 2 smart person *She is the brain in our class.* Col: beat one's brain in – batter someone in the head   brain-fart – forget a simple item one should know automatically   no-brainer – obvious or easy   on the brain – think about obsessively   pick someone's brain – ask an expert for information on their topic without paying them   rack one's brain – to think hard

brake (break) /br**Ayk**/ [brakes, braked, braking] *noun* something used to stop movement *Apply the brake when you come to a stop sign.* • *verb* slow speed *I brake for turtles.* Col: emergency brake – a brake used by hand to stop movement   hand brake – same as emergency brake   parking brake – same as emergency brake

break (brake) /br**Ayk**/ [breaks, broke, broken, breaking] *noun* a scheduled stop from work or activity *We'll take a 15 minute break and return to class at 10:30.* • *verb* divide something into pieces *I fell off my bike and broke my leg.* Col: break away – separate   break down – stop working   break even – no money lost or gained at the end of the event   break in – train, work the newness out   break into – illegally enter a place   break out – 1 a rash on the skin 2 acne 3 to escape from a place   break through – make sudden significant progress   break up – end a relationship   break a leg – theater term used to wish someone luck   break bread – bond with others while sharing food   break ground – start building a construction project   break one's back – work very hard   break someone's heart – make someone sad or disappointed   break the bank – spend more money than you have or can get   break the ice – start a friendly conversation with a stranger   break wind – fart   deal breaker – non-negotiable item in an agreement

buffet /bu f**Ay**/ [buffets] *noun* 1 long flat piece of dining room furniture for storing dishes *The silverware is in the buffet.* 2 assortment of food where people serve themselves *We are going out for dinner for Chinese buffet.*

café /ka **fAy**/ [cafes] *noun* coffee shop *My husband has coffee and reads the paper every morning in the café on the corner.*

cake /**kAyk**/ [cakes, caked] *noun* a sweet baked food *Chocolate cake is a birthday party favorite.* • *verb* cover with a thick layer *The car was caked in mud.* Col: **have one's cake and eat it too** – not necessary to compromise   **sell like hot cakes** – sell very quickly   **piece of cake** – easy to do   **take the cake** – sarcastic for worst

came /**kAym**/ *verb* past tense of *come* draw closer *He came to class 10 minutes late.* Col: **This is where I came in.** – bow out of an exciting story retold   **whole world came crashing down around you** – catastrophic event   **There are plenty more where that came from** – easy to replace

care /**kAyr**/ [cares, cared, caring] *noun* 1 close attention to *Please handle the crystal with care.* 2 supervision *The children are in the care of the babysitter.* • *verb* 1 expression of interest *I don't really care what movie we go to see.* 2 to assist or supervise *I care for my aging mother.* Col: **care of** – at the address of, written on envelopes, abbreviated as c/o   **care package** – a package received from a loved one   **take care** – a way to say goodbye   **take care of** – pay bills, baby sit or provide nursing

change /**ChAynj**/ [changes, changed, changing] *noun* 1 something different *I don't like change.* 2 coins *Do you have change for a dollar?* • *verb* to become different *He changed as he got older.* Col: **a change is as good as a rest** – doing a different task revitalizes as much as doing nothing   **change hands** – pass from one owner to another   **change of heart** – decide against   **change one's mind** – select something different   **change one's tune** – to adjust one's attitude or opinion   **the change** – menopause

chaos /**kA** yos/ *noun* complete confusion and disorder *After the break-in the office was in chaos.*

collocation /ko lu **kAy** Shun/ [collocations, collocated, collocating] *noun* small group of words that goes together for reason to create an image *English speakers communicate using collocations not grammar.* • *verb* when random words go together to make meaning *Put collocates with up and with to mean tolerate.*

danger /**dAyn** jEr/ [dangers] *noun* something that may cause harm *Eating fast food everyday is a danger to your health.* • *adj* [dangerous] very unsafe *Playing with fire is dangerous.* Col: **danger is my middle name** – a risk taker   **danger pay** – extra money paid for a dangerous job   **fly in the face of danger** – take risks   **stranger danger** – advice for children to be cautious of people they don't know

date /**dAyt**/ [dates, dated, dating] *noun* 1 the fruit from a palm tree *I eat dates with my coffee.* 2 a time in the past, present or future, specified by day, month, or year *Check the dates on your calendar and tell me when you are available.* 3 an appointment, meeting or scheduled event *They set their wedding date for next summer.* • *verb* 1 find the age of something *They use science to date the fossils they find.* 2 to go out with someone *Sarah and John have been dating for three months.* • *adj* not current *Her clothes are dated.* Col: **best-before date** – the best time to eat, drink or use something before it goes bad   **blind date** – a romantic meeting arranged for two strangers   **bring someone up-to-date** – to give someone the most current information   **hot date** – a passionate meeting between two people   **out-of-date** – not current   **to date** – up until now   **up-to-date** – current

day /**dAy**/ [days] *noun* the opposite of night, the time between when the sun comes up and the sun goes down *I go to school during the day.* • *adj* relating to the time between when the sun comes up and the sun goes down *As a family we enjoy taking day trips.* Col: all in a day's work – part of the job, not out of the ordinary *An apple a day keeps the doctor away.* – *proverb* that supports healthy eating at the end of the day – basically bad hair day – nothing seems to be going right starting with hair call it a day – finish work day after day – over and over day in and day out – same as day after day day off – a day when you don't have to go into work or school different as night and day – used to describe opposites don't give up the day job – no talent, usually for singing in this day and age – this period in time it'll be a cold day in hell – never plain as day – obvious save for a rainy day – to keep an amount of money for an emergency in the future wouldn't give the time of day – can't get someone's attention

education /e ju **kAy** shun/ *noun* formal learning *I received my education from a private college.* educational software – computer programs dedicated to learning Col: level of education – highest completed stage of education: elementary, high-school, post-secondary, college, university

eh (A) /**Ay**/ *interj* notably Canadian, looking for agreement *It looks like it is going to rain eh?*

eight (ate) /**Ayt**/ [8, eights] *noun* cardinal number between seven and nine eight *Eight is too many hot dogs for one person!* • *adj* eight in number *A spider has eight legs.* Col: behind the eight ball – in a difficult position, billiards term

eraser /Ey **rAy** sEr/ [erasers] *noun* small piece of rubber for removing pencil print. *I need an eraser to rub out my mistakes.*

err (air, heir) /**Ayr**/ [errs, erred, erring] *verb* make a mistake *We erred on the side of caution with our building budget.* Col: To err is human, to forgive divine. – *proverb* about forgiving because everyone makes mistakes

exchange /eks **ChAynj**/ [exchanges, exchanged, exchanging] *verb* trade *We exchanged phone numbers and I was sure he would call.* • *noun* the place and act of trade *She sold her Bell shares on the stock exchange.* Col: exchange student – organized inter-country student swap foreign exchange – international money changers

face /**fAys**/ [faces, faced, facing] *noun* 1 front part of the head including eyes, nose, and mouth *She has a beautiful face.* 2 front of a mountain, building or watch *They climbed the face of Mt. McKinley.* • *verb* 1 look or turn toward *Please face the front of the class.* 2 a brave front *He was upset when the dog died but put on a brave face and didn't cry.* Col: about-face – turn 180 and leave at face value no hidden meaning be as plain as the nose on one's face – obvious be in your face – angry or nag blow up in one's face – didn't work out can't see one's hand in front of one's face – poor visibility from fog or snow come face to face – confronted cut one's nose off to spite one's face – prepared to pay a big price to hurt another disappear off the face of the earth – vanish face off – drop the puck to start play in a hockey game face head-on – deal with it – accept face off against – fight face only a mother could love – not attractive face the consequences – take responsibility for bad decisions face the facts – accept face the music – experience the consequences of one's actions face to face – in person face one's fears – deal with them fall flat on one's face – failed completely after some build up fill

HOW DO YOU SAY? PRONUNCIATION DICTIONARY

face – eat too much   fly in the face of – take a risk   game face – aggressive look to intimidate opponents   get out of my face – leave   have egg on face – look foolish after bad behavior   I'd rather face a firing squad than do... – dread   keep a straight face – no laughing in a funny situation   laugh in the face of danger – cavalier   long face – sad   look in the face – eye to eye   lose face – lose respect   make a face – express negativity as a facial gesture   not just a pretty face – smart   on the face of it – surface   put a brave face on – hide fear   put one's face on – wear make-up   put your game face on – an angry look to intimidate opponents   red in the face – blushing   save face – retain respect   set in a type face – font   slam the door in one's face – abrupt   slap in the face – insult   stuff your face – over eat   talk till you are blue in the face – no one is listening   two-faced – inauthentic   what's his face – can't remember a person's name   wipe the smile off one's face – threat   written all over one's face – revealing emotions with facial expressions

fair (fare) /fAyr/ [fairer, fairest] *adj* 1 according to the rules without favor to one side or the other *It was a fair fight.* 2 beautiful *He won the hand of the fair maiden.* 3 light skinned *She is too fair to go out in the sun.* 4 average, not bad *We had fair weather on the weekend.* • *noun* exhibition *They showed their horses and pumpkins at the fair.* Col: All's fair in love and war – *proverb* deceit is allowed in important circumstances   fair and square – equal treatment   fair game – okay to attack or abuse   fair play – by the rules   fair shake – good treatment even if it wasn't deserved   fair to middling – not good, not bad   Fair's fair. – nothing to argue about in the contest   fair-haired – blond   fair-haired boy – preferred child   fair-weather friend – only there when times are good   more than one's fair share of – extra   No fair! – cheated   the fair sex – women

fare (fair) /fAyr/ *noun* price of a ticket *Bus fare goes up every few years.*

flame /flAym/ [flames, flamed, flaming] *noun* bright, moving colors produced by fire: *The flames from the campfire rose high into the night sky.* • *verb* 1 burst into or make fire *The embers flamed back up when he poured gas on them.* 2 strong love *Her heart flamed with passion.* Col: burst into flames – caught fire   drawn like a moth to a flame – naturally attracted   fan the flames – make emotions more intense   flamed out – lost energy   go up in flames – destroy by fire   old flame – former love interest, boyfriend/girlfriend

game /gAym/ [games, gamer, gamest] *noun* 1 activity for fun *The kids made a game out of folding the laundry* 2 organized sport activity *We watched a football game on Monday night.* 3 hunted wild animals *Hunting for big game can be expensive and dangerous.* • *adj* daring or willing *Are you game for some tennis?* Col: a game and a half – extra entertaining or exciting   a numbers game – play the odds   a shell game – con for money   a whole new ball game – different topic, new problem   a zero-sum game – no further ahead after effort and expense   ahead of the game - anticipate   at the top of game – peak performance or success   at this stage of the game – his point in the middle of a process   back in the game – left for a while and is now back   fair game – legal target   game is up – over   game plan – action plan   got game – enthusiasm   name of the game – point   new to the game – beginner   not all fun and games – serious   off game – not performing as well as usual   play a waiting game –

/ Ay / is Gray

wait as a strategy　play the game – participate in life　the only game in town – highest interest at the moment　throw a game – lose on purpose　two can play at that game – manipulation that works for both

gave /g**Ay**v/ *verb* past tense of *give* 1 transfer something *I gave him my coat.* 2 perform an action *She gave a speech.* 3 make someone have or feel something *The English course gave me confidence* 4 organize an event *We gave him a party* 5 bend or break *The break-wall gave due to the force of the water.* Col: gave a break – showed generosity　gave away – handed the bride to her future husband at the wedding ceremony　gave in – concede defeat　gave off – emitted　gave out – broke　gave up – quit

grain /gr**Ay**n/ [grains] *noun* 1 crops of cereal plants *The farmer planted wheat, corn and barley this year.* 2 the pattern of lines in a piece of wood *Oak has a yellow color and a wide grain.* 3 a small amount of something *Grains of sand from the beach are stuck in my socks.* Col: go against the grain – to not follow common practice　grain of truth – a little bit true and the rest is questionable

grape /gr**Ay**p/ [grapes] *noun* juicy red, green or purple fruit that grows on vines and is used for making wine *Grapes grow in warm sunny climates.* Col: sour grapes – jealousy from the fable the Fox and the Grapes

grate (great) /gr**Ay**t/ [grates, grated, grating] *noun* 1 metal pattern of bars *Homeless people sleep where warm air comes up through the grate in the sidewalk.* 2 metal bracket in a fireplace *Throw another log on the grate.* • *verb* cut finely *I like carrots grated on top of my salad.* Col: grate on one's nerves – annoy, perhaps unintentionally

gray (grey) /gr**Ay**/ [grays, grayer, grayest] *adj* the color between black and white *Her hair turned gray when she was in her forties.* • *noun* the color. *Gray is a good color for a winter coat.* Col: gray area – lacking clear rules　gray matter – brain　shades of gray – many slight differences that might not matter

great (grate) /gr**Ay**t/ [greater greatest] *adj* 1 large amount or degree. *There was a great turnout for the election* 2 important, successful, or famous. *Meryl Streep is a great actress.* 3 better than good *It was a great day.* 4 parents' grandparents *My great grandfather came to Canada from Ireland in 1925.* 5 very *We caught a great big fish.* Col: a great deal of – excess amounts　didn't turn a hair – there was no reaction　go to great lengths – effort　going great guns – making good or fast progress　great minds think alike – self congratulating comment　life's great mysteries – marvel at nature or the unknown　no great shakes – not very good　Oh, that`s just great! – sarcastic remark meaning not great at all　take great pains – work hard and carefully　the great beyond – afterlife　the greatest thing since sliced bread – describing something new and wonderful

gauge /g**Ay**j/ [gauges] *noun* tool for measuring *The gas gauge is broken in my car and I never know if I'll run out of gas.* • *verb* measure *The speedometer gauges speed.*

H /**Ay**ch/ [H's] *noun* the eighth letter of the Latin alphabet *House starts with an H.* Col: h-e-double-hockey-sticks – said by Canadians to avoid saying the word hell　what the h – said to avoid saying the word hell

hair (hare) /h**Ay**r/ [hairs] *noun* thin thread that grows from the top of the head *Brush your hair.* Col: a hair's breadth – very close　bad hair day – nothing seems to be going right starting with hair　by a hair – small margin　hair-raising – scary　have by the short and curlies – powerless against　haven't seen hide nor hair of – not seen at all　in the cross hairs –

aiming at   let hair down – relax   make hair stand on end – scare or enrage   not a hair out of place – perfect   part hair – divide in a line   put hair on chest – spicy food   put hair up – fancy hair-do   run fingers through hair – touch with affection or romance   split hairs – dwell on silly details

hare (hair) -/hAyr/ [hares] noun rabbit *The tortoise won the race against the hare in the famous fable.* Col: the March Hare – Alice in Wonderland character

haste /hAyst/ [hasten] noun moving quickly *In his haste he made many mistakes.* Col: Haste makes waste. – proverb that warns against rushing and making costly mistakes   make haste – to hurry

hay (hey) /hAy/ [hays, hayed, haying] noun grass or other plant used to feed farm animals *The hay for the cows is in the barn.* • verb bringing in the hay *The men haying need gloves and long sleeved shirts.* Col: a role in the hay – impulsive sex   hay-fever – allergy to nature   hit the hay – to go to bed   it's like looking for needle in a haystack – unlikely to find   Make hay while the sun shines. – proverb take the present opportunity

heir (air, err) /Ayr/ [heirs] noun one with the right to receive another's property after that person dies *Prince Charles is the heir to the throne in England.*

hey (hay) /hAy/ interj 1 used to attract attention *Hey, you!* 2 informal greeting *Hey, how are you?* 3 used to express surprise *Hey! When did you get here?*

intimidation /in ti mu dAy Shun/ noun cause fear. *The bully used intimidation to get what he wanted.*

J /jAy/ [J's] noun the tenth letter of the Latin alphabet *July starts with a J.*

jade /jAyd/ [jaded] noun 1 a semiprecious stone, usually green *Jade is my favorite gemstone.* 2 a shade of the green *Her favorite color is jade.* • adj cynical *After her date with Bob, she became jaded about men.*

K /kAy/ [K's] noun the eleventh letter of the Latin alphabet *King starts with a K.* Col: k – text, informal for ok or okay   K2 – second highest summit in the world   K9 – a dog

late /lAyt/ [later, latest] adj 1 after the expected time. *I was late for school yesterday.* 2 near the end of a period of time. *We will be there by late afternoon.* 3 dead *The late John Smith.* • adv after the expected time *School started late because of the storm.* Col: Better late than never. – proverb value in appearing however late   she's late *(whispered)* – a woman's menstrual period is overdue, she is possibly pregnant   It's never too late. – proverb try, start, apologize no matter how much time has passed   late bloomer – didn't accomplish anything until they were older

made (maid) /mAyd/ [make, made, making] verb past tense of *make* construct *We made sandwiches for lunch.* Col: a match made in heaven – perfect love relationship, destiny   a self-made man – earned his money and success on his own   have it made –success/security   made for each other – good or bad, the people are a match   Made in ___ – manufactured in the named country   made to measure or tailor made is a perfect or custom fit   not made of money – high expectations or entitlement   Rules were made to be broken. – proverb it's okay to think for oneself and not always blindly follow silly rules   show what you are made of – show good qualities like courage in an adverse situation   they broke the mould when they made you – unique, very special   You made your bed now lie in it. – proverb one must suffer the consequences of bad decisions

maid (made) /mAyd/ [maids] noun female servant *My parents hired a maid to clean twice a week.* Col: an old maid – a rude reference to an unmarried woman   maid of honor – primary attendant of the bride   **maiden aunt** – unmarried aunt   **maiden voyage** – ship's first trip

mail (male) /**mAyl**/ [mails, mailed, mailing] *verb* send by post *I mailed the letters yesterday.* • *noun* postal system *The check is in the mail.* Col: **return mail** – immediate reply, the day the letter is received   **snail mail** – postal service not email which is much faster

make /**mAyk**/ [makes, made, making] *verb* 1 produce or build *They make their own clothes.* 2 cause to happen *You make me laugh.* 3 force *They made me do my homework before I could go to the movies.* 3 hire or promote *They made him the store manager.* 4 earn money *She makes $60,000 a year.* 5 selected *I made the team.* • *noun* type of product *Honda is a popular make of car.* Col: **Absence makes the heart grow fonder.** – *proverb* love someone more after some time apart   **barely make out** – difficult to read, hear or see something   **clothes make the man** – appearances are important   **Haste makes waste.** – *proverb* hurrying is costly through mistakes   **kiss and make up** – end a lover's spat or fight   **make a federal case out of it** – sarcastic, too much fuss over something unimportant   **make a mistake** – error   **make amends** – apologize and fix a damaged relationship   **make believe** – imagination   **make do** – use what you have   **make off with** – steal   **Make hay while the sun shines.** – *proverb* take the present opportunity   **make it** – achieve success   **make over** – create a new look   **make that up** – lie   **Many hands make light work.** – *proverb* helpers makes the work easier   **Practice makes perfect.** – *proverb* improve, do it over and over   **that makes two of us** – same here or I agree   **Two wrongs don't make a right.** – *proverb* it is not okay to do the wrong thing because someone else was bad

male (mail) /**mAyl**/ [males] *noun* the masculine sex *There were 10 males and 11 females in the class.* • *adj* about men or boys *Security is a male-dominated industry.* Col: **male chauvinist pig** – out-of-date man who believes men are superior to women

May /**mAy**/ [Mays] *prop noun* fifth month of the year *Mother's Day is the second Sunday in May.* • *helping verb* 1 possibility *It may rain.* 2 permission *May I go to the washroom?* Col: **April showers bring May flowers.** – *proverb* reminding after annoying (bad) rain flowers (good) come   **be that as it may** – none-the-less   **devil-may-care** – carefree   **may as well** – no reason not to   **May the best man win.** – good sportsmanship   **Sticks and stones may break my bones but names will never hurt me.** – *proverb* sensible response to name calling   **to whom it may concern** – formal address to the opener of the letter

mistake /mu**stAyk**/ [mistakes] *noun* error *How many mistakes did you have on your spelling test?* Col: **by mistake** – by accident   **make a mistake** – error   **mistake someone for someone else** – confuse identity

nail /**nAyl**/ [nails, nailed, nailing] *noun* thin pointed piece of metal hammered to attach pieces of wood together – *She hammered nails into the wall of the cabin and hung up the coats.* 2. The hard growth the ends of your fingers and toes – *Trim your toenails or you'll wear holes in your socks.* • *verb* fasten with nails *The restaurant tables are nailed to the floor so no one can steal them.*   **a nail-biter** – an exciting nerve-racking event   **another nail in his coffin** – bad decision bringing someone closer to being fired or rejected   **as tough as nails** – emotionally or physically strong   **final nail in the coffin** – no going back or recovery from this point   **For want of a nail the shoe was lost...** – *proverb* that says fix small problems before they become big   **hit the nail on the head** — word or action done exactly right   **nailed him/her** — caught in some illegal/unethical act   **nailed it** — excelled in a task

name /**nAym**/ [names, named, naming] *noun* 1 label of a person or group *My name is Judy Thompson.* 2 reputation *Our company has a good name.* • *verb* the act of giving a name. *They are naming the new baby after her aunt.* Col: **a big name** — famous or important person   **a household name** — commonly known person or product   **call names** — verbally insult   **clear name** — defend reputation   **drop names** — use of important people in order to make oneself feel important   **have one's name on it** — well suited to   **I didn't catch your name.** — didn't hear it when you arrived   **in name only** — married but living separately   **know by name** — familiar with   **make a name for** — be successful   **name after** — give a parent or friend's name to your baby   **good name** — reputation   **in his/her name** — ownership   **in the name of** — use as a reason to do something   **name in lights** — Broadway   **name is mud** — bad reputation   **name names** — expose others   **name of the game** — the purpose   **on a first-name basis** — friends   **A rose by any other name would smell as sweet.** — *proverb* names don't matter   **take one's name in vain** — disrespect   **terrible at names** — forget names   **worthy of the name** — maintain the good reputation   **you name it** — anything you want

nation /**nAy** shun/ [nations] *noun* a country and its citizens — *Canada became a nation in 1867.*

neighbor /**nAy** bEr/ [neighbors] *noun* one who lives nearby *My neighbor is having a barbecue.* Col: **Good fences make good neighbors** — *proverb* it is easy to be friendly if no one trespasses   **next-door neighbor** — lives closest

observa**tion** /ob zEr **vAy** shun/ [observations] *noun* 1 perceive through one of the senses *The nurse made the observation the rash was spreading.*

occupa**tion** /ok yUw **pAy** Shun/ [occupations] *noun* job *Teaching English is my occupation.*

opera**tion** /o pE **rAy** shun/ [operations] *noun* 1 The work of a business or organization *The Blue Jay's operation is located in Toronto.* 2 people working together to accomplish something *The rescue operation was successful.* 3 surgery *His heart operation was successful.*

organiza**tion** /Or gu nIy **zAy** shun/ [organizations] *noun* 1 a group formed for a purpose *The U.N. is an international organization.* 2 the process of making things run *The organization of the event is her responsibility.*

page /**pAyj**/ [pages, paged, paging] *noun* 1 one side of a piece of paper *The title is at the top of the first page.* 2 attendant *For two summers he worked for the government as a page.* • *verb* call someone in a public place by a public address system — *The airport paged Mr. Smith who left his wallet at the check-in.* Col: **on the same page** — agreement   **take a page from someone's book** — adopt one of their good policies   **turn the page** — move on to the next matter/issue

pain (pane) /**pAyn**/ [pains] *noun* 1 hurt *I have a pain in my lower back.* 2 difficult or unpleasant to do *Working late is a real pain!* Col: **chronic pain** — never goes away   **feeling no pain** — drunk   **growing pains** — physical or emotional discomfort from growth   **No pain no gain.** — *proverb* work until it hurts to improve   **pain in the ass** — nuisance   **painful reminder** — sad or uncomfortable memory   **pain in the neck** — annoying   **take great pains** — effort

paint /**pAynt**/ [paints, painted, painting] *noun* a mix of colored liquid to cover a surface *We used blue paint to decorate the dining room.* • verb – cover with paint *She painted the dining room blue.* Col: **as exciting as watching paint dry** – not exciting   **coat of paint** – one layer of paint   **paint a picture** – describe the obvious in detail   **paint the town red** – have fun   **paint oneself into a corner** – into a difficult position

pane (pain) /**pAyn**/ [panes] noun a section of glass in a window. *The golf ball broke one pane in the front window.*

paper /**pAy** pEr/ [papers, papered, papering] noun 1 thin material made from wood or rice used to write on *He wrote his phone number on a piece of paper.* 2 short form for newspaper *I read about it in yesterday's paper.* 3 an essay *The students have to write a paper as part of their course.* 4 official documents *They need to sign the papers to complete the deal.* • verb decorating walls with wall paper *We are papering the living room.* Col: **looks good on paper** – the reality may be different   **not worth the paper it is written on** – worthless   **paper chase** – an activity that takes many documents   **paper trail** – documented history   **paper weight** – small heavy object that keeps papers on the desk   **put it on paper** – write a contract

payment /**pAy** munt/ [payments] noun 1 money given in exchange *He made monthly payments of $300 on his car loan.* Col: **down payment** – lump sum paid up front for a big purchase   ___ **is payment enough** – no money is required

place /**plAys**/ [places, placed, placing] noun 1 space, building, area, or location *The library is a quiet place to study.* • verb set or put *She placed the bowl on the table.* Col: **A woman's place is in the home.** – proverb about traditional roles   **all over the place** – scattered   **as if one owned the place** – confident   **be in the right place at the right time** – lucky   **be out of place** – awkward   **between a rock and a hard place** – in a difficult situation   **Don't spend it all in one place.** – spend money wisely   **fall into place** – progress   **go places** – success   **happy place** – in one's mind   **have friends in high places** – wealthy powerful friends   **heart is in the right place** – kind   **in the first place** – beginning a list of arguments   **in the wrong place at the wrong time** – unfortunate, unlucky   **know one's place** – mind one's manners, don't be bold   **nice place you have here** – home   **not a hair out of place** – tidy   **cannot be in two places at one time** – can only do so much   **out of place** – doesn't belong   **place an order** – buying   **place at a premium** – value   **place for everything, and everything in its place** – organized and structured   **place in jeopardy** – in danger   **place of business** – work   **put in place** – reprimanded   **tear a place apart** – looked carefully for something   **There is a time and a place for everything.** – proverb about different behavior that is appropriate for different occasions   **there's no place like home** – from the Wizard of Oz   **turn a place upside down or inside out** – looking for something   **Your place or mine?** – for sex   **one's place in the sun** – utopia

plain (plane) /**plAyn**/ [plainer, plainest] adj 1 easy to see or hear *The flag was in plain view in the center of town.* 2 ordinary, not special *He was a little plain but very kind.* • noun a large flat area with no trees *Cowboys graze cattle on the plains.* Col: **in plain language** – direct, simple clear explanations   **plain as day** – out in the open, not hidden, obvious **plain as the nose on your face** – obvious **plain Jane** – not beautiful

plane (plain) /**plAyn**/ [planes] *noun* 1 short form of airplane *We took a plane to Montreal.* 2 level of thought or activity *Visual learners operate on a different plane.* 3 tool used to smooth wooden surfaces *He used a plane on the top of the door.*

plate /**plAyt**/ [plates, plated, plating] *noun* 1 flat dish on which food is served or eaten *Put some rice on your plate.* 2 flat piece of metal with words or numbers stamped in it. *Cars need license plates to legally drive on the road.* • *verb* cover with a thin layer of metal *The cutlery is plated with silver.* Col: **a lot on his plate** – very busy, lots of responsibilities **clean up one's plate** – eat all the food on their plate **full plate** – very busy **have one's head on a plate** – severely reprimand **step up to the plate** – baseball term for taking action

play /**play**/ [plays, played, playing] *noun* a story to be acted out on stage *There is a new play on Broadway.* • *verb* take part in a game or have fun *Let's play soccer.* Col: **a play on words** – a joke using a word with two meanings **All work and no play makes Jack a dull boy.** – *proverb* don't work too hard **child's play** – easy **fair play** – by the rules **foul play** – illegal **If you play with fire, you'll get burned.** – *proverb* if you do dangerous things you'll get hurt **play a joke on** – trick **play by ear** – play an instrument without lessons or written music **play cat and mouse** – toy with a victim **play devil's advocate** – ask the tough questions **play dirty** – cheat **play footsie with** – touch feet in a sexual way **play for keep** – forever **play hardball** – serious business **play innocent** – pretend not to know what is going on **play it safe** – be conservative **play possum** – play dead **play the field** – date many people at once **play the ponies** – bet on horse races **power play** – an advantage **When the cat is away the mice will play.** – *proverb* people don't work as hard when their boss is away

potato /pu **tAy** du/ [potatoes] *noun* large white root vegetable with brown skin *I like to have a baked potato with my steak dinner.* Col: **couch potato** – lazy person who watches too much TV **hot potato** – controversial or unpleasant issue or topic **mashed potatoes** – popular dish of cooked, crushed potatoes **meat and potatoes** – traditional North American dinner meal **small potatoes** – not much value or worth bothering about

rail /**rAyl**/ [rails] *noun* 1 two long metal tracks trains roll on *They are fixing the rails and the train has to detour.* 2 the railway system *We went to Calgary by rail.* 3 a bar that runs between two posts as a barrier *The fence was in fairly good shape we only had to replace a few rails.* • *verb* complain loudly. *The public railed against further tax hikes.* Col: **back on the rails** – making good progress after a setback **thin as a rail** – too skinny

rain (reign, rein) [rains, rained, raining] /**rAyn**/ *noun* drops of water that fall from the sky *The rain ruined our holiday.* • *verb* wet weather *It rained all week.* Col: **come rain or shine** – hold an event regardless of the weather **doesn't have the sense to come in out of the rain** – not smart or judged for being different **I hate to rain on your parade** – bring bad news to a happy event **raining cats and dogs** – heavy rain **right as rain** – all is well **take a rain check** – say yes to an invitation but for a future date **When it rains it pours.** – *proverb* bad news seems to come all at once

range /**rAynj**/ [ranges, ranged, ranging] *noun* 1 stove top *The range usually has four burners.* 2 group of things that are different but belong to the same type.

TLC provides a range of business services. 3 distance over which something can be seen or heard *The boat was still within range of the hurricane warning and returned to shore.* 4 line of mountains *The mountain range stretched for 1000 miles.* • verb 1 limits within which amounts can vary. *Her children range in age from 2 to 19 years.* Col: **close range** – proximity   **driving range** – golf practice   **free range chickens** – raised outdoors in a natural space   **home on the range** – from an old cowboy song about the plains   **range of motion** – scope of ability to move a joint or body part   **within range** – near enough

rate /rAyt/ [rates, rated, rating] *noun* 1 cost of services *What are the overnight rates in this hotel?* 2 number of times over a period of time *Her heart rate is 60 beats per minute.* 3 speed *The water is flowing through the pipe at a rapid rate.* • verb assess ability *He is rated as one of the best players in the world.* Col: **at any rate** – regardless   **first rate** – top quality   **going rate** – current price   **he/she rates** – deserves   **second rate** – substandard

ray /rAy/ [rays] *noun* beam of light *Rays light shone through the cracks in the curtains.* Col: **catch some rays** – suntan   **ray of hope** – tiny bit of hope   **ray of sunshine** – positive force or influence

reign (rain, rein) /rAyn/ [reigns, reigned, reigning] *noun* period of rule by a king or queen *The Olympics were hosted by Great Britain during the reign of Queen Elizabeth.* • verb ruling a domain *My husband reigns over the garage and workshop.*

rein (rain, reign) /rAyn/ [reins] *noun* part of a bridle for stopping and steering a horse *The reins got tangled in her fingers and the horse stopped.* Col: **loose rein** – a degree of freedom   **rein in** – stop or slow   **tight rein** – controlling

relation /ru lAy Shun/ [relations] *noun* 1 blood connections *All our relations are coming to the family reunion.* 2 interaction between people, countries, organizations, etc. *We have excellent relations with China.* Col: **intimate relations** – sex   **the poor relations** – family members with no money

safe /sAyf/ [safes, safer, safest] *adj* 1 free from risk, harm or danger *It is safe to swim here.* 2 cautious *Safe drivers have fewer accidents.* • noun 1 strong metal box used to keep valuables *Leave your passport and jewelry in the hotel safe.* 2 condom – *He always carries a safe in his wallet, just in case.* Col: **a safe bet** – sure thing   **be on the safe side** – cautious   **in safe hands** – in good care   **play it safe** – prepare for any possible outcome   **safe and sound** – home and well after being lost or delayed   **Safe home.** – parting remark to departing visitors

sail (sale) /sAyl/ [sails, sailed, sailing] *noun* large piece of cloth use to propel a boat *His boat has a blue sail.* • verb 1 travel across water by boat or ship *We sailed around the West Indies on our cruise.* 2 move gracefully through the air *The baseball sailed through the air and over the fence.* Col: **sail along** – moving forward easily   **sail through** – to succeed easily   **set sail** – begin a journey   **took the wind out of his sails** – deflated his enthusiasm

sale (sail) /sAyl/ [sales] *noun* an exchange of things or services for money *The biggest sale he ever made was his house.* Col: **close a sale** – complete the transaction to the new owner   **for sale** – offered for money   **no sale** – denied permission   **on sale** – reduced price   **fire sale** – severely reduced price   **garage, lawn or yard sale** – selling unwanted things to the public from one's driveway or yard

same /sAym/ *adj* identical *We go to the same hotel every year.* Col: **all the same to me** – no preference   **big long song and dance** – elaborate excuses   **cut from**

the same cloth – similar values and disposition   I'll have the same – identical food or drink order   in the same ballpark – close to a agreement in a general sense   in the same boat – situation   it's the same old story – familiar old excuse   live under the same roof – in the house or dwelling   not in the same league – not as good as   on the same page – understand one another clearly   one and the same – identical   on the same wavelength – similar in thought and approach   same difference – no difference   same here – my experience too   same old same old – nothing changing that probably should   same to you – reflect back wishes either good or bad   speak the same language – understand one another   tar with the same brush – accuse all members of a group of one bad behavior   two sides of the same coin – closely connected ideas

say /sAy/ [says, said, saying] verb 1 make words with one's mouth – *What did you say?* 2 express in words, spoken or written *Say it in an email.* • noun opinion *I want a say in which car we should buy.* Col: anything you say – submission   can't say for sure – unsure   Do as I say, not as I do – doesn't like to be judged, only to give orders   have the final say – last word   I'll say – wholeheartedly agree   let's say – imagine for a minute   Need I say more? – case closed   needless to say – obvious   Never say die – persevere   never say never – stay hopeful   saying a mouthful – big impact   Say cheese! – smile for the camera   say grace – pray before a meal   say in a roundabout way – indirectly   Say no more – I understand, agree and have already started   say the word – give permission   Say what? – question in disbelief   Say when – prepared to start and activity or stop filling a glass   Says who? – challenge an idea   smile when you say that – threat   sorry to say – report bad news   That's easy for you to say. – your overall position is better to say the least – sarcastic   What can I say? – I can't do anything about the misfortune   What do you say? – greeting   What do you want me to say? – plea in an irresolvable situation   wouldn't say boo to a goose – very timid   you can say that again – wholeheartedly agree   You don't say. – I'm surprised   having said that – adding an opinion to one already stated   you can say that again – you strongly agree

scale /skAyl/ [scales] noun 1 a device for weighing *Heavy people avoid the bathroom scale.* 2 small shiny chips of fish skin *Fish scales are used to make lipstick shiny.* 3 units of measure along a line *Is there an inch or centimeter scale on that ruler?* verb climb *Rock climbers scale mountains and cliffs for sport.* Col: musical scales – practice exercises for learning to play an instrument   scale back or scale down – reduce

shade /shAyd/ [shades, shaded, shading] noun 1 shadow caused by blocking light *The big trees provide shade in the yard.* 2 tint or hue of color *Sapphire is my favorite shade of blue.* 3 roll-up window curtain *Pull the shades down in the afternoon to keep the house cool in summer.* • verb protect from light *The house is shaded by big trees.* Col: shady character – suspicious   shady deal – illegal transaction   have it made in the shade – well-off, no financial worries

shake /shAyk/ [shakes, shook, shaking] verb move back and forth quickly *Shake the crumbs out of the table cloth.* • noun slang for a drink made with ice cream *I'll have a chocolate shake with my hamburger.* Col: a fair shake – honest treatment   hand shake – traditional greeting gesture in many cultures   no great shakes – not good   shake a leg – hurry   shake like a leaf – tremble

shame /shAym/ [shames, shamed, shaming] *noun* bad feeling as a result of doing something wrong *His drug addiction brought shame to his parents.* • *verb* make someone feel badly *We shamed him into paying his debts.* Col: **crying shame** – a terrible pity **Fool me once, shame on you; fool me twice, shame on me.** – *proverb* don't make the same mistake twice **for shame** you know better **put to shame** – bested **shame on you** – scolding one who behaves badly and shouldn't

slay (sleigh) /slAy/ [slays, slew, slaying] *verb* 1 kill violently *St George slew the dragon with his sword.* 2 slang for amuse *That comedian slays me.*

sleigh (slay) /slAy/ [sleighs] *noun* open carriage on runners for traveling over snow. *Santa Claus drives a big red sleigh.*

snake /snAyk/ [snakes, snaked, snaking] *noun* long thin reptile with no legs *The snake was sleeping on the rocks.* • *verb* moving from side to side *The ivy snaked up the side of the house.* Col: **snake along** – move forward by swinging from side to side **snake charmer** – con man **snake in the grass** – dishonest **snake oil** – fake medicin

soiree /swo rAy/ [soirees] *noun* evening party *We were all invited to the soiree at the neighbors.*

space /spAys/ [spaces, spaced, spacing] *noun* 1 the area that contains the universe *The rocket was launched into space.* 2 empty spot in a sequence *Leave a space between each word in a sentence.* • *verb* manage empty area *Space the chairs evenly along the back wall.* Col: **outer space** – everything beyond the Earth's atmosphere **space station** – space craft capable of supporting people **spaced out** – mentally unfocused **take up space** – no value **waste of space** – useless

spade /spAyd/ [, spades] *noun* 1 pointed shovel *Use a spade to dig a hole to plant the tree.* 2 the black suit in playing cards shaped like a pointed leaf *The Queen of Spades is worth 13 points in Hearts.* Col: **ace of spades** – highest value playing card **black as the ace of spades** – pitch black, totally dark **call a spade a spade** – say the truth, straightforward talk **in spades** – good fortune

square /skwAyr/ [squares, squared, squaring] *noun* 1 shape with four equal sides □ *Circles, squares and triangles are three basic shapes.* 2 meeting place in the center of a town *The town council is putting up the Christmas tree in the square.* • *verb* shaping something into right angles *He squared off the edges of the wood to make a table top.* Col: **back to square one** – start over **be there or be square** – show up or be judged as unreliable **fair and square** – honest dealings **square dance** – traditional dance **square meal** – meat, potatoes and vegetables **square up with someone** – pay a debt of money or a favor **square deal** – good for all parties **square off** – prepare to fight **square peg in a round hole** – not a good fit, out of place **three square meals a day** – good treatment **square root** – math term for a number times itself

stake (steak) /stAyk/ [stakes, staked, staking] *noun* 1 piece of wood or metal pointed at one end *That stake marks the corner of the property.* 2 a share or investment *What is your stake in the family business?* • *verb* officially marking out an area *The father staked out a corner of the farm to give to his son.* Col: **burn at the stake** – destroy, from witches killings in the past **raise the stakes** – increase the risk or importance **stake a claim** – establish ownership of mineral rights, property or an idea **stake your reputation** – support a person or belief with all you own **stake out** – mark territory or lay in wait to catch a bad guy **pull up stakes** – move away

stage /stAyj/ [stages, staged, staging] *noun* 1 raised platform for public performances *The kitchen table made a perfect stage for the children's puppet show.* 2 part in a series of development *Learning English happens in stages, not all at once.* **Col:** **at this stage of the game** – now, currently   **center stage** – focus of attention   **not at this stage** – not now   **set the stage** – context or atmosphere before sharing a story   **stage coach** – horse-drawn transportation   **stage two cancer** – progression

state /stAyt/ [states, stated, stating] *noun* 1 condition *The old building was in a bad state.* 2 country *The new president spoke to the state immediately after the election.* 3 part of an area under one government *There are 52 states in the USA.* • *verb* declare or say *He stated the only way he would come was with his family.* • *adj* having to do government *She works for the state department.* **Col:** **fine state of affairs** – sarcastic remark for a bad situation   **state of flux** – up and down   **state of mind** – attitude   **state of the art** – most modern technology   **state of the union address** – president's message   **stating the obvious** – literal

statement /stAyt munt/ [statements] *noun* 1 a declaration *The lawyer made a statement to the press on behalf of his client.* 2 financial accounting *We get a statement from VISA every month.* **Col:** **bank statement** – report of financial activity and balance   **statement of accounting** – printed record of financial charges

station /stAy Shun/ [stations, stationed, stationing] *noun* 1 position or place one usually works *The work stations at the donut store are clean and efficient.* 2 building for special organizations *The fire station is next to the bus station.* 3 position in life *It's my station to serve others.* • *verb* assigned position *He was stationed in South Korea.* **Col:** **marry beneath your station** – lower social ranking   **panic stations** – urgency, high anxiety and quick actions   **play station** – electronic toy   **police station** – official building   **work station** – area set up for accomplishing specific tasks

steak (stake) /stAyk/ [steaks] *noun* choice cut of meat *Grilled steaks are a popular summer meal.* **Col:** **steak and kidney pie** – traditional British dinner pastry   **steak house** – restaurant   **steak knife** – sharp table knife   **steak sauce** – tangy condiment especially for beef   **steak tartar** – high quality beef finely chopped, spiced and raw   **t-bone steak** – thick tender cut of beef good on the barbeque.

straight (strait) /strAyt/ [straighter, straightest] *adj* 1 without a curve. *Use a ruler to draw a straight line.* 2 honest *He was straight with us about how long the classes would take.* 3 slang for heterosexual *Jane is gay but her sister is straight.* • *adv* 1 directly *He came straight home after school.* 2 upright *Stand up nice and straight.* **Col:** **as straight as an arrow** – honest   **can't see straight** – too angry or emotional to function normally   **can't think straight** – too tired or distracted to think clearly   **straight from the horse's mouth** – information from the source   **get the facts straight** – without interpretation or exaggeration   **Give it to me straight** – tell me the unpleasant truth   **keep a straight face** – serious   **keep things straight** – fully disclose, open communication   **keep to the straight and narrow** – strictly honest and legal   **set the record straight** – correct misinformation   **shoot straight from the hip** – blunt or overly direct   **sit up straight** – fix your posture and your behavior   **straight ahead** – in front of, forward   **straight face** – no laughing   **straight man** – the serious partner in a comedy team   **straight out** or **straight up** – direct clear or blunt message   **straight shooter** – honest   **straight talk**

46

– open conversation about a sensitive subject   **straightaway** – immediately   **the straight and narrow** – honest

strait (straight) /str**A**yt/ [straits] *noun* 1 narrow waterway *Drive slowly and carefully through the straights to avoid other boats.* 2 serious trouble or circumstances *With the economic collapse the country was in difficult straits.* Col: **dire straits** – serious financial trouble, no immediate income   **Straits of___** – geographical name for a specific waterway

strange /str**A**ynj/ [stranger, strangest] *adj* 1 unknown *That is a strange dog.* 2 unusual or odd *That is a strange thing to say.* • *adv* odd or unusual *He dresses strangely.* Col: **strange but true** – odd fact

stranger /str**A**yn jEr/ [strangers] *noun* 1 new to an area *The stranger is from overseas.* 2 person unknown *There was a stranger hanging around the school so I called the police.* Col: **make strange bedfellows** – people usually opposed work together for a common purpose   **no stranger to…** - well aware of   **perfect stranger** – unknown   **stranger danger** – advice for children to be cautious of people they don't know   **Truth is stranger than fiction.** – *proverb* events that really happen that are more fantastic than fantasy

suede (swayed) /sw**A**yd/ *noun* soft brushed leather *I love the feel of suede but it is hard to take care of.* • *adj* made of suede *Suede jackets are on sale at the mall.*

swayed (suede) /sw**A**yd/ [sways, swayed, swaying] *verb* past tense of *sway* rock back and forth *The rope swayed from the top of the flagpole.*

table /t**A**y bul/ [tables] *noun* flat-topped furniture for setting things on *The pine table in the kitchen belonged to her grandmother.* Col: **clear the table** – take dirty dishes away after a meal   **coffee table** – low wide table in front of the living room couch   **drink someone under the table** – consume more alcohol   **lay one's cards on the table** – fully disclose one's plans   **set the table** – place cutlery and dinnerware on the kitchen or dining room table before a meal   **table a motion** – postpone the discussion of an item at a meeting   **table tennis** – ping pong   **turn the tables** – reverse or backfire a situation on someone   **wait on tables** – food server, work as a waitress or waiter

tail (tale) /t**A**yl/ [tails, tailed, tailing] *noun* 1 the part of an animal's backbone that sticks out behind it *Happy dogs wag their tails.* 2 end of a object *The kite needs a longer tail.* 3 one side of a coin *I always choose tails and my sister always picks heads.* • *adj* last or in the rear *The caboose is at the tail end of the train.* • *verb* follow *The detective tailed the suspect across three states.* Col: **bright-eyed and bushy-tailed** – wide awake and ready for action   **can't make heads nor tails of** – can't understand   **freeze one's tail off** – be very cold   **has the world by the tail** – happy, everything is going well   **have a tiger by the tail** – have a big or dangerous problem   **heads or tails** – make a decision by flipping a coin   **in two shakes of a lamb's tail** – soon, very quickly   **nose to tail** – following closely one after the other   **on coattails** – clinging to the power or glory of another   **tail after** – follow   **tail between legs** – shame   **tail off** – fade away   **the tail end of** – very last part   **the tail wagging the dog** – minor players making the decisions   **turn tail** – run away   **shirt tail** – bottom of a long shirt

take /t**A**yk/ [takes, took, taking] *verb* 1 seize or hold in one's hands *Take the milk and put it in the fridge.* 2 carry or bring *Take a coat it might rain.* 3 transportation *The kids take the bus to school.* 4 accept *We take book orders online* 5 tolerate – *I can't take the hot weather.* 6 make or do *Take pictures of the new baby.* 6 swallow *Take your medicine before bed.* • *noun* money generated at an event or in a business *What was the take from bingo last night?* `Col:` give and take – compromise   has what it takes – have the skills and resources for success   It takes all kinds – note and appreciate or despair of differences   It takes one to know one – retort to an insult   It takes two to tango. – *proverb* a situation that did not get created by one person   like a duck takes to water – natural ability   take one's breath away – awe, surprise and impress   take a cold shower – thinking too much about sex   take one's hat off to – acknowledge a job well done   take one's life – suicide   take one's life in one's hands – put oneself in serious danger   take one's time – go slowly   take someone's life – homicide   take someone's part – support them in an argument or position   take someone down a peg – criticize   take a back seat – given less importance   take a bath – lose money in an investment   take a beating – lose badly in a fight or sports activity   take a bite out of – small part   take a blind notice – ignore   take a bow – a gesture of accepting acknowledgement   take a break – rest   take a chance – risk   take a chance on – risk by believing in something or someone else   take a cold shower – suggestion to cool down sexually   take a collection up – gather money for charity   take a course – register for school   take a crack at – try   take a deep breath – slow down, get control of emotions   take a dim view – don't like   take a dirt nap – fall down   take a fancy to – start to like   take a gander – look at   take a guess – guess for fun   take over – assume control   take pictures – photography   take turns – play nicely, be

considerate of others   takes care of that – finishes   takes getting used to – not nice at first but gets better over time   That's settled – finished   That takes the cake! – good or bad it's remarkable   You pays your money and you takes your chances .– do one's best then accept what happens

tale (tail) /**tAyl**/ [tales] *noun* 1 story *Read me the tale about Peter Rabbit.* 2 lie *Don't tell tales or no one will believe you when you tell the truth.* `Col:` old wives' tale – story that has endured but might not be true   tall tale – lie

taste /**tAyst**/ [tastes, tasted, tasting] *noun* 1 one of the five senses by which flavor is perceived *Taste is not as important at sight or hearing.* 2 sense of style *She has great taste in clothes.* • *verb* experience flavors on the tongue *This soup tastes too salty.* `Col:` tastes funny – has an odd flavor   a taste of one's own medicine – receive a sample of bad treatment that one has been giving others   developed a taste for – a desire for a special food or experience   in bad or poor taste – rude or vulgar comments or behavior   leave a bad taste in one's mouth – memory of an unpleasant experience   no accounting for taste – accept that people like different things   want something so badly one can taste it – really want something

their (there, they're) /**ThAyr**/ *adj* 1 the possessive form of *they* belonging to them *Their house is the green one.* 2 his or hers when the gender of the owner is unknown *Someone left their keys on the desk.*

there (their, they're) /**ThAyr**/ *adv* that place *Stay there and we'll pick you up later.* • *noun* place *We went there on our holiday.*

they /**ThAy**/ *pron* 1 replacing people or things *What are they doing on the weekend?* 2 people or things already mentioned. *If your friends come, they should bring extra food.* 3 people in general *They say it will*

/ Ay / is Gray

be a long winter. 4 he or she if the gender of the person is not known. *There was a phone call for you. They will call back.* Col: **They broke the mould when they made you.** — one of a kind, special **They don't make them like they used to.** — blame modern manufacturing as poor quality

they're (their, there) /ThAyr/ *contr* they are *They're coming to school with us.*

today /tu dAy/ [todays] *noun* 1 this day *Today is sunny.* 2 present time in general *Kids today are comfortable using computers.* Col: **Here today gone tomorrow.** — *proverb* things exist for only a short time

tomato /tu mAy du/ [tomatoes] *noun* juicy red (or yellow) fruit that seems more like a vegetable. *Please slice some tomatoes for the salad.*

trade /trAyd/ [trades, traded, trading] *noun* 1 exchange *The car was a good trade for the motorcycle plus cash.* 2 job that requires a particular skill *He is a plumber by trade.* • *verb* exchange *He traded his motorcycle plus cash for a car.* Col: **a roaring trade** – business is going well with lots of sales   **jack of all trades but master of none** – does many things well but nothing really well   **ply one's trade** – use work skills   **trade in** – use an old model as part of the pay for a new one   **trade secret** – a secret way of making more money or sales   **trade show** – conference or exposition in an industry   **trade for** – exchange without money   **trade off** – get rid of or sacrifice in an exchange   **trade up** – get better products   **traded insults** – said nasty things to each other   **tricks of the trade** – special knowledge associated with each profession

train /trAyn/ [trains, trained, training] *noun* 1 a line of railroad cars pulled by a locomotive *I'm taking the train into the city at 8:00.* 2 extra material on a dress that trails behind *The bride's train was eight feet long.* • *verb* 1 teaching a person or animal new behaviors through repetition *He trained his dog to pull a small wagon.* 2 program of physical activity *She trained for the Olympics with a foreign coach.* Col: **gravy train** – access to money   **train of thought** – series of ideas   **train one's sights** – focus on a goal in the future

tray /trAy/ [trays] *noun* a flat, open piece of wood or metal for carrying food. *Please put the tea cups on the tray and take it into the kitchen.*

vain (vane, vein) /vAyn/ [vainer, vainest] *adj* 1 overly concerned with one's own appearances *She is so vain she can't stop looking at herself in the mirror!* 2 without success *He struggled in vain to improve his spoken English.*

vane (vain, vein) /vAyn/ *noun* thin flat surfaces designed to turn in the wind *The weather vane on the barn is shaped like a rooster.*

vein (vain, vane) /vAyn/ [veins] *noun* 1 small tube for taking blood back to the heart for more oxygen *Surface veins are unsightly but harmless* 2 ore inside of rock *There are veins of gold around Dawson City.* Col: **struck a vein** – found a significant amount of precious metal for mining

waist (waste) /wAyst/ [waists] *noun* part of the body above the hips and below the chest *Women years ago had much smaller waists.*

wait (weight) /wAyt/ [waits, waited, waiting] *verb* stay in one place until a planned event happens *Wait for me!* Col: **can't wait** – looking forward to   **Good things come to he who waits.** – *proverb* be patient   **have to wait** – delayed   **hurry up and wait** – a process like airplane travel that alternates between hurrying and stopping   **on the waiting list** – on an actual list of people in line for an opportunity   **Time waits for no man.** – *proverb* that encourages action, life is precious and short don't waste it   **wait on tables** – serve food in a restaurant, waitress or waiter **wait a minute** – have a new idea **wait for the other shoe to drop** – negative connotation, standing by for the inevitable **wait on someone hand and foot** to serve someone too well **wait one's turn** – let everyone ahead of finish their turn **wait something out** – remain until the end before taking action. **wait up** – I'm coming, so wait **wait up for** – don't go to sleep until someone arrives **wait-and-see attitude** – tentative **waiting room** – lounge outside a professional's office **worth the wait** – appreciate something that took a long time

waste (waist) /wAyst/ [wastes, wasted, wasting] *noun* 1 garbage *He used the waste from building the house to make a shed.* • *verb* spend in a careless way for little or no return *They wasted their money on a motor home they only use once a year.* • *adj* useless material *Our waste station separates recyclable materials.* Col: Don't **waste your breath.** – no point talking they aren't listening **waste basket** – garbage pail **Waste not want not.** – *proverb* don't waste and there will always be enough, repurpose **waste of time** – no point doing it **waste away** – deteriorate

way (weigh) /wAy/ [ways] *noun* 1 a path *Is this the way to the park?* 2 manner *He has a kind gentle way about him.* 3 distance *The mountains are a long way from here.* Col: **a one-way ticket** – not coming back **a two-way street** – give and take **a way of life** – lifestyle **all the way** – sex **any way you slice it** – one conclusion **any way, shape, or form** – not particular **be in a bad way** – bad physical or emotional health **be laughing all the way to the bank** – lucky turn of fortune **by the way** – did you know **come a long way** – improved **cry all the way to the bank** – success as a result of another's misfortune **do the hard way** – bad choices **either way** – no matter **feel one's way** – learn **find a way around** – resourceful **get in the way** – not helping **get one's own way** – indulged **go a long way toward** – it helps **go all the way** – sex **go back a long way** – history **go out of your way for** – extend oneself for another **go the way of the dodo** – extinct **have a way with** – natural affinity **Have it your way** – concede **in a big way** – grandiose **in a family way** – pregnant **in a way** – sort of **in harm's way** – in danger **inch way along** – slowly progress **Keep out of my way** – threat **know way around** – expert **lead the way** – we'll follow you **look the other way** – ignore **Love will find a way** – triumph **make way in the world** – survive **No way!** – not a chance **no way, José** – no **not know which way to turn** – confused and overwhelmed **on the way** – coming **other way round** – backwards **out of the way** – private **pave the way for** – assist **right-of-way** – go first **rub the wrong way** – annoy **take the easy way out** – maybe not the right way, no integrity **That's the way the cookie crumbles** – destiny **the coward's way out** – suicide **There's more than one way to skin a cat.** – *proverb* resourceful **to put it another way** – rephrase **under way** – started **The way to a man's heart is through his stomach** – *proverb* to capture a husband a woman should feed him well **way to go** – congratulations **Where there's a will there's a way!** – determination will always succeed **will go a long way** – great effort **work one's way to the top** – success through effort

wear (where) /wAyr/ [wears, wore, wearing] *verb* 1 put on as in clothes *Wear a bathing suit when you go swimming.* • *noun* the condition of being worn *The*

/ Ay / is Gray

wear on the tire shows the wheels are not straight. `Col:` **be the worse for wear** – suffered physically from an experience   **wear and tear** – deterioration from use   **wear away** – erode   **wear more than one hat** – has many jobs or responsibilities   **wear my fingers to the bone** – physically works hard   **wears his heart on his sleeve** – all his emotions are plainly seen   **wears the pants in the family** – makes the family decisions

weigh (way) /wAy/ [weighs, weigh, weighing] *verb* 1 measure with scales. *This suitcase weighs 40 lbs.* 2 consider *Let's weigh the pros and cons.* `Col:` **weigh a ton** – excessively heavy

weight (wait) /wAyt/ [weights] *noun* 1 heaviness *How much does he weigh?* 2 equipment lifted because of their heaviness *He lifts weights at the gym as part of his exercise program.* `Col:` **a big weight off one's shoulders** – relieved of the burden of responsibility   **carry one's weight** – one's share of the work and responsibility   **carried a lot of weight** – was influential in an important event   **weight of the world** – burden

where (wear) /wAyr/ *adv* Wh question, in what place *Where are my glasses?* • *conj* place *I am going where I can find a drink.* `Col:` **Where are they now?** – wondering about people from the past

HOW DO YOU SAY? PRONUNCIATION DICTIONARY

Chapter 2
/a/ is Black

Chapter 2
/a/ is Black

a /a/
abdomen /ab du mun/
acid /a sud/
act /akt/
adult /a dult/
advertise /ad vEr tIyz/
advertisement /ad vEr tIyz munt/
Africa /a fru ku/
after /af dEr/
alphabet /al fu bet/
am /am/
an /an/
and /and/
angle /aN gul/
angry /an grEy/
animal /a nu mul/
answer /an sEr/
ant (aunt) /ant/
apple /a pul/
apricot /a pru kot/
as /az/
ask /ask/
ass /as/
asthma /az mu/
at /at/
attack /a tak/
attraction /u trak Shun/
aunt (ant) /ant/
automatic /o du ma dik/

back /bak/
bad /bad/
bag /bag/
balance /ba luns/
banana /bu na nu/
band /band/
basket /bas get/
bath /baTH/
bladder /bla dEr/
black /blak/
blanket /blaNg kut/
branch /branCh/
brass /bras/

cabbage /ka buj/
calendar /ka lu dEr/
calf /kaf/
camera /kam ru/
can /kan/
Canada /ka nu du/
candidate /kan du dAyt/
cantaloupe /kan tu lOwp/
canvas /kan vus/
capital (capitol) /ka pu dul/
capitol (capital) /ka pu dul/
cash /kaSh/
cat /kat/
chance /Chans/
chapter /Chap dEr/
crab /krab/
crack /krak/

Dad /dad/
dam /dam/
damage /da muj/

elastic /Ey la stik/
example /eg zam pul/
expansion /eks pan Shun/

family /fam lEy/
fast /fast/
fat /fat/
flag /flag/
flat /flat/
fragile /fra jul/

gas /gas/
glass /glas/
glasses /gla suz/
grandmother /gra mu ThEr/
grass /grass/
gravel /gra vul/

had /had/
hafta /haf tu/
ham /ham/

/ a / is Black

hammer /ha mEr/
hand /hand/
hang /haNg/
happen /ha pun/
happy /ha pEy/
has /haz/
hasta /has tu/
hat /hat/
have /hav/

jam /jam/
January /jan yU we rEy/

lamb /lam/
land /land/
language /laN gwuj/
last /last/
laugh /laf/

mad /mad/
man /man/
manager /ma nu jEr/
manual /man yU wul/
map /map/
mass /mas/
match /maCh/
math /maTH/

natural /na Chu rul/

pad /pad/
pancreas /pan krE yus/
passed (past) /past/
past (passed) /past/
pasta /pa stu/
piano /pE ya nOw/
plaid /plad/
planet /pla nut/
plant /plant/

radish /ra duSh/
ran /ran/
raspberry /ras be rEy/
rat /rat/
reaction /rE yak Shun/

sad /sad/
salad /sa lud/
salmon /sa mun/
sand /sand/
sandwich /sam wuj/
Saturday /sa dEr dAy/
shall /Shal/
smash /smaSh/
splash /splaSh/
stamp /stamp/

tacks (tax) /taks/
tax (tacks) /taks/
than /Than/
that /That/
traffic /tra fik/
transport /trans pOrt/

vacuum /va kyUwm/
value /val yUw/

wax (whacks) /waks/
whacks (wax) /waks/

yam /yam/

a /a/ *indefinite article* used before a noun when the subject is not known to the listener *I just bought a house.*

abdomen /ab du mun/ [abdomens] *noun* front part of the body *The stomach is in the abdomen.*

acid /a sud/ [acids] *noun* a sour chemical that dissolves in water *The acid I spilled killed these plants.* • *adj* a mean, unfriendly quality *He made an acid comment about my presentation; I guess he didn't like it.* Col: **acid rain** – rain full of pollution   **stomach acid** – enzymes in the stomach used to digest food

act /akt/ [acts, acted, acting] *noun* 1 performance *The stand-up comedian has a great act.* 2 section of a play *He forgot his lines in the third act.* • *verb* 1 behavior *He acted out of kindness.* 2 professional performance *Brad Pitt acts in the movies.* Col: **act of faith** – trusting the outcome will be good   **act of God** – divine intervention   **act out** – charades, physically demonstrate   **act your age** – stop behaving like a child   **acting out** – behaving badly   **balancing act** – trying to do more than one thing at a time   **caught in the act** – interrupted while doing something wrong   **clean up one's act** – behave oneself properly   **get one's act together** – get organized, start moving forward   **solo act** – success doing things on one's own   **tough act to follow** – an excellent performance

adult /a dult/ [adults] *noun* fully grown person *Adults pay admission, children get in for free.*

advertise /ad vEr tIyz/ [advertises, advertised, advertising] *verb* call attention to products in order to sell *Companies advertise in newspapers, magazines, billboards and on TV.* Col: **advertise for** – put the word out for something desired   **advertise in** – a magazine or newspaper or periodical   **advertise on** – television, DVD

advertisement /ad vEr tIyz munt/ [advertisements] *noun* a public message intended to sell *I saw an advertisement on TV for English lessons.* Col: **walking advertisement** – a person dressing and behaving in a way that promotes a certain product

Africa /a fru ku/ *prop noun* the second largest continent *Africa is south of Europe between the Atlantic and Indian oceans.*

after /af dEr/ *prep* behind in place or in time *Friday is the day after Thursday.* • *adv* later *She went home after the party.* • *conj* following an event *His game improved after he took some lessons.* Col: **a man/woman after my own heart** – similar tastes, values and disposition   **after all** – putting things into perspective at the end   **after the fact** – adding new information following an event, often a crime   **happily ever after** – a happy ending to a story   **look after** – take care of   **shortly after** – a short time following an event   **time after time** – repeatedly

alphabet /al fu but/ [alphabets] *noun* list of symbols representing sounds, put together to make words *A, B, and C are the first three letters of the Latin alphabet.* Col: **alphabet soup** – soup made with letter-shaped noodles   **alphabetical order** – in the order letters occur in the alphabet

am /am/ *verb* first person singular form of the verb to *be* exist *I am Canadian.* Col: **I yam what I yam** – from the cartoon *Popeye*, it means authentic, accepting of self

an /an/ *indefinite article* used before a noun when the subject is not known to the listener and the word following it begins with a vowel sound *I saw an elephant.*

and /and/ *conj* 1 in addition *The actress is beautiful and talented.* 2 joining two related and important ideas *I wrote the exam and I passed.* Col: **and so on** – to keep going in the same way or style and **then some** – much more **and/or** – to choose one or both **over and over** – repeat

angle /aN gul/ [angles, angled, angling] *noun* two straight lines touch at one point *Each angle in a square is 90 degrees.* Col: **angle towards** – turn to face camera **angle** – direction from which a picture is taken **knowing all the angles** – aware of short cuts and tricks to complete task more quickly **right angle** – 90 degrees **wide angle lens** – camera lens for taking landscape pictures

angry /aN grEy/ [angrier, angriest] *adj* strong negative feeling *I'm angry with my son for leaving his new bike in the rain.* • *verb* to cause extreme anger *She angered her teacher when she bullied the younger children.* Col: **anger management** – behavior training to control temper

animal /a nu mul/ [animals] *noun* a living thing that can move and eats other living things *Dogs are my favorite animals.* Col: **animal lover** – one who has pets and likes all kinds of animals **animal rights** – laws regulating bad treatment of creatures **animal shelter** – provides care for lost or abandon pets **party animal** – goes to many parties and gets carried away **stuffed animal** – a soft toy in the shape of a specific animal **take an animal in** – shelter a wounded or homeless animal **wild animal** – an animal that lives in nature

answer /an sEr/ [answers, answered, answering] *noun* 1 response to a question *She knew the answers to all the questions on the test.* 2 solution to a problem *The answer to your money problems is to get a better job.* • *verb* give an answer *She didn't answer him when he asked her what was wrong.* Col: **answer the call of duty** – sign up for the military **answer the call of nature** – go pee **answer the door** – go to the door and open it when someone knocks or rings the doorbell **answer the phone** – pick up the phone and speak when it rings **answer to one's prayers** – an event that solves a big problem **not taking no for an answer** – insistent

ant (aunt) /ant/ [ants] *noun* a small insect that lives in groups with other ants *There are ants in the sugar bowl.* Col: **ant hill** – a small rise in the ground where ants live **ants in one's pants** – jumpy, agitated or restless **carpenter ants** – ants that destroy houses **The Ants and the Grasshopper** – children's fable with a message to work before one plays

apple /a pul/ [apples] *noun* a round red, green or yellow fruit *I had an apple at snack time.* Col: **Adam's apple** – a small bump seen at the front of a man's neck **apple pie** – a round, sweet dessert made with apples, flour and sugar **compare apples and oranges** – two things that are very different. **How about them apples?** – What do you think about that? **the Big Apple** – New York City

apricot /a pru kot/ [apricots] *noun* a small, juicy round orange colored fruit *I like apricots fresh or dried.* • *adv* light orange color *She wore an apricot scarf.* Col: **apricot jam** – fruit spread made with apricots to eat with bread **apricot brandy** – strong alcoholic drink made from apricots

as /az/ *conj* showing comparison *The room is as wide as it is long.* Col: **as a matter of fact** – actually **as if** – not likely or something that might be true **as of** – up to a certain time **as is** – an item that will be sold with no changes to its current condition **as well as** – in addition

ask /ask/ [asks, asked, asking] *verb* 1 request *She asked to borrow the car.* 2 question *He asked, How much it cost?"* Col: **ask around** - make inquires **Ask a stupid question, you'll get a stupid an-**

swer – the question is too silly to deserve a proper response   Ask me no questions, I'll tell you no lies - I'm not going to share the information   ask after – inquire about the health of a friend or relative   ask back – invite for a return visit   ask in – invite into a home   ask out – invite on a date   ask over – invite to visit or play   ask for one's hand – propose marriage   ask for the moon – too much   ask for trouble – risk   asking price – the price a seller hopes for but could accept less   couldn't ask for more – totally happy with someone or something   Don't ask – bad news   Don't ask me – I don't know   I couldn't ask you to do that – it's too much   If there is anything you need, don't hesitate to ask – sincere offer of help   If you ask me – offer an unwanted opinion   If you don't see what you want, please ask – shopkeepers offer   It doesn't hurt to ask – the answer could be yes   It's better to ask for forgiveness than permission – take a chance without permission   no questions asked – no consequence for a confession   Shoot first, ask questions later – act quickly   You asked for it – you deserve the negative consequences of your actions   yours for the asking – free, easy to obtain

ass /as/ [asses] *noun* 1 donkey *An ass is smaller than a horse with longer ears* 2 vulgar slang for a vain, self-important stupid person *That ass cut right in front of me!* 3 vulgar slang for buttocks, anus, sex *Look at the ass on her.* Col: ass is on the line – job is in jeopardy   ass over tea kettle – tumbling fall   be on ass – micro- manage   bust ass – work hard   chew someone's ass off – yell at someone   cover one's ass -ensure one can't be blamed or criticized later   flat on one's ass – fell down on one's butt   get ass – sex   get one's ass in gear – get moving   get off one's ass – get up and get to work   Get your ass over here! – come here   half-assed – incomplete work or poorly done   haul ass – go fast, perhaps to escape   It will be your ass! – threat about possible consequences   kick ass – a great job   kick some ass – win a fight   kiss ass – try too hard to please a boss or teacher   Kiss my ass! – go to hell   make an ass of – make a fool of one's self   not give a rat's ass – don't care   pain in the ass – nuisance   smart ass – mouthy, rude   talk out of one's ass – don't know what you are talking about   tight ass – cheapskate   tits and ass – R rated display of woman's breasts and buttocks   work one's ass off – work hard

asthma /az mu/ *noun* a disease of the lungs that makes it difficult to breathe *My son had asthma as a child but it went away when he was a teenager.*

at /at/ *prep* 1 place or direction *The desk is at the front of the room.* 2 a condition *They are at war.* 3 time *We will meet at noon.* Col: at least – the smallest thing that can happen or be done   at once – now, immediately   stand at attention – stand up straight with arms at sides

attack /u tak/ [attacks, attacked, attacking] *verb* start a fight *He attacked me with a knife.* Col: fatal attack – causes death   heart attack – the heart stops beating from shock or disease   panic attack – symptoms of extreme fear leaving one unable to act   terrorist attack – violent action to harm and cause fear in another group of people   under attack – violently acting against

attraction /u trak Shun/ [attracts, attracted, attracting] *noun* 1 a feeling of being drawn towards *There was some attraction to Bob a year ago but not now.* 2 an appealing event *The pandas were the main attraction at the zoo.* Col: fatal attraction – drawn to something harmful   main attraction – the part of a show that is the most exciting **tourist attraction** – interesting to people visiting from other places **romantic attraction** – love connections between two people

aunt (ant) /ant/ [aunts] *noun* mother's sister or father's sister *My aunt took care of me while my parents went on a second honeymoon.*

automatic /o du ma dik/ *adj* without effort or thinking *Breathing is automatic.* Col: **automatic pilot** – a computer that controls the airplane **automatic transmission** – a car with no manual gear stick

back /bak/ [backs, backed, backing] *noun* 1 part of the body above the bum below the neck *I didn't recognize her because I only saw her back.* 2 location to the rear of a building *We went around to the back of the house when no one answered the front door.* • *verb* reverse *I backed the car over my son's bike.* Col: **back and forth** – can't decide or change direction forward and back in a rocking motion **back door** – unobserved, not in plain view from the street **back up** – reverse or store data in a computer in another location **behind my back** – harm someone without their knowledge

bad /bad/ [worse, worst] *adj* not good or nice *Smoking is a bad decision.* Col: **bad apple** – one in a group who acts badly and gets others to do the same **bad blood** – unresolved conflict between families **bad feeling about** – sixth sense, anticipating disaster **bad mouth** – speak poorly about **bad to the bone** – evil **go bad** – food or people that rot **going from bad to worse** – declining **not bad** – so so, almost good **take the good with the bad** – accept the whole **too bad** – unfortunate

bag /bag/ [bags, bagged, bagging] *noun* soft-sided container for carrying things *Use bags to carry your food home from the store.* • *verb* put thing in bags *The clerk bagged the groceries for me.* Col: **bag of bones** – very thin **grab bag** – bundle of different goods **I'm bagged** – very tired **bag of tricks** – surprises **shoulder bag** – a purse or bag with a strap over the shoulder **sleeping bag** – a large padded bag made for a person to sleep in **tea bag** – a small bag with very small holes and tea inside it

balance /ba luns/ [balances, balanced, balancing] *noun* 1 ability to hold a position without falling *He lost his balance and fell off the ladder.* 2 of equal weight or importance *To lose weight, one needs a balance between eating and exercise.* 3 the difference between the money owed and paid *After today's payment, our bank balance is $2,500.* • *verb* find equilibrium *The seal balances a ball on his nose.* Col: **balance of power** – the bigger share of power held by a party or individuals **balance sheet** – business document that gives a snapshot of the financial situation **balance the books** – accounting term for ensuring everything has been included and accounts balance **delicate balance** – taking equal care of two important things

banana /bu na nu/ [bananas] *noun* a long, narrow, sweet, yellow fruit that is peeled before eating *I eat a banana with breakfast every day.* Col: **banana republic** – small, poor country with a weak or corrupt government **banana spilt** – large dessert with ice cream between two halves of a banana

band /band/ [bands, banded, banding] *noun* 1 a group of musicians who play regularly together *We hired a really good band for the dance.* 2 a group of people who move or act together *They were attacked by a band of thieves.* 3 a narrow flat piece of material used for decoration or tying things together *His hat had a black band around it.* Col: **arm band** – cloth worn around the upper arm for a reason **band together** – form a group   marching band – organized group of walking musicians for parades   rock band – a band of musicians that plays rock and roll music   strike up the band – get organized and begin   wedding band – a ring worn on the left hand of married people

basket   /**ba** skut/ [baskets] *noun* container made of woven wood strips or grass *She put all the apples in a basket to carry them home.* Col: basket case – emotional wreck   gift basket – basket full of many small items given as a present   picnic basket – designed to carry food to be eaten outdoors   put all one's eggs in one basket – risk losing everything   waste-paper basket – small garbage container used mostly for paper refuse

bath   /**baTH**/ [baths, bathed, bathing] *verb* the washing of the entire body *She bathed her son because he was dirty.* • *noun* water used for a bath *The maid ran a warm bath for the duchess.* Col: bath towel – very large towel   bubble bath – foam soap bubbles in a bath for fun or luxury

bladder   /**bla** dEr/ [bladders] *noun* organ in the body that holds urine *His bladder was starting to feel full.* Col: full bladder – need to pee

black   /**blak**/ [blacks, blacker, blackest] *adj* the darkest color *Most of my students have black hair.* • *noun* the color *Black is flattering on almost everyone.* Col: black and blue – badly bruised   black and white – very clear, having only one meaning   black eye – purple around the eye from bruising   black hearted – evil   black out – lose electricity or go unconscious   black sheep – the one person who is different or strange   black tie – very formal event   pitch black – no light at all

blanket   /**blaNg** kut/ [blankets, blanketed, blanketing] *noun* a cloth cover for a bed *It will be cold tonight, here is an extra blanket.* • *verb* to cover something with a layer *She blankets her horse in winter.* Col: born on the wrong side of the blanket – parents were not married.   security blanket – gives a feeling of safety or confidence   wet blanket – a negative person who ruins the fun for others

branch   /**branCh**/   [branches, branched, branching] *noun* 1 a smaller piece growing from the trunk of a tree *They cut off the tree branch that was touching the phone wires.* 2 a smaller office that is part of a larger business with many locations *The Royal Bank has a branch in our neighborhood.* • *verb* diverge *The stream branched off the main river.* Col: branch manager – one in charge of a company branch   branch of government – part of government responsible for specific field

brass   /**bras**/ *adj* shiny yellow-orange metal *They have a brass lamp on the table.* • *noun* musical instruments made of brass including horns and trumpets *The brass adds a rich, sharp quality to the sound of an orchestra.* Col: bold as brass – courageous or rude   brass ring – achievement   get down to brass tacks – focus on work details   top brass – those in charge of an entire organization/military

cabbage   /**ka** buj/ [cabbages] *noun* a round vegetable with large green leaves *We made coleslaw with cabbage and shredded carrots.* Col: cabbage patch – garden where cabbages are grown

calendar   /**ka** lun dEr/ [calendars] *noun* table showing the days, weeks and months of a year *There is a calendar on the wall in my class.* Col: calendar girl – pinup model   calendar year – January 1 – December 31

calf   /**kaf**/ [calves] *noun* 1 baby cow *The cow wouldn't let us touch her calf.* 2 lower back part of the leg *I stretch my calves before I run.*

camera   /**kam** ru/ [cameras] *noun* a device for taking pictures *I have a cam-*

era in my phone. Col: **camera crew** – people who take the pictures for TV or movies   **digital camera** – electronic camera that uses no film   **on camera** – to be in a picture taken with a camera   **video camera** – camera that takes moving pictures

can /kan/ [cans, canned, canning] *noun* a small metal container *I bought a can of peas.* • *verb* 1 ability *I can play the piano quite well.* 2 permission *You can leave when you have finished the test.*

Canada /**ka** nu du/ *pr noun* second largest country in the world *Ottawa is the capital of Canada.* Col: **Canada goose** – a large wild bird from Canada that flies south for the winter   **Canada Day** – celebrated July 1 each year

candidate /**kan** du dAyt/ [candidates] *noun* someone competing for a job or elected position

cantaloupe /**kan** tu lOwp/ [cantaloupes] *noun* a large round melon, rough and brown on the outside, juicy and orange on the inside *I like cantaloupe in fruit salad.*

canvas /**kan** vus/ [canvases] *adj* rough, heavy material used for tents and work clothes *He wore his canvas shirt for hiking in the woods.* • *noun* treated material pulled tight for artists to paint on *The artist set up his canvas and began to paint.* Col: **blank canvas** – a place to design anything but have not yet begun

capital (capitol) /**ka** pu dul/ [capitals] *noun* 1 large set of alphabet letters *Names begin with capitals.* 2 money *One needs capital to start a business.* 3 the city where the government of a country is located *London is the capital of England.*

capitol (capital) /**ka** pu dul/ *noun* building where the lawmakers meet *The representatives are leaving the capitol.*

cash /kaSh/ [cashes, cashed, cashing] *noun* money in the form of coins and paper bills *He didn't have enough cash in his pocket, so he paid with a credit card.* • *verb* get money for a check *You can cash that check at the bank.* Col: **cash cow** – a product or business that brings in a lot of money   **cash in** – exchange for what is owed   **cash is king** – good to have in a recession to purchase bargains   **cash out** – exchange casino chips for money before leaving   **cold hard cash** – currency not credit

cat /kat/ [cats] *noun* 1 small furry pets with pointed ears and long whiskers *She always bought her cat the best pet food.* 2 felines, large animals related to cats *The tiger is part of the cat family.* Col: **cat burglar** – a professional thief   **cat fight** – women in conflict   **Cat got your tongue?** – speechless   **Curiosity killed the cat.** – *proverb* about minding one's own business   **fat cat** – rich and powerful   **fraidy cat** or **scardy cat** – timid   **house cat** – a pet cat that lives inside with the family   **let the cat out of the bag** – to tell a secret prematurely   **look what the cat dragged in** – surprise guest   **wild cat** – a large cat that lives in nature   **wildcat strike** – illegal strike

chance /**Chans**/ [chances, chanced, chancing] *noun* 1 opportunity *I had a chance to study art in Italy, so I took it.* 2 luck *Poker is a game of chance.* • *verb* risk *We inverted in pork bellies and chanced losing everything.* • *adj* random *We met by chance encounter at the market.* Col: **by chance** – because of luck   **chance of a lifetime** – rare opportunity   **fat chance** – sarcastic for unlikely   **not a chance** – never   **take a chance** – try something that may not work

chapter /**Chap** dEr/ [chapters] *noun* 1 main section of a book *Grass is Black is divided into sixteen sound/color chapters.* 2 branch of an organization or club *Toronto has Rotary and many other service club chapters.*

crab /krab/ [crabs] *noun* a sea animal with a hard shell and large claws, popular as food *Crab is delicious and expensive.* Col: **crab walk** – move with both hands and both feet on the ground **crabby** – short tempered

crack /krak/ [cracks, cracked, cracking] *noun* 1 small break in a surface making a line or small opening *There was a crack in the cup and some tea leaked out.* 2 narrow opening *You can't see through the cracks between the boards.* 3 loud sharp sound *We heard a crack of thunder when the storm started.* 4 slang for street drug *She was smoking crack on the street corner.* • *verb* 1 break and cause a snapping sound *The nuts cracked in the vice.* 2 break down mentally. *He got promoted too soon and cracked under the pressure.* Col: **crack down** – limit bad behavior **crack of dawn** -very early **crack open** – open beer or wine **crack the case** – to solve a crime **crack the whip** – take charge to make sure work gets done **crack up** – burst out laughing **have first crack at** – first try **slip between the cracks** – went unnoticed **You're on crack.** – you're crazy

Dad /dad/ [dads] *noun* informal word for father *My dad takes me to all the ball games.*

dam (damn) /dam/ [dams, dammed, damming] *noun* barrier built across water to control flow *The dam broke and the town flooded.* • *verb* make a barrier for water *We dammed the river.*

damn (dam) /dam/ *interjection* curse to express anger or regret *Damn! I hit my thumb with the hammer.* Col: **Damn it!** or **God damn it.** – swearing because one is annoyed **give a damn** – care about **not worth a damn** – worthless

damage /da muj/ [damages, damaged, damaging] *noun* 1 harm that makes a thing less useful or less valuable *Fire caused the damage to the wiring, so the lights wouldn't work.* 2 injury that affects ability *The accident caused damage to his back, so he couldn't work anymore.* • *verb* ruin *The car damaged the bicycle badly in the collision.* Col: **damage control** – minimize consequences after a mishap **What's the damage?** – How much is this going to cost?

elastic /u la stik/ [elastics] *noun* 1 a rubber band *I use elastics to teach my students about word stress.* • *adj* the quality that stretches and returns to original shape *My jeans have an elastic waist that is really comfortable* **elastic band** – a band made of rubber that stretches and used to hold things together **elastic waistband** – an elastic in the waist of a skirt or pants

example /eg zam pul/ [examples] *noun* model or sample *The dog is an example of a popular pet.* Col: **classic example** – a word, picture, person or thing often linked to what is being described **for example** – additional information to clarify meaning **make an example of** – punish one to deter others **prime example** – perfect model

expansion /ek span shun/ [expansions] *noun* making something bigger *The expansion of the highway will make it easier to get to Ottawa.*

family /fam ley/ [families] *noun* 1 a group of people who are related ⋔ *My family came from Ireland.* 2 a related group of plants or animals *Lions, tigers, and leopards are all part of the cat family.* Col: **family affair** – private, only family members included **family resemblance** – looking like those related to one **family values** – beliefs that put families first **like family** – a friend so special that you think of them as family **one big happy family** – a group of people who are happy working together **royal family** – a group of related people at the head of a country **runs in the family** – characteristic common from generation to generation in a family

fast /fast/ [faster fastest, fasts, fasted, fasting] *adj* quick *He is a fast worker.* • *verb* go without food for a period of time *Muslims fast during Ramadan.* Col:

fast food – cheap food of poor quality prepared quickly   fast friends – loyal   fast track – quick route   going nowhere fast – no progress   hard and fast rule – no flexibility   make a fast buck – make money in a short period of time   pull a fast one – successfully deceive

fat /fat/ [fatter, fattest] *adj* too large and heavy *He should eat less and exercise more because he is too fat.* • *noun* cooking substance especially for frying food *He fried the chicken in fat.* Col: big fat – extra emphasis   chew the fat – gossip   fat and sassy – healthy   fat cat – a wealthy person   fat chance – unlikely   not over until the fat lady sings – still a small unlikely chance one's team will win   trim the fat – remove everything that is not needed

flag /flag/ [flags, flagged, flagging] *noun* ⚑ colorful piece of cloth with a special design representing a country, city, or other specific group or place *The flag of Canada has a red maple leaf.* • *verb* mark to look at carefully later *She flagged some of the comments as important.* Col: flag them down – call over to help   raise the flag – put the flag up at the top of the pole   red flag – indicating a possible problem   wave a white flag – surrender   wrap one's self in the flag – patriotic action

flat /flat/ [flatter, flattest] *adj* not round or bumpy *The top of a table is flat.* Col: fell flat on one's face – embarrassed from a public failure   flat broke – out of money   flat on one's back – sick in bed   flat rate – money paid for services based on the job   flat tire – a wheel that has lost some of its air   flats – women's shoes without high heels

fragile /fra jul/ *adj* easily broken *Bullies often have fragile egos.*

gas /gas/ [gases] *noun* 1 one of the three states of matter that is neither solid or liquid *Oxygen is a gas.* 2 mix of combustibles used to heat homes and cook *I cook with gas at home.* 3 fuel used to run vehicles *I need to put gas in the car.* Col: cooking with gas – making good progress   gas guzzler – big engine in a vehicle that uses lots of fuel   gas up – to put gas in a car   natural gas – gas used to make stoves work and heat homes   pass gas – fart

glass /glas/ [glasses] *noun* 1 smooth, hard material, usually transparent, used for windows, decorations, and dishes *Windows are made of glass.* 2 container to drink out of *She poured some juice in my glass.* Col: glass ceiling – invisible limit to women's corporate advancement   looking glass – mirror   People who live in glass houses shouldn't throw stones. – *proverb* about speaking carefully   rose-colored glasses – optimist   see the glass as half full or half empty – optimist or pessimist   the man in the glass – the only person one answer to is oneself   wine glass – ♀ goblet shape especially for wine

glasses /gla suz/ [glasses] *noun* short form of eyeglasses, lenses in frames to help one see 👓 *Honey, have you seen my glasses?* Col: sun-glasses – tinted to protect eyes from the glare of the sun

grandmother /gra mu ThEr/ [grandmothers] (grandma, granny, nana) *noun* mother of a person's parent *My grandmother likes to bake cookies.*

grass /grass/ [grasses] *noun* 1 plant with thin green leaves that grows all over the world *They planted grass in front of the house.* 2 slang term for marijuana *He smoked some grass before class.* Col: cut the grass – trim the lawn   grass roots – ordinary people   green as grass – inexperienced   snake in the grass – sly, unpopular person   The grass is always greener on the other side of the fence. – *proverb* people think they would be happier if their circumstances were different

gravel /**gra** vul/ [gravels, gravelled, gravelling] *noun* small pieces of stone for driveways and country roads. *They filled the potholes in their driveway with fresh gravel.* • *verb* to cover with small bits of stone *They gravel the roads every spring.* `Col:` **gravel-voiced** – speaks with a low, rough, raspy voice

had /**had**/ [has, having] *verb* past tense of *have* 1 hold *I had a book in my hand.* 2 own *I had a house in Vancouver but I sold it.* 3 cause something to happen *I had the dress made for my wedding.* `Col:` **had enough** – can no longer tolerate a situation

hafta /**haf** tu/ *contr* have to, spoken word only *English is Stupid Students are Not Chapter Four /I hafta go home./*

half /**haf**/ [½, halves] *noun* one of two equal parts of something *I ate half of the apple and she ate the other half.* • *adv* nearly 50% *The glass is half full.* • *adj* approximately a half *Give him half a chance.* `Col:` **half baked** – incomplete or crazy **half done** – not finished **half time** – break in the middle of a sporting event **in half** – two equal parts **see the glass as half full or half empty** – optimist or pessimist

ham /**ham**/ [hams] *noun* smoked pig meat *We had ham for dinner.* `Col:` **ham sandwich** – sliced ham between two pieces of bread **such a ham** – silly person

hammer /**ha** mEr/ [hammers, hammered, hammering] *noun* carpenter's tool with a flat steel surface for pounding in nails *He framed up the shed with wood, a hammer and nails.* • *verb* use a hammer *He hammered the nails into the wood.* `Col:` **hammer home** – impress important information on others by repeating it often **hammer out** – decide on the details of an agreement **hammer away** – work hard at something until it is done `Col:` **hammer toe** – a problem with the second toe that causes pain

hand /**hand**/ [hands, handed, handing] *noun* part of the body at the end of the arm with fingers attached 👋 *She held the flowers in her hand.* • *verb* giving something to someone *She handed me a five-dollar bill for her share of lunch.* `Col:` **by hand** – made without machines **hand in hand** – two people's hands joined together or people working together to do a task **hand of cards** – cards held by one player during a card game **hand over** – give **hand out** – charity `Col:` **hand over fist** – quickly and continuously **hand over hand** – place one arm on top of the other **lend a hand** – help **on the other hand** – look at something in a different way

hang /**haNg**/ [hangs, hanged, hanging] *verb* 1 attach an object to an overhead object *Baskets of flowers hang from the front porch.* 2 attach decorations to a wall *Pictures, posters and photographs hang in the front room.* 3 die from being suspended with a rope around the neck and suspending them *The man who killed the child was hanged.* `Col:` **get the hang of** – improving at a new skill **hang in there** – be patient, the situation will improve **hang on** – wait **hang out** – spend time in a favorite place **hang out with** – spend time with friends in a certain place **hang up** – put the telephone down on the receiver to disconnect

happen /**ha** pun/ [happens, happened, happening] *verb* 1 take place, occur *Many small car accidents happen in parking lots.* 2 by chance or luck *I happened to run into her at the market and asked her for tea.* `Col:` **as it happens** – luck, coincidence **happen upon** – find by chance **it happens** – things happen for no reason **minute it happened** – exact time **What happened?** – share the story

happy /**ha** pEy/ [happier, happiest] *adj* feeling the opposite of sad *We were all happy to see the new baby.* `Col:` **couldn't be happier** – completely happy with all areas of life   happily ever after – traditional end to fairy tales   happy accident – coincidence   happy camper – content with their life or situation   happy couple – a couple about to be married or newly married   happy ending – a good finish to a story   happy hour – cheap drinks in a bar from about 5-7pm   not a happy camper – someone who is angry, sad, or upset about a situation

has /haz/ [had, having] *verb* third person singular present tense of *have* 1 hold *She has a book in her hand.* 2 own *He has a house and a cottage.* 3 cause an event to happen *She has her hair done every week.* Col: a has-been – once famous, no longer popular   has got game – excited about an activity and performing well

hasta /has tu/ *contr* has to, spoken word only, *English is Stupid, Students are Not* Chapter Four /*He hasta go home.*/

hat /hat/ [hats] *noun* a piece of clothing worn on the head *I wear a hat in the winter to keep my head and ears warm.* Col: hat in hand – beg for   hats off to you – congratulations   I'll eat my hat – be very surprised if a particular event occurs   old hat – familiar or routine   pass the hat – collect money to help the unfortunate   pull out of a hat or pull a rabbit out of a hat – magically make appear   take my hat off – show honor or admiration   wear many hats – have many occupations

have /hav/ [has, had, having] *verb* 1 hold *I have a book in my hand.* 2 own *They have a house in Vancouver.* 3 cause to happen *I have my hair done every week.* Col: coulda – contraction of could have   have a crush on – like very much romantically   have a secret – private information   have it in for – dislike and intend harm   have it out – argue until the problem is resolved   have pain – headache, toothache, a sore throat...   have to – must   have to do with – about or related   shoulda – contraction of should have   to have and to hold from this day forward – marriage vows   What are we having for dinner? – what food   Who are we having for dinner? – which guests   woulda – contraction of would have

jam /jam/ [jams, jammed, jamming] *verb* 1 stuck *The car ran off the road and was jammed between two trees.* 2 slang for informally playing music together *The band jammed in his garage every weekend.* • *adj* fixed in place unable to work properly *The window is jammed and I can't open it.* • *noun* 1 difficult or awkward situation *I'm in a jam because I'm supposed to work tomorrow and my son is sick.* 2 sweet jelly made from fruit *She put strawberry jam on her toast.* Col: get out of a jam – out of a tricky situation   in a jam – small tricky situation   jam session – musicians informally playing together   jam something up – clog   PB&J – peanut butter and jam   traffic jam – too many cars on the road stopped or moving very slowly

January /jan yU we rEy/ [Jan., Januarys] *prop noun* first month of the year *New Year's Day is January 1ˢᵗ.* Col: as slow as molasses in January – moves very slowly

lamb /lam/ [lams] *noun* 1 baby sheep *That ewe always has twin lambs.* 2 meat from a young sheep *Mint sauce is good with lamb.* Col: gentle as a lamb -simile for kind, caring and calm   quiet as a lamb – very quiet   two shakes of a lamb's tail – quickly

land /land/ [lands, landed, landing] *noun* 1 solid part of the earth not under water *Pine trees only grow on land.* 2 property, often without buildings on it *He bought land in Florida and plans to build a big house.* • *verb* return to land after being in the air *The pilot landed the plane.* Col: land a fish – catch a fish   land a job – get a job that many others applied for   land on one's feet – to get out of a tricky situation and look good   **lay of the land** – the overall picture of operations   **native land** – country of birth   **Never-never land** – Peter Pan's magical land where children never grow up   **no man's land** – deserted place   **promise land** – place of abundance and opportunity

language /laNg wuj/ [languages] *noun* a system of signals for communication *Europeans often speak more than one language.* Col: EFL – English as a Foreign Language   ELL – English as a Learned Language   ESL – English as a Second Language   **dirty language** – vulgar, profane   **first language** – native language, learned in early childhood   **Now you are talking my language.** – said what I have been waiting to hear   **second language** – a learned language different from one's first language   **sign language** – an official language used mostly by those who are deaf   **speak my language** – understand me, my values and expectations   **strong language** – swearing, profanity   TESL – Teachers of English as a Second Language   TESOL – Teacher of English to Speakers of Other Languages

last /last/ *adj* at the end *She was last in line at the bank.* • *verb* keep going or be useful for a long time *These shoes lasted for ten years.* Col: **at last** – finally, after a long wait   **last time** – never happen again   **last words** – words someone says just before they die   **last name** – family or surname   **last of all** – the final point

laugh /laf/ [laughs, laughed, laughing] *verb* show pleasure with smiles, movement and noise *He laughs at all my jokes.* • *noun* funny *She is a laugh a minute.* Col: **a good laugh** – something funny   **be laughing all the way to the bank** – satisfaction of financial success after struggle   **laugh at** – make fun of   **last laugh** – satisfaction of success after being ridiculed   **lol** – text for laugh out loud   **no laughing matter** – a serious situation someone thought was funny

mad /mad/ [madder, maddest] *adj* 1 angry *The teacher is mad the students arrive late every day.* 2 crazy *After her son was killed by a drunk driver the mother went mad and shot the driver.* Col: **as mad as a hatter** – to be crazy   **as mad as a hornet** – to be crazy   **as mad as a March hare** – to be crazy from Alice in Wonderland   **barking mad** – UK crazy   **Don't get mad, get even.** – advice for directing one's anger   **hopping mad** – very angry   **fighting mad** – angry enough to take serious action   **hopping mad** – very angry   **in a mad rush** – in a hurry   **like mad** – actively   **mad about** – love   **so mad I could scream** – angry and frustrated   **stark raving mad** – out of control

man /man/ [men, manned, manning] *noun* 1 ♂ adult male person, opposite of woman *A man would not normally wear a dress.* 2 piece used in a board game *You have to place your man on the first square then roll the dice.* • *verb* manage ongoing business in person *Someone has to stay in the office and man the phones.* Col: **a yes man** – agrees with authority regardless of personal beliefs   **Clothes make the man.** – *proverb* appearances are important   **dirty old man** – pervert   **every man for himself** – don't count on co-operation   **every man has his price** – his soul can be bought   **family man** – family first   **hangman** – word game   **hit man** – hired killer   **ladies' man** – heartbreaker   **low man on the totem pole** – the one with least authority/power   **man after my own heart** – similar values or tastes   **Man cannot live by bread alone.** – *proverb* his spirit needs to be nourished   **man enough** – a grown-up who takes ownership or responsibility for the situation   **man for all seasons** – good at everything

man of few words – quiet   **man of his word** – honest   **man of means** – rich, powerful   **man of the cloth** – priest   **man of the world** – educated and well traveled   **man on the street** – average man   **or a mouse?** – coward   **man's best friend** – dog   **man's got to do what a man's got to do** – destiny   **man's man** – ruggedly masculine   **man-to-man** – grown-up talk   **may the best man win** – good sport wishing good luck   **man on the street** – average guy   **not the man he used to be** – diminished somehow   **Oh, man!** – surprise or frustration   **One man's loss is another man's gain.** – *proverb* when one person loses something another person gets it   **one's own man** – independent   **right-hand man** – trusted assistant   **see a man about a horse** – pee   **self-made man/woman** – earned his/her money and success on their own   **stick man** – simplest drawing   **take it like a man** – don't cry   **the man** – authority or an honorable individual   **the odd man out** – doesn't fit in   **The way to a man's heart is through his stomach** – to capture a husband a woman should be a good cook   **Time waits for no man.** – *proverb*, life moves forward don't miss out   **You can't keep a good man down.** – *proverb* about recovering from setbacks

manager /ma nu jEr/ [managers] *noun* someone in charge of a business or department *The manager said I could have the day off work.* Col: **bank manager** – local branch head   **campaign manager** – manages a person's attempt to get elected

manual /man yU wul/ [manuals] *noun* book of instructions *The new stove came with a manual.* • *adj* with the hands *Raking the lawn is a manual activity.* Col: **instruction manual** – book of directions   **manual labor** – physical work   **manual transmission** – automatic gear shift   **training manual** – learning guide

map /map/ [maps, mapped, mapping] *noun* drawing that shows geography and locations *We needed a map to find Joe's cottage.* • *verb* make a representation of an area *They mapped the area around the lake over 100 years ago.* Col: **follow the map** – use as a guide   **map out** – draw a sketch or plan   **off the map** – vanish completely   **on the map** – recognition   **put on the map** – bring notoriety to a small place   **treasure map** – guide to fortune   **wipe off the map** – take out of existence   **world map** – atlas of Earth

mass /mas/ [masses] *noun* 1 large amount *The astronomer spotted a large mass in outer space.* 2 science term, related to weight as a property of matter *Mass is affected by gravitational forces.* 3 lump *They found a mass on her lung.* 4 Roman Catholic church service *Mass is at midnight on Christmas Eve.* • *adj* large group or number *Thousands of people took part in a mass protest against coal emissions.* Col: **critical mass** – point after which a struggle becomes easier or there is no turning back   **mass marketing** – campaign to a large group of people   **mass media** – television, radio, movies, and newspapers   **mass graves** – grave where many people are buried together   **mass production** – produce in large quantities using machinery

match /matCh/ [matches, matched, matching] *verb* 1 the same as *The color of the curtains has to match the color of the sofa.* 2 correctly go together with *Match each question with the right answer.* • *noun* a small stick with an ignitable tip used to light fires *He lit the barbeque with a match.* Col: **a good match** – go well together   **a match made in heaven** – a perfectly happy marriage   **be no match for** – the opponent is vastly superior   **match up** – find paired items   **match**

wits – intellectual contest   **meet one's match** – meet one's social and intellectual equal   **mix and match** – select from a limited number of items   **shouting match** – yelling back and forth in argument   **strike a match** – to light a match   **tennis match** – a game of tennis   **whole shooting match** – all and everything

math /maTH/ [maths] *noun* the science of using numbers, short form for mathematics *Math was her best subject in school.* Col: **do the math** – calculate the expense before making a decision   **math problem** – a puzzle solved using numbers

natural /na ChE rul/ *adj* 1 occurring in nature *It is natural for a mother to love her child.* 2 from nature, not artificial *Everything I cook with is natural.* Col: **die of natural causes** – disease or old age not accident or murder   **naturally gifted** – born with an ease for performing specific skills   **natural gas** – combustible fuel tapped from underground   **natural light** – daylight, sunlight   **natural resource** – products like water, trees and minerals found in nature and used by humans   **second nature** – skill that came easily without study or practice

pad /pad/ [pads, padded, padding] *noun* 1 thick piece of cloth used to protect or to soak up liquid *She put a pad under the vase so it would not scratch the table.* 2 bottom of an animal's foot *My dog cut his pad on the ice.* 3 sheets of paper bound together *She took out a writing pad and made notes.* 4 (slang) where a person lives *He showed his girlfriend his new pad.* • *verb* thicken with material *She padded her bra to make her breasts seem bigger.* Col: **heating pad** – a thin square electrical cushion that can be plugged in to provide heat   **key pad** – a set of numbered keys on a keyboard or calculator   **launch pad** – place from which rockets are sent into space   **pad of paper** – several small sheets of paper bound with glue   **pad out** – going to sleep   **pad the bill** – overcharge

pancreas /**pan** krE yus/ [pancreases] *noun* organ in the body that makes digestive juices and insulin *The pancreas makes insulin for digesting sugar.*

passed (past) /**past**/ [passes, passed, passing] *verb* past tense of *pass* go by *He passed the ball to his brother.* Col: **passed out** – unconscious either fainted or asleep

past (passed) /**past**/ *adj* time gone by *In years past we visited the cottage.* • *prep* move in front of and beyond *The soldiers paraded past the king.* • *noun* before the present *Don't dwell in the past.* Col: **blast from the past** – music or nostalgia old rock and roll song   **a thing of the past** – history   **can't see past the end of one's nose** – too busy focusing on self to see what is really important   **in the past** – in a time that has now finished   **live in the past** – too much time thinking about the past   **not put it past** – suspect   **past its best before date** – food that may be too old to eat   **past caring** – don't care anymore   **past prime** – best days are behind   **past event** – something that happened in the past   **past tense** – form of a verb showing an action that occurred in the past   **slip past** – sneak around undetected

passed (past) /**past**/ *verb* past tense of *pass* go by *The red car passed me on a double yellow line.* Col: **passed away** – deceased

pasta /**pa** stu/ [pastas] *noun* noodles made from flour, eggs and water *Spaghetti is a pasta.*

piano /pE **ya** nOw/ [pianos] *noun* large musical instrument with a keyboard and wire strings *I learned to play the piano as a child.* Col: **piano bar** – cocktail lounge with a piano player as entertainment

plaid /plad/ [plaids] *noun* a colorful fabric with distinctive horizontal and vertical stripes *Each Scottish clan has a family plaid called a tartan.* Col: **plaid shirt** – farmer or woodsman's garment **plaid skirt** – often part of a private school uniform

planet /pla nut/ [planets] noun large ball of rock and metal that circles the sun. *We live on the planet Earth.* Col: **from another planet** – not a mainstream thinker or out of touch **What planet are you from?** – extremely naïve or misinformed

plant /plant/ [plants, planted, planting] *noun* 1 living organism not an animal and cannot move on its own *The rose is a beautiful plant.* 2 where things are made with machinery *There is a large steel plant in Hamilton.* • *verb* move dirt, place plants in the ground and snug the dirt back around *I plant tomatoes every year.* Col: **house plant** – a plant that is grown in a pot indoors **plant a garden** – put seeds or plants in prepared soil outdoors **plant a seed** – start a process that will develop later **plant on** – maliciously place incriminating evidence on an innocent person **treatment plant** – a processing center where water is made clean

radish /ra dish/ [radishes] *noun* a small round red vegetable with a white centre *I put radishes in the salad for color more than taste.*

ran /ran/ [runs, ran, running] *verb* past tense of *run* travel quickly *It was raining so I ran all the way home from school.* Col: **ran away** – left home **ran off** – printed copies or walked out on responsibilities **ran out** – none left **ran the business** – managed or was in charge of a business **ran through** – covered quickly

raspberry /ras be rEy/ [raspberries] *noun* a small tart red bumpy fruit that grows on thorny sticks *I had raspberries on my cereal.* Col: **blow a raspberry** – fake a fart sound pumping air under one's armpit **give someone a raspberry** – made rude noise with their mouth

rat /rat/ [rats, ratted, ratting] *noun* 1 a large rodent *They found a rat in the garbage can.* 2 one who lies, cheats, or steals *That rat tricked me out of my savings.* • *verb* inform authority about another's wrong doing *He ratted on his brother who was stealing from the company.* Col: **dirty rat** – a sneaky unlikeable person who harms others **lab rat** – a rat used for scientific experiments **pack rat** – hates to throw things out so they keep junk **rat around** – waste time **rat out** – tell authorities of another's wrong doing **rat race** – competitive urban lifestyle **rug rat** – toddler **smell a rat** – suspect trickery

reaction /rE yak Shun/ *noun* response *The puppy's reaction to the fireworks was to hide.* Col: **delayed reaction** – response some time after the event **gut reaction** – response from feelings more than facts **knee-jerk reaction** – automatic response, without thinking **mixed reaction** – a variety of responses to an announcement

sad /sad/ [sadder, saddest] *adj* 1 unhappy feeling *I have some sad news.* 2 in bad condition *That old sofa is in sad shape.* Col: **long sad story** – dramatic account not taken seriously by the listener **sad state of affairs** – not good management or conditions **sad truth** – unfortunate, but true **sad to say** – sorry to report **sadder but wiser** – learned a hard lesson through loss

salad /sa lud/ [salads] *noun* a concoction of fresh vegetables served in a bowl *He made a salad with lettuce, tomatoes, cucumbers, carrots and onions.* Col: **salad dressing** – sauce for salad **side salad** – not the main meal

salmon /sa mun/ *noun* salt water food fish that lays its eggs in fresh water *We* *had grilled salmon for dinner.* Col: **salmon pink** – orangey-pink color

sand /sand/ [sands, sanded, sanding] *noun* fine bits of crushed rock found on beaches and in the desert *The beach had white, soft sand.* • *verb* rub with granular paper to make smooth *Beth stripped and sanded the old table before staining it.* Col: **built on sand** – poor foundation **bury one's head in the sand** – choose not to see the obvious **draw a line in the sand** – beyond which action will be taken, warn **grain of sand** – a single piece of finely crushed stone **sand castle** – small castle-shaped structure, made with wet sand **sand down** – rub rough edges off with sand paper **sand dune** – hill of sand **sands of time** – hourglass

sandwich /sam wuj/ [sandwiches, sandwiched, sandwiching] *noun* meat, cheese or spreads between two slices of bread *David made tuna sandwiches for lunch.* • *verb* stuck between *The TV remote was sandwiched between the couch cushions.*

Saturday /sa dEr dAy/ [Sat., Saturdays] *prop noun* the day after Friday *I don't have to work on Saturday.* Col: **Saturday night special** – concealed pistol

shall /shal/ *helping verb* used to make the future tense, formal and not widely used *I shall have a cup of tea.* Col: **Shall we?** – an invitation **What shall we do?** – What would you like to do today?

smash /smash/ [smashes, smashed, smashing] *verb* 1 break into small pieces *The window smashed when it broke.* 2 slang for very drunk *He was smashed at the party.* • *noun* slang for very popular *The movie was a smash.* Col: **smash in** – crush inwards **smash through** – break a blockade **smash to bits** – violently break into very small pieces **smash hit** – very popular movie, show, or song **smash up** – break

splash /splash/ [splashes, splashed, splashing] *noun* the act or sound of displacing liquid *Add a splash of lemon to your water.* • *verb* spray liquid around *The kids were splashing in the pool.* Col: **make a big splash** – social impact, **splash-down** – space craft landing in the sea

stamp /stamp/ [stamps, stamped, stamping] *noun* small piece of paper with a design used to show postage has been paid *You need to put a stamp on that letter before you mail it.* • *verb* pound with the foot *Stamp on the fire to put it out.* Col: **rubber stamp something** – accept officially without looking **stamp of approval** – acceptance **stamp out** – stop forever

tacks (tax) /taks/ *noun* plural of tack, a push pin *The teacher uses tacks to hold up the map.* Col: **as sharp as a tack** – clever **tack down** – attach to the floor with small nails **tack up** – attach to the wall with push pins **get down to brass tacks** – focus on details of work

tax (tacks) /taks/ [taxes, taxed, taxing] *noun* money paid to the government *The tax on the money earned is income tax.* • *verb* money taken by the government on top of the purchase price *Western governments tax the middle classes excessively.* • *adj* about tax *Property taxes increase with no increase in services.* Col: **income tax** – paid on the amount of money made in a year **sales tax** – paid on purchases **sin tax** – heavy tax on things that are bad like liquor **tax and spend** – high taxes and loose spending **tax break** – less tax is paid **tax cut** – pay less tax **tax grab** – the government takes extra tax for a small new service

than /than/ *conj* compare two things *My dog is bigger than that dog.*

that /that/ [those] *adj* point out or distinguish something from a distance in place or time *That man over there is the manager.* • *pron* distinguish or emphasize *That is a good idea.* • *conj* connect two clauses *I know that they are coming to the wedding.*

traffic /tra fik/ *noun* cars, trucks, and people moving along a road *The traffic at five o'clock is very heavy.* • *verb* buy and sell illegal goods *They traffic in illegal drugs.* Col: **go play in the traffic** – sarcastic suggestion meant to be funny meaning get out of here permanently **rush-hour traffic** – large volume of traffic when people travel in and out of the city for work **stuck in traffic** – severe delay **tie traffic up** – cause delay **traffic cop** – controls the flow of cars, trucks and vans **traffic jam** – too many cars on the road stopped/moving slowly

transport /**tran** zpOrt/ [transports, transported, transporting] *verb* carry big things from one place to another *Trucks transport food from the farm to the market.* • *noun* delivery *The transport of goods is a multi-billion dollar industry.* Col: **public transport** – individuals pay for traveling on the system **transportation system** – network for moving things over distance **transported into joy** – moved to happiness

vacuum /**va** kyUwm/ [vacuums, vacuumed, vacuuming] *noun* totally empty space *Draw air out of a container to create a vacuum.* • *adj* about sucking in air *The vacuum cleaner is in the hall closet.* • *verb* clean using a vacuum machine *The kids vacuum their rooms on Saturday mornings.*

value /**val** yUw/ [values, valued, valuing] *noun* 1 amount of money an item is worth *This ring has a value of $3,000.00.* 2 non-monetary contribution *His reputation added value to the company.* • *verb* set a price *The jeweler valued the ring for the insurance policy.* Col: **commercial value** – how much the public will pay **entertainment value** – enjoyment **take at face value** – exactly as presented, nothing hidden **value added** – improve the monetary quality of a product **value judgment** – an opinion based on personal beliefs

wax (whacks) /**waks**/ [waxes, waxed, waxing] *noun* greasy material that is hard when it's cold and soft when it's warm used for making candles *The wax dripped from the candle onto the table cloth.* • *verb* get larger *The moon waxes until it is full.* Col: **wax and wane** – get bigger and smaller by turns like the moon **wax on** – practice dutifully, until a behavior is automatic **wax paper** – paper covered with wax used for wrapping food **whole ball of wax** – everything

whacks (wax) /**waks**/ *verb* plural of whack which means hit *He whacks the desk with his ruler when he wants the students' attention.* • *noun* a smack *I gave my son a whack for touching the knife.* Col: **out of whack** – not working **whack something off** – finish quickly **patty whacks** – birthday slaps on the butt, one for every year

yam /**yam**/ [yams] *noun* oval orange root vegetable, similar to sweet potato *Yams are high in nutrition and I like them better than potatoes.* Col: **I yam what I yam** – from the cartoon *Popeye*, authentic, accepting of self

Chapter 3
/Ey/ is Green

Chapter 3
/Ey/ is Green

achieve /u ChEyv/
agree /u grEy/
appeal /u pEyl/
appear /u pEyr/
appreciate /u prEy ShE yAyt/

B (be bee) /bEy/
be (B, bee) /bEy/
bean (been) /bEyn/
beat (beet) /bEyt/
bee (B, be) /bEy/
beef /bEyf/
been (bean) /bEyn/
beet (beat) /bEyt/
belief /bu lEyf/
believe /bu lEyv/
between /bu twEyn/
breathe /brEyTh/

C (sea, see) /sEy/
cheap /ChEyp/
cheek /ChEyk/
cheese /ChEyz/
chief /ChEyf/
clear /klEyr/
complete /kum plEyt/
cream /krEym/

D /dEy/
dear (deer) /dEyr/
deep /dEyp/
deer (dear) /dEyr/
degree /du grEy/
delete /du lEyt/
detail /dEy tAyl/
disease /du zEyz/
dream /drEym/

E /Ey/
east /Eyst/
eat /Eyt/
engineer /en jun Eyr/
equal /Ey kwul/
even /Ey vun/

fear /fEyr/
feeble /fEy bul/
feed /fEyd/
feel /Eyl/
feet /fEyt/
female /fEy mAyl/
field /fEyld/
free /frEy/
freeze /frEyz/
frequent /frEy kwunt/

G (gee) /jEy/
gee (G) /jEy/
green /grEyn/

hear /hEyr/
heat /hEyt/
here /hEyr/

idea /Iy dE yu/
increase /in krEys/

jeans /jEynz/

keep /kEyp/
key (quay) /kEy/
knee /nEy/

lead /lEyd/
leaf /lEyf/
lean /lEyn/

machine /mu ShEyn/
meat (meet) /mEyt/
meet (meat) /mEyt/
medium /mEy dE yum/

/ Ey / is Green

museum /myUw zE yum/

naive /nI yEyv/
near /nEyr/
need /nEyd/
needle /nEy dul/
niece /nEys/

P (pea, pee) /pEy/
pea (P, pee) /pEy/
peace (piece) /pEys/
peach /pEyCh/
pee (P, pea) /pEy/
people /pEy pul/
period /pEy rE yud/
piece (peace) /pEys/
pizza /pEyt zu/
please /plEyz/
police /pu lEys/

quay (key) /kEy/

reach /rEyCh/
read (reed) /rEyd/
reason /rEy zun/
receipt /ru sEyt/
reed (read) /rEyd/

sea (C, see) /sEy/
seam /sEym/
season /sEy zun/
seat /sEyt/
secret /sEy krut/
see (C, sea) /sEy/
seed /sEyd/
seem (seam) /sEym/
serious /sEy rE yus/
scene (seen) /sEyn/
seen (scene) /sEyn/

sheep /ShEyp/
sheet /ShEyt/
ski /skEy/
sleep /slEyp/
sneeze /snEyz/
steal (steel) /stEyl/
steam /stEym/
steel (steal) /stEyl/
street /strEyt/
suite (sweet) /swEyt/
sweet (suite) /swEyt/

T (tea, tee) /tEy/
tea (T, tee) /tEy/
teach /tEyCh/
tee (T, tea) /tEy/
teen /tEyn/
teeth /tEyTh/
these /ThEyz/
three /THrEy/
tree /trEy/

V /vEy/
VISA /vEy zu/

we (wee) /wEy/
we'll (wheel) /wEyl/
weak (week) /wEyk/
wee (we) /wEy/
week (weak) /wEyk/
wheel (we'll) /wEyl/
wreath /rEyTH/

year /yEyr/

Z /zEy/ USA
zucchini /zUw kEy nEy/

HOW DO YOU SAY? PRONUNCIATION DICTIONARY

achieve /u **ChEyv**/ [achieves, achieved, achieving] *verb* reach a goal through effort, accomplish *The student achieved recognition for her volunteer efforts.*

agree /u **grEy**/ [agrees, agreed, agreeing] *verb* 1 have the same opinion as another *She agrees that spelling in English is crazy.* 2 allow to happen *He agreed to the offer for his car.* 3 suits or works for *Marriage agrees with him.* 4 subject and verb have the same number or gender *They agree with his idea.* Col: **agree to disagree** — accept a difference of opinion **come to an agreement** — the process of agreeing

appeal /u **pEyl**/ [appeals, appealed, appealing] *noun* 1 attract interest *The white, sandy beaches have special appeal to summer tourists.* 2 a formal request, also in law *The lawyer asked the judge for an appeal.* • *verb* 1 request urgently *The earthquake victims appealed to the world for aid.* 2 enjoy *The scent of spring flowers appeals to me.* 3 request another trial *The thief appealed to the judge for a new trial.*

appear /u **pEyr**/ [appears, appeared, appearing] *verb* 1 shows up *The dog appeared suddenly from around the corner.* 2 seems *It appears as though dinner will be late.*

appreciate /u **prEy** ShE yAyt/ [appreciates, appreciated, appreciating] *verb* grateful *I appreciate the help I got putting the dictionary together.*

B (be, bee) /**bEy**/ [B's] *noun* 1 the second letter of the Latin alphabet *Boy starts with a B.* 2 the second major grade level for school *I got a B on my test.* Col: **ABC's** — the Latin alphabet

be (B, bee) /**bEy**/ *verb* 1 exist *I am a teacher.* 2 take place *The game is tomorrow.* 3 linking subject and predicate for a) identity *I am Canadian.* b) condition *The shirt was dirty.* c) quality *The shirt was cheaply-made.* d) opinion *The shirt is too expensive.* e) total *There are two shirts in the bag.* f) cost *Each shirt is $25.*

bean (been) /**bEyn**/ [beans] *noun* 1 vegetable plant which has a long pod and edible seeds *My kids would eat pork and beans for lunch every day.* 2 one of the seeds inside the long pod *If I taste a lima bean in my salad I spit it right out.* Col: **be full of beans** — high energy   **Jack and the Beanstalk** — classic children's fairy tale   **not worth a hill of beans** — of no value

beat (beet) /**bEyt**/ [beats, beat, beating] *verb* 1 hit over and over *The boy beat the dog that stole his lunch.* 2 defeat in a sporting activity *The Toronto Maple Leafs beat the Edmonton Oilers.* 3 stir quickly and with effort *She beat three eggs together to add to the cake batter.* 4 movement of the heart when pumping blood *Her heart beat quickly after the run.* • *noun* the main accent in music *She tapped her feet to the beat of the music.* Col: **beat a path to door** — in demand   **beat a retreat** — leave quickly   **beat around the bush** — avoid asking directly   **beat brains out** — severe violence   **beat head against the wall** — futile effort   **Beat it!** — go away   **beat oneself up** — self critical   **beat the clock** — time is critical   **beat the daylights out of** — severely injure in a fight   **beat the pants off** — win by a large margin   **beat the rap** — got off a legal charge   **beat the socks off** — win by a large margin   **beat the system** — made money from a system that usually takes one's money   **beat the tar out of/beat to a pulp/beat to within an inch of one's life** — severe beating   **beat to it** — got there first   **beat to the punch** — got to the prize first   **Beats me?** — I don't know   **can't beat that** — good deal   **heart skips a beat** — romantic interest   **If that don't beat all!** — shock   **If you can't beat them, join them.** — *proverb* meaning to join the enemy you can't defeat   **There is no point beating a dead horse.** — *proverb* don't continue to discuss a matter that is done   **without missing a beat** — with no hesitation

bee (B, be) /bEy/ [bees] noun 1 a flying insect that makes honey *The bee flew from flower to flower before heading to the hive.* 2 group work on a big project *They had a barn-raising bee after their barn burned down.* Col: a bee in one's bonnet – annoyed   spelling bee – spelling contest   the bee's knees – awesome   the birds and the bees – talk about where babies come from

beef /bEyf/ noun 1 the flesh of a cow, steer or bull that is used as food *The roast beef was very tender.* 2 a complaint *He had a few beefs about his new summer schedule.* Col: beef up – strengthen, add to increasing quantity   have a beef with – minor conflict   Where's the beef? – content

been (bean) /bEyn/ {also said /bin/ see Pink} verb past participle of to *be* exist *How have you been?*

beet (beat) /bEyt/ [beets] noun plant with a dark red root used as a vegetable *My father loves pickled beets.* Col: turn beet red – blush from embarrassment

belief /bu lEyf/ [beliefs] noun a strong opinion *It is my firm belief there is an easy way to learn English.* Col: contrary to popular belief – against current general thought

believe /bu lEyv/ [believes, believed, believing] verb 1 accept as being true *I believe my teacher.* 2 think *I believe she went to the hospital yesterday.* 3 have faith in *She believes in the power of faith.* Col: believe it or not – it's true even if one does not believe it   believe me – some reason not to   Believe nothing of what you hear, and only half of what you see. – proverb cautioning against second and first hand information   Believe you me! – sincerity   can't believe ears – incredulous   couldn't believe eyes – too good or bad to be true   don't believe I've had the pleasure – we haven't met   hard to believe – skeptical   have to be seen to be believed – information is so great I cannot be believed until proven with sight   I can't believe it! – incredulous   I don't believe it! – skeptical   I don't believe this! – denial   I'll believe it when I see it. – skeptical but will believe when proof given   If you believe that, you'll believe anything! – gullible   lead to believe – deceived   make believe – imagination   Seeing is believing. – proverb it is hard to accept what hasn't been experienced   You better believe it. – conviction   You can't expect me to believe that. – don't believe and chastise

between /bu twEyn/ prep 1 at, into or across a space separating (two things) *Put the plate between the knife and fork.* 2 a period of time separating two points *I normally eat breakfast between 7 and 9 o'clock.* 3 share *We'll have one ice cream sundae between us.* 4 to and from *They drove between New York and Boston every month to distribute products.* Col: between a rock and a hard place – between two difficult situations   between you and me – a secret

breathe /brEyTh/ [breathes, breathed, breathing] verb 1 take air into the lungs and release it *The doctor told the patient to breathe deeply.* 2 allow air to move through *Cotton breathes and plastic doesn't.* Col: breathe a sigh of relief – relief   breathe new life into – refresh   breathe easy – relax   breathe one's last breath – die   breathe down someone's neck – micromanage or annoy with too much attention   don't breathe a word – secret   live and breathe a topic – spend all one's time on one thing

C (sea, see) /sEy/ [C's] noun 1 the third letter in the Latin alphabet *Cat starts with a C.* 2 third major level of grade for school *I got a C on my test.* 3 note in the musical scale □ *Sing Happy Birthday to you in the key of C.* Col: C – Roman numeral 100   C minor – musical chord or key

cheap /ChEyp/ [cheaper, cheapest] *adj* 1 not expensive *Dinner for only $5 is cheap!* 2 poor quality *The cheap new shirt fell apart in the wash.* 3 doesn't like to spend money *His father was too cheap to leave the server a good tip.* Col: **cheap shot** – cruel or underhanded comment **cheapskate** – doesn't like to spend money **dirt cheap** – really inexpensive **on the cheap** – spend little money **talk is cheap** – talk doesn't cost anything, let's see action

cheek /ChEyk/ [cheeks] *noun* 1 the side of the face below the eye *He had a mole on his left cheek.* 2 slang for a buttock (butt) *The left cheek of his pants had grease on it.* 3 rude talk *Mind your cheek when you are speaking to a teacher.* Col: **butt cheeks** – bottom (bum) **cheeky** – lack of respect **tongue in cheek** – said as a joke but with truthful undertone **turn the other cheek** – ignore abuse or an insult

cheese /ChEyz/ [cheeses] *noun* firm dairy food made from milk *Cheese is food in every culture.* Col: **big cheese** – the boss **cheesed off** – angry **cheesy** – cheese in taste or of poor quality **cut the cheese** – fart, pass gas **Say cheese!** – smile for a photo

chief /ChEyf/ [chiefs] *noun* 1 leader of a tribe or aboriginal group *The chief wore a magnificent headdress during the ceremony.* 2 head of an organization *He was the chief of the training group.* 3 most important *The gun was the chief piece of evidence at the murder trial.* Col: **chief cook and bottle washer** – one in charge usually of the home **chief of staff** – head of a hospital **chieftain** – leader of the tribe

clear /klEyr/ [clears, cleared, clearing, clearer, clearest] *adj* 1 transparent or see through *The glass lenses were clear.* 2 something easy to understand *It was clear from the instructions what had to be done.* 3 nothing in the way *The pathway was clear to walk down.* 4 amount of money earned after all expenses *As a director at the company, she clears $2,000 a week.* • 1 found innocent of breaking the law *After a month-long trial, Jorge was cleared of all charges.* 2 make free of *Clear the path.* • *adv* in a clear way *I can hear him loud and clear.* Col: **clear as a bell** – clearly explained **clear as mud** – sarcastic for not understood, too complicated **clear away** – remove **clear conscience** – haven't done anything bad or regrettable **clear-cut** – decisive or well defined or cut down all the trees **clear-headed** – think clearly **clear name** – restore reputation **clear out** – leave **clear sailing** – nothing in the way **clear the air** – talk to relieve built-up tension **clear the way** – get out of the way or make a path **clear throat** – ahem **clear up** – resolve **coast is clear** – unobstructed **crystal clear** – understood **free and clear** – no debt or obstruction **in the clear** – free **out of the clear blue sky** – an idea or interruption from nowhere **read you loud and clear** – understand your intention

complete /kumplEyt/ [completes, completed, completing] *verb* 1 finished *With the final answer entered, the crossword puzzle was complete.* 2 fill in the answers *When applying for a job, you often have to complete an application form.* 3 to make whole or perfect *After finding the missing piece, the students were able to complete the puzzle of Canada.*

cream /krEym/ [creams, creamed, creaming, creamier, creamiest] *noun* 1 the fatty part of milk *She takes 2% cream in her coffee.* 2 a soft, smooth substance in cosmetics *The base cream was very light.* • *adj* off-white or a very pale yellow color *The bride wore a pale cream dress.* • *verb* 1 mix together until smooth *Cream the butter and sugar together.* 2 slang for beat by a large score *The home football team creamed the other team 40-2 last night.* Col: **cream of the crop** – the best part ice cream – smooth, sweet dessert made from frozen milk and fruit   ice cream cone – hand held ice cream treat

D /dEy/ [D's] *noun* 1 the fourth letter of the Latin alphabet *Dog starts with a D.* 2 the fourth major level of grade for school/work *I got a D on my test.* Col: **D** – Roman numeral 500   **D Day** – day of reckoning

dear (deer) /dEyr/ [dears, dearer, dearest] *adj* 1 much loved *The puppy was very dear to the little boy.* 2 used at the beginning of a letter *Dear sir/madam* 3 expensive *That antique watch is very dear.* • *noun* loved one *Good morning dear.* Col: **Dear John** – break up letter   **dear to one's heart** – loved   **cost one dearly** – emotional or financial price was very high   **hang on for dear life** – secure yourself   **Oh dear!** – surprise, pity, disappointment or panic

deep /dEyp/ [deeper, deepest] *adj* 1 far below the surface or edge *The well is very deep.* 2 below the surface *They always plant their seeds 6 inches deep.* 3 very dark shade *Her dress was a deep red.* Col: **Beauty is only skin deep.** – *proverb* about values what is inside is more important   **between the devil and the deep blue sea** – choose from two unpleasant options   **deep down** – in one's soul   **deep freeze** – very cold weather   **deep pockets** – rich   **deep-six** – bury or dispose of   **dig deep** – try harder   **go off the deep end** -crazy   **in deep** – emotional or financial hardship   **in deep shit** – big trouble   **in deep water** – in trouble   **in too deep** – can't recover   **knee-deep in** – some trouble   **one's deepest sympathy** – very sorry for the death of a loved one   **run deep** – emotionally   **still waters run deep** – quiet people feel strongl   **take a deep breath** – inhale fully

deer (deer) /dEyr/ *noun* a four-legged wild animal which eats grasses; the males usually have antlers *There was a deer with her fawn in the field with the cows.*

Col: **like a deer in the headlights** – glazed-over frightened stare

degree /du grEy/ [degrees] *noun* 1 unit for measuring temperature *20° is a pleasant temperature.* 2 stage or step *He is feeling better to some degree.* 3 title from finishing a university program *She graduated with a degree in electrical engineering.* 4 a unit of measure of angles *A right angle is ninety degrees.* Col: **180° turn** – turn to face the opposite direction   **by degrees** – small stages   **nth degree** – maximum   **third degree** – questioning   **to a degree** – to a limited extent

delete /du lEyt/ [deletes, deleted, deleting] *verb* remove *Her name was deleted from the list.* Col: **delete key** – computer key used to erase

detail /dEy tAyl/ [details, detailed, detailing] *noun* 1 a small piece of information *I want to hear all the details about your trip.* • *verb* go into particulars *She detailed a floral pattern around the bottom of her wedding dress.* Col: **down to the last detail** – thorough   **gory details** – tell the juicy gossip

disease /du zEyz/ [diseases] *noun* sickness *Dutch Elm disease killed most of the elm trees.*

dream /drEym/ [dreams, dreamed/dreamt, dreaming] *noun* 1 series of pictures in the mind while sleeping *In his dream, Jose was driving a sports car.* 2 ambition *Her dream was to become a doctor.* 3 beautiful or nearly perfect *The car was a dream to drive.* • *verb* 1 imagine *Olivier dreamed about winning the lottery.* 2 pictures in sleep *She was dreaming about riding horses when her alarm woke her up.* Col: **American dream** – own ones home   **be in a dream world** – unrealistic   **broken dreams** – unfulfilled   **dream-boat** – gorgeous man   **dream come true** – receive a much desired goal   **dream in color** – dream big   **Dream on!** – not going to happen   **dream up** – imagine or create   In your dreams! – snub an offer   like a dream – very easily   pipe dream – unrealistic want   wet dream – sex dream   wildest dreams – beyond any dream   wouldn't dream of – never

E /Ey/ [E's] *noun* 1 the fifth letter of the Latin alphabet *East starts with an E.* 2 the short form of east *She lives on Queen St. E.* `Col:` **E=MC²** – formula for energy   **e** – prefix for electronic

east /Eyst/ *noun* 1 the direction that the sun rises *If your bedroom window faces east, you'll wake up early.* 2 the eastern part *According to the map, we could find the river to the east of downtown.* *adj* from the east *There's an east wind bringing rain.* `Col:` **East is east and west is west** – sides so different they never agree

eat /Eyt/ [eats, ate eating] *verb* 1 consume food *I normally eat three times a day.* 2 destroy gradually *The high rate of inflation eats away at the buying power of the dollar.* `Col:` **a bite to eat** – a meal   **dog eat dog** – competitive   **eat alive** – over power   **eat and run** – eat and leave early   **eat away at** – erode   **eat crow** – admit a mistake   **eat for breakfast** – dominate   **eat hat** – very surprised   **eat heart out** – pine emotionally   **eat humble pie** – admit error   **eat in** – prepare meal at home   **eat it up** – eat it all or savor   **eat like a bird** – eat little   **eat like a horse** – eat a lot   **eat like a pig** – too much or messy   **Eat my shorts!** – go to hell   **eat out** – dine in a restaurant   **eat out of house and home** – eat so much need to sell the house to pay for groceries   **eat through** – bore a hole   **Eat up!** – finish   **eat words** – admit a mistake   **Eat, drink, and be merry, for tomorrow we die.** – *proverb* about life's impermanence   **I'll eat my hat.** – in shock   **Let them eat cake.** – forget about others, one has one's own problems   **so clean one could eat off the floor** – clean and sanitary   **You eat with that mouth?** bad language

engineer /en jun Eyr/ [engineers, engineered, engineering] *noun* 1 person trained and qualified in engineering (electrical, mechanical, systems etc) *His degree is in electrical engineering.* 2 a person who controls an engine or other machine *His father is an engineer for the railway.* • *verb* 1 arrange for *He engineered a surprise party for his wife.* 2 design or make *The bridge is engineered to handle six lanes of traffic.*

equal /Ey kwul/ [=, equals, equaled, equaling] *adj* 1 the same in amount, size, or number *The recipe includes equal amounts of oil and water.* 2 having the same rights or status *Under Canadian law, men and women have equal rights.* • *verb* in mathematics, the word which signals the answer *Two times two equals four. 2x2=4* `Col:` **all things being equal** – if two situations are similar in other ways   **first among equals** – a bit higher

even /Ey vun/ *adj* 1 level *The two pictures were even on the wall.* 2 a number that can be divided by two with no remainder *Four is an even number.* 3 neither owe nor have money owed *After the two hundred dollars was paid, the brothers were even.* `Col:` **an even break** – fair opportunity   **even so** – however   **even Steven** – repaid the debt   **even though** – despite the fact   **get even with** – revenge

fear /fEyr/ [fears, feared, fearing] *noun* strong negative emotion caused by the threat of danger, pain, etc. *You could see the fear in his face.* • *verb* when something unpleasant happens *He feared the sound of sirens in the night.* `Col:` **fear of God** – intimidate   **Fools rush in where angels fear to tread.** – *proverb*, foolish people take dangerous risks   **for fear of** – avoid risking   **never fear** – I'll save you

feeble /fEy bul/ [feebler, feeblest] *adj* 1 weak *All they could see was a feeble old man being helped into a wheelchair.* 2 not having energy or force *It was a feeble attempt at apologizing for the error.* Col: **feeble excuse** – lame reason   **feeble-minded** – weak minded

feed /fEyd/ [feds, fed, feeding] *verb* 1 eat *The wild birds are feeding on the birdseed.* 2 make grow *If you feed your plants with fertilizer, they will grow better.* 3 flow into another *The Smoky River feeds into the Peace River.* *noun* food, especially for farm animals *Feed for cattle can affect the amount of fat in the meat.* Col: **chicken feed** – insignificant amount of money   **Don't bite the hand that feeds you.** – *proverb* meaning treat the provider with respect   **Feed a cold and starve a fever.** – *proverb* advice about health care   **spoon-feed** – help too much

feel /Eyl/ [feels, felt, feeling] *verb* 1 search for using touch *He felt the rough surface of the rock.* 2 affected by emotions *She felt sad when her friend moved away.* 3 opinion or belief *He felt sure he had been there before.* Col: **cop a feel** – boob touch   **feel a draft** – moving air   **feel at home** – comfortable   **feel blue** – sad or depressed   **feel for** – sympathize   **feel free** – no hesitation   **feel honor bound** – integrity   **feel light-headed** – dizzy   **feel under the weather** – ill   **feel guilty** – to blame   **feel hard done-by** – cheated   **feel in bones** – intuit   **feel like a new person** – well again   **feel oats** – act silly   **feel one's way** – move slowly and carefully   **feel out** – pre-assess   **feel out of things** – not connected to the group   **feel sick to stomach** – nauseous   **feel the pinch** – short of cash   **feel up to** – well and capable   **feel like a million bucks** – really healthy and fit   **get the feel of** – try it   **make feel small** – bully   **make one's presence felt** – have an effect that is noticed even if not seen   **not feeling oneself** – out of sorts

feet /fEyt/ *noun* 1 plural form of *foot* People have two feet. 2 measure of distance *There are twelve inches in a foot.* Col: **a load off feet** – sit down   **back on feet** – recovered physical or financial health   **balls of feet** – thick part of underfoot where toes attach   **carried out feet first** – dead   **cold feet** – changed one's mind too nervous   **dead on feet** – exhausted   **drag feet** – move slowly   **feet of clay** – move very slowly   **feet on the ground** – practical   **get feet wet** – start new activity   **get some weight off feet** – sit   **get to feet** – stand up   **have itchy feet** – want to travel   **have the world at feet** – much potential   **have two left feet** – can't dance   **in stocking feet** – socks no shoes   **jump in with both feet** – fully commit   **keep feet on the ground** – be realistic or not too enthusiastic   **land on both feet** – come out well after an upset or problem   **patter of tiny feet** – have babies   **put feet up** – sit and recline   **run off feet** – over worked   **six feet under** – dead or buried   **spring to feet** – jump up   **stand on one's own two feet** – make one's own decisions   **sweep off feet** – passionate love   **think on feet** – think quickly   **throw oneself at feet** – beg

female /fEy mAyl/ [females] *noun* member of the sex that can have children or produce eggs *A female was seen driving the stolen car.* • *adj* being a member of the sex that has children *The female bird is often brown, not colorful like the male.* Col: **female intuition** – sixth sense

field /fEyld/ [fields] *noun* 1 an open area of land, often used for animal feeding or growing crops *The corn in the field was ready to harvest.* 2 area of work or study *Her field of expertise is adult education.* 3 part of a record in a database *The date field had been left empty.* • *adj* grown in a field *She prefers field tomatoes to those artificially grown.* Col: **field questions** – take questions from an audience have a field day – chance to enjoy an activity like criticizing in the field – working away from one's main office area out in left field – wrong play the field – dating more than one person at a time

free /frEy/ [freer, freest, frees, freed, freeing] *adj* 1 no restrictions *He was free to plan his future.* 2 no cost *The sign said newspapers were free.* • *verb* 1 set free *The soldiers freed the political prisoners.* 2 independent *The United States is a free country.* [Col:] as free as a bird – without limits break free – sever ties feel free – open invitation footloose and fancy-free – carefree and happy for free – at no cost free agent – no contract free and clear – no debts free and easy – casual free hand – can you help free ride – no obligation free spirit – unconventional free-for-all – out of control free rein – lose control free up – make available go scot-free – unpunished home free – safe, in the clear It's a free country! – say what one thinks without fear The best things in life are free. – *proverb* about values There's no such thing as a free lunch. – *proverb* there is some obligation Why buy a cow when you can get milk for free? or Why buy the pig when you can get the sausage for free? – rude comment no reason to marry if the sex is available

freeze /frEyz/ [freezes, froze, freezing] *verb* 1 turn into solid by cold *Freeze some more ice cubes for the party.* 2 prevent from being changed *The bank is freezing his account until the divorce is settled.* 3 very cold *I should have brought a coat, I'm freezing.* • *adj* the state of frozen *Freeze-dried vegetables taste almost like fresh.* [Col:] freeze tail off – be very cold freeze to death – die of cold freeze up – blocked by ice freeze wages – no chance of a raise when hell freezes over – never

frequent /frEy kwent/ *adj* repeated or often *She was a frequent visitor to the art museum.*

G (gee) /jEy/ [G's] *noun* 1 the seventh letter of the Latin alphabet *Goat starts with a G.* 2 slang for one thousand *He paid 30 's for the car.* [Col:] g force – force of gravity

gee (G) /jEy/ *interj* expresses surprise and support. *Gee you look terrific!* [Col:] Gee whiz! – exclamation Gee That's too bad. – sympathy

green /grEyn/ [greens, greener, greenest] *adj* 1 the color of grass *The grass was a deep green.* 2 not yet ripe *The apples were too green to eat.* 3 not experienced *He bought a green horse and trained it himself.* • *noun*, 1 vegetables *Greens are superfoods that should be eaten every day.* 2 the color *Green has been adopted to represent the environmental movement.* [Col:] get the green light – permission go green – change habits to protect the environment green around the gills – nauseous green as grass – inexperienced green backs – money green belt – large protected land around cities and urban areas green eyed monster – jealousy Greenpeace – global protection activist organization green thumb – good gardener green with envy – jealous

hear (here) /hEyr/ [hears heard, hearing] *verb* 1 identify sounds with the ear *We hear the next door neighbor practicing drums in his garage.* 2 listen to and judge *The judge heard the evidence then made his decision.* 3 be told *He heard from his boss that the contract had been signed.* [Col:] can't hear myself think – too loud could hear a pin drop – quiet didn't hear a peep out of – silent good to hear your voice – reassuring hear about – gossip or news hear from – recent contact hear of – know about hear out – listen to hear through the grapevine – informal source or gossip I hear and I forget. I see and I remember. I do and I understand. – Confucius about the best way to learn.   I hear you. – understand   like to hear oneself talk – talks to much even when no one is listening   make oneself heard – shout   never hear the end of it – a story that will be retold   Now hear this! – pay attention   See no evil, hear no evil, speak no evil. – proverb caution to avoid gossip   sorry to hear that – sympathy   will not hear of – denial   won't hear a word against – loyal

heat /hEyt/ [heats, heated, heating] noun 1 energy, the state of hot *The summer heat was too much for the elderly.* 2 blame *China is taking the heat for poor air quality.* • verb make or become hot *Heat the water to boiling before adding the tea bag.* • adj intense 1 *The conversation was heated.* Col: heat of the moment – decisions made with passion not thinking   If you can't stand the heat stay out of the kitchen. – proverb if one can't stand the pressure of a situation they should get out   in a dead heat – tied   in heat – sexual excitement   take the heat – blame   the heat is on – pressure   turn up the heat – pressure

here (hear) /hEyr/ adv this place, or at this location *Stay here and wait for me to come back and get you.* • noun introduction *Here's Johnny.*

idea /Iy dE yu/ [ideas] noun a thought or image formed in the mind *The artist's idea was to create a sculpture that children could play on.* 2 a concept *The idea for the sound dictionary came from the color chart.* Col: bright idea – clever thought   flirt with the idea – think about doing it but decide not to   put ideas into one's head – suggest trouble to get into   rough idea – an estimate   The very idea! – not approve   What's the big idea? – disapprove or chastise

increase /in krEys/ [increases, increased, increasing] verb become bigger in size *The size of the debt increased each day.*

jeans /jEynz/ [jeans] noun pants made of heavy cotton *Susan's black jeans look great on her.* Col: blue jeans – denim slacks

keep /kEyp/ [keeps, kept, keeping] verb 1 possession *Normally a lawyer keeps the original copy of a will.* 2 remain in a certain condition *Lettuce keeps better in the refrigerator.* 3 fulfill a commitment *Her husband kept his promise to call every night while he was away.* 4 make regular entries *The captain kept a log of the ship's activities.* Col: A man is known for the company he keeps. – proverb friends are an indicator of the character of a person   An apple a day keeps the doctor away. – proverb that supports healthy eating   for keeps – permanently   How are you keeping? – haven't seen for a awhile, How are you?   keep at – continue doing   keep back – stay a distance away   keep down – not throw up food   keep one's temper – control one's anger   keep to – follow   keep to oneself – avoid contact with others   keep up – not fall behind   keep up with the Joneses – compete with the neighbors in social status and belongings   play for keeps – forever

key (quay) /kEy/ [keys keyed, keying] noun 1 a piece of metal cut to open a lock ↩ *The key for the front door was hidden under the mat.* 2 a button that operates a machine or makes a musical instrument play a sound *A piano has more white keys than black ones.* 3 a list of codes that provides understanding *The answer key was at the back of the textbook.* • verb entering data using a keyboard *The typists keyed the information into the database.* Col: church key – bottle opener   key up – become nervous   low key – casual   off key – off pitch in music   turn-key – ready to go   under lock and key – safe

knee /nEy/ [knees, kneed, kneeing] *noun* the joint between the thigh and the lower leg *Her knees were sore after scrubbing the floor.* • *verb* hit with the knee *She kneed him in the groin when he got too close.* `Col:` **bring one to their knees** – surrender or destroy **knee deep** – heavily involved **knee high to a grasshopper** – short, indication of the age of a child **knee-jerk reaction** – automatic **learn at one's mother's knee** – learned very young **put one over the knee** – spank **the bees knees** – fantastic

lead /lEyd/ [leads, led, leading] *noun* in first position *She took the lead at the beginning and held it for the entire race.* 2 chief part in a play or movie *Sean Connery played the lead in many of the James Bond movies.* 3 a clue *The lead given by the witness helped the police put the criminal behind bars.* • *verb* 1 show the way *Jean is leading the parade in his old Cadillac.* 2 set a course or direction *That road leads to town.* `Col:` **All roads lead to Rome.** – proverb about destiny **follow the leader** – child's game **lead a charmed life** – things seem to go his way **lead a dance** – dictate moves **lead a dog's life** – lazy or easy **lead a double life** – undercover **lead astray** – bad influence **lead by the nose** – dominate **lead down the garden path** – take advantage of an innocent person **lead off** – take a head start **lead on** – we'll follow **lead on a merry chase** – long pursuit with no result **lead the field** – first in a race **lead the pack** – dominant one **lead the way** – we'll follow **lead with** – play first card **one thing leads to another** – chain of events **You can lead a horse to water, but you can't make him drink.** – proverb meaning can't force a person to take a suggestion

leaf /lEyf/ [leafs, leaves, leafed, leafing] *noun* 1 the flat green part of a plant that grows from the stem *The last leaf fell off the tree before the first snowfall.* 2 a single piece of paper in a book, with each side called a page *A leaf had been torn out of the book.* 3 extra sections to make a table bigger *The table leafs were stored in the bedroom.* • *verb* 1 sprout leaves *The trees leafed out early this year* 2 glance through a book *He leafed through a magazine in the waiting room.* `Col:` **leaf through** – turn over the pages of a book/magazine without reading in detail **take a leaf out of a person's book** – imitate **turn over a new leaf** – resolve to improve conduct or performance

lean /lEyn/ [leans leaned/leant, leaning,] *adj* 1 thin *She was lean when she came out of the hospital.* 2 having little fat *The meat was very lean.* • *verb* 1 on an angle from the perpendicular *The ladder was leaning against the house.* 2 rely on *Her aging mother leans on her more and more.* `Col:` **lean times** – little money **lean and mean** – ready to fight

machine /mu ShEyn/ [machines, machined, machining] *noun* equipment that requires power and does a particular task *The washing machine broke down on Tuesday.* • *verb* work on equipment using machines *The metal was machined into a pipe.* `Col:` **is a machine** – tireless worker

meat (meet) /mEyt/ [meats] *noun* 1 the flesh of animals for food *Meat, potatoes and vegetables is a standard dinner.* 2 the edible part of fruits, nuts, eggs, shellfish *The meat of the lobster is very sweet.* `Col:` **dead meat** – in big trouble **meat-and-potatoes** – basics **meat market** – selection of men/women to date

meet (meat) /mEyt/ [meets, met, meeting] *verb* 1 come together at the same place and time *We can meet in front of the movie theatre at 7 p.m.* 2 be introduced to *My sister met her future husband at my birthday party.* 3 come into contact with *Their lips met in a kiss.* 4 satisfy *The company met the standards for safety outlined by the government.* `Col:` **gone to meet one's**

maker – dead   make ends meet – making just enough money to survive   meet halfway – compromise   meet one's match – social and intellectual superior   meet up – connect in person   more than meets the eye – hidden qualities or information   never the twain shall meet – never agree or exist together

medium /mEy dE yum/ [mediums] *noun* 1 middle size *That jacket is a medium and you need a large.* 2 means or a tool *Art is a good medium for self expression.* 3 clairvoyant *The medium gets paid to contact the deceased.* • *adj* middle or average *He has a medium build.* Col: happy medium – compromise in the middle

museum /myUw zE yum/ [museums] *noun* a building where historical or artistic things of interest are displayed for people to enjoy *This old cannon should be in a museum.*

naïve /nI yEyv/ *adj* simple and trusting *The girl was very naïve when she first moved to the big city.*

near /nEyr/ [nearer, nearest] *adv* 1 close by *The school is near their new home.* 2 not far, closely *In the near future we'll take a vacation.* • *verb* draw closer *The kids got excited as we neared grandma's house.* Col: from near and far – gathered from great distances to one place   in the near future – soon   near death experience – almost die able to share the experience   nearest and dearest – closest family and friends all together   so near and yet so far – almost achieved but to finish is difficult

need /nEyd/ [needs, needed, needing] *verb* require *He needed help with his homework.* 2 necessary *Pets need to be fed and watered every day.* Col: A friend in need is a friend indeed. – *proverb* good friend one can count on in bad times   I don't need this! – fed up   I need it yesterday. – urgent   if need be – necessary   If there's anything you need, don't hesitate to ask. – offer of help   in hour of need – in trouble   need doing – chores and tasks   need head examined – crazy   need I remind you – reminding you now   Need I say more? – clear?   need like a hole in the head – don't need   That's all I need! – sarcastic for don't need   We need to talk. – relationship is over or in jeopardy

needle /nEy dul/ [needles, needled, needling] *noun* 1 a very thin small pointed piece of steel with a hole in one end (eye) used for sewing *The sewing needle was too small for the heavy denim material.* 2 a slender stick without an eye used in knitting *The knitting needles were stuck in the ball of yarn.* 3 a slender indicator on a dial *The needle on the speedometer read 120 km/hr.* 4 an injection using a syringe *Many people are afraid of needles.* 5 slender leaf on an evergreen tree *The needles on the fir tree were turning yellow because of the lack of rain.* • *verb* tease or harass *The teenage boy loved to needle his sister about her nose.* Col: have pins and needles – tingling sensation from a pinched nerve   looking for a needle in a haystack – impossible to find   on pins and needles – anticipation

niece /nEys/ [nieces] *noun* the daughter of a brother or sister *My niece looks like my sister and me.*

P (pea, pee) /pEy/ [P's] *noun* 1 the sixteenth letter of the Latin alphabet *People starts with a P.* 2 *abbr* for page *The definition can be found on p18.* Col: mind your P's and Q's – manners   PJ's – pajamas

pea (P, pee) /pEy/ [peas] *noun* 1 a round green seed in a pod that is eaten as a vegetable *The peas were freshly picked from the garden.* 2 the plant that produces this vegetable *The peas were planted in early May.* Col: like two peas in a pod – similar   pea brain – slang for a stupid person

HOW DO YOU SAY? PRONUNCIATION DICTIONARY

peace (piece) /pEys/ noun 1 freedom from war *The country had waited ten years for the war to end and for peace to follow.* 2 quiet *The peace she found in the garden was heavenly.* Col: **at peace** – calm and complete **hold one's peace** – to keep silent **keep the peace** – prevent conflict **leave in peace** – go away **make peace** – bring together **peace of mind** – calm, no worries **Peace out.**- close a conversation **rest in peace** – to a dead person, wish eternal tranquility

peach /pEyCh/ [peaches] noun 1 a juicy round fruit with a yellowish red fuzzy skin *The peach was ripe on the tree.* • adj 1 with or about the fruit *The peach tree was covered in blossoms.* 2 a color, yellowish/red *The peach chiffon outfit complemented her skin tone.* Col: **peaches and cream** – lovely skin or a variety of corn on the cob **She's a peach.** – she is kind and gentle

pee (P, pea) /pEy/ [pees, peed, peeing] verb urinate *The puppy peed on the rug.* • noun urine *The pee was in the toddler's potty.. Yeah!* Col: **take a pee** – urinate

people /pEy pul/ [person] noun 1 human beings *People travel to work on the bus.* 2 large group of humans related by blood or nationality *My father's people come from Ireland.* Col: **People who live in glass houses shouldn't throw stones.** – proverb don't criticize others with the same faults you have **You can fool some of the people all of the time, and all of the people some of the time, but you can't fool all of the people all of the time.** – quote from Abraham Lincoln

period /pEy rE yud/ [periods] noun 1 punctuation mark after a complete sentence – . – *A period at the end of a sentence is expressed as a pause when speaking.* 2 a specific section of time *I have lunch during third history period.*

piece (peace) /pEys/ [pieces, pieced, piecing] noun 1 a portion separated from the whole *The piece of pie was too big for one person.* 2 a musical or written work *That piece of music was popular in the 60's.* 3 a token used to make moves in a board game *The pieces of the Monopoly game were in the plastic bag.* 4 slang for gun *The gangster bought his piece on the black market.* Col: **a conversation piece** – interesting artifact to talk about **a piece of the action** – share in the excitement or profits **a piece of the pie** – share profits **all in one piece** – safe and well **be a nasty piece of work** – jerk **bits and pieces** – odds and ends **fall to pieces** – breakdown **give a piece of one's mind** – yell at **go to pieces** – emotionally upset **in one piece** – not broken up **in pieces** – fragmented **pick to pieces** – criticize **pick up the pieces** – support after devastation **piece of cake** – easy **piece together** – figure out **pull to pieces** – analyze **say one's piece** – give opinion **take a piece out of** – yell at **tear to pieces** – destroy **thrill to pieces** – make happy **thrilled to death** – happy and excited

pizza /pEyt zu/ [pizza] noun round baked Italian bread crust covered in cheese, tomato sauce and other toppings *The neighbors come over for pizza on Friday nights.*

please /plEyz/ [pleases, pleased, pleasing] verb 1 make happy *The little boy wanted to please his parents.* 2 wishes *He does whatever he pleases.* • adv a polite way of making a request *Please sit in the front row.* Col: **Check, please.** – bring the bill **disease to please** – overly nice **if you please** – indignant **less than pleased** – angry **One moment, please.** – wait **please oneself** – do what one likes **pleased as Punch** – happy (from Punch and Judy) **pleased for** – happy you're happy **pleased to meet you** – greeting **pleased with** – satisfied **Pretty please?** – silly beg **We aim to please.** – try hard **You cannot please everyone.** – do your best then be satisfied

police /pu **lEys**/ [polices, policed, policing] *noun* group responsible for enforcing the law 🚓 *The police were called to control the riot.* *verb* control using police officers *The officers policed the streets looking for vandals.*

quay (key) /**kEy**/ [quays] *noun* pier *The containers on the quay waited to be loaded onto the ship.*

reach /**rEyCh**/ [reaches, reached, reaching] *verb* 1 stretch out an arm in order to touch or grab something *He reached for the can of coffee on the top shelf.* 2 arrive at *They reached their destination at midnight.* 3 accomplish *They reached their goal in a month.* 4 make contact with *His sister reached him via Skype.* • *noun* 1 distance one can extend their arm *The reach of the basketball player was amazing.* 2 the extent of someone's influence *Oprah's reach impacts the whole world.* Col: **reach out** – offer help

read (reed) /**rEyd**/ [reads, read, reading] *verb* 1 follow and understand the meaning of words *The students enjoy reading their books.* 2 speak written words out loud *The mother reads to her small son every night.* 3 interpret the importance of *A teacher reads the faces of her students to know when they understand.* 4 copy or transfer data *The computer reads and stores files.* Col: **read as** – one's understanding **read between the lines** – look for hidden meaning **read cover to cover** – all **Read 'em and weep.** – you lose, my hand (card game) can't be beaten **read for** – as a service **read from** – which text or book **read into** – assume meaning not intended by the writer **read like a book** – understand another's thoughts and feelings **read lips** – skill of the deaf **read minds** – psychic **Read my lips!** – listen to me **read one rights** – arrested **read the fine print** – details **read the writing on the wall** – the obvious **read the riot act** – threaten **read the runes** – fortune telling **read to** – out loud **read up on** – study **read you loud and clear** – understand your intentions **take it as read** – no tricks

reason /**rEy** zun/ [reasons, reasoned, reasoning] *noun* explanation *The detour in the road was the reason they were late.* • *verb* reach conclusions by thinking logically *He reasoned that the extra cost for the flooring would increase the value in their home.* Col: **all the more reason for** – more support for an argument **by reason of** – because of **it stands to reason** – logical **listen to reason** – be influenced **no earthly reason** – can't think of any reason **no rhyme or reason** – cliché, without logic **reason with** – discuss with the intentions of changing their mind **with good reason** – obviously true **within reason** – within boundaries of common sense

receipt /ru **sEyt**/ [receipts] *noun* 1 receive *The receipt of the lottery money allowed them to pay off their mortgage.* 2 a printed record of payment *He needed the receipt to exchange his jeans for a bigger size.* Col: **in receipt of** – having received

reed (read) /**rEyd**/ [reeds] *noun* 1 a water plant with tall firm stems *The ducks made their nests in the reeds.* 2 part of the mouthpiece of a wind instrument that vibrates *The reed in his clarinet often gets replaced.*

scene (seen) /**sEyn**/ [scenes] *noun* 1 place where an event happened *He took pictures at the scene of the accident.* 2 section of a play or movie *"To be or not to be…" Act 3 Scene 1 of Hamlet* 3 an emotional outburst *Don't make a scene in front of the kids.* Col: **behind the scenes** – in secret **don't make a scene** – control your behavior **scene of the crime** – where an illegal event took place **set the scene** – supply background information to support a story

sea (C, see) /**sEy**/ [seas] *noun* 1 body of salt water covering most of the planet Earth. *His dream was to sail the seven seas.*

2 a specific smaller body of salt water. *It is called the Mediterranean Sea.* 3 a large area or quantity *Parliament Hill was a sea of red hats on Canada Day.* Col: **at sea** – in a ship on the water **at sea level** – level of the surface of the ocean, zero altitude **between the devil and the deep blue sea** – chose between two unpleasant options **from sea to sea** – coast to coast **put out to sea** – to leave land for the open water on a ship **sail the seven seas** – around the world *There are plenty of fish in the sea.* – *proverb* lots of better choices for romance

seam (seem) /**sEym**/ [seams] *noun* 1 the line where two pieces of cloth are sewn together/two edges meet *The seam on his pants ripped when he bent over.* 2 a layer of coal in the earth *The coal seam was deep in the earth.* Col: **bursting at the seams** – full of excitement or emotion **come apart at the seams** – break down or disintegrate emotionally

season /**sEy** zun/ [seasons, seasoned, seasoning] *noun* 1 the four divisions in the year; spring, summer, fall, winter *Spring is the season of renewal and rebirth.* 2 a schedule of shows, sporting events etc. *The baseball season was just about to start.* 3 a time when something is plentiful and enjoyed often *The raspberry season is short.* • *verb* add flavor with salt, herbs etc *The chicken was seasoned with lemon and herbs.* • *adj* become more experienced *He was a seasoned player after three years in the big leagues.* Col: **come into season** – female ready for breeding **in season** – ripe and ready to eat **off season** – slow for business

seat /**sEyt**/ [seats seated, seating] *noun* 1 chair or object for sitting on *The seats in the theatre were very uncomfortable.* 2 the part of the chair that someone sits on *The car seats were covered with dog hair.* 3 a Member of Parliament *The seat was won by a member of the Green Party.* 4 part of pants that covers the buttocks *The seat of his jeans was covered in grass stains.* • *verb* 1 arrange a place for sitting *The ushers seated the bride's family on the left and the groom's family on the right.* Col: **at the edge of one's seat** – excited or engage in the action **be seated** – sit down **by the seat of one's pants** – close call **fly by the seat of one's pants** – try a difficult activity without preparation or experience **have a seat** – sit down **in the driver's seat** – in control **in the hot seat** – interrogated **ringside seat** – close to the action **take a seat** – sit down

secret /**sEy** krut/ [secrets] *noun* information hidden on purpose *The secret about the baby's real father was kept for over twenty years.* • *adj* private, meant to be kept from others *She kept her diary in a secret hiding place.* Col: **Can you keep a secret?** – I have one I want to tell you **carry a secret to the grave** – never tell **keep a secret** – not tell **trade secret** – special knowledge related to specific industries *Your secret is safe with me.* – I won't tell

see (C, sea) /**sEy**/ [sees, saw, seeing] *verb* 1 look at *Can you see the airplane?* 2 experience or witness *I saw the robbery happen.* 3 come to understand *I see what you mean.* 4 date a girlfriend or boyfriend. *Jane has been seeing Matt for over a year.* Col: **as far as I can see** - what I understand with this information presented **as I see it** – my opinion **be glad to see the back of** – couldn't wait for them to leave *Believe nothing of what you hear, and only half of what you see.* – *proverb* cautioning against second and first hand information **can't see past the end of nose** – won't look, closed mind or blind **can't see hand in front of face** – impaired visibility, fog or snow *Can't see the forest for the trees.* – *proverb* can't see what is important for focusing on details **Could I see you again?** – request for another date

/ Ey / is Green

didn't see it coming – blindsided   haven't seen hide nor hair of- haven't seen any sign of   I'll believe it when I see it. – skeptic   let's see – consider   Long time no see. – haven't seen you for a while   Monkey see, monkey do. – copy   see with naked eye – no lens   see a man about a dog – pee   see eye to eye – agree   see fit – appropriate   see home – walk home with   see in hell first – never see into – get more information   See no evil, hear no evil, speak no evil. – *proverb* meaning avoid gossip   see off – from place of departure   see out – stay until   see over – supervise   see red – angry   see stars – dizzy, from a blow   see the color of money – show me the money   see the error of ways – repent   see the glass half empty – pessimist   see the glass half full – optimist   see the last of – never return   see the light – understand one's mistakes, or suddenly believe   see the sights – tourist   see things – sixth sense   see through – not fooled   See ya – bye-bye   See you later, alligator. – bye   see one's way to – possible   There's none so blind as those who will not see. – *proverb* about denial   wait and see – be patient   What you see is what you get. – straight goods, no tricks   You see? – do you understand?

seed /sEyd/ [seeds, seeded, seeding] *noun* 1 plant's way of reproducing *The seeds needed to be dried.* 2 beginning *The seeds of change were planted in the public's mind.* • *verb* sow seeds *The farmer seeded the field in corn.* Col: go to seed – a plant stops flowering or person stops taking care of their looks   seed money – start up cash

seem (seam) /sEym/ [seems, seemed, seeming] *verb* to give the impression of *Her new boyfriend seems nice.* Col: Things are seldom what they seem. – *proverb* warning things are often not as they appear

seen (scene) /sEyn/ *verb* past tense form of see Col: Children should be seen and not heard – children should be quiet   seen as – perceived

serious /sEy rE yus/ *adj* 1 responsible, dedicated *The new student is serious about learning to speak English.* 2 intention to marry *They are serious about each other and plan to marry next year.* Col: dead serious – not kidding   get serious – stop kidding around   serious about someone – in love

sheep /shEyp/ *noun* a grass-eating animal with a thick wooly coat *The wolves have eaten the sheep.* Col: separate the sheep from the goats – divide the competent from the incompetent   the black sheep of the family – the one who is different, usually bad   wolf in sheep's clothing – seems pleasant but is evil inside

sheet /shEyt/ [sheets] *noun* 1 a large rectangular piece of fabric used on a bed to either lie on or under *The sheets on the bed needed to be washed.* 2 a broad thin flat piece of paper or metal *I need a sheet of paper for the photocopier.* 3 a wide stretch of water, ice, flame, falling rain etc. *The road was a sheet of ice after the freezing rain.* Col: a clean sheet – start over   sheet lightning – wide lightning   three sheets to the wind – drunk   white as a sheet – very pale from fear or illness

ski /skEy/ [skis, skied, skiing] *noun* 1 a long fiberglass piece of equipment for travelling over snow *His skis are stored in the garage, waiting for snow.* 2 long rounded pieces of metal for under an aircraft *The airplane had skis to land on water.* • *verb* sport on skis *They skied effortlessly across the frozen lake.* Col: après ski – social time after ski   ski bum – one who loves to ski and does as often as possible

sleep /slEyn/ [sleeps, slept, sleeping] *noun* 1 unconscious rest required by people and animals *Their sleep was disturbed by the thunderstorm.* 2 discharge found in the corners of the eyes after sleep *The little boy had to wash the sleep out of his eyes in the morning.* • *verb* 1 be or fall asleep *I couldn't sleep so I read my book.* 2 have a sexual relationship *They had been sleeping together for a month before they told anyone about their relationship.* Col: **beauty sleep** – needs in order to feel healthy and look attractive **cry oneself to sleep** – weep until sleep comes **didn't sleep a wink** – stayed awake all night **drift off to sleep** – fall gently to sleep **go to sleep** – fall asleep or tingling sensation **Let sleeping dogs lie.** – *proverb* warning not to stir up trouble **lose sleep over** – worry **put to sleep** – humanely destroy **sleep around** – sexually active **sleep in** – get up late **sleep like a log** – deep **sleep off** – a hangover **sleep on it** – decided tomorrow **sleep over** – stay at a friend's overnight **sleep through** – didn't wake **sleep tight** – sleep well **sleep together** – have sex **sleep with** – have sex **sleeping giant** – dormant problem **sleeping partner** – sex partner

sneeze /snEyz/ [sneezes, sneezed, sneezing] *noun* a sudden outburst of air from the nose and mouth *His sneeze could be heard in the next room.* • *verb* have a sneeze *He sneezed when he smelled the flowers.* Col: **not to be sneezed at** – important

steal (steel) /stEyl/ [steals, stole, stealing] *verb* 1 take without permission *The thief stole her jewelry.* 2 move quietly *The cat stole through the backyard and surprised the birds.* 3 baseball term for taking a base during a pitch *The player tried to steal second base.* • *noun* unexpected easy task or good bargain *At $5 each, the t-shirts were a steal.* Col: **steal a one's heart** – capture one's affection **steal**

one's thunder – draw attention away at their big moment **steal the show** – outshine others

steam /stEym/ [steams, steamed, steaming, steamier, steamiest] *noun* 1 the gas that water turns into from boiling *The steam from the kettle fogged the window.* • *adj* cook food in steam *The recipe called for steamed beans.* • *verb* 1 treat with steam *Steam your dress to take out the wrinkles.* 2 move under the power of steam *The train steamed down the railway tracks.* Col: **all steamed up** – angry **blow/let off steam** – release built-up energy **full steam ahead** – onward **lose steam** – run out of energy **pick up steam** – speed up **run out of steam** – lose energy **under one's own steam** – without help

steel (steal) /stEyl/ [steels] *noun* durable metal made of iron and carbon *The steel in the walls kept the building from falling.* Col: **have a mind like a steel trap** – quick and smart **nerves of steel** – courageous **steel against** – fortify

street /strEyt/ [streets] *noun* public road *The streets were quiet on Sunday night.* • *adj* 1 suitable for wearing everyday *Street clothes are fine to go to the zoo.* 2 homeless *Street people go to a shelter at night.* Col: **a two-way street** – both parties contribute **easy street** – the good life **man on the street** – ordinary guy **street smarts** – knowledge and experience to survive in the city

suite (sweet) /swEyt/ [suites] *noun* rooms or furniture that forms a set *Our hotel suite outside of the city cost the same as a room downtown.*

sweet (suite) /swEyt/ [sweets, sweeter, sweetest] *noun* candy *The sweets are in the cookie cupboard.* adj 1 taste of sugar *The tea was too sweet.* 2 smell or sound pleasant *The flowers smelled sweet.* 3 pretty, charming *She has a sweet nature.* 4 fond of *The teenager was sweet on the waitress.* Col: **A rose by any other name would smell as sweet.** – *proverb* nature is more important than name it is called **revenge is sweet** – hurting enemies feels good **short and sweet** – to the point **sweet and sour** – mix of tastes **sweet nothings** – love talk **sweet talk** – charm **sweet tooth** – likes sugar **Sweet!** – Great! **Take the bitter with the sweet.** – *proverb* advising accept the good with the bad

T (tea, tee) /tEy/ [T's] *noun* 1 the twentieth letter of the Latin alphabet *Time starts with a T.* 2 T-shaped *The road comes to a T-intersection.* 3 a T-shirt *She wore a pink T.* Col: **suit to a T** – exactly **TNT** – dynamite **T-shirt** – light garment with short sleeves

tea (T, tee) /tEy/ [teas] *noun* 1 water poured over herbs to make a drink *Herb tea before bed helps me sleep.* 2 social gathering in the afternoon with tea and cakes *Jane is coming over for tea.* Col: **not for all the tea in China** – no **not one's cup of tea** – don't like it **one's cup of tea** – like it

teach /tEyCh/ [teaches, taught, teaching] *verb* instruct *The lifeguard teaches swimming during the week.* Col: **teach someone a lesson** – punish or get even with a bad guy **Those who can, do; those who can't, teach.** – *proverb* people who can't do anything well enough to make a living at it, become teachers **You can't teach an old dog new tricks.** – *proverb* it is difficult to make one change when they have been doing something for a long time

tee (T, tea) /tEy/ [tees] *noun* a short peg with a dip in the top to hit a golf ball off *My son-in-law uses bright orange tees.* 2 raised area where a golf game begins – *The golfers met at the first tee.* Col: **tee off** – start **teed off** – angry **to a tee** – perfectly

teen /tEyn/ [teens] *noun* 1 short form for teenager *Teens like to go to the mall to hang out with their friends.* 2 numbers from 13 through 19 *When temperatures are in the teens, you need a coat.* Col: **teen idol** – music or movie star popular with young people

teeth /tEyTh/ *noun* 1 plural of tooth *Her teeth are perfectly straight and she has no cavities.* Col: **a kick in the teeth** – betrayal **armed to the teeth** – research done and ready to argue **by the skin of teeth** – close call **cut teeth** – first project at a new skill from when babies cut teeth **get teeth into** – focus on **get the bit in one's teeth** – run away with opinions **give eye teeth for** – want badly **grit teeth** – repress anger **lie through teeth** – lie **like pulling teeth** – extract information from a reluctant source **pull teeth** – extract **scarce as hen's teeth** – rare **show teeth** – threaten **sink teeth into** – in depth

these /thEyz/ *adj* plural of *this These chairs need to be moved.* Col: **one of these days** – someday

three /THrEy/ [3, threes] *noun* cardinal number between two and four *Three is the number of sides in a triangle.* • *adj* three in number *A tricycle has three wheels.* Col: **phony as a three-dollar bill** – not authentic, two-faced **the three R's** – reading writing and arithmetic, basic education also stands for Reduce, Reuse and Recycle **three sheets in the wind** – drunk **three square meals a day** – fair treatment, can't complain **three strikes and you are out** – three chances to succeed **three-ring circus** – lots of action **Two is company but three's a crowd.** – *proverb* asking the third party to leave

tree /trEy/ [trees] *noun* 1 a big plant with a trunk and branches which grows tall *The maple tree is taller than the house.* 2 a diagram which shows relationships by lines as branches *The decision tree showed five options on how to solve the problem.* Col: **bark up the wrong tree** – wrong about a reason or source **cannot see the forest for the trees** – missing the big picture paying too much attention to details **family tree** – map of decedents **money doesn't grow on trees** – be careful of spending because the amount is limited **out of one's tree** – crazy

V /vEy/ [V's] *noun* 1 twenty-second letter of the Latin alphabet *VISA starts with a V.* 2 Roman numeral five. *The index is on page* V. 3 short form for volt *The toy car runs on a 12 v battery.* [Col:] **V** – Roman numeral 5 **V-neck** – shape of a garment's neckline

VISA /vEy zu/ [visas] *noun* 1 a brand of credit card *She paid for it with her VISA.* 2 passport document that allows entry into a country *Her student visa is for a year.*

we (wee) /wEy/ *pron* the speaker and at least one other person *We danced until midnight.*

we'll (wheel) /wEyl/ *contr* we will future *We'll finish the assignment before we leave school.*

weak (week) /wEyk/ [weaker, weakest] *adj* lacking strength and energy *I can't watch horror movies because I have a weak stomach.* [Col:] **A chain is as strong as its weakest link.** – *proverb* about the importance of all members of a group **a week spot for** – special feelings for **as weak as a kitten** – no physical strength **The spirit is will but the flesh is weak.** – *proverb* people can't always do what they know they should **weak at the knees** – so overcome with emotion one feels like they may fall down

wee (we) /wEy/ *adj* very small *The wee boy couldn't reach the top of the table.*

week (weak) /wEyk/ [weeks] *noun* 1 duration of seven days, usually from Sunday to Saturday *There are 52 weeks in a year.* 2 seven days devoted to a specific theme *Education Week falls in October.* [Col:] **by the week** – 7 days at a time **week in, week out** – same old **weeks on end** – a long time **work week** – Monday to Friday

wheel (we'll) /wEyl/ [wheels] *noun* 1 a round frame used to move machinery *The wheels on the bicycle needed air.* 2 moving forces *The wheels of industry slow down in a recession.* [Col:] **asleep at the wheel** – not paying attention **at the wheel** – driving **behind the wheel** – driving **big wheel** – boss or big shot **don't reinvent the wheel** – use existing tools and methods **fifth wheel** towing adaption **hell on wheels** – energetic character, trouble-maker **put shoulder to the wheel** – work **set of wheels** – vehicle **set the wheels in motion** – start **spin wheels** – working but not getting ahead **squeaking wheel gets the oil** – noisy person gets attention **the wheels are turning** – thinking **wheel and deal** – dicker **wheel around** – turn quickly **wheel off** – leave quickly

wreath /rEyTH/ [wreaths, wreathed, wreathing] *noun* circular decoration of greenery to show respect or on front doors at Christmas time. *The children place wreaths at the war memorial on Remembrance Day.*

year /yEyr/ [years] *noun* 365 days *The calendar year starts January 1.* [Col:] **autumn years** – old age **by the year** – future **donkey's years** – long time **getting on in years** – older **leap year** – every fourth year has 366 days **leap year day** – February 29 only exist during a leap year, every four years **light years** – the distance light travels in a vacuum in one year **light years away** – far in the distant future **Not in a million years!** – never **one's sunset years** – old age **ring in the new year** – party December 31 until after midnight to celebrate the changing of the year **school year** – in Canada runs from September until June **seven-year itch** – critical time in a marriage, one partner strays **take years off** – look younger **twilight years** – old age **up in years** – getting older

year after year – regularly **year in, year out** – continually **year round** – all year

Z /zEy/ USA [Z's] *noun* the American pronunciation of the twenty-sixth letter of the Latin alphabet *Zebra starts with a Z.* Col: **catch some z's** – take a nap **from A to Z** – everything **Zzz's** – notation for sleeping

zucchini /zUw **kEy** nEy/ [zucchinis] *noun* dark green summer squash shaped like a cucumber *I get zucchini for free because my neighbor always grows too many.* Col: **zucchini bread** – sweet loaf made from zucchini squash

Chapter 4
/e/ is Red

Chapter 4
/e/ is Red

America /u me ri ku/
any /e nEy/
attention /u ten Shun/

bed /bed/
bell /bel/
bent /bent/
berry /be rEy/
best /best/
better /be dEr/
bread /bred/
breath /breTH/

carry /ke rEy/
carriage /ke rij/
celery /sel rEy/
cent (scent, sent) /sent/
center, centre /sen tEr/
chemical /ke mu kul/
check /Chek/
cherry /Che rEy/
chest /Chest/
connection /ku nek Shun/
contest /kun test/
credit /kre dut/

dead /ded/
death /deTH/
debt /det/
December /du sem bEr/
deck /dek/
delicate /de lu kut/
depend /du pend/
develop /du ve lup/
desk /desk/
desert /de sErt/
digestion /du jes jun/
direction /dur ek Shun/
dress /dres/

echo /e kOw/
edge /ej/
effect /u fekt/
egg /eg/
electric /u lek trik/
elephant /e lu funt/
eleven /u le vun/
end /end/
engine /en jun/
error /e rEr/
essay /e sAy/
event /u vent/
ever /e vEr/
every /ev rEy/
ex (X) /eks/
exit /ek sut/ or /eg zit/
expert /eks pErt/

F /ef/
February /fe byU we rEy/
feather /fe ThEr/
friend /frend/
get /get/
general /je nu rul/
guess /ges/
guest /gest/

head /hed/
health /helTH/
hell /hel/
help /help/

intelligence /in te lu junz/
invention /in ven Shun/

jello /je lOw/
jelly /je lEy/

kettle /ke dul/

/ e / is Red

L /e**l**/
lead (led) /**led**/
leather /**le** ThEr/
led (lead) /**led**/
left /**left**/
leg /**leg**/
lemon /**le** mun/
let /**let**/
letter /**le** dEr/
lettuce /**le** dus/
level /**le** vul/
lieute**n**ant / lUw **te** nunt/

M /e**m**/
many /**me** nEy/
marry (merry) /**me** rEy/
measure /**me** ZhEr/
men /**men**/
merry (marry) /**me** rEy/
my**self** /mIy **self**/

N /e**n**/
neck /**nek**/
nephew /**ne** fyUw/
never /**ne** vEr/
next /**nekst**/
No**vem**ber /nOw **vem** bEr/

parent /**pe** runt/
pen /**pen**/
pencil /**pen** sul/
penny /**pe** nEy/
pleasure /**ple** ZhEr/
present /**pre** zunt/
pretzel /**pre** tzul/

question /**kwes** jun/

read (red) /**red**/
ready /**re** dEy/
record /**re** kErd/
red (read) /**red**/
reference /**ref** runs/
re**gret** /ru **gret**/
regular /**reg** yu lEr/
rent /**rent**/
repre**sent** /re pru **zent**/
re**spect** /ru **spekt**/
resume /**re** zu mAy/
rest /**rest**/

S /e**s**/
said /**sed**/
scent (cent, sent) /**sent**/
schedule /**She** jU wul/, /**ske** jU wul/
second /**se** kund/
se**lec**tion /su **lek** Shun/
self /**self**/
send /**send**/
sentence /**sen** tuns/
seven /**se** vun/
shelf /**Shelf**/
separate /**se** pu rAyt/
Sep**tem**ber /sup **tem** bEr/
sex /**seks**/
sense /**sens**/
sent (cent, scent) /**sent**/
smell /**smel**/
stem /**stem**/
step /**step**/
stretch /**strech**/
special /**spe** Shul/
sug**gest** /su **jest**/
sweatshirt /**swet** ShErt/

HOW DO YOU SAY? PRONUNCIATION DICTIONARY

tell /tel/
ten /ten/
tenant /**te** nunt/
test /test/
them /Them/
then /Then/
thread /THred/
together /tu **ge** ThEr/
twelve /twelv/

umbrella /um **bre** lu/

very /ve rEy/
vest /vest/

weather (whether) /we ThEr/
Wednesday /wenz dAy/
welcome /wel kum/
well /wel/
went /went/
west /west/
wet /wet/
when /wen/
whether (weather) /we ThEr/

X (ex) /eks/

yellow /ye lOw/
yesterday /yes dEr dAy/
yes /yes/

Z /zed/ CAN

/ e / is Red

America /u **me** ri ku/ [USA] *prop noun* 1 the United States of America *English is the mother tongue of 82% of the people in America.* Col: **Central America** —nations from Mexico to Panama   **North America** – includes Canada, the United States and Mexico   **South America** – continent south of Panama   **the Americas** – land mass including North, South, Central America and the Caribbean

any /e nEy/ *adj* one of several *Choose any chocolate bar you want.* • *pron* negative *There aren't any students here.* • *adv* to a degree *Do I look any older?* Col: **A rose by any other name would smell as sweet.** – *proverb* characteristics are more important than names   **any number of** – unspecified   **any old thing** – don't fuss   **any port in a storm** – desperate   **any Tom, Dick, or Harry** – random individual   **any way you slice it** – one answer   **at any cost** – regardless of cost   **at any rate** – oh well   **Don't give me any of your lip!** – don't be rude to me   **Don't let it go any further.** – stop the conflict now   **Don't take any wooden nickels.** – *proverb* be careful, don't be tricked   **go to any length** – great effort   **in any case** – no matter   **in any event** – whatever   **Is there any truth to?** – verify a rumor   **no one will be any the wiser** – our little secret   **not by any stretch of the imagination** – no way   **not going to win any beauty contests** – unattractive   **not in any way, shape, or form** – absolute no   **pull any punches** – speak directly without holding any opinions back   **ring any bells** – remember

attention /u **ten** Shun/ *noun* 1 focus awareness *The teacher asked for the student's attention.* 2 recognition *Young children need a lot of attention.* 3 military maneuver *The soldiers stood at attention for the inspection.* Col: **attention span** – length of time a person can focus   **call to one's attention** – point out   **center of attention** – focal point   **grab someone's attention** – attract their interest   **pay attention** – listen

bed /bed/ [beds] *noun* 1 furniture for sleeping *The child slept in his mother's bed.* 2 flower garden *He pulled the weeds from the flower bed.* Col: **a bed of nails** – unpleasant experience   **as easy as falling out of bed** – ridiculously easy   **bed down** – retire for the night   **bed-and-breakfast** – overnight room with breakfast   **bed head** – messy morning hair   **bed sores** – skin irritations from lying in bed for a long time   **bedridden** – confined to bed   **Early to bed and early to rise, makes a man healthy, wealthy, and wise.** – *proverb* on the importance of getting sleep   **get up on the wrong side of bed** – wake up crabby   **go to bed with** – have sex with   **in bed with** – doing business with as a partner   **make the bed** – tidy it   **not a bed of roses** – not easy   **put to bed** – not talk about again   **sick in bed** – ill and lying down   **You've made your bed now lie in it.** – *proverb* to suffer the consequences of one's own bad decisions

bell /bel/ [bells] *noun* upside down, hollow, metal, musical instrument *The church bells ring on Sunday mornings.* Col: **all the bells and whistles** – extra trimmings   **clear as a bell** – understood   **Hell's bells!** – OMG, surprise   **It rings a bell.** – vague recollection or memory   **saved by the bell** – spared at the last moment   **sound as a bell** – healthy   **with bells on** – dressed in finery

bent /bent/ [bends, bent, bending] *verb* past of *bend* 1 double over *He bent over to pick strawberries.* 2 curved *The tree bent in the wind.* Col: **bent on** – committed   **bent out of shape** – angry, upset or annoyed   **hell bent for leather** – going fast

berry /bɛ rEy/ [berries] noun small sweet fruit *My favorite berries are blueberries.* [Col:] brown as a berry – suntanned

best /best/ [good, better, best] adj superlative of good *I have the best teacher.* [Col:] all the best – wish someone well at best – odds of most favorable outcome at one's best – in top shape at the best of times – the highest outcome one can expect be on best behavior – manners best be going – time to leave best bet – odds on best friend – closest friend best man – groomsman, male witness at wedding best of luck – good wishes best part of – most enjoyable or biggest portion best-case scenario – most favorable possible outcome *Best-laid plans of mice and men often go astray.* – proverb life does not always go according to plan bff – best friends forever bring out the best in – conditions that foster highest performance come off second best – lost do one's best – apply oneself *Experience is the best teacher.* – proverb that supports learning by doing for the best – rationalize a bad experience give it best shot – utmost effort Give my best to – pass on wishes have best interest at heart – good intentions *Honesty is the best policy.* – proverb about integrity hope for the best – wish *Hope for the best and prepare for the worst.* – proverb to have a good attitude but be practical in the best of health – healthy *Laughter is the best medicine.* – proverb about the healing powers of laughter and happiness make the best of a bad situation – resourceful in crisis man's best friend – dog may the best man win – good sport mother knows best – defer one's best shot – try hardest put best foot forward – start off with good effort second best – less quality Sunday best – formal clothes the best of both worlds – great success from two spheres the best of a bad lot – least bad of an unsavory group *The best defense is a good offense.* – proverb attack is the best protection *The best things in life are free.* – proverb about values with the best of them – as good as the experts work out for the best – a bad experience won't seem so bad in time

better /bɛ dEr/ [good, better, best] adj comparative of good, superior *Kim's grades are better than Chris's.* [Col:] all better – everything is OK now better be going – time to leave better half – spouse or life partner better off – in a more satisfactory position for better or worse – marriage vows to remain together no matter what happens get better – get well or improve *It is better to have loved and lost than never to have loved at all.* – proverb the risk and cost of love is worth it

bread /bred/ [breads, breaded, breading] noun baked food made from flour, yeast *Whole wheat bread is better for you.* [Col:] bread and butter – main income breaking bread – eating meal with friends and family know on which side your bread is buttered – behave respectfully toward the bread winner/boss *Man cannot live by bread alone.* – proverb people need art and friends, more than the bare essentials in life the best thing since sliced bread – exciting new invention

breath /breTH/ [breaths] noun inhalation and exhalation of air *I could see my breath in the cold air.* [Col:] all in one breath – speak quickly without stopping to breath breath of fresh air – a nice change in the same breath – say two different opinions one after the other out of breath – unable to breath take one's breath away – in awe under one's breath – complain quietly so no one hears waste one's breath – voice an opinion that no one listens to

carry /**ke** rEy/ [carries, carried, carrying] *verb* transport *Carry your identification with you always.* Col: **cash and carry** – small purchases   **carry a torch** – secretly love   **carry on** – continue   **carry-on luggage** – cabin bags not checked in   **carry out** – continue and finish   **carry over** – postpone

carriage /**ke** ruj/ [carriages] *noun* vehicle, buggy *The Queen's carriage was pulled by six white horses.* Col: **carriage trade** – steady business clientele

celery /**sel** rEy/ *noun* long, green stalked vegetable *Celery is the only food that has less calories than it takes to eat it.*

cent (scent, sent) /**sent**/ [¢, cents] *noun* North American 1¢ coin *A penny and a cent are the same thing.* Col: **not worth a cent** – worthless   **two cents worth** – personal opinion

chemical /**ke** mi kul/ [chemicals] *noun* a combination of elements *Chlorine is a chemical used to clean swimming pools.* Col: **chemical warfare** – harmful chemical weapons   **chemical soup** – mix of toxic liquids

center, **cen**tre /**sen** tEr/ [centers, centered, centering] *noun* 1 middle *Place the candle in the center of the cupcake.* • *verb* find the physical or emotional midpoint *Before her speech she took a deep breath and centered her energy.* 2 building with a special purpose *Center for the Arts* Col: **center of attention** – the focus of a group of people   **center of gravity** – point where weight is dispersed evenly on all sides

check /**Chek**/ [checks, checked, checking] *verb* 1 proofread *The teacher will check your answers.* 2 limit, restrain *The police will keep the protesters in check.* • *noun* 1 bankable note used instead of money *We accept cash or check.* 2 physical contact in hockey *The referee gives a 2 minute penalty for a rough check.* Col: **bounced check** – insufficient funds   **check up** – medical examination   **check in** – register into hotel   **check out** – leaving the hotel   **check it out** – verify, examine   **check in on** – visit a patient   **checkmate** – winning move in chess game   **checkpoint** – official roadblock for inspection purposes   **take a rain check** – postpone until future date

cherry /**Che** rEy/ [cherries] small round red pitted fruit *The cherry blossoms were beautiful in spring.* Col: **cherry picking** – choose the best requiring little effort   **Life is a bowl of cherries.** – life is good

chest /**Chest**/ [chests] *noun* 1 upper portion of human body covering ribs *He had a scar on his chest after heart surgery.* 2 storage cabinet *The blankets are stored in the chest.* Col: **barrel-chested** – physically broad in chest region   **chest of drawers** – dresser   **get something off one's chest** – talk about a problem or concern   **hope chest** – storage container for items for future married life   **play one's cards close to one's chest** – private about thoughts and intentions   **treasure chest** – where pirate's store valuables

connection /ku **nek** Shun/ [connections, connected, connecting] *noun* 1 tie, association, attachment *The internet connection is being installed.* 2 friend, relative, acquaintance *I have some connections in the real estate industry.* • *verb* hooked up *We are connected to the internet.* Col: **a good connection** – a helpful contact person   **in connection with** – relating to   **stay connected** – stay in touch

contest /kun **test**/ [contest, contested, contesting] *verb* challenge or fight *We contested the will my mother made after she lost her mind.*

credit /**kre** dut/ [credits, credited, crediting] *noun* 1 trust, faith, pat on the back *You should get more credit for all your hard work.* 2 acknowledgement of actors' performances *Watch the credits at the end of the movie.* • *verb* debt *Credit my account.* Col: **buy on credit** – use a credit card   **credit card** – plastic card used to purchase things   credit bureau – organization that investigates one's ability to pay   give credit where credit is due – acknowledge work well-done   take credit for – accept praise for something done well

dead /ded/ *adj* 1 not living *My car battery is dead.* 2 emotionless *Our relationship was dead so we divorced.* Col: dead right – 100% correct   dead wrong – 100% wrong   dead ringer – identical appearance to another   dead as a doornail – lifeless   dead set against – very opposed   dead on one's feet – exhausted   dead tired – extremely tired   over my dead body – refuse   wouldn't be caught dead – wouldn't do it

death /deTH/ [deaths] *noun* end of life *What was the cause of death?* Col: at death's door – very sick   death warmed over – look very ill   death wish – unconscious desire for something bad to happen   frighten to death – extremely scared   frozen to death – very cold   worked to death – complaint about extremely hard work

deck /dek/ [decks, decked, decking] *noun* 1 platform off a building with no roof *We sunbath on the deck in the afternoon.* 2 pack of playing cards *There are 52 cards in a deck* • *verb* knock down *She decked the thief as he was trying to escape.* Col: all hands on deck – everyone help   clear the deck – everything out of the way in preparation   decked out – dressed up   hit the deck – get out of bed   on deck – present, next to go

debt /det/ [debts] *noun* sum of money owed *Her student debt was paid off before she got married.* Col: in someone's debt – owe   out of debt – no longer owing   pay one's debt to society – spend time in prison

Decem**ber** /du sem bEr/ [Dec., Decembers] *prop noun* twelfth month of the year *December is the last month of every year.* Col: May-December relationship – spouses with large age gap

delicate /de lu kut/ [delicates] *adj* 1 fragile, fine, not robust *Wash your delicate laundry in cold water.* 2 sensitive *I have delicate skin.* Col: delicate flower – sensitive person   delicate matter – sensitive issue   in a delicate condition – pregnant

depend /dEy pend/ [depends, depended, depending] *verb* rely on *It depends on how much time I have.* Col: depend on – rely on   that all depends – there are other factors to consider

develop /du ve lup/ [develops, developed, developing] *verb* grow, mature *This exercise will help you develop muscles.* Col: developing idea – evolving line of thinking   developing skill – improve ability   well developed – physically impressive

desk /desk/ [desks] *noun* 1 office furniture, table *We share a desk at work.* 2 service area of business *Visit the information desk at the entrance.* Col: away from one's desk – unavailable but at work   desk job – employment in an office environment   help desk – location to call for service or assistance   news desk – media info area

desert /de sErt/ (deserts) *noun* dry sandy area with no plants *Camels are one of the few animals that can cross the desert.*

diges**tion** /du jes jun/ *noun* process of absorbing food into body *Eat slowly for better digestion.*

direc**tion** /dIy rek Shun/ [directions] *noun* 1 way, route *Can you give me directions to the hospital?* 2 guidance *The councilor helped me find some direction for my life.* Col: go in all directions – disorganized and scattered   give direction – advise, order   right direction – correct route   wrong direction – incorrect route

dress /dres/ [dresses, dressed, dressing] *noun* article of clothing women wear *Beth looks sexy in her little black dress.* • *verb* 1 put clothes on *The little girl*

/ e / is Red

needed help to dress in the morning. 2 decorate *It was her job to dress the department store window.* 3 cover a wound *The nurse began to dress the soldier's wounds.* Col: **dress down Fridays** – casual attire at week's end   **dress for success** – wear good clothing to create a good impression   **dress up** – wear formal clothes   **dress someone down** – yell at   **dress the salad** – put sauce on it   **dressed to the nines** – wear nice or sexy clothes   **dressed to kill** – dress up or sexy

echo /e kOw/ [echoes, echoed, echoing] *noun* sound waves bouncing back from a large surface *The echo in the Grand Canyon can be heard for miles.* • *verb* produce an echo *The music echoed through the village.* Col: **Little Sir Echo** – name for a toddler who repeats everything they hear

edge /ej/ [edges, edged, edging] *noun* 1 margin, boundary *Don't stand too close to the edge of the cliff.* 2 advantage *Salespeople who speak more than one language have an edge.* 3 sharp part of a tool *The knife edge is sharpened with a stone.* • *verb* slowly move closer *The baby edged toward the pail of toys.* Col: **cutting edge** – very current innovation   **double edged sword** – problems with either option   **edge by** – move carefully past   **edgy** – nervous   **on edge** – tense   **over the edge** – crazy   **rough around the edges** – uneducated low class person

effect /Ey **fekt**/ [effects, effected, effecting] *noun* result, consequence *The effect of pollution is climate change.* • *verb* influence *How can we effect a change?* Col: **a bad effect** – negative impact   **domino effect** – causes an automatic result which continues   **go into effect** – a law or regulation becomes valid   **in effect** – in reality   **snowball effect** – increases in size or importance at an increasing rate   **to that effect** – like that

egg /eg/ [eggs, egged, egging] *noun* unborn species *A chicken lays an egg.* 2 breakfast food *Cook my egg sunny side up.* • *verb* encourage *My brother said he wanted to go skydiving so I egged him on.* Col: **bad egg** – often in trouble   **egg on** – encourage   **egghead** – nerd, know-it-all, intellectual   *Don't put all your eggs in one's basket.* – *proverb* about diversifying   **nest egg** – money saved for future

electric /u lek trik/ *noun* powered by electricity *The hybrid car is electric and gas powered.* Col: **electric performance** – emotional and impressive presentation

elephant /el u funt/ [elephants] *noun* largest land mammal *African elephants have big ears.* Col: **a memory like an elephant** – a good memory   **elephant in the room** – important topic not being discussed   **white elephant** – not useful but big and costly

eleven /u le vun/ [elevens] *noun* number after ten and before twelve *The corner store was open from 7:00 am to 11:00 pm.* Col: **eleventh hour** – at the last minute

end /**end**/ [ends, ended, ending] *noun* 1 conclusion *Finally it was the end of the movie.* 2 result, outcome *In the end he went to live with his grandmother.* • *verb* finale *The game ended in a tie.* Col: **a means to an end** – method or strategy to accomplish a goal   **all's well that ends well** – ended well after a bit of trouble   **dead end** – no exit   **end of the line** – final limit   **end of one's rope** – no more patience   **end up** – finish up   **end result** – consequences   **in the end** – ultimately   **see light at the end of the tunnel** – there's a good outcome in the future

engine /en jun/ [engines] *noun* motor, machine *This engine runs on gas and electricity.* Col: **search engine** – internet research tool

error /e rEr/ [errors] *noun* mistake *It was an error to drive through a stop light.* Col: **in error** – by mistake   **see the error of one's ways** – acknowledge mistakes

103

trial and error — trying something new without fearing failure

essay /**e** sAy/ [essays] *noun* short piece of writing *My English essay is due tomorrow and I haven't started it.*

event /**Ey** vent/ [events] *noun* situation, happening *The wedding was the biggest event of the year.* `Col:` blessed event — birth of a child   coming event — future occasion   in any event — whatever occurs   special event — special occasion   unlikely event — probably not

ever /**e** vEr/ *adj* at any times *When will you ever finish this work?* `Col:` everlasting — without ending   forever and ever — time without end   live happily ever after — fairy tale ending   whenever — no special time limit

every /**ev** rEy/ *adv* each, single *Every child got a balloon.* `Col:` at every turn — all the time   every man for himself — look after one's self   every Tom, Dick and Harry — everyone   every which way — in all direction

ex (X) /**eks**/ [ex's] *noun* slang for former *My ex is great about picking up the kids.*

exit /**ek** sut/ or /**eg** zit/ [exits, exited, exiting] *verb* go out, departure *Please exit by the rear door.* • *noun* route, way out *There were four exits on the airplane.* `Col:` exit strategy — plan for escape leave   fire exit — emergency route out

expert /**eks** pErt/ [experts] *noun* specialist *The experts were called in to fix the chimney.* • *adj* specialist *Thompson Language Center generates expert speaking teachers.* `Col:` expert witness — a person with authority in an area important to a trial

F /**ef**/ [F's] *noun* 1 the sixth letter of the Latin alphabet *Five starts with an F.* 2 slang short form of fuck *What the F is going on!* `Col:` F off — avoiding swearing for go away   f u — avoiding swearing for go to hell

February /**fe** byU we rEy/ [Feb., Februarys or Februaries] *prop noun* second month of the year *Valentine's day is February 14th.*

feather /**fe** ThEr/ [feathers, feathered, feathering] *noun* outer bird covering, plume *Chicken feathers are plucked off before the bird is cooked.* • *verb* make more comfortable *The bride feathered her new home with matching drapes and throw pillows.* `Col:` birds of a feather — similar people   Birds of a feather flock together. — *proverb* about people with similar values and interests socializing regularly   feather in one's cap — a reward or recognition for achievement   feather one's nest — make a home more comfortable or beautiful   feather weight — very light; weight category for boxers; an insult to ones intelligence   knock over with a feather -extreme surprise   light as a feather — extremely light

friend /**frend**/ [friends] *noun* buddy, companion *The friends you make at school last your whole life.* `Col:` best friend — number one closest friend   fair weather friend — friend only in good times   friends in high places — influential friends   friend or foe — Are you a friend or an enemy?   make a friend — form a friendship   man's best friend — a dog   to unfriend — remove name from Facebook

get /**get**/ [gets, got, getting] *verb* 1 acquire *I get my fruits and vegetables at the market.* 2 become *I get angry when students regularly come to school late.* 3 arrive *I get to school at 8:00 every day.* 4 understand *I get what you are saying about colors and vowel sounds.* `Col:` get a life — find something better to do than bother me   get something off one's chest -share a secret that is held as a burden   get the lion's share — have the biggest percentage   get on with it — hurry up and complete an unpleasant task   get up and go — physical energy   get back

– revenge get by – barely manage financially get off the hook – escape responsibility get along – co-operate get to – permission get over – recover from get around to – deal with later get out of – escape responsibility get a head-start – advantage get personal – intimately involved get out of hand – become uncontrolled get the hang of – become more skillful at a new task get carried away – exaggerate or overdo get a bite – eat get one's life together – regain control of one's purpose get off – be found innocent get one's wires crossed – misunderstand get on one's nerves – annoy get real – become realistic get a second wind – have a burst of energy after tiring get wind of something – overhear

general /je nu rul/ [generals] *adj* normal, usual *Parks and libraries are for the use of the general public.* • *noun* military rank *The general inspected the soldiers.* Col: general store – local store with a wide range of merchandise in general – usually

guess /ges/ [guesses, guessed, guessing] *verb* estimate *I guess there are about 200 people at my school.* • *noun* the estimate *What is your guess?* Col: educated guess – predict based on research and prior knowledge Guess what? – conversation starter I guess – suppose, maybe I agree it's anyone's guess – hard to determine second guess – predict what another is thinking

guest /gest/ [guests] *noun* visitor *He was a guest in her house.* Col: be my guest – help yourself guest house – accommodation separate from main home guest of honor – special visitor guest room – room set aside for visitors

head /hed/ [heads, headed, heading] *noun* 1 part of body held up by the neck *He had no hair on his head.* 2 top, peak *She is the head of the English department.* • *verb* 1 lead *He headed up the new advertizing team.* 2 move forward *Head towards the exit and it's the door on the left.* Col: a good head – reliable person bed head – messy morning hair dead head – remove flower blossoms; hazardous log just under water surface dickhead /shithead – asshole, dislikable person head in the clouds – unaware or unrealistic head of the class – student with the highest marks head out – start a journey head over heels – deeply in love head start – earlier start head to – go somewhere head up – manage a team head-on collision – accident in which two cars collide face to face heads and shoulders above – much better than others heads or tails – call when flipping a coin in game of chance in over one's head – taking on tasks that one cannot handle keep a cool head – stay calm lose one's head – lose self-control make a lot of headway – good progress off the top of one's head – without thinking or preparation over one's head – beyond one's understanding pig-headed – stubborn thick in the head – not intelligent turn heads – get attention two heads are better than one - more input, better result use one's head – plan before acting on something use one's head – think logically

health /helTH/ [healthy] *noun* well-being, condition *Exercising is good for your health.* Col: health and safety – workplace conditions healthy, wealthy and wise – ultimate goals in life to one's health – toast, wish for long life

hell /hel/ [hells] *interj* a bad word, *slang word of surprise or dismay* Oh Hell! • *noun* a dark place of torment and suffering *Go to hell.* Col: a hell of a – extremely, good or bad a living hell – long-term tortuous conditions all hell broke loose – suddenly chaotic be shot to hell – plans ruined beat the hell out of – physically hit   catch hell – get in trouble   come hell or high water – no matter what   fight like hell – furiously combat   for the hell of it – for fun   get the hell out – angry command   Give them hell! – sporting cheer   go through hell – painful period   go to hell in a hand-basket – fell into decay   Go to hell! – swear at   don't have a chance in hell – no possibility   don't have a snowball's chance in hell – no possibility   have been to hell and back – returned from a bad experience   hell-bent on – committed to   Hell hath no fury like a woman scorned. – *proverb* beware of a woman whose love has not been returned   hell on earth – unpleasant life   hell on wheels – badly behaved   hell to pay – serious consequences   Hell's bells! – surprised or annoyed   hell-bent for leather – go fast   It'll be a cold day in hell – not going to happen   knock the hell out of – took a toll on health   like a bat out of hell – fast   put through hell – made suffer   raise hell – make a big fuss   scare the hell out of – frighten   sure as hell – probably bad   the child from hell – badly behaved child   The road to hell is paved with good intentions. – *proverb* it is not enough to mean well, one has to produce results   to hell and gone – far away   to hell with – don't bother when hell freezes over – never

help /**help**/ [helps, helped, helping] *verb* assist *Can I help you?* • *noun* 1 assistance, aid *The neighbor is offering us help.* 2 paid employees *The help eat before or after their shift.* `Col:` beyond help – too mentally or physically ill   couldn't help it – couldn't prevent it   good help is hard to find -condescending comment about employee's productivity   Help! – an emergency call   help me – a plea for assistance   help out – assist   help yourself – serve yourself or accept what is offered   every little bit helps – thank for small but appreciated donation   seek professional help – for mental illness

intelligence /in **te** lu junz/ *noun* 1 ability to learn and process information quickly *Dolphins have a lot of intelligence.* 2 secret information gathered by governments *Spies collect foreign intelligence.*

invention /in **ven** Shun/ [inventions] *verb* make a new device *The wheel was a great invention.* `Col:` Necessity is the mother of invention. – proverb one will think of a way to do something important

jello /**je** lOw/ [jellos] *noun* fruit flavored gelatin dessert *My kids love jello as a dessert but not as a salad.*

jelly /**je** lEy/ [jellies, jellied] *noun* gelatin jam or dessert *I like grape jelly on toast.* • *adj* the quality of jelly *Jellied salad is often eaten at barbecues.* `Col:` jelly belly – fat stomach   jelly fish – poisonous sea creatures

kettle /**ke** dul/ [kettles] *noun* vessel for boiling water *Put the kettle on the stove.* `Col:` a fine kettle of fish – difficult situation   pot calling the kettle black – hypocritical comments

L /**el**/ [L's] *noun* the twelfth letter of the Latin alphabet *Lemon starts with an L.* `Col:` L – Roman numeral 50   L-shaped – right angled   L-7 – slang for person who does not fit in

lead (led) /**led**/ [leads] *noun* heavy blue-gray metal *Lead pencils are not lead but graphite.* `Col:` go over like a lead balloon – unfavorable idea   lead astray – misguided   lead down the garden path – cheated or taken advantage of   lead to believe – taught or informed   lead the way – provided direction and inspired others

leather /**le** ThEr/ [leathers] *noun* animal skin dried and processed *Leather is usually made from cow hide.* • *adj* made from leather *Leather purses cost more and last longer.* `Col:` hell bent for leather –

/ e / is Red

running away quickly   leather back – type of turtle

led (lead) /**led**/ *verb* past tense of *lead* guide *The dog lead the children safely out of the woods.*

left /**left**/ *noun* 1 opposite of right *My classroom is on the left inside the main door.* 2 remainder *After shopping I had three dollars left in my purse.* • *verb* past tense of *leave* depart *He left after lunch.* Col: a left-handed compliment – contains hidden criticism   hang a left – turn to the left   left-handed – writes with one's left hand   lefty – left-handed person   left wing – liberal political view   left in – remained   left out – excluded   out in left field – badly mistaken   leftovers – food remaining from previous meal   the left hand doesn't know what the right hand is doing – lack of communication   two left feet – can't dance

leg /**leg**/ [legs, legged, legging] *noun* 1 lower limb of body *He broke his leg falling down the stairs.* 2 supporting portion of furniture *The hall table has three legs.* 3 section of journey *The last leg of the journey was through England.* Col: Break a leg! – wish good luck before an event or performance   can talk the hind leg off a horse – talks too much   costs an arm and a leg – expensive   get up on hind legs – an animal rising up o two back legs   doesn't have a leg to stand on – no rational supporting arguments   have legs – wine quality   He puts his pants on one leg at a time – human like the rest of us   leg up on – an advantage   on its last legs – end of its usefulness   pull one's leg – joke or tease   sea legs – get accustomed to a new job   Shake a leg! – hurry up   show some leg – sexy flash of the top of a woman's leg   stretch legs – exercise a bit   tail between legs – cowardly   to have a hollow leg – eats a lot

lemon /**le** mun/ [lemons] *noun* 1 sour yellow citrus fruit *Lemons are available in the supermarket all year round.* 2 substandard, always breaking down *Unfortunately, my last car was a lemon.* •*adj* 1 flavor of the fruit *Lemon pie is my husband's favorite* 2 bright yellow color *They painted their kitchen lemon yellow.* Col: a real lemon – poorly made, always breaking down   lemon fresh – clean crisp smell

let /**let**/ [lets, let, letting] *verb* 1 allow *Let me take your hat and coat.* 2 rent *I have a room to let.* Col: let off – go freely   let out – alter clothing to increase size; release from jail   Let sleeping dogs lie. – proverb don't revisit an issue already solved   let the cat out of the bag – reveal a secret   let up – stop pushing   live and let live – don't judge others

letter /**le** dEr/ [letters] *noun* 1 one of 26 symbols in the writing alphabet *Capitalize the first letter of the first word of a sentence.* 2 written communication *I prefer to send an e-mail than write a letter.* Col: a four letter word – a swear word, profanity   a man of letters – a professional   a red letter day – an important day   Dear John letter – denotes the end of a romantic relationship   French letter – condom   letterhead – official stationery   the letter of the law – exactly as it is written vs. the spirit of the rule   to the letter – exact

lettuce /**le** dus/ *noun* leafy vegetable, base for salads *Romaine lettuce is used for making caesar salad.*

level /**le** vul/ [levels, leveled, leveling] *noun* 1 storey of a building *The coffee shop is on the ground level of the mall.* 2 flat, even *The bookcase isn't level and it drives me nuts.* 3 tool with a bubble of fluid to indicate flat *The bricklayer used a level with each row of bricks.* 4 rank of authority *Take your complaint to a higher level.* • *verb* 1 make even *Level the gravel before the sidewalk gets poured.* 2 flatten *They* leveled the old building to make space for the new one. `Col:` **at sea level** — at the ocean's surface   **do one's level best** — perform to best ability   **find one's own level** — find the position or rank that suits a person the best   **level-headed** — logical, sensible   **level playing field** — all have equal chance   **on the level** — honest, straight forward

lieutenant /lUw **te** nunt/ [lieutenants] *noun* an officer's rank in the military *My cousin was recently promoted to lieutenant.*

M /**em**/ [M's] *noun* 1 the thirteenth letter of the Latin alphabet *Money starts with an M.* `Col:` **M** — Roman numeral 1000

many /me nEy/ *adj* numerous *There are many new students every September* `Col:` **finger in too many pies** — involved in too many different projects at once   **have one too many** — drunk   **in many respects** — many ways   **many 's the time** — often   **Many are called but few are chosen.** — *proverb* a number of people want position but few attain it   **Many hands make light work.** — *proverb* the value of helpers   **many moons ago** — a long time ago   **one too many** — alcoholic drinks   **There's many a good tune played on an old fiddle.** — *proverb* usefulness in old age   **Too many chiefs and not enough Indians** — *proverb* about more management than workers   **Too many cooks spoil the broth.** — *proverb* that too many people trying to manage a project end up ruining it   **Too many irons in the fire** — *proverb* about spreading oneself to thin and being ineffective

marry (merry) /me rEy/ [marries, married, marrying] *verb* 1 wed *Will you marry me?* 2 connect *Let's marry these two theories together to get the best solution.* `Col:` **marry beneath oneself** — marry someone of lower social status   **marry for money** — status not love   **marry into** — marry money   **marry off** — find spouse for a daughter to be rid of her   **marry up** — marry into a higher social or economic class   **not the marrying kind** — one who should or wants to remain single

measure /**me** ZhEr/ [measures, measured, measuring] *verb* size, quantity, scale *The tailor will measure you for your new suit.* • *noun* procedure *An emergency escape plan in case of fire is a good safety measure.* `Col:` **beyond measure** — extremely high degree   **for good measure** — a little extra   **made-to-measure** — suit perfectly   **measure up** — meet expectations   **Measure twice, cut once.** — *proverb* the wisdom of being meticulous

men /men/ *noun* plural of man *How many men are in the class?*

merry (marry) /me rEy/ [merrier, merriest] *adj* happy, cheery *Everyone had a merry time at the family reunion.* `Col:` **eat, drink and be merry** — enjoy oneself   **Merry Christmas** — greeting at Christmas time   **merry-go-round** — carousel, amusement park ride   **the more the merrier** — more people make an event more fun

myself /mIy **self**/ *pron* first person reflexive personal pronoun *I count on myself the most.* `Col:` **by myself** — without assistance   **keep oneself busy** — occupied with work and tasks   **make oneself clear** — make oneself understood   **me, myself and I** — emphatically personal

N /en/ [N's] *noun* 1 the fourteenth letter of the Latin alphabet *Number starts with an N.* `Col:` **nth degree** — the utmost

neck /nek/ [necks, necked, necking] *noun* 1 body part connecting the head to the rest of the body *I got a sore neck from working at the computer all day.* 2 narrow part of bottle *The cork is stuck in the neck.* • *verb* slang for kissing *The teenagers neck in lover's lane at the end of the country road.* `Col:` **breathe down one's neck** — micromanage, harass another   **breakneck speed** — very fast   **bottle-**

/ e / is Red

neck – too much traffic in a narrow section of road   **neck on the line** – in a risky situation   **neck of the woods** – nearby, familiar location   **neck and neck** – a close tie   **neck with** – kiss passionately   **pain in the neck** – annoying   **risk one's neck** – to take a chance   **stick out one's neck** – take a risk   **up to one's neck in** – overwhelmed

nephew /**ne** fyUw/ [nephews] *noun* son of brother or sister *We are going to my sister's for my nephew's birthday.*

never /**ne** vEr/ *adv* not ever, no way *Never cross the street without looking both ways.* Col: **almost never** – very rarely   **Better late than never.** - *proverb* better to show up late then not at all   **It never rains but it pours.** – *proverb* things finally happen in great numbers   **never a dull moment** – things are interesting all the time   **never fails** – can count on it   **never the twain shall meet** – two people or things will never meet   **never-never land** – not paying attention, originally from the story of Peter Pan   **never say never** – always a possibility   **now or never** – pressure to act   **Well, I never!** – shock and indignation

next /**nekst**/ *adj* following, beside *The next time you come to school late, you have to report to the office.* • *adv* nearest that follows *Buy a notebook on your next visit to the mall.* Col: **better luck next time** – try again   **next door neighbor** – close neighbors   **next in line** – succession   **next to nothing** – almost nothing   **next to no time** – happened quickly   **next of kin** – closest relatives of a dead person

Novem**ber** /no **vem** bEr/ [Nov., Novembers] *prop noun* eleventh month *American Thanksgiving is in November.*

parent /**pe** runt/ [parents, parented, parenting] *noun* father or mother of a child *Parents love their children.* • *verb* actively raise children *We parent differently than we were parented.* Col: **Parent, it's a verb** – take control of your children

pen /**pen**/ [pens] *noun* 1 ink writing device *Write your answers in pen, not pencil.* 2 enclosure for animals *The pigs are in the pen for the night.* 3 prison *You get 5 years in the pen for theft.* Col: **pen pal** – friend one writes to   **pig pen** – dirty, messy place   **put pen to paper** – begin composing or writing   **The pen is mightier than the sword.** – *proverb* knowledge and education solves more than violence

pencil /**pen** sul/ [pencils, penciled, pencilling] *noun* thin, wood, erasable, writing tool *Teacher, may I borrow a pencil?* • *verb* use the erasable writing tool *She penciled her corrections in on her paper.* Col: **pencil case** – zippered case for holding pencils   **pencil pusher** – office worker   **pencil sharpener** - small sharp blade in a tiny box for scraping points on a wooden pencils   **pencil thin** – fine line or too skinny

penny /**pe** nEy/ [¢, pennies] *noun* one cent coin 1¢ *It used to cost a penny for a piece of candy.* Col: **a penny for your thoughts** – tell me what you are thinking about   **costs a pretty** penny – is expensive   **lucky penny** – superstition, found penny brings good fortune   **penny stock** – stock market investment valued under one dollar   **Take a penny leave a penny.** – a jar at the cash register where clients can take a penny if they are short

pleasure /**ple** ZhEr/ *noun* 1 enjoyment *Eating good food is a pleasure.* Col: **business before pleasure** – work before play   **it's a pleasure** – response to "thank you"   **my pleasure** – response agreeing to assist or help or meet someone   **the pleasure is mine** – response to "thank you"   **with pleasure** – eagerly agree to help

present /**pre** zunt/ [presents presented, presenting] *noun* 1 now *Action happening now is the present.* 2 gift 🎁 , *I need* to buy a present for the birthday party. • verb introduce *I would like to present our guest speaker.* `Col:` **for the present time** — in the moment   **past, present and future** — tenses   **the present is a gift** — don't dwell on the past or future   **live in the present** — live in the moment

pretzel /**pre** tzul/ [pretzels] noun crisp, salted biscuit in the shape of a knot or stick. *The kids like to snack on pretzels in front of the TV.*

question /**kwes** jun/ [questions] noun interrogative form *Do you have a question?* • verb 1 doubt, concern *I question their policy.* 2 ask questions *You may question the professor at the end of the lecture.* `Col:` **a question of time** — will happen sooner or later   **beg the question** — invites a new topic   **beyond question** — no doubt   **burning question** — intense point of discussion   **in question** — a point of disagreement   **leading question** — first point of discussion   **no question** — no argument   **open to question** — open for comment and review   **out of the question** — impossible   **pop the question** — ask to marry   **Q & A** — questions and answers   **without question** — no doubt or — without argument

read (red) /**red**/ verb past tense of *read* study *Have you read the newspaper today?* `Col:` **well-read** — educated

ready /**re** dEy/ [readier, readiest] adj 1 prepared *Get yourselves ready for the storm.* 2 eager `Col:` **at the ready** — prepared for action   **good and ready** — impatient to start   **ready or not** — action is starting   **ready to order** — place order at a restaurant   **ready, willing and able** — eager and capable   **rough and ready** — eager for anything

record /**re** kErd/ [records] noun 1 written account *The librarian kept records in the basement.* 2 highest score *Wayne Gretzky holds the record for goals scored in hockey.* 3 round flat disk where sounds have been copied *The old phonograph plays records.*

red (read) /**red**/ [reds, redder, reddest] adj the color of blood *Primary colors are yellow, blue, and red.* • noun the color. *Red and green are Christmas colors.* `Col:` **catch red-handed** — catch in the act of breaking the law   **don't have a red cent** — no money at all   **in the red** — debt, owe more than one makes   **like a red flag to a bull** — provoke rage   **out of the red** — out of debt   **paint the town red** — celebrate   **red eye** — all night flight   **red head** — person with red hair   **red herring** — takes attention away from the main topic   **red ink** — corrections   **Red sky at night, sailors delight, red sky in the morning sailors take warning.** rule of thumb weather indicator   **red tape** — official or bureaucratic paperwork   **red-blooded** — patriotic   **red-carpet treatment** — special treatment   **red-hot** — desirable   **red-letter day** — fantastic news   **roll out the red carpet** — treat someone like royalty   **run a red light** — traffic violation, not stop at a red signal   **see red** — become very angry   **the red-light district** — prostitutes   **the red, white and blue** — American flag   **turn beet red** — flushed with embarrassment

reference /**re** fruns/ [references, referenced, referencing] noun quotation *Put your reference in the footnote.* 2 testimonial *Can you be my reference for my job application?* `Col:` **reference book** — book of data   **reference check** — investigation into one's background   **reference point** — base standard   **reference section** — research area in library   **with reference to** — regarding

re**gret** /ru **gret**/ [regrets, regretted, regretting] verb 1 sorrow *I regret not seeing my father before he died.* 2 polite apology *I regret not being able to attend the dinner.* 3 to have second thoughts *I regret my decision.* `Col:` **no regrets** — without guilt   with regret — feeling of sadness

regular /**reg** yu lEr/ [regulars] *adj* usual *Thursday is a regular school day but Friday is a holiday.* *noun* coffee order, one milk one sugar *I'll have a regular.* `Col:` a regular guy — a good man   regular as clockwork — on schedule   regular mail — not email, not courier   to be regular — not constipated

rent /**rent**/ [rents, rented, renting] *noun* payment to landlord *We pay our rent at the beginning of each month.* • *verb* to lease something rather than owning it *We rent our home.* `Col:` rent-to-own — agreement in which the rent applies to home purchase   rent controls — system to keep rents within fixed governmental guidelines

re**pres**ent /re pru **zent**/ [represents, represented, representing] *verb* 1 act as *It is unfortunate the letters of the Latin alphabet don't represent English sounds.* 2 serve as an agent *Lawyers represents their clients in court.*

re**spect** /re **spekt**/ [respects, respected, respecting] *verb* 1 appreciation *He respects your position.* 2 look up to *Respect your elders.* `Col:` pay one's respects — attend a funeral or visitation   have respect for — hold in high regard   with all due respect — polite way to begin a disagreement   with respect to — with reference to

re**sume** /re zu mAy/ [resumes] *noun* curriculum vitae (c.v.), work history *Bring three copies of your resume to the job interview.*

rest /**rest**/ [rests, rested, resting] *noun* 1 sleep or relax *Did you get any rest last night?* 2 surplus *Give the dog the rest of your dinner.* • *verb* lean, prop *Rest your head on my shoulder.* • *verb* relax *Please be quiet the patient is resting.* `Col:` at rest — idle, stopped   come to rest — come to a stop   final resting place — grave   give it a rest — stop annoying behavior   lay to rest — bury   put mind to rest —

become peaceful about   rest area — picnic area on highway   rest assured — be confident of   rest one's case — conclude arguments   rest in peace — in the afterlife   rest up — take a break

S /**es**/ [S's] *noun* the nineteenth letter of the Latin alphabet *Summer starts with an S.* `Col:` SOS — Morse Code distress signal (· · · — — — · · ·)

said /**sed**/ [says, said, saying] *verb* past tense of *say* spoke *My teacher said I was going a good job.* `Col:` after all is said and done — when the argument is over   easier said than done — not an easy task   he said, she said — gender disagreement   no sooner said than done- act upon one's word quickly   The less said the better. — *proverb* be quiet and let the issue fade   well said — good point, concisely spoken   when all is said and done — in the end

scent (cent, sent) /**sent**/ [scents, scented, scenting] *noun* 1 sense of smell *Dogs have a good sense of smell.* 2 perfume *The scent of roses wafted in through the window.* • *verb* detect by smell *The dog scented a rabbit and ran off to find it.* `Col:` throw off the scent — give false information to stop others from discovering a secret

schedule /**She** jU wul/, /**ske** jU wul/ [schedules, scheduled, scheduling] *noun* timetable of events *The train schedule is posted on the bulletin board.* • *verb* written plan for future activities *People schedule their holidays for when the kids are out of school.*

second /**se** kund/ [2nd, seconds, seconded, seconding] *noun* an instant, tick of the clock *There are sixty seconds in a minute.* *adj* ordinal number after first, before third *Today is her second day in school.* • *verb* side with *I second the motion.* `Col:` just a second — wait   on second thought — after some thought one changes one's mind   second best — not the winner   second class — not most important   second hand — previously owned   **second fiddle** – not the first choice or best player   **second guess** – try to predict   **second nature** – a natural talent   **second wind** – burst of energy after being tired   **second to none** – the best   **split second** – very quickly   **without a second thought** – without hesitation

selection   /su lek Shun/ [selections] noun choice *This store has more selection in the produce department.*

self   /**self**/ noun one's own character *She was ill last week but she is back to her old self now.*   Col: **full of one's self** – arrogant   **self directed learning** – (SDL) online education   **self esteem** – good healthy opinion of oneself   **self help** – improve oneself   **self made man** – earned their success not inherit   **self storage** – temporary accommodation for one's possessions   **selfless** – unselfish   **To thine own self be true.** – proverb about recognizing one's own values and acting on them

send   /**send**/ [sends, sent, sending] verb transmit, deliver *Send me a postcard.*   Col: **send a signal** – transmit a message   **send back** – return   **send for** – request for the presence of   **send off** – celebration before a trip   **send to** – destination

sentence   /**sen** tuns/ [sentences, sentenced, sentencing] noun a complete thought including a subject and a verb. *Sentences end in periods, question marks or exclamation marks.* • verb pass legal judgment on *He was sentenced to thirty days in jail for breaking the law.*   Col: **Marriage isn't a word, it's a sentence.** – play on words

seven   /**se** vun/ [7, sevens] noun the cardinal number after six, before eight *He is seven years old.*   Col: **24/7** – all the time   **in seventh heaven** – extremely happy   **seven year itch** – belief in a high risk of infidelity after seven years

shelf   /**shelf**/ [shelves] noun 1 board used to hold items *If I had a shelf in the kitchen I could put cookbooks on it.* 2 reef, sandbank *Fishing is great on the continental shelf off the coast.*   Col: **off the shelf** – ready-made not custom made   **on the shelf** – on hold   **shelf life** – recommended product storage time

separate   /**se** pu rAyt/ [separates, separated, separating] verb detach *The teacher separated the students who wouldn't stop talking.*   Col: **separate but equal** – segregated but of equal value   **separate off** – divide from the whole   **separate the men from the boys** – a difficult task not all will complete   **separate the wheat from the chaff** – divide what is useful from the rest

September   /sup **tem** bEr/ [Sept., Septembers] prop noun ninth month of the year *The school years starts in September.*

sex   /**seks**/ [sexes] noun 1 gender *Do you know the sex of your baby?* 2 intercourse *Safe sex will prevent unwanted pregnancy.*   Col: **the fairer sex** – outdated term for women   **opposite sex** – the other gender   **sex appeal** – desirability   **sex kitten** – sensual young woman   **sex object** – dehumanizing someone for sex only   **sexpot** – seductive woman

sense   /**sens**/ [senses, sensed, sensing] noun 1 feeling, perception *I have a sense the weather is going to change.* 2 practical knowledge *My father has good business sense.* 3 meaning, point *War, what's the sense of it all?* • verb perceive *I sense you don't agree with me.*   Col: **bring to one's senses** – cause one to return to logical state of mind   **common sense** – practical, logical   **horse sense** – common sense   **in a sense** – in a manner or way   **knock some sense into** – suggestion physical force   **make sense** – logical   **No scents makes good sense.** – ban on perfume   **nonsense** – silly, unintelligible   **sense of humor** – ability to appreciate and make jokes

/ e / is Red

sixth sense – receive information beyond the ordinary five senses

sent (cent, scent) /**sent**/ [sends, sent, sending] *verb* past tense of *send* carried to another place *I sent your book special delivery.* Col: **heaven sent** – unexpected windfall

smell /**smel**/ [smells, smelled, smelling] *verb* detect odors *I smell dinner cooking.* • *noun* 2 aroma *The smell of gas filled the air.* Col: **smell a rat** – suspicious   **smells fishy** – suspicious   **smell like a rose** – appear innocent or to be successful   **smell to high heaven** – bad odor or bad deal   **wake up and smell the coffee** – pay attention to the obvious

stem /**stem**/ [stems, stemmed, stemming] *noun* 1 plant stalk *Tulip stems are long.* 2 slender part of wineglass *Hold the glass by the stem to keep the wine cool.* • *verb* 1 stop liquids *He stemmed the flow of blood with direct pressure on the wound.* 2 branch out *Our company is stemming into other states.* • *adj* about stems *I'd like to buy a dozen long stemmed roses.* Col: **from stem to stern** – from one end to another nautical term   **stem from something** – originate from   **stem the tide** – slow down the inevitable

step /**step**/ [steps, stepped, stepping] *noun* stair *Go up the steps to the second floor.* 2 progress of action *Tell me the six steps to speaking English.* • *verb* walking movement *Step forward out of the shadows.* Col: **baby steps** – proceed in small steps   **march in step** – conform   **one step at a time** – progress in a measured fashion   **side step** – avoid an issue   **step aside** – to not interfere   **step by step** – in a logical order   **step-family** – relatives one gains from second marriage   **step ladder** – climbing device to reach heights   **step on it** – go faster   **step out** – adulterous affair   **step out of line** – misbehave   **step right up** – come forward   **two step** –

country and western dance   **step up to the plate** – take responsibility

stretch /**stretCh**/ [stretches, stretched, stretching] *verb* reach, extension *This exercise requires you to stretch your arms out.* • *noun* distance or period of time *This stretch will be over soon.* Col: **by any stretch of the imagination** – as much as anyone could imagine   **home stretch** – close to task completion   **it's a stretch** – an exaggeration   **stretch marks** – marks on skin from weight gain or pregnancy   **stretch the truth** – almost a lie

special /**spe**Shul/ [specials] *adj* different, exceptional *New Years is a special day* • *noun* good deal *Watch for specials at the grocery store.* Col: **daily special** – restaurant meal of the day   **early bird special** – cheaper price at specific times   **special edition** – newspaper for extraordinary occasion   **special effects** – stage or cinema props to create illusion   **special interest groups** – lobbyists

suggest /su **jest**/ [suggests, suggested, suggesting] *verb* 1 imply, hint *What wine do you suggest with veal?* 2 propose, recommend *I suggest you finish your homework before you watch TV.*

sweatshirt /**swet** shErt/ [sweatshirts] *noun* loose, casual, fleece top worn for warmth *Bring an extra sweatshirt to camp.*

tell /**tel**/ [tells, told, telling] *verb* 1 say, inform *Please tell me where the bus stop is.* 2 narrate *I will tell the story from the beginning.* Col: **show and tell** – demonstrate and describe   **tell a tale** – oral story   **tell-all** – book which reveals wicked details about another   **tell off** – reprimand   **tell on** – inform on   **to tell tales** – lie about someone

ten /**ten**/ [10, tens] *noun* 1 the cardinal number between nine and eleven *The baby has ten fingers and ten toes.* Col: **nine times out of ten** – usually   **ten commandments** – biblical reference wouldn't touch with a ten foot pole — avoid completely

tenant /**te** nυnt/ [tenants] *noun* a person or a leaseholder who rents space *The tenants must pay their rent on time.* **Col:** tenant-in-common — co-owner on title

test /**test**/ [tests, tested, testing] *noun* an exam *A test is not as important as an exam.* • *verb* to formally assess *The teacher tests the students after every learning unit.* **Col:** acid test — indisputable proof   litmus test — indicator of acidity   put to the test — challenge   test drive — try before buying   test out — try   test the waters — check for suitability   test of time — lasts for a long period

them /**Them**/ *pron* 1 things already mentioned *If they want a ride to school tell them to get into the car.* 2 he or she when the person is not know. *Someone phoned for you but I told them you were out.* **Col:** If you can't beat them join them. — *proverb* if one can't win, consider joining the other team   pack them in — draw a lot of people to an event   them or us — competition   You can't win them all. — *proverb* good sport about losing

then /**Then**/ *adv* — at that past time *Back then we used to walk to school.* 2 soon after or next *We had dinner then we went out for ice cream.* **Col:** every now and then — from time to time   then again — re evaluating

thread /**THred**/ [threads, threaded, threading] *noun* 1 thin fiber *There is thread hanging from your skirt.* 2 theme or sequence of events *There is a thread of logic holding all of spoken English together.* • *verb* put through a tiny space *The sewer threaded her needle before she began to sew.* **Col:** hanging by a thread — precariously   lose the thread — stop understanding the meaning of a story   loose thread — unfinished business   pick up the thread — start again   thread-bare — extremely worn out   thread one's way through — carefully choose a path

together /tυ **ge** ThEr/ *adv* at the same time *We only need to take one car if we go to school together.* **Col:** get one's act together — get organized   hang out together — spend time with each other   let's get together — let's meet   live together — share a dwelling as husband and wife without getting married   pull oneself together — get hold of one's emotions   thrown together — haphazard meeting or collection

twelve /**twelve**/ [12, twelves] *noun* the number between eleven and thirteen *There are twelve eggs in a dozen.*

umbrella /um **bre** lu/ [umbrellas] *noun* waterproof material stretched over a frame that folds up. ☂ *Bring your umbrella it looks like it is going to rain.*

very /**ve** rEy/ *adv* 1 extremely *He was very excited about his birthday party.* **Col:** Thank you very much. — a heart-felt thank you   that very thing — exactly that   The very idea! — outrage   very good — indication of approval or consent   very last — absolute end   very much so — a great degree

vest /**vest**/ [vests] *noun* a sleeveless piece of clothing worn over a shirt *A three-piece suit includes a vest.* **Col:** vest — grant power or control

weather (whether) /**we** ThEr/ [weathers, weathered, weathering] *noun* atmospheric conditions *The weather will be cold today.* • *verb* wear away due to the climate *The shingles are badly weathered and we need a new roof.* **Col:** fair-weather friend — friend only in good times   under the weather — ill   weather permitting — only if it isn't raining or snowing   weather the storm — survive a difficult time

Wednesday /**wenz** dAy/ [Wed., Wednesdays] *prop noun* the fourth day of the week *Wednesday is hump day, half way through the week.* **Col:** Ash Wednesday — the first Wednesday in Lent (Christian)

welcome /wel cum/ [welcomes, welcomed, welcoming] *interj* 1 warm greeting *Welcome!* • *noun* warm reception *Canada gave the Royals a warm welcome.* • *verb* receive with pleasure *I welcome a good program for learning crazy English.* Col: **wear out one's welcome** – stay too long **welcome aboard** – generous acceptance **welcome mat** – a mat at the door **You're welcome.** – a polite response to being thanked

well /wel/ [wells] *noun* – hole in the ground for water *Our old well dried up and we had to dig a new one.* • *adv* 1 in good health *I don't feel weel.* 2 better than good *Your homework is well done.* 3 thoroughly *My son is well versed in teaching English.* Col: **well-being** – welfare, happiness, contentment **well done** – well cooked meat; compliment **well-heeled** – rich **well-placed** – advantageous position **well-to-do** – rich **Well, well, well.** – imagine that

went /went/ [goes, went going] *verb* the past tense of *go* travel *I went to university in the city.* Col: **went south** – didn't work out

west /west/ *noun* the point on the horizon where the sun sets *The sun rises in the east and sets in the west.* Col: **go west, young man** – the future is in the west **out west** – in the western part of North America **wild west** – cowboy and Indian period

wet /wet/ [wetter, wettest] *adj* soaked in fluid usually water *It's too wet to play in the park.* Col: **get one's feet wet** – begin a new activity **wet behind the ears** – inexperienced or immature **wet blanket** – spoiled or a pessimistic person **wet one's whistle** – have a drink **wet t-shirt contest** – a contest involving women **wet one's self** – pee one's pants **You're all wet.** – you don't know what you are talking about

when /wen/ *adv* Wh question, at what time *When does school start?* • *conj* during the time *He will have to get a job when he goes to university.* Col: **When the cows come home** – not soon

whether (weather) /we ThEr/ *conj* introduce a choice *Whether we go on a picnic or to the zoo we'll have fun.*

X (ex) /eks/ [X's] *noun* 1 the twenty-fourth letter of the Latin alphabet *X-ray starts with an X.* 2 Roman numeral for ten Col: **Xbox** – video game console **X-rated** – adults-only

yellow /yel Ow/ [yellows, yellower, yellowest] *adj* the color of lemons and bananas *Primary colors are yellow, blue, and red.* • *noun* the color. *My kids love yellow jello in the summertime. adj* 1 golden, lemony color 2 spineless, cowardly 3 sensational, shoddy Col: **yellow bellied** – cowardly **yellow streak** – cowardly **yellow journalism** – distasteful, lurid writing

yesterday /yes tEr dAy/ [yesterdays] *noun* 1 the day before today *Yesterday was Tuesday.* • *adv* on the day before today *Did you go to school yesterday?* Col: **need it yesterday** – urgently needed **not born yesterday** – not naive **yesterday's man** – a man whose time has passed

yes /yes/ [yeses] *adv* positive response *Yes, you can borrow a pencil.* • *noun* a vote in favor of *The community voted yes to building a new library.* Col: **yes man** – a person who agrees with everything regardless of what he personally believes

Z /zed/ CAN [Z's] *noun* the Canadian pronunciation of the twenty-sixth letter of the Latin alphabet *Zebra starts with a Z.* Col: **from A to Z** – everything **Zzz** – sleeping

HOW DO YOU SAY? PRONUNCIATION DICTIONARY

Chapter 5
/Iy/ is White

Chapter 5
/Iy/ is White

aisle (I'll, isle) /Iyl/
acquire /u kwI yEr/
apply /u plIy/
aye (eye, I) /Iy/

bike /bIyk/
bite (byte) /bIyt/
bright /brIyt/
buy (by, bye) /bIy/
by (buy, bye) /bIy/
bye (buy, by) /bIy/
byte (bite) /bIyt/

child /ChIyld/
China /ChIy nu/
choir /kwI yEr/
crime /krIym/
cry /krIy/

design /du zIyn/
desire /du zI yEr/
dime /dIym/
divide /du vIyd/
drive /drIyv/
dry /drIy/

excite /ek sIyt/
expire /ek spI yEr/
eye (aye, I) /Iy/

fight /fIyt/
fine /fIyn/
fire /fI yEr/
five /fIyv/
flight /flIyt/
Friday /frIy dAy/
fry /frIy/

giant /jI yunt/
guide /gIyd/

height /hIyt/
hi (high) /hIy/
high (hi) /hIy/

I (aye, eye) /Iy/
ice /Iys/
I'll (aisle, isle) /Iyl/
iron /I yErn/
island /Iy land/
isle (aisle, I'll) /Iyl/
July /ju lIy/

kind /kIynd/
knife /nIyf/
knight (night) /nIyt/

library /lIy bre rEy/
light (lite) /lIyt/
like /lIyk/
lime /lIym/
line /lIyn/
lion /lI yun/
live /lIyv/

mind /mIynd/
mine /mIyn/
my /mIy/

nice /nIys/
night (knight) /nIyt/
nine /nIyn/

/ Iy / is White

papaya /pu pI yu/
pi (pie) /pIy/
pie (pi) /pIy/
pineapple /pIy na pul
pipe /pIyp/
price /prIys/
private /prIy vut/
prize /prIyz/

quiet /kwI yut/
quite /kwIyt/

rhyme /rIym/
rice /rIys/
ride /rIyd/
right (write) /rIyt/
righteous /rIy Chus/
ripe /rIyp/
rye /rIy/

science /sI yuns/
side /sIyd/
sign /sIyn/
size /sIyz /
smile /smIyl/
society /su sI yu dEy/
spice /spIys/
spiral /spIy rul/
style /stIyl/
surprise /su prIyz/

thigh /THIy/
tie /tIy/
tiger /tIy gEr/
tight /tIyt/
time (thyme) /tIym/
tire /tI yEr/
thyme (time) /tIym/
triangle /trI yaN gul/
try /trIy/

vine /vIyn/
violent /vIy lunt/

while /wIyl/
whine (wine) /wIyn/
white /wIyt/
whiteboard /whIyt bOrd/
why (Y) /wIy/
wide /wIyd/
wife /wIyf/
wild /wIyld/
wind /wIynd/
wine (whine) /wIyn/
wire /wI yEr/
wise /wIyz/
write (right) /rIyt/

Y (why) /wIy/

HOW DO YOU SAY? PRONUNCIATION DICTIONARY

aisle (I'll, isle) /**Iyl**/ [aisles] noun a long passage between rows *The soup is in aisle 4.* Col: rolling in the aisles – laughing   walk down the aisle – get married

acquire /u kwI yEr/ [acquires, acquired, acquiring] verb get *She acquired the car when her grandmother died.*

apply /u plIy/ [applies, applied, applying] verb 1 use extra effort *If you apply yourself in school you'll get more out of it.* 2 request *He applied for a job at the bakery.* 3 put in contact *She applied glue to the back of the pictures to make them stick to the page.*

aye (eye, I) /Iy/ [ayes] noun a yes vote *There were more ayes than nays.* • adv yes *All in favor say aye.* Col: Aye aye – response to a command or request based on historic nautical term   Aye, laddie – affirmative response, based on historic Gaelic language

bike /bIyk/ [bikes, biked, biking] noun short for bicycle two-wheeled transportation 🚲 *The kids ride their bikes to school when it isn't raining.* • verb ride a bike *I bike with my friends.*

bite (byte) /bIyt/ [bites, bit, biting] noun to put teeth into *Eve took a bite of the apple.* • verb to cut with teeth *She bites her fingernails when she is nervous.* Col: bite off more than one can chew – take on a task too difficult or time consuming   bite one's tongue – avoid making controversial remarks   bite someone's head off – yell at someone   Don't bite the hand that feeds you. – proverb about treating one's provider with respect   His bark is worse than his bite. – he is aggressive but harmless   I'll bite – I'm interested   take a bite out of – reduce   won't bite you – don't be afraid

bright /brIyt/ [brighter, brightest] adj 1 giving off a shine or glow *The bare bulb with no lampshade is too bright.* 2 strong colors, or shine *The room was decorated in bright yellows and pinks.* 3 intelligent *She is a bright student.* Col: bright and early – wake or arrive early for an event or appointment   bright as a button – smart and lively   bright-eyed and bushy tailed – alert and full of energy   bright future – good prospects   bright idea – great, clever idea   look on the bright side – be optimistic

buy (by, bye) /bIy/ [buys, bought, buying] noun a bargain purchase *There were great buys at the yard sale.* • verb 1 pay for something *I need to buy groceries, there is nothing in the fridge.* 2 agreement *I don't buy your theory that English is so difficult.* Col: buy a round – pay for drinks   buy into – accept theory   buy off – pay for discretion   buy on credit – pay later   buy on time – pay in installments   buy sight unseen – pay before seeing   buy time – stall the inevitable   buy way in – pay for part ownership   buy way out – bribe to avoid penalties for bad behavior   buy for a song – inexpensive   Why buy a cow when you can get milk for free? or Why buy the pig when you can get the sausage for free? – rude, no reason to marry if the sex is available

by (buy, bye) /bIy/ prep 1 beside or near *The house is by the lake.* 2 through another's action *She was hit by a bus.* 3 past *I drove by the store.* 4 not later than *I will be there by 7:30.* 5 used in measuring area *The room is 12 feet by 14 feet.* Col: by and large – mostly but not all   by the seat of one's pants – in a way based on intuition and experience or without equipment   by the way – comment in passing   by and by – eventually

bye (buy, by) /bIy/ [byes] noun formal good-bye *Bye, see you later!* Col: good-bye and good riddance – farewell and I'm happy you are gone   good-bye for now – see you again   kiss something good-bye – opportunity is lost forever

byte (bite) /bIyt/ [bites] noun unit of computer information *A byte is usually equal to eight binary bits.*

/ Iy / is White

child /chIyld/ [children] *noun* a young human *The child was playing in the sandbox.* Col: **child abuse** – criminal neglect or mistreatment of a child **child's play** – easy **foster child** – provide care for another's child **it takes a village to raise a child** – communities contribute to the raising of children, not just the parents **love child** – born out of wedlock **poster child** – perfect example **spare the rod and spoil the child** – spanking children can be a good idea **with child** – pregnant

China /chIy nu/ *prop noun* 1 country in Asia *There are more students learning English in China than there are people in the United States.* 2 a hard, delicate dish made from baked clay *She never uses her best china.* Col: **face like a china doll** – beautiful and delicate **like a bull in a china shop** – clumsy **not for all the tea in China** – not for any price

choir /kwI yEr/ [choirs] *noun* organized group of singers often in church *She sang in the choir for 40 years.* Col: **preach to the choir** – those who already agree

crime /krIym/ (crimes) *noun* against the law *Stealing is a crime.* Col: **crime doesn't pay** – in the end criminals get caught and are punished severely **make the punishment fit the crime** – penalize according to the crime committed **partners in crime** – illegal conspirators or best friends

cry /krIy/ [cries, cried, crying] *verb* 1 tears fall because of emotion *She cried when her dog died.* 2 call out or yell *She cried for help.* Col: **a far cry from** – very different **cry all the way to the bank** – bad event turned into lots of money **cry-baby** – cries too easily **cry bloody murder** – scream **cry eyes out** – weep bitterly Col: **cry for joy** – cry from happiness **cry like a baby** – unabashed **cry oneself to sleep** – upset **cry wolf** – call for help when none was needed to manipulate others **cry your** heart out – broken hearted **Don't cry over spilled milk.** – *proverb* don't worry about things that can't be undone **for crying out loud** – expression of irritation **hue and cry** – loud protest **not knowing whether to laugh or cry** – filled with mixed emotions **shoulder to cry on** – a friend who helps in difficult circumstances

design /du zIyn/ [designs, designed, designing] *noun* 1 style or floor plan *We have the open concept design in our house.* 2 pattern *Yellow roses is the design on our china.* • *verb* create plans *I designed the house myself.* Col: **have designs on** – romantically interested **more by accident than by design** – an unplanned course of action

desire /du zI yEr/ [desires, desired, desiring] *noun* strong longing or sexual want *The sight of her in a bathing suit filled him with desire.* • *verb* wish for or want *They desired to move to the United States.* Col: **leave a lot to be desired** – lacking

dime /dIym/ [10¢, dimes] *noun* North American 10¢ coin *Ten dimes equal one dollar.* 2 slang quantity of illegal drugs for $10 *A dime of coke was found in his car.* Col: **a dime a dozen** – plentiful with little or no value **nickel and dime** – argue over a small amount of money **not worth a dime** – of little value **stop/turn on a dime** – agile

divide /du vIyd/ [÷, divides, divided, dividing] *verb* 1 separate into sections *Let's divide the chocolate bar in two.* 2 mathematical operation $10 \div 2 = 5$ Col: **divide and conquer** – policy for growing power **divided by** – math operation of division

drive /drIyv/ [drives, drove, driving] *noun* 1 travel in a vehicle *We went for a drive in the country.* 2 part of a computer *Where is the disk drive on your computer?* 3 organized group effort *Our church group held a food drive.* • *verb* travel by car *They drive into the city on Saturdays.* Col: **drive a hard bargain** – settle a deal without giving up too much drive a price down/up — outside factors influence the price drive a wedge between — emotionally or physically separate people drive around the bend — make crazy drive at — what is your point? drive batty — make one crazy drive crazy — cause one to feel anger, frustration or confusion drive home — get an effective message across in a discussion drive in — outdoor movie theater drive into the ground — overwork to the point of exhaustion drive one out of mind — make one crazy drive through — on the spot service without leaving the car drive to distraction — make one crazy drive to drink — make one drink alcohol to cope drive up the wall — make one crazy

dry /drIy/ [dries, dried, drying, dryer, driest] adj 1 with little water or moisture *My skin feels dry in the winter.* 2 funny without laughing *His dry sense of humor confuses me because I can't tell when he is being serious.* • verb remove the moisture *Please dry the dishes.* Col: bleed someone dry — take all of their money dry as a bone — without any moisture dry as dust — no moisture or very dull topic of discussion dry run — a rehearsal or practice dry out — quit drinking alcohol dry spell — unproductive period of time high and dry — safe and secure like watching paint dry — long, boring experience not a dry eye in the house — an emotional experience that affected an audience

excite /ek sIyt/ [excites, excited, exciting] verb stimulate *The visit from Santa Claus excited the children.*

expire /ek spI yEr/ [expires, expired, expiring] verb end *Their contract expired in May.*

eye (aye, I) /Iy/ [eyes, eyed, eying] noun 1 sight organ that allows animals to see 👁 *She has beautiful blue eyes.* 2 observe skillfully *You have a good eye for color.* • verb look at *The students eyed their teacher with surprise when she showed up late.* Col: an eye for an eye — revenge catch someone's eye — to get someone's attention give someone the eye — meaningful glance in the eyes of — in the opinion of keep an eye on — watch or protect keep an eye out for — watch for keep one's eyes peeled — fixed observation keep one's eyes open — watch carefully only have eyes for — in love, interested in only one thing or person see eye to eye — agree with the eye of the storm — quietly calm in the center of furious action to make eyes at — to flirt with

fight /fIyt/ [fights, fought, fighting] noun conflict *A fight broke out in the school yard.* • verb conflict *Soldiers fight for our right to free speech.* Col: a fighting chance — a small but real possibility fight a losing battle — undertaking a task or challenge that is impossible fight against time — hurry to meet a deadline fight back — retaliate fight fire with fire — use the same methods that one's opponent is using on them fight it out — struggle for dominance fight to the finish — fight until one party is dead fight tooth and nail — use extreme effort to achieve a goal pick a fight — start a disagreement

fine /fIyn/ [fines, fined, fining, finer, finest] noun penalty *He had to pay a fine for parking in the wrong place.* • verb order payment for breaking a minor law *The government fined the man for working illegally.* • adj of good quality *The weather is fine today.* Col: Come on in, the water's fine! — invitation to try cut a fine figure — handsome in formal clothes cut it fine — close timing everything's going to be fine — a calming suggestion or advice to an agitated individual fine and dandy — old fashioned expression of satisfaction fine art — high quality original art work fine by me — statement of agreement

/ Iy / is White

fine figure of a man – handsome   fine how do you do – sarcastic for an unpleasant situation   fine kettle of fish – predicament   fine line – a distinction between two things that are very similar   fine-tune – sensitive or delicate adjustment   fine with me – acceptance of a situation   go over with a fine-tooth comb – carefully examine   have down to a fine art – refined practiced skill   not to put too fine a point on it – too precise   read the fine print – examine the details   You're a fine one to talk! – examine one's own actions before criticizing others

fire /flyr/ [fires, fired, firing] *noun* the flame that results from burning *The fire started in the basement.* • *verb* 1 shoot a gun *The police officer fired her gun at the burglar.* 2 rapidly question *The officer fired questions at the suspect.* 3 let go from employment *The police officer was fired for coming to work drunk.* 4 slang for excited *The citizens were all fired up about the green belt.* **Col:** be under fire – attacked by opposing forces   catch on fire – ignite   fight fire with fire – return aggression with aggression   fire away – ask questions   fired up – excited or motivated   have fire in one's eye – angry or determined expression   on fire – in flames or a high state of energy   set a fire under – motivate or pressure   set fire to – start something on fire

five /flyv/ [5, fives] *noun* cardinal number that comes after four and before six *Humans have five fingers on each hand.* • *adj* five in number *There are five women in my class.* **Col:** five-finger discount – stealing   give me five – sideways slapping of hands is a gesture of friendship   high five – congratulatory gesture slapping palms in the air with another   nine-to-five – regular day job   take five – take a short break

flight /flIyt/ [flights] *noun* 1 travel by plane *My flight leaves at 9:00.* 2 traveling through the air *A bird in flight is a beautiful thing.* 3 run away *The fugitive took flight when he saw the police car.* 4 a set of stairs *We had to walk up five flights when the elevator was broken.* **Col:** flight of fancy – imaginative ideas   flights of stairs – levels of stairs   have a nice flight – a salutation given as a person departs on a plane journey   in flight – while flying   in full flight – escaping rapidly   take flight – start flying or escape quickly   top flight – the highest level of a job or sport

Friday /frIy dAy/ [Fri., Fridays] *prop noun* last day of the work week after Thursday and before Saturday *People like to leave work early on Fridays.* **Col:** girl Friday – a worker with a wide range of office duties   Good Friday – Easter holiday   man Friday – worker with a wide range of helpful basic duties   TGIF thank God it's Friday! – joy that the work week is almost over

fry /frIy/ [fries, fried, frying] *noun* potato cut into sticks and cooked in oil *Burgers and fries is fast food and not a nutritious meal.* • *verb* 1 cook in a fat *Eggs fried in bacon fat with toast and bacon is a popular breakfast.* 2 get burned *I fried at the beach without sunscreen.* **Col:** French fries – long thin cuts of potato deep fried in oil   frying something up – to cook in a pan over the heat or to make some plans   have bigger fish to fry – more important things to do   small fry – children or people who are perceived to be unimportant

giant /jI yunt/ [giants] *noun* extra large person real or imaginary *The castle was guarded by a family of giants.* •*adj* extra large *The micro chip was a giant step forward in technology.* **Col:** a gentle giant – tall, strong and quiet   a sleeping giant – powerful and waiting

guide /gIyd/ [guides, guided, guiding] *noun* leader *The guide led us through the forest.* • *adj* reference *Our guide book helped us find the way.* • *verb* lead along

The librarian guided us to the reference section. `Col:` **a guiding light** – a mentor or example   **Let your conscience be your guide.** – *proverb* about making the most moral decision

height /**hIyt**/ [heights] *noun*   1 distance from base to top *The height of the wall is eight feet.*   2 the measurement from the top of the head to the ground *His height is proportional to his weight.*   3 the top, the highest point *He is at the height of his career.* `Col:` **at the height of one's powers** – maximum strength   **fear of heights** – phobia of being up high

hi (high) /**hIy**/ *interj* an informal greeting, Hello *Hi, how have you been?*

high /**hIy**/ [higher, highest] *adj*   1 vertical distance *The tree is 20 feet high (6 m).*   2 greater than average *Commuters ride a high-speed train to work.*   3 elevated rank, dignified *She is a high official of the government.* • *noun*   1 related to emotions *He was on a high after getting straight A's on his report card.*   2 slang for intoxicated, using illegal drugs *He got high on marijuana before the concert.* `Col:` **come hell or high water** – unstoppable   **friends in high places** – powerful friends   **from on high** – from the boss   **get off high horse** – stop being arrogant   **go sky-high** – rise alarmingly   **high and mighty** – arrogant   **high as a kite** – intoxicated   **high jinks** – silly behavior   **high roller** – big spender `Col:` **highly-strung** – nervous   **hold head high** – be proud   **hold in high regard** – esteemed   **in high gear** – moving quickly   **it's high time** – long overdue   **knee-high to a grasshopper** – small child   **leave high and dry** – abandon   **live high on the hog** – enjoying luxury   **pile it high and sell it cheap** – get rid of it   **riding high** – life is going well   **search high and low** – look everywhere   **stink to high heaven** – smell really bad

I (aye, eye) /**Iy**/ [I's] *pron* oneself, the one who is speaking or writing *I would stay longer if I could.* • *prop noun* the ninth letter of the Latin alphabet *Ice cream starts with an I.* `Col:` **dot the i's and cross the t's** – finish final details   **I** – Roman numeral 1   **I spy with my little eye** – child's game where one guesses what another has spied in the room

ice /**Iys**/ [ices, iced, icing] *noun* frozen water *Be careful not to slip on the ice.* • *verb* decorate a cake *We iced the birthday cake with chocolate icing.* `Col:` **break the ice** – speak first   **ice over** – freeze   **put something on ice** – postpone   **skating on thin ice** – in a risky situation

I'll (aisle, isle) /**Iyl**/ *contr* I will future *I'll go to the store to buy some milk.*

iron /**I yErn**/ [irons, ironed, ironing] *noun*   1 element *Steel is made from iron and other additives.*   2 hot appliance used to remove wrinkles from material *The iron must heat up before it can be used.*   3 chains *The prisoner was transported in irons.* • *adj*   1 great strength *He had an iron will.*   2 strict *The king ruled with an iron fist.* • *verb* remove wrinkles with an iron *Ironing removes wrinkles from fabric.* `Col:` **Iron Age** – period of history from 1100 BC when humans started making tools with iron   **iron it out** – reach an agreement   **pump iron** – lift weights   **rule with an iron hand** or **fist** – strict controls   **Strike while the iron is hot.** – *proverb* about acting quickly before the opportunity is gone

island /**Iy land**/ [islands] *noun* land surrounded by water *We went on a vacation to the island of Hawaii.* `Col:` **desert island** – an isolated island in the middle of the ocean   **No man is an island.** – *proverb* humans need company   **Treasure Island** – classic story by Robert Louis Stevenson

isle (aisle, I'll) /**Iyl**/ [isles] *noun* a small island *Many sea birds nest on the isle at the mouth of the river.*

July /**ju lIy**/ [Jul., Julys] *prop noun* the seventh month of the year *July is the* hottest month of the year. Col: born on the 4th of July – patriotic

kind /kIynd/ [kinds] noun group of similar things, people or animals, a type *What kind of dog is that?* • adj nice and helpful *He was kind enough to give me a drive home.* Col: it takes all kinds – accept there are many different types of people   kind of – slang for slightly   one of a kind – unique   two of a kind – two similar people

knife /nIyf/ [knives, knifed, knifing] noun thin sharp blade with a handle used for cutting *He cut the cucumber with a knife.* • verb stab or cut with a knife *The criminal knifed the woman and ran.* Col: go under the knife – undergo surgery   on a knife edge – in a precarious position   twist the knife – adding pain to pain   cut the air with a knife – tension

knight (night) /nIyt/ [knights, knighted, knighting] noun 1 soldier on horseback from the Middle Ages *The knights protected the king.* 2 chess piece *Knights move in an L pattern.* • verb formal title from the Queen *The Queen knighted Elton John for his contribution to music.* Col: knight in shining armor – helps in a difficult situation   white knight – gives money to a company to prevent it from being bought out

library /lIy bre rEy/ [libraries] noun 1 a center from where books may be borrowed *Libraries provide reading material and resources to the public.* 2 a room especially designed for books and reading. *The rest of the family stays out of father's library.*

light /lIyt/ [lights, lit, lighting, lighter, lightest] noun 1 energy from the sun that allows animals to see *It is too dark, please turn on the lights.* 2 a traffic signal *A green light means go.* 3 sunshine *He walked from the tunnel and into the light.* 4 a lamp *Turn off the lights when you leave the room.* 5 understanding *After he saved the puppy, I saw him in a new light.* • adj 1 pale in color *She wore a light pink shirt.* 2 not heavy *This box is much lighter than the other.* • verb 1 set on fire *Please light the candles on the birthday cake.* 2 become brighter *His face lit up with a smile.* Col: A heavy purse makes a light heart. – proverb for the security of having lots of money makes people carefree   A light purse makes a heavy heart. – proverb no money is worrying   a light sleeper – wakes at the slightest noise   all sweetness and light – positive, happy, loving disposition   as light as a feather – little weight   at first light – dawn   be the light of one's life – most loved person   bring to light – come to attention   come to light – facts recently revealed   give the green light – give permission   in a good light – favorable impression   in light of – considering certain facts   in the cold light of day – harsh reality   light a fire under – motivate   light at the end of the tunnel – positive future after a difficult time   light-headed – dizzy   lights out – sleep time   light years away – far distant future   make light of – trivialize, seem unimportant   make light work of – finish quickly   Many hands make light work. – proverb, work goes faster with lots of helpers   not to see the light of day – in hiding or imprisoned   out cold – asleep or unconscious   out like a light – fast asleep   run a red light – break the law by not stopping at a traffic signal   see in a new light – reevaluate   see the light – understand   shed light on – make clear   the red-light district – sex trade area of the city   travel light – bring only the bare essentials   trip the light fantastic – dance enthusiastically

like /lIyk/ [likes, liked, liking] verb 1 enjoy *She likes to dance.* 2 fond of *He likes the girl with long dark hair.* 3 want or desire *I like going to the beach.* • adj 1 resemble *The girl looks like her mother.* 2 expected of *It isn't like her to be late.* •

HOW DO YOU SAY? PRONUNCIATION DICTIONARY

interj affectation of notably young North American girls *He like looked at me and like smiled and it was like so funny.* **Col:** likes and dislikes – personal preferences   the likes of which – something similar   would like – want, desire

lime /lIym/ [limes] *noun* 1 small green citrus fruit *Juice made from lime is my favorite.* 2 calcium oxide powder used in cement *Lime is extremely caustic and will burn your eyes.* **Col:** lime-light – fame

line /lIyn/ [lines, lined, lining] *noun* 1 continuous mark *There is a white line down the center of the road.* 2 boundary *The Mason Dixon line is the boundary between the North and the South in the States.* 3 row of people or things *A line of people waited to get into the concert.* 4 a rope or string *Hang your wet clothes on the line outside.* 5 a collection of products *The store carries several different lines of cosmetics.* 6 sentence delivered by an actor *He had to learn his lines before rehearsal.* • *verb* 1 draw lines on *I lined the page with a grid pattern.* 2 insert an inner layer *The boots were lined with fur.* **Col:** bring into line – create order or agreement   drop someone a line – to call/write   feed, give, or hand one a line – to mislead/trick with words   get a line on – gain insight or information   get in line – to form a line with others or to act according to the rules   hold the line – pause   in line for – due to receive   in the line of duty – while performing police or military job   line of thinking – general way of thinking   line something up – arrange a meeting or business deal   line up – form an orderly pattern   on the line – at risk   out of line – improper or unacceptable behavior   read between the lines – understand an implied underlying message not directly stated

lion /lI yun/ [lions] *noun* large member of the cat family native to Africa and northern India *The male lion has a dark hairy mane around his neck.* **Col:** March comes in like a lion, and goes out like a lamb. – *proverb* about the season change from winter to spring in March   the lion's share – the larger share

live /lIyv/ [lives, lived, living] *adj* 1 in an active life state *I would never eat lobster because they cook them live.* 2 able to explode *The field was full of live ammunition.* 3 viewed by an audience, not pre-recorded *We watched the Olympics live on television.* **Col:** a live wire – wire carrying electricity or an energetic person

mind /mIynd/ [minds, mined, mining] *noun* thinking and remembering part of the brain *noun* 1 *I have been reviewing the pronunciation lesson in my mind.* 2 beliefs and opinions *That girl speaks her mind.* 3 awareness *Please keep in mind that some people are allergic to peanuts.* • *verb* look after *The nanny minds the children while the parents are at work.* **Col:** blank mind – no thoughts on a subject   blow one's mind – extreme shock in either joy or disbelief   change one's mind – reverse opinions   don't mind me – ignore me   give a piece of one's mind – tell off   great minds think alike – people who agree like to congratulate one another   have a mind of one's own – independent thinker   have a mind to do something – have almost decided to do it   have a one-track mind – focus on only one thing   keep in mind – remember   know one's own mind – be clear about one's own beliefs and values   lose one's mind – go insane   mind your own business – don't meddle in other's affairs   mind's eye – imagination   never mind – don't bother   take a load off one's mind – release from worry

mine /mIyn/ [mines, mined, mining] *pron* belongs to me *That book is mine.* • *noun* 1 a man-made hole in the ground used to remove minerals *Sudbury is home to the Big Nickel mine.* 2 a type of explosive device hidden under the ground *Land mines killed many people in*

/ Iy / is White

World War II. • *verb* dig in the ground for minerals *Gold diggers mine in the Yukon.* Col: **back to the salt mines** – time to get back to work   **gold mine of information** – great resource   **mine for** – prospect   **sitting on a gold mine** – a business or object of great valuable   **what's mine is yours** – property in marriage   **your guess is as good as mine** – I don't know either   **your place or mine** – suggestive invitation for sex

my /mIy/ *adj* belonging to me *Have you seen my new car?*

nice /nIys/ [nicer, nicest] *adj* 1 friendly, pleasant, kind *She is a very nice girl.* 2 pretty, attractive *That is a nice jacket.* 3 pleasing, enjoyable *We had a very nice time at dinner.* Col: **Have a nice day!** – friendly parting expression   **Mr. Nice Guy** – friendly to a fault   **nice break** – unexpected opportunity   **Nice going!** – sarcastic for bad job   **nice to see you** – friendly greeting   **nice weather** – typical conversation starter

night /nIyt/ [nights] *noun* the time of darkness between sunset and dawn *It rained all night.* Col: **call it a night** – go to bed or leave a party   **dead of night** – middle of the night   **fly by night** – contractor who does a bad job then leaves town with the money   **make a night of it** – celebration   **night and day** – opposites   **night hawk** – one who consistently stays up late   **night life** – clubs and drinking   **night on the town** – wild evening fun out in the city   **night owl** – stays up late at night   **one-night stand** – one time sex with a stranger   **ships that pass in the night** – two people who meet intimately but briefly and move on

nine /nIyn/ [nines] *noun* cardinal number between eight and ten *Nine is very late for children to go to bed.* • *adj* nine in number *There are nine students in the advanced class.* Col: **A cat has nine lives.** – old wives' tale about how often cats escape death   **dressed to the nines** – dressed up, stylish   **nine lives** – being very lucky   **nine times out of ten** – almost always   **nine-to-five** – regular day job   **on cloud nine** – in love, happy   **the whole nine yards** – the entire amount or the whole way

papaya /pu pI yu/ [papayas] *noun* a tropical tree with yellow fruit, or the fruit itself *Papayas are available in most supermarkets all year around.*

pi (pie) /pIy/ [pi's, □] *noun* mathematical ratio of a circle's circumference to its diameter *Pi = 3.14... it never repeats.*

pie (pi) /pIy/ [pies] *noun* a baked pastry shell filled with fruit or meat *Apple pie and ice cream is an all American dessert.* Col: **as easy as pie** – very easy   **cow pie** – disks of cow manure   **eat humble pie** – admit a mistake   **have a finger in many pies** – involved in many different projects at once   **nice as pie** – a friendly person   **pie eyed** – drunk   **pie in the sky** – idealistic hope   **shut your pie hole** – rude expression to be quiet

pineapple /pIy na pul/ [pineapples] *noun* tropical plant with a large sweet yellow fruit *Pineapple and strawberry make a great smoothie.*

pipe /pIyp/ [pipes, piped, piping] *noun* 1 tube used to transport liquids or gases from one place to another *The water pipes in my house are leaking.* 2 a thin tube with a mouthpiece connected to a small bowl used for smoking tobacco *The man sat in his chair and smoked a pipe.* 3 musical instrument made of multiple tubes that are blown into *I play the pipe.* • *verb* carry through a pipe *The water is piped from the lake into the city.* Col: **pipe down** – be quiet   **pipe dream** – wish or dream that is impossible to achieve   **pipe up** – speak up   **put that in your pipe and smoke it** – tell one to accept what is even if it is not desirable   **set of pipes** – singing voice

price /prIys/ [prices, priced, pricing] *noun* 1 a sum of money charged for goods or services *The price of gas is always rising.* 2 an amount of money high enough to change one's mind *Everyone has their price.* • *verb* 1 mark a value on *The shirt was priced at 50% off.* 2 determine the price of *My boss wanted me to price the books before buying them.* `Col:` asking price – not the firm price   at any price – no matter the cost   drive the price up or down – market influences   *Every man has his price.* – *proverb* it is possible to bribe people   pay a price – suffer for   price on one's head – reward to catch   price one has to pay – a sacrifice one has to make   put a price on it – say what it costs   quote a price – state in advance the estimated cost   roll prices back – to reduce the cost   selling price – price paid

private /**prIy** vut/ [privates] *adj* 1 personal *My diary is private, no one else is allowed to read it.* 2 away from public *He had a private room in the hospital.* 3 owned by a person or business *Do not go past that marker, it's private property.* • *noun* low ranked soldier in the army *When you join the army, you start off as a private.* `Col:` in private – without others present   private eye – private detective   private parts – genitals

prize /**prIyz**/ [prizes] *noun* a reward *First prize was a gold cup*

quiet /**kwI y**ut/ [quiets, quieted, quieting, quieter, quietest] *adj* 1 without sound, silent *When no one else was home, the house was very quiet.* 2 calm *The spa was peaceful and quiet.* 3 not busy *Business is quiet today.* • *verb* make quiet *Would you quiet your child?* •*noun* absence of noise *The quiet of the weekend is soothing after a hectic week.* `Col:` be quiet – don't talk or make noise   keep quiet – don't talk   keep quiet about – don't tell anyone   on the quiet – secretly   peace and quiet – little noise, calmness   quiet as a mouse – silent   quiet down – an order demanding less noise

quite /**kwIyt**/ *adv* 1 almost *He is not quite done his homework.* 2 large degree *This jacket is quite warm.* 3 really *Are you quite sure that is what the boss said?* `Col:` quite a change – very different   quite a few – several   quite a ways – a long distance   quite a while – a long time   quite something – amazing

rhyme /**rIym**/ [rhymes, rhymed, rhyming] *noun* 1 have the same sound. *Parents read nursery rhymes to their small children.* 2 poem that has the same sounds *Rhyming is an important part of most poems.* • *verb* match two rhyming words *Night rhymes with light.* `Col:` to rhyme with something – words that create a poetic pattern of sounds together   without rhyme or reason – not making sense, without logic

rice /**rIys**/ *noun* type of grain seed *I always order rice when I go to a restaurant.*

ride /**rIyd**/ [rides, rode, riding] *noun* 1 carnival activity *We went on all the rides at the fair.* • *verb* 1 travel on an animal or machine *I would rather ride a horse than a train.* 2 carried *She was riding the wave of fame.* 3 slang, make fun of *He rides his friend about his ugly shirt.* `Col:` go along for the ride – join in without actively participating   let something ride – relaxed attitude to a problem   ride a wave – take advantage of opportunities   ride on one's coat-tails – success by association not one's own merits   ride out the storm – simply wait for a difficult period to end   take for a ride – cheat someone   *There's no such thing as a free ride.* – *proverb* beware of hidden or non-monetary expectations

right (write) /**rIyt**/ [rights] *adj* 1 the direction to the east when facing north *Make a right turn after the stop sign.* 2 correct *You gave the right answer!* • *noun* 1 permission guaranteed by law *Everyone has the right to free education in Canada.* 2 morals *The criminal doesn't know right from wrong.* • *adv* 1 in the proper way

The boots didn't fit right. 2 directly *The bear walked right up to me.* • *verb* 1 repair *My mission was to right the world's wrongs.* 2 return to position *He righted the sailboat before it tipped.* Col: **get it right** – to do or understand correctly **have one's heart in the right place** – to be a person who is kind and helpful **in one's right mind** – sane **in one's own right** – alone, independently by oneself **to be in the right** – to be correct **to go right** – turn to the right or work honestly **right away** – immediately **right off the bat** – immediately

righteous /rIy Chus/ *adj* honorable, concerned with right and wrong. *The minister was more self-righteous than a truly good person.*

ripe /rIyp/ [riper, ripest] *adj* a fully grown food ready to be harvested *If you want the best taste, you must wait until the fruit is ripe.* Col: **ripe for** – ready **ripe old age** – very old **the time is ripe** – the right time

rye /rIy/ [ryes] *noun* a grain used in cereal, flour and whiskey *He ordered a rye and coke from the bartender.*

science /sI yuns/ [sciences] *noun* 1 facts related to the natural world *I always wanted to study space science.* 2 particular branch of science *Chemistry is a type of science.* Col: **blind someone with science** – confuse with technical terms **have down to a science** – know how to do a skill or process really well

side /sIyd/ [sides, sided, siding] *noun* 1 edge *The side of my house is covered in ivy.* 2 a specific location *I live on the south side of the city.* 3 a part away from the center *I jumped to the side of the road to avoid the car.* 4 one of two opposing groups or teams *Are you rooting for the blue side or white side?* 5 lineage *I get my looks from my Mom's side.* • *verb* agree with *The judge sided with the victim.* Col: **from all sides** – every direction **on the bright side** – be optimistic **off to one side** – away from center **on the side** – food not included **side by side** – beside each other **talk out of both sides of one's mouth** – say different things to different people on the same subject **to take sides** – join forces with one team/group **two sides of the same coin** – two similar points of view on the same issue

sign /sIyn/ [signs, signed, signing] *noun* 1 board or poster with public information *Always stop at stop signs.* 2 gesture *Waving your hand is a sign for 'Goodbye'.* 3 a symbol *In math 'X' is a multiplication sign.* • *verb* 1 autograph *George Clooney signed my napkin.* 2 use hand motions to communicate *I learned to sign so I could communicate with deaf people.* Col: **a sign** – an indication **show signs** – give an indication **sign away** – give up ownership **sign for** – signing one's name to prove receipt **sign in** – write down one's name **sign of the times** – an indication of current conditions or situation **sign off on** – provide approval **sign on** – join **sign on the dotted line** – make official by signing a document **sign out** – indicate that one is leaving **sign over** – hand over ownership **sign up** – join

size /sIyz/ [sizes, sized, sizing] *noun* 1 a physical measurement *The size of that baby is very unusual.* 2 a numbered scale indicating big or small *I am determined to go down from size 14 to size 10.* • *verb* 1 measure *The movers sized up the bookcase to see if it would fit in the hall.* Col: **all shapes and sizes** – a wide variety **cut down to size** – criticize one who is too confident **Pick on somebody your own size.** – don't be a bully **size a person up** – judge a person **that's the size of it** – that's the way it is **try it on for size** – test before buying

smile /smIyl/ [smiles, smiled, smiling] *noun* facial expression with the corners of the mouth turned up to show happiness *A smile is understood in every language.* • *verb* expression of happiness *I* smiled at the new student and she smiled back. **Col:** be all smiles – look pleased   crack a smile – grin   flash a smile – smile quickly   keep smiling – encouraging phrase   put a smile on one's face – make one smile   smile from ear to ear – wear a broad smile   smile at – look at with a happy expression   wipe that smile off one's face – take this situation seriously

society /su sI yu dEy/ [societies] *noun* a community who share background and culture *North American society is known for its wastefulness.* 2 the world of the rich *At the age of 16, girls are entered into society through a ball.* 3 a club *My cousin belongs to the Music Society of America.* **Col:** high society – wealthy class of people   society girl – a stylish young woman from a wealthy family

spice /spIys/ [spices, spiced, spicing] *noun* substance used to flavor food *This sauce needs a little more spice.* 2 adds excitement *Add a little spice to your life!* • *verb* 1 add flavor *I need something to spice up this soup.* 2 add interest *I spiced up my outfit with a bright red purse.* **Col:** spice up – make more interesting   Variety is the spice of life. – *proverb* different people and experiences make life more interesting

spiral /spIy rul/ *noun* a continuous curve that winds around *The thin wire spine of the notebook is a spiral.* *adj* shape of curling around *Spiral notebooks are great for students.*

style /stIyl/ [styles, styled, styling] *noun* 1 manner *He talks in a slow and soothing style.* 2 characteristic *My house is decorated Japanese style.* 3 being in fashion *Men's hats have gone out of style.* • *verb* 1 create *The hairdresser styled her hair after cutting it.* **Col:** cramp one's style – limit or prevent a person expressing themselves in style – fashionable   out of style – no longer fashionable   spend money like it's going out of style – spend a lot of money quickly with no regard to value   style after – imitate

surprise /su prIyz/ [surprises, surprised, surprising] *noun* startled *I was surprised and happy when he proposed.* • *verb* unexpected *He surprised me with flowers when it wasn't our anniversary.* **Col:** come as no surprise – will not be a surprise   surprise party – arranged in secret for the guest of honor   take by surprise – startle

thigh /THIy/ [thighs] *noun* 1 the upper part of the leg *My thighs were sore after a walking up so many stairs.*

tie /tIy/ [ties, tied, tying] *noun* 1 emotional attachment *Our school ties kept us together.* 2 a clothing item that is wrapped around one's neck *Professional men used to wear ties to work.* • *verb* 1 fasten together *She taught her son to tie his shoelaces.* 2 equal score *We tied for second place in the competition.* could do with one arm tied behind ones back – bragging that a task is so easy   hands are tied – unable to help   fit to be tied – angered or agitated   sever ties – break off relationships   tie down – restricted or married   tie one into – involve or connect   tied one on – got drunk   tie up – bind together or hinder   tied up – busy   tied to mother's apron strings – dominated by one's mother

tiger /tIy gEr/ [tigers] *noun* a large, yellow and black striped member of the cat family *Tigers live in the jungle.* **Col:** have a tiger by the tail – control something powerful and dangerous   paper tiger – a company or organization that seems powerful but is not

tight /tIyt/ [tights, tighter, tightest] *adj* 1 fitted closely *These shoes are too tight.* 2 fastened firmly *I made sure the knot was tied tight.* 3 taut *A man can walk across a tight rope.* 4 closely *I held my daughter tight.* **Col:** hold on tight – grasp firmly and not let go   in a tight spot – a difficult or dangerous situation   keep a tight rein – control firmly   run a tight ship – control a well – organized business or organization   sit tight – wait, stay   tight as a drum – stretched to the extreme   tight ass – a cheap person or a person who is stern and inflexible   tight race – close race up tight – a tense and inflexible person

time (thyme) /tIym/ [×, times, timed, timing] *noun* 1 the duration of existence, the passing of days, months, years *Time seems to go faster when you're having fun.* 2 exact moment of the day *Does 7:00 seem like a good time for dinner?* 3 a measured period *We waited to be seated at a table for a long time.* 4 experience *Remember that time when we went ice skating?* • *verb* 1record the duration of an event *We timed how long she could hold her breath.* 2 multiplication $2 \times 4 = 8$ Col: a good time – a happy experience   A good time was had by all – everyone had fun   a hard time – difficult period   A stitch in time saves nine. – *proverb* about fixing small problems before they become big   ahead of time – early   ahead of one's time – having innovative ideas   all in good time – no rush   all the time – constantly   arrange for some time – to meet and talk   at no time – never   at one time – in the past   at some time sharp – punctual   at times – periodically or sometimes   at the present time – now   at the same time – simultaneously   Better luck next time. – sorry, try again   bide time – waiting patiently   big time – prosperity   buy on time – payment schedule   buy time – find a shortcut   devil of a time – problems   do time – go to prison   Don't waste your time. – no point   fight against time – urgency   find the time – squeeze into a busy schedule   for the time being – present   from time to time – occasionally   give a hard time – cause problems for   hardly have time to breathe – busy   have a lot of time for – like them   have a whale of a time – lots of fun   have time on hands – extra time   have time on side – youth   have time to kill – not doing anything   having the time of one's life – best experience ever   He puts his pants on one leg at a time. – he's human like the rest of us   how time flies – goes quickly   I'm having quite a time. – difficulties   in due time – eventually   in good time – early   in no time – quickly   in the nick of time – at the last second   in the right place at the right time – lucky break   in the wrong place at the wrong time – unlucky break   in time – eventually   It's about time! – Where have you been?   it's high time – long overdue   just in time – last minute   kill time – waste time   legend in one's own time – notoriety before one is dead   living on borrowed time – supposed to be dead by now   Long time no see. – haven't seen you for a while   make good time – no delays   make time for – fit one into a busy schedule   make up for lost time – spend quality time together to repair separation   mark time – watch the clock   Maybe some other time. – not now   no time like the present – do it now   not give the time of day – ignore   only a matter of time – eventually   one at a time – in order individually   on own time – not at work   on time – punctual   once upon a time – phrase that begins fairy tales   pressed for time – in a hurry   quality time – no distractions   race against time – hurry for a deadline, urgency   right on time – punctual   run out of time – didn't finish   serve time – prison   spend time in – visited   stall for time – manipulate to get more time   stand the test of time – durable   take time out – a break   take up time – wasting time   tell time – read a clock   the time is ripe – opportunity is now   There is a time and a place for everything. – *proverb about good manners*   There's no time to lose. – *hurry*   third time's the charm – *success after two failures*   time after time – *repeatedly*   Time and tide wait for no man. – *proverb about not wasting one's life*   Time flies when you're having fun. – *fun activities seem to go quickly*   time has come – *the moment to act is now*   Time is a great healer. – *proverb about the healing powers of time*   Time is money. – *capitalist value*   Time is of the essence. – *critically important*   Time is up. – *no more opportunity*   time off – *vacation*   time off for good behavior – *less punishment for being a good prisoner*   time on hands – *not doing anything*   time out – *take a break*   Time to call it a day. – *work is finished*   Time to call it a night. – *go to bed*   time to hit the road – *leave*   time will tell – *don't know now*   times tables – *multiplication chart*   two-time – *cheat on*   You're wasting my time. – *not interested*

tire /tI yEr/ [tires, tired, tiring] *noun* the outer part of a wheel filled with air *We need winter tires on our car.* • *verb* 1 weaken, lose strength *I tire easily, that's why I take the elevator.* `Col:` spare tire – *extra tire in case of a flat*   around the waist tire of – *bored or lose interest*   tire out – *get tired*   tire one out – *to exhaust a person*

thyme (time) /tIym/ *noun* an herb *This chicken needs to be seasoned with a little rosemary and thyme.*

triangle /trI yaN gul/ [triangles] *noun* 1 geometric figure with three sides Δ *The child learned how to draw squares and triangles at school today.* 2 percussion instrument in the shape of a triangle *The triangle hangs beside the drums.* `Col:` love triangle – *a romantic situation where two people are in love with the same person*

try /trIy/ [tries, tried, trying] *verb* 1 attempt *She has to try and find a job.* 2 taste *Try the smoked salmon.* 3 legal process *The guy was tried for murder.* `Col:` If at first you don't succeed, try and try again – *never give up*   These things are sent to try us – *accept a bad situation that can't be changed*   try on for size – *listen to a new idea*   try out – *show up, play for the coaches and hope to be chosen for the team.*

vine /vIyn/ [vines] *noun* climbing plant *All we saw in Italy were vines dripping with grapes.* `Col:` die on the vine – *destruction of an idea or project*   wither on the vine – *gradual destruction of an idea or project*

violent /vIy lunt/ [violently] *adj* 1 brutality *That boy was always violent and aggressive with the other children.* 2 caused by a strong force *The violent storm raged outside.* 3 bad temper *She always had a violent temper.*

while /wIyl/ *noun* short period of time *My friend will be staying for a while.* • *conj* 1 during this time *I can't speak to you while you're texting.* 2 although *While I still don't agree, you do have a point.* `Col:` make it worth your while – *make a situation profitable*   see you in a while – *in the near future*   it takes a while – *it takes time*   while away one's time – *to waste time*   worth one's while – *worth one's time*

whine (wine) /wIyn/ [whines, whined, whining] *verb* annoying sulking noise *What is that child whining about?*

white /wIyt/ [whites, whiter, whitest] *adj* the lightest color *I prefer white milk to chocolate milk.* 2 pale *Her skin was as white as snow.* • *noun* clear part of a raw egg *The recipe calls for egg whites.* `Col:` black and white – *straight forward with no ambiguity*   in black and white – *in writing*   lily white – *predominantly Caucasian*   white as a sheet – *very pale complexion often related to fear or illness*   white as the driven snow –

/ ɪy / is White

innocent   white bread – ordinary or boring   white-collar worker – office worker   white elephant – a large, expensive and useless object that one can't get rid of   white knuckle – frightening   white lie – small insignificant lie   white trash – uneducated white people   whiter than white – a person incapable of being corrupted

whiteboard /whɪyt bOrd/ [whiteboards] *noun* shiny white display boards for non-permanent markers. *I use black and red markers on the whiteboard to separate writing and speaking.*

why /wɪy/ *adv* Wh question, for what reason *Why is the sky blue?* Col: that's why – ending statement that emphasis an explanation   Why buy a cow when you can get milk for free? or Why buy the pig when you can get the sausage for free? – rude no reason to marry if the sex is available   Why not? – demanding request for explanation

wide /wɪyd/ [wider, widest] *adj* 1 measurement from side to side *The desk must be at least 3 feet wide.* 2 large range or scope *After years of studying chimps, she had a wide understanding of them.* Col: blow/break wide open – expose   be wide open – available, as in a sporting situation   cut a wide swath – left a wide path   far and wide – many places and great distances   give a wide berth – stay away from   whole wide world – everywhere   wide of the mark – missed the target

wife /wɪyf/ [wives] *noun* 1 a woman who is married *She would make a good wife someday.* 2 the woman whom a man is married to *I love my wife very much.* Col: a good husband makes a good wife – if a man wants a good wife he needs to be a good husband   How's the wife? – phrase used by one friend to another inquiring about their spouse

wild /wɪyld/ [wilder, wildest] *noun* a deserted area *I lived in the wild for years.* • *adj* 1 uncultivated *There are wild strawberries growing behind my house.* 2 not tamed *The forest is full of wild animals.* 3 without discipline, *This party is going to be wild!* 4 crazy *He went wild when he found out he had lost the scholarship.* Col: go wild – act crazy   hog wild – out of control   not in one's wildest dreams – never   run wild – live in nature or be crazy   sew one's wild oats – do silly things in one's youth   wild about – love   wild and wooly – exciting   wild blue yonder – far-away place   wild card – an unknown element or person   wild goose chase – a failed hunt

wind (wined) /wɪynd/ [winds, wound, winding] *verb* 1 curvy, turning *The path winds through the jungle.* 2 turn in a tight circle *Wind the yarn into a ball.* 3 tighten *Wind up the clock for it to keep working.* Col: all wound up – be nervous, tense, full of unused energy   wind around – make a turn   wind back – return to a starting place   wind down – slow down and relax   wind around one's little finger – have control over another person   wind onto – coil around   wind up – arrive somewhere by accident   wind up with – end up being with

wine (whine) /wɪyn/ [wines] *noun* alcohol made from fermented grapes *I like to have a glass of red wine with dinner.* Col: wine and dine – woo, entice

wire /wɪ yEr/ [wires, wired, wiring] *noun* 1 a long thin strand of metal *Many of our fences are made of wire.* 2 strings of metal used to conduct electricity *My phone isn't working, I think a telephone wire must be broken.* • *verb* 1 install electrical wires *They wired my house for electricity yesterday.* 2 send by cable *He wired the money to my bank account.* Col: by wire – sent by cable   down to the wire – last possible minute   have one's wires crossed – experience confusion or misunderstanding   live wire – wire carrying electricity or an energetic person   under the wire – right before a deadline   wired in – electrically installed   wired up – attached with a wire

wise /wIyz/ [wiser, wisest] *adj* 1 good judgment from experience *The years had made him wise.* Col: **penny wise and pound foolish** – save on little things but splurge on big items   **wise-guy** – smart aleck   **wise up** – become smart in the ways of the world   **wise to** – aware of another's wicked intensions   **word to the wise** – good advice

write (right) /rIyt/ [writes, wrote, writing] *verb* 1 print letters onto a surface *Write your name on the line, please.* 2 present ideas *She wrote her thoughts in a diary.* 3 create literary works *Paul McCartney wrote many Beatles songs.* 4 job producing written material *I write ESL text books.* Col: **nothing to write home about** – nothing special   **write away for** – request   **write down** – make a note   **write off** – dismiss   **write out** – make a copy   **write to** – send a letter or email to   **write up** – an article or report

Y (why) /wIy/ [Y's] *noun* 1 the second last letter in the Latin alphabet. *Yellow begins with a Y.* 2 stands for an unknown number in math *I calculated y by using this equation 10 □ 8 = y .* Col: **the Y** – short for the YMCA community center originally the Young Men's Christian Association   **y chromosome** – genetic code of males   **Y-fronts** – men's underwear

Chapter 6
/i/ is Pink

Chapter 6
/i/ is Pink

addition /u **di** Shun/

been /**bin**/
big /**big**/
bit /**bit**/
bitch /**biCh**/
bitter /**bi** dEr/
blister /**bli** sdEr/
brick /**brik**/
bridge /**brij**/
bring /**briNg**/
build /**bild**/
business /**biz** nus/
busy /**bi** ZEy/

children /**Chil** drun/
chili (chilly) /**Chi** lEy/
chilly (chili) /**Chi** lEy/
chin /**Chin**/
city /**si** dEy/
committee /ku **mi** dEy/
competition /com pu **ti** Shun/
condition /kun **di** Shun/
contiguous /kun **tig** yU wus/

decision /du **si** Zhun/
dictionary /**dik** Shu ne rEy/
did /**did**/
different /**dif** runt/
distance /**dis** duns/
division /du **vi** Zhun/
drink /**driNgk**/

English /**iNg** lish/
existence /eg **zi** stuns/

fiction /**fik** Shun/
fill /**fil**/
finger /**fiN** gEr/
fish /**fish**/
fix /**fiks**/
flamingo /flu **miN** gOw/
flipper /**fli** pEr/

gift /**gift**/
gimme /**gi** mEy/
give /**giv**/
grip /**grip**/
gym (Jim) /**jim**/

hiccough/**hiccup** /**hi** kup/
him (hymn) /**him**/
hip /**hip**/
his /**hiz**/
history /**hi** strEy/
hymn (him) /**him**/
hypocrite /**hi** pu krit/

if /**if**/
ill /**il**/
impulse /**im** puls/
in (inn) /**in**/
increase /**in** krEys/
industry /**in** du strEy/
ink /**ink**/
inn (in) /**in**/
insect /**in** sekt/
instrument /**in** stru munt/
interest /**in** trust/
into /**in** tUw/
is /**iz**/
it /**it**/

kick /**kik**/
kid /**kid**/
kiss /**kis**/

lift /**lift**/
limit /**li** mit/
linen /**li** nun/
lip /**lip**/
liquid /**li** kwud/
list /**list**/
listen /**li** sun/
little /**li** dul/
live /**liv**/

/ i / is Pink

liver /**li** vEr/

middle /**mi** dul/
military /**mi** lu te rEy/
milk /**milk**/
minute /**mi** nut/
mix /**miks**/
mystery /**mi** strEy/

nickel /**ni** kul/

opinion /u **pin** yun/
original /u **ri** ju nul/

physical /**fi** zu kul/
pick /**pik**/
picture /**pik** ChEr/
pig /**pig**/
pin /**pin**/
pink /**piNgk**/
political /pu **li** du kul/
position /pu **zi** Shun/
pretty /**pri** dEy/
print /**print**/
prison /**pri** zun/

quick /**kwik**/

religion /ru **li** jun/
rhythm /**ri** Thum/
rib /**rib**/
ring /**riNg**/
river /**ri** vEr/

scissors /**si** zErz/
serendipity /se run **di** pu dEy/
shift /**Shift**/
ship /**Ship**/
shit /**Shit**/
sick /**sik**/
silly /**si** lEy/
silver /**sil** vEr/
simple /**sim** pul/
sing /**siNg**/
single /**siN** gul/
sister /**sis** dEr/
sit /**sit**/
six /**siks**/

skin /**skin**/
splint /**splint**/
spring /**spriNg**/
sticky /**sti** kEy/
still /**stil**/
swim /**swim**/
system /**sis** dum/

thick /**THik**/
thin /**THin**/
thing /**THiNg**/
think /**THiNgk**/
this /**This**/
ticket /**ti** kut/
tin /**tin**/
tip /**tip**/
trick /**trik**/
twist /**twist**/

until /un **til**/
unwilling /un **wi** liNg/

which /**wiCh**/
whistle /**wi** sul/
will /**wil**/
wind /**wind**/
windbreaker /**win** brAy kEr/
window /**win** dOw/
wing /**wiNg**/
winter /**win** tEr/
wish /**wiSh**/
witch /**wiCh**/
with /**wiTh**/
women /**wi** mun/
wrist /**rist**/

zipper /**zi** pEr/

addition /u **di** Shun/ [additions] noun 1 mathematical process *In primary school, we learned addition, subtraction, multiplication and division.* 2 building on to a house *The neighbors built an addition on the back of their house.* Col: **in additional to that** – expand an idea or add facts **in addition** – furthermore or also

been /**bin**/ {also said /**bEyn**/ see Green} verb past participle of *to be* exist *How have you been?* Col: **a has been** – person no longer popular or famous **been there, done that** – already visited or already accomplished

big /**big**/ [bigger, biggest] adj large, huge *Celine Dion is a big star.* Col: **big cheese** – boss **go over big** – warmly received **in a big way** – on a grand scale **make it big** – to be a big success **talk big** – exaggerate **The bigger they are, the harder they fall.** – proverb about prominent people having more to lose so their down fall appears more severe **the big picture** – in the larger scheme of things

bit /**bit**/ [bits] noun 1 small amount *I have a bit more homework to do.* 2 part of a drill tool *The bit broke when it hit a piece of steel.* 3 part of a horse's bridle *Put the bit in his mouth and the reins over his head.* • verb past tense of *bite* cut with teeth *Snow White bit the poisoned apple and fell into a deep sleep.* Col: **a little bit** – a small piece **bit by bit** – slowly, one small step at a time **champ at the bit** – impatient **do one's bit** – help or contribute **just a bit** – only a little **not a bit** – not at all

bitch /**biCh**/ [bitches, bitched, bitching] noun swearing, a bad word for difficult female *My boss is a bitch.* • verb complain *I have been bitching about my boss for years.* Col: **son of a bitch** – difficult man or situation

bitter /**bi** dEr/ [bitterer, bitterest] adj 1 sharp, not sweet taste *This medicine tastes bitter.* 2 unpleasantly cold weather *It was a bitter morning in December when the storm started.* Col: **bitter sweet** – both good and bad feelings about an event **bitter pill to swallow** – unpleasant situation that must be accepted **leaves a bitter taste in one's mouth** – lingering unpleasant feelings **to the bitter end** – stay to the very last despite hardships

blister /**bli** sdEr/ [blisters, blistered, blistering] noun pocket of clear fluid under the skin from rubbing, insect bite or burn *They got blisters on their feet from running the marathon.* • verb cause bubbles on a surface *Too much sun blisters your skin.*

brick /**brik**/ [bricks, bricked, bricking] noun 1 hard, block-shaped, building material *They live in a house made of brick.* 2 cube shape or form *Grandma bought a brick of ice cream.* • verb building with bricks *They bricked up the fireplace they didn't use.* Col: **brick shit house** – solid and well-built **like a ton of bricks** – suddenly, with major impact **run into a brick wall** – find difficulty continuing forward

bridge /**brij**/ [bridges, bridged, bridging] noun 1 a structure over a river or roadway *We took the bridge over the Hudson into Manhattan.* 2 control station of a ship *The captain gave the order from the bridge.* 3 card game played with four people *The neighbors come over for Bridge once a month.* • verb span a gap *The English Phonetic Alphabet bridges written to spoken English.* Col: **bridge of one's nose** – top of the nose where eyeglasses sit **bridge the gap** – a temporary solution to a problem **cross that bridge when we come to it** – deal with a situation when it arises, but not before **water under the bridge** – in the past, all over with now

bring /**briNg**/ [brings, brought, bringing] verb come carrying something *Please bring a salad to the dinner party.* Col: **bring about** – cause to happen **bring down** – cause to fail **bring forward** –

present ideas or information **bring out** – highlight **bring tears to one's eyes** – create such emotion one cries **bring up** – vomit or raise a child or present an idea

build /**bild**/ [builds, built, building] *verb* 1 construct *We built our house with wood.* 2 accumulate *Build your wealth through hard work.* • *noun* human fitness *The body builder had huge muscles.* Col: **build in** – incorporate into **build on** – add to the original structure or discussion **build up** – increase size or strength

business /**biz** nus/ [businesses] *noun* occupation, work or trade in which a person is engaged to earn money *He owns his own business.* Col: **business as usual** – continue with normal activity **do your business** – spoken to remind a child or dog to go to the bathroom **have no business in** – no authority or right **mean business** – be serious **mind one's own business** – do not interfere **none of your business** – not your concern

busy /**bi** ZEy/ [busier, busiest] *adj* many things to do. *Mothers with small children have busy lives.* Col: **busy as a bee, busy as a beaver** – doing many things **busy body** – meddles in other people's business, **get busy** - start working, keep busy – stay occupied **the phone is busy** – someone is already talking on the line

children /**chil** drun/ *noun* plural of child *The children are playing in the street.* Col: **acting like children** – displaying annoying youthful behavior **Children should be seen and not heard.** – *proverb* suggesting children be quiet around adults

chili (chilly) /**Chi** lEy/ [chilies] *noun* a hot red spice Put chili on your hotdog to spice it up. Col: **chili peppers** – hot peppers from Mexico **chili powder** – spice made from dried ground chili peppers **chili con carne** – spicy stew with beef, tomatoes, beans and onions

chilly (chili) /**Chi** lEy/ [chilies] *adj* lack of warmth, a cool temperature or atmosphere *Her relationship with her ex-husband was chilly.*

chin /**Chin**/ [chins] *noun* lowest part of human face *She has a pointed chin.* Col: **chin-ups** – physical exercise pulling the body up until the chin is level with a high bar **chin chin** – toast to good fortune **keep one's chin up** – remain positive and keep going **take it on the chin** – endure misfortune without complaint

city /**si** dEy/ [cities] *noun* a large town *We moved from the country to the city when I was ten.* Col: **city slicker** – a dishonest, fancy dresser from the city **you can't fight city hall** – you can't win over the rules of the system

committee /ku **mi** dEy/ [committees] *noun* a group of people working together in an official role for a common purpose *The town formed a special committee to run the annual fair.* Col: **ad hoc committee** – a short term working group set up for a specific purpose **steering committee** – group which determines order of business activities

competition /com pu **ti** Shun/ [competitions] *noun* 1 a rivalry between people, businesses or sports teams *They are in a swimming competition this weekend.* 2 demand for the same resources *In the forest, the competition for light drives growth.* Col: **no competition** – easy victory **stiff competition** – talented, experienced opponent

condition /kun **di** Shun/ [conditions, conditioned, conditioning] *noun* 1 state of health *He is fit and in good condition.* 2 medical term referring to an ailment *She has a heart condition.* 3 requirement of a legal contract *The condition of sale required payment by a specific date.* • *verb* actively improving condition *Her training conditioned her body for the big race.* Col: **air conditioning** – mechanical system to cool a building **in mint condition** –

perfect shape   **in no condition** – not able   **on condition** – with stipulation   **out of condition** – not in good physical shape

contiguous /kun **tig** yU wus/ *adj* share a common boarder *The US has 48 contiguous states.*

decision /du **si** Zhun/ [decisions] *noun* to come to a conclusion *The judge handed down his decision.* `Col:` **arrive at a decision** – to conclude   **reach a decision** – to conclude   **split decision** – conclusion not shared by the whole group

dictionary /**dik** Shu ne rEy/ [dictionaries] *noun* a resource book that lists words in a logical order and includes spelling meaning and function of many words *Old dictionaries are useless because students have to know what a word means and how to spell it before they can use one.* `Col:` **sound dictionary** – groups words by sound not letters in order to help students spell crazy English

did /**did**/ [does, did, doing] *verb* past tense of *do* used to *I did do my homework but my dog ate it.* `Col:` **Didja __?** – Did you, contraction   **Didjer __?** – Did your contraction

different /**di** frunt/ [differently] *adj* 1 unlike in form, quality, amount *The food was different from anything she had ever tasted.* 2 contrasting *They had different opinions.* • *adv* not the same *She remembers the details differently.* `Col:` **as different as night and day** – complete opposites   **different strokes for different folks** – different people make different choices   **march to a different drummer** – an individual who does not follow the norm   **sing a different tune** – changed their story

distance /**dis** duns/ [distances, distanced, distancing] *noun* 1 extent of space between two objects or places *The distance between the two houses is one kilometer.* 2 a point or area that is far away *She lives at a great distance from her job.* 3 emotional separation *There was a distance between the sisters where once they had been so close.* • *verb* make separate *He distanced himself from his friends when they started experimenting with drugs.* `Col:` **go the distance** – work to complete a challenge   **keep your distance** – stay away   **long distance** – not a local call   **put some distance between** – move away from   **within walking distance** – close enough to walk there

division /du **vi** zhun/ [÷, divisions] *noun* 1 physical or emotional separation *A division formed between the students who wanted to study grammar and the ones who wanted more speaking.* 2 mathematical process *In primary school, we learned addition, subtraction, multiplication and division.* 3 section of an organization *She works in the accounting division of the company.* `Col:` **subdivision** – concentration of houses built at the same, time in the same area

drink /**driNgk**/ [drank, drinks, drinking] *verb* 1 swallow liquid *We drink coffee every morning.* 2 alcohol *He drank heavily and his wife left him.* 3 take in or appreciate through the senses *He drank in the beauty of the sunrise and was filled with peace.* • *noun* a type of beverage *Tea is the most popular drink in the world.* `Col:` **drink someone under the table** -contest to drink more and remain more sober than an opponent   **drink to** – toast one's success   **drink up** – consume entire beverage   **go for a drink** – meet at a bar

English /**iN** gliSh/ *prop noun* 1 relating to people from England *People from England are usually English.* 2 relating to the language of English *They speak English in North America.* `Col:` **English muffin** – small, round bread, split and toasted   **in plain English** – speak clearly and simply   **Queen's English** – RP received pronunciation, refined and proper, grammatically correct

existence /eg **zis** tuns/ [existences] *noun* the state of being *Our existence on earth is short-lived.*

/i/ is Pink

fiction /**fik** shun/ *noun* 1 creative writing based on the author's imagination *J. K Rowling writes children's fiction.* • *adj* about fiction *She is a fiction writer.* Col: **fact or fiction** — true or false   **truth is stranger than fiction** — things that actually happen are sometimes more fantastic than things made up

fill /**fil**/ [fills, filled, filling] *verb* 1 put into a container *Fill the jug with water.* 2 repair a cavity in the mouth *The dentist filled my tooth.* 3 meet a need *He filled the position without interviewing any outside candidates.* 4 purchase an order of specific medicine *She filled the prescription at the pharmacy.* • *noun* dirt that is pushed into a hole *Put some fill in that hole.* Col: **clean fill wanted** — looking for dirt with no rocks or garbage   **fill in** — complete a form   **fill in for** — replace someone who is temporarily missing   **fill in the blanks** — make an educated guess about the missing information   **fill out** — complete a form or become fatter

finger /**fiN** gEr/ [fingers, fingered, fingering] *noun* 1 one of five digits on a hand *He put the ring on her finger and asked her to marry him.* 2 one part of a glove *The liner has come out of the fingers in my glove.* • *verb* touch *He fingered the smooth white pearls of the necklace.* Col: **give the finger** — rude gesture using an upward motion of middle finger   **ring finger** — next to baby finger, where wedding band is worn   **wrap around one's finger** — to have significant influence over another   **work one's fingers to the bone** — work very hard

fish /**fish**/ [fishes, fished, fishing] *noun* 1 type of cold blooded vertebrate living in water ← *Cod is a delicious white fish.* 2 children's card game *Go Fish!* • *verb* catch fish with a hook/bait *They fished for salmon in the ocean.* Col: **big fish in a small pond** — false sense of superiority where the test group is small   **bigger fish to fry** — more important issues need attention   **go fish** — try again   **like a fish out of water** — out of place   **not the only fish in the sea** — encouragement following a break up to know that there are many (better) opportunities for love

fix /**fiks**/ [fixes, fixed, fixing] *verb* repair or mend *I fixed the broken handle on the door.* Col: **fix someone up** — arrange a romantic encounter with a stranger for a friend   **get a fix** — dose of an illegal drug   **in a fix** — in an awkward situation

flamingo /flu **miN** gOw/ [flamingos] *noun* large bright pink tropical wading bird *A flock of flamingos is a spectacular sight.*

flipper /**fli** pEr/ [flippers] *noun* 1 flat wide swimming shoe *You can swim quickly if you wear flippers.* 2 flat wide limbs for water animals. *Dolphins, whales and seals have flippers.*

gift /**gift**/ [gifts] *noun* 1 a present given voluntarily 🎁 *She bought a birthday gift for her daughter.* 2 special talent or aptitude *His musical ability was only one of his many gifts.* Col: **Don't look a gift horse in the mouth.** — *proverb* there is probably something wrong with it but be gracious   **hostess gift** — a small present for the hostess that shows thanks   **regift** — take a gift you received and did not like and give it to someone else

gimme /**gi** mEy/ *contr* give me, spoken word only *English is Stupid Students are Not Chapter Four* Col: **Gimme a break** — don't annoy me or get me in trouble   **Gimme, gimmie never gets.** — ask nicely   **Gimme some skin.** — slap hands in friendly greeting

give /**giv**/ [gave, gives, giving] *verb* 1 donate *We give food to the food bank for the poor.* 2 convey *Give directions to the taxi driver.* Col: **give a hand** — applaud or help   **give in** — submit or surrender   **give one a run for one's money** — attempt to defeat another and almost succeed give something a fair shake — honest or unbiased treatment   give the devil his due — give deserved credit to someone even if you don't like them   give up — surrender or concede   give up the ghost — to die or to stop   give your best shot — try your hardest or best

grip /**grip**/ [grips, gripped, gripping] verb hold tightly *Grip the railing so you don't fall.* Col: come to grips with — begin to dealing with a bad situation   get a grip — regain self control

gym (Jim) /**jim**/ [gyms] noun a place to exercise, often in a school or public building *Let's go to the gym for a workout.* Col: hit the gym — go for a workout   jungle gym — children's physical activity structure

hiccough or **hiccup** /**hi** kup/ [hiccoughs, hiccoughed, hiccoughing] noun sudden gulp of air *Drinking soda gave the child hiccoughs.* • verb a series of throat spasms *She hiccoughed after eating too fast.*

him (hymn) /**him**/ pron object referring to males *Give him the pen.*

hip /**hip**/ [hips] noun body joint connecting the leg to the torso at the pelvis *She fell off her horse and broke her hip.* • adj an attitude that is stylish and currently in vogue *She was hip to the latest fashions.* Col: Hip hip hurrah! — a cheer of congratulations   hip of beef — section of cow meat   hip hop — style of street music and dance   joined at the hip — inseparable

his /**hiz**/ pron possessive referring to ownership by a male *His pen is on his desk.*

history /**hi** strEy/ noun 1 reference to the past, antiquity *WW2 is part of our history.* 2 subject in school *We studied history and geography last year.* 3 experience *We are no longer married but we share 20 years of history.* Col: a history of — repeated past action   go down in history — remembered   make history — do something significant that will be remembered   the rest is history — familiar story   you're history — you're fired

hymn (him) /**him**/ [hymns] noun church music *'Ode to Joy' by Johan Sebastian Bach is my favorite hymn.*

hypocrite /**hi** pu krit/ [hypocrites] noun a person who behaves the opposite to what they say they believe. *The doctor smokes even though he knows smoking is bad for him.*

if /**if**/ conj 1 introducing a condition *If we don't leave now we will be late.* 2 exclaiming *If only they had come on time.* 3 whether *Ask if he plans to come tonight.* Col: as if — sarcastic comment, don't believe something will happen   if and when — possibility of something happening   no if's ands or buts — no excuses

ill /**il**/ [iller, illest] adj sick, unwell, unhealthy *I felt ill after eating shellfish.* • noun malicious, harmful *Social ills like drug and alcohol addiction are difficult to treat.* Col: house of ill repute — prostitution   ill advised — bad advice   ill at ease — uncomfortable   ill behaved — badly behaved   ill-gotten gains — illegal booty   ill mannered — rude or vulgar   ill tempered — nasty disposition, unfriendly or crabby   ill wind blowing — bad news coming   Never speak ill of the dead. — proverb meaning don't speak badly of people who have passed on

impulse /**im** pulse/ [impulses] noun sudden notion, urge, desire *I gave in to a nasty impulse to buy chocolate bars at the check-out counter.* Col: impulse shopping — unplanned buying

in (inn) /**in**/ prep location within *Mobile is in Alabama.* • adj current fashion *Bell bottoms were in during the 1970's.* • adv available *Is he in?* Col: all in — fully committed   all in all — considering everything   ins and outs — knows everything including any extra information about an industry or business

/ i / is Pink

in the know – current and aware   **the in crowd** – popular group

increase /**in** krEys/ [increases, increased, increasing] *verb* add on *We increased the square footage of our home when we closed in the porch.* • *noun* rise in *This summer there has been an increase in average temperature.* Col: **on the increase** – more frequently

industry /**in** du strEy/ [industries] *noun* 1 business, commercial enterprise *They work in the textile industry.* 2 hard work or effort *He shows industry and ingenuity at work.* Col: **captain of industry** – wealthy capitalist businessman

ink /**ink**/ [inks] *noun* fluid in pens *I always write with blue ink.* Col: **red ink** – debt

inn (in) /**in**/ [inns] *noun* small hotel *I prefer to stay at wayside inns than big fancy hotels.*

insect /**in** sekt/ *noun* bug small creature, usually with wings, pairs of legs and a three-part body *The mosquito is a pesky insect.*

instrument /**in** stru munt/ [instruments] *noun* 1 device for playing music *The violin is a fine instrument.* 2 medical tools *The dentist uses special instruments to take care of teeth.*

interest /**in** trust/ [interests, interested, interesting] *noun* 1 attention, concern *I am interested in what you have to say.* 2 financial compensation paid or earned *They made 12% interest on their money.* 3 hobby *Students have different interests outside of class.* • *verb* curiosity *Collecting butterflies collection interests me more than any other hobby.* Col: **best interests at heart** – do something with good intentions   **draw interest** – earn interest   **in the interest of** – concerning   **keen interest in** – strong interest   **person of interest** – watched by authorities for various reasons   **vested interest** – personal biased

into /**in** tUw/ *prep* 1 indicating action to a point *His car ran into a tree.* 2 within *He walked into the room.* 3 interested in as a hobby *He's into learning the guitar.*

is /**iz**/ *verb* present tense of to *be* third person singular *He is rich.*

it /**it**/ *subject* or *object pron* third person singular *It is cold.* Col: **cut it out** – stop annoying   **easy does it** – proceed cautiously   **hit it big** – unexpectedly do well   **jump on it** – seize the opportunity   **like it or not** – accept it even if you do not like it   **sleep on it** – delay decision to give time to think

kick /**kik**/ [kicks, kicked, kicking] *verb* strike with one's foot *He kicked the ball.* • *noun* good feeling *They get a kick out of concerts.* Col: **get a kick** – receive enjoyment   **kick a habit** – stop a bad habit   **kick butt** – do something very well   **kick oneself** – upset with oneself for behaving foolishly   **kick back** – relax or illegal pay   **kick at the can** – try something   **kick the bucket** – die   **kick up one's heels** – party, enjoy

kid /**kid**/ [kids] *noun* 1 slang for child *How many kids do you have?* 2 baby goat *The nanny goat had twin kids every spring.* • *verb* jest or joke *Are you kidding me?* Col: **a kid in a candy store** – happy   **handle with kid gloves** – handle a sensitive person or situation gently, calmly or cautiously   **just kidding** – joking around   **kids' stuff** – childish or for children   **no kidding** – it's true

kiss /**kis**/ [kisses, kissed, kissing] *noun* caress or touch with the lips *Give your old grandma a kiss!* • *verb* touch with the lips to express affection *We kissed goodbye at the airport.* Col: **blow a kiss** – send a kiss with a blowing gesture   **French kiss** – deep passionate   **K.I.S.S.** – Keep It Simple Stupid   **kiss and make up** – stop fighting   **kiss and tell** – ungentlemanly to reveal intimate details about a love relationship   **kiss good bye** – gone forever   **kiss my ass** – rude way of expressing anger   **kiss of death** – end of   **kiss your money goodbye** – danger of losing all your money   kissed off – left to avoid responsibility   sun kissed – lightly tanned   S.W.A.K. – Sealed With A Kiss – letters sent with love

lift /**lift**/ [lifts, lifted, lifting] *verb* raise up or elevate *The crane lifted the cargo from the dock.* • *noun* 1 a ride with someone *Can you give me a lift.* 2 a positive feeling *Coffee gives me a lift first thing in the morning.* Col: **face lift** – cosmetic surgery to remove wrinkles from the face   **lift off** – plane or rocket ascent   **not lift a finger** – put forth no effort to help or work

limit /**li**mit/ [limits, limited, limiting] *noun* boundary *We live within the city limits.* • *verb* restrain *She limits the amount of alcohol he drinks.* Col: **limited edition** – few prints or models, of interest to collectors   **off limits** – forbidden area   **speed limit** – posted maximum   **time limit** – deadline   **the sky is the limit** – no limit   **within limits** – working within some restrictions

linen /**li**nun/ [linens] *noun* 1 natural fabric *The table cloth and tea towels are made of linen.* 2 household fabric goods collectively *Hotel linens are often stolen.* • *adj* for or made of linen *Put the sheets and towels away in the linen closet.* Col: **air one's dirty linen in public** – revealing personal matters

lip /**lip**/ [lips] *noun* 1 upper and lower exterior edges of the mouth *Her lips are ruby red.* 2 sass or back talk *Don't give me any lip.* 3 edge or rim of a cup or bowl *The lip of the cup was chipped.* Col: **bite one's lip** – say nothing about..   **button your lip** – be quiet   **give someone lip** – rude or back talk   **lick one's lips** – shows eagerness   **lips are sealed** – keep a secret   **pay lip service** – insincere or say it with no intention of doing it   **read my lips** – pay attention to what I say   **tight lipped** – angry or not saying

liquid /**li**kwud/ [liquids] *noun* fluid *Water is a liquid.* • *adj* easily accessed assets, cash *In case of emergency, our liquid assets are cash and some bonds.* Col: **solid, liquid, gas** – states of matter   **liquid asset** – cash or items easily converted to cash   **liquid lunch** – beer instead of food

list /**list**/ [lists, listed, listing] *noun* series of names, words or items *Take a shopping list to the grocery store and you'll spend less money.* • *verb* 1 record or itemize *He listed all his previous jobs on his resume.* 2 tilting of ship to one side *The boat listed to port.* Col: **blacklisted** – identified as a troublemaker   **hit list** – list of those you plan to kill   **waiting list** – in line for a service   **wish list** – things wanted

listen /**li**sun/ [listens, listened, listening] *verb* pay attention *Many people listen to the radio while driving their cars.* Col: **listen to reason** – accept logical arguments   **listen up** – slang for pay attention   **Stop look and listen before you cross the street, use your eyes and use your ears, before you use your feet.** poem to teach small children to cross the street safely

little /**li**dul/ [littler, littlest] *adj* small, brief, insignificant, unimportant *I'm a little tired but not ready to go to bed.* Col: **a little bird told me** – gossip   **every little bit helps** – even small contributions make a difference   **give a little** – effort or money   **Great oaks from little acorns grow.** – *proverb* for possibility   **in a little bit** – soon   **little bird told me** – gossip   **little by little** – progress slowly   **A little knowledge is a dangerous thing.** – *proverb*, overconfidence can result bad decisions   **little or nothing** – small amount   **little people** – abnormally small people or dwarfism   **little white lie** – lie that does little harm   **Oh, ye of little faith** – success against the odds   **too little, too late** – what little was offered was offered too late

/ i / is Pink

to allow success   twisted around one's little finger — controls another

live /**liv**/ [lives, lived, living] *verb* exist, function, reside, dwell *I live on a farm in Canada.* `Col:` As I live and breathe! — fantastic   have to live with — endure   haven't lived — inexperienced   He who fights and runs away, lives to fight another day. — *proverb* about discretion   I can live with that — tolerate   live in a dream world — unrealistic   live in an ivory tower — protected or separate from reality   learn to live with — accept   live a lie — under false pretenses   live and learn — always learning through experiences   live and let live — accept others and their ways   live beyond means — spend more than earn   live dangerously — risk takers   live down — until shame fades   live for the moment — carefree   live hand to mouth — poverty   live happily ever after — end of a fairy tale, it all works out   live high off the hog — well   live in — help in the house   live in hope — optimistic   live in sin — share a house and bed with someone who is not married   live in the past — not accept progress or change   live it up — enjoy oneself   live like a king — lavishly   live off the land — farm   live on borrowed time — past best before date or die imminently   live on nerves — tense   live on own — independently   live on the edge — risk taker   live out days — until death   live out of a suitcase — travel   live through — survive   live to a ripe old age — die old   live to tell the tale — survive   live together — cohabitate as a couple without being married   live under the same roof — same dwelling   live up to — honor   live within means — budget   live on the edge — take many risks   People who live in glass houses shouldn't throw stones. — *proverb* to be careful about accusing others of things you also do   words to live by — good advice

liver /**li** vEr/ [livers] *noun* 1 organ in the body which cleanses blood from toxins *Alcohol abuse damaged his liver.* 2 edible animal organ meat *I had liver and onions for dinner last night.* `Col:` lily-livered — not brave

middle /**mi** dul/ [middles] *noun* center, core, midpoint *The middle of a tornado is called the eye.* `Col:` in the middle of something — busy   Middle Ages — 1000 AD to 1500 AD   middle age — forties and fifties   middle class — average income, working people   middle management — higher than workers lower than executive   middleman — go-between or agent   middle of the road — moderate or average

military /**mi** lu te rEy/ *noun* armed forces *The government called in the military to help citizens after the earthquake.* `Col:` military intelligence — armed forces secret information gathers and processors   military precision — accurate

milk /**milk**/ [milks, milked, milking] *noun* nourishing fluid produced by female mammals *My children always drink milk with their meals.* • *verb* draw liquid from *Dairy farmers milk their cows every morning and every night.* `Col:` don't cry over spilt milk — don't fuss about little things you can't change   land of milk and honey — a happy prosperous place, utopia   milk the system — exploit or take unfair advantage of aid   the milk of human kindness — natural empathy and caring   Why buy a cow when you can get milk for free? — rude *proverb* meaning why marry when you can have sex without the commitment

minute /**mi** nut/ [minutes] *noun* 1 one sixtieth of an hour *We are leaving in ten minutes.* 2 small amount of time *You only have a minute to get ready.* 3 recorded notes taken of meetings *The secretary recorded the minutes of the meeting.* `Col:` a laugh a minute — funny person   at the last minute — just before the opportunity closes   every minute counts —

urgent   hold on a minute – rethinking   just a minute – wait for a short time or process a flash of insight   talks a mile a minute – speak very quickly   up to the minute – current   wait a minute – wait, I just thought of something important   when you get a minute – I need your help when you are available

mix /**miks**/ [mixes, mixed, mixing] verb combine ingredients in cooking, drinks or social settings *We mixed sugar, flour and eggs to make cookies.* Col: mix and match – complementary clothing styles and colors   mix and mingle – be sociable   mix up – confuse   mix something up – combine things to create something to eat   mixed feelings about – some positive and some negative   mixed marriage – couple from different ethnic backgrounds

mystery /**m**i strEy/ [mysteries] noun 1 secret or unsolved problem *Who stole the purse? It is a mystery.* 2 type of written story *Steven King writes scary mysteries.* Col: one of life's great mysteries – a common question that we will never know the answer to

nickel /**ni** kul/ [5¢, nickels] noun 1 North American 5¢ coin *He gave her five nickels for her quarter.* 2 type of metal *Nickel is mined in Sudbury* 2 • adj about nickel *Sudbury has nickel mines.* Col: Don't take any wooden nickels. – proverb be careful and take care of oneself   nickel and dime – petty bargaining, cheapskate   on one's nickel – I pay, my treat

opinion /u **pin** yun/ noun belief, view, theory, finding, assessment *It is my opinion that religion and politics should be separate.* Col: difference of opinion – disagree   form an opinion – develop an idea   IMHO – text for *in my humble opinion*, only what I think   in my humble opinion – only what I think, maybe patronizing   it's a matter of opinion – subjective arguable point   keep one's opinions to oneself – be quiet

original /u **ri** ju nul/ [originals] noun first of its kind, one that is copied *The lawyer keeps the originals and the purchaser receives a copy.* • adj first *Kate Middleton wore an original Jenny Packham.*

physical /**fi** zu kul/ [physicals] noun a medical checkup *I go to the doctor for a physical every year.* • adj solid, concrete *Children spend too much time in front of electronics, they need more physical activity.* Col: get physical – become more aggressive, more active, or get sexually involved   physical education – school subject about physical activity   physically fit – in good physical shape

pick /**pik**/ [picks, picked, picking] verb select *We pick our friends but we are born to our family.* Col: a pick-me-up – rejuvenator   bone to pick – point of disagreement to talk about   have pick of – first choice   pick a fight – aggravate   pick a lock – open without key   pick and choose – select one thing and leave another   pick apart – criticize   pick brain – ask for ideas   pick-me-up – makes one feel better   pick off – shoot with rifle or remove by scratching with fingernails   pick on – tease, harass or bully   pick pocket – steel from someone's pocked or bag in secret   pick up – give someone a ride or connect for a sexual opportunity   pick up after – tidy someone else's mess   pick up on – understand   pick-up sticks – child's game   pick up the bill – pay for   pick up the pace – go faster   pick up the pieces – regain emotional composure   pick up the slack – work harder   pick up the tab – pay the bill   take your pick – choose whichever you like

picture /**pik** ChEr/ [pictures, pictured, picturing] noun 1 image or visual representation *We hung the picture of the children in the living room.* 2 perfect example, model *She was the picture of health.* • verb imagine *I always pictured we would grow old together.* Col: A picture is worth a thousand words. – *proverb* meaning images deliver messages better than words **get the picture** – understand **picture perfect** – flawless

pig /**pig**/ [pigs] *noun* 1 big fat barnyard animal that eats anything and has many babies at a time *Pork and bacon come from pigs.* 2 a rude person *He was a pig to his wife and she left him.* Col: **bleeding like a stuck pig** -bleeding profusely **making a pig of oneself** – eating too much, bad table manners **pig pen** – messy place **pig sty** – messy place **pigskin** – American football **pigging out** – eating a lot **sweat like a pig** – perspire **This little piggy went to market…** – children's rhyme to say while wiggling a baby's toes **when pigs fly** – unlikely to happen **Why buy the pig when you can get the sausage for free?** - no reason to marry if the sex is available

pin /**pin**/ [pins, pinned, pinning] *noun* fastener like a safety pin or jewelry brooch *She put pins in the bottom of her hem to hold it up.* • *verb* 1 fasten, affix *She pinned her hem before she sewed it.* 2 to hold down or restrain *They pinned the thief to the ground and called the police.* Col: **neat as a pin** – tidy **pin down** – hold someone accountable for times or facts **pin up** – picture of sexy idol **pins and needles** – tingling sensation from impinged nerve **push pin** – thumb tack **so quiet you could hear a pin drop** – very quiet **stick pin** – jewelry **straight pin** – sewer's tool

pink /**pink**/ [pinks, pinker, pinkest] *adj* the color from mixing white and red *She stepped on a wad of pink gum and it stuck to the bottom of her shoe.* • *noun* the color *Pink is a popular color for lipstick.* Col: **in the pink** – peak of health **pink dollar** – lesbian economy **pink slip** – you are fired **see pink elephants** – drunk **tickled pink** – ecstatic or happy

political /pu **li** du kul/ *adj* concerning government, bureaucracy and diplomacy *People who run for office are political.* Col: **political football** – an issue that doesn't get solved, just passed around **politically correct** – careful not to offend or social sensitive **political science** – study of government systems

position /pu **zi** shun/ *noun* 1 location, place, viewpoint *We are in a good position to see the parade.* 2 status, class *He has a high ranking position in the military.* 3 posture or pose *Hold that position in yoga.* Col: **in an awkward position** – a socially difficult situation **jockey for position** – compete for a good position **make your position clear** – tell people what you think **missionary position** – standard sexual position **pole position** – advantage

pretty /**pri** dEy/ [prettier, prettiest] *adj* attractive, lovely *She is a pretty girl* • *adv* to a degree, 70% *It was a pretty nice day.* Col: **costs a pretty penny** – expensive **not a pretty sight** – unpleasant looking **not just a pretty face** – smart as well as beautiful **pretty as a picture** – beautiful **pretty much** – almost **pretty please** – begging request **pretty early** – quite early **sitting pretty** – in a good position

print /**print**/ [prints, printed, printing] *noun* 1 copy of original artwork *We have a Picasso print on our wall.* 2 pattern on fabric *The print on her dress was flowery.* • *verb* 1 basic lettering *Students print in Grade One and write in Grade Three.* 2 create paper copies *Print the legal documents, then sign them and send them back.* 3 publish *'English is Stupid, Students are Not' was printed in Canada.* Col: **in print** – book available **license to print money** – company that makes money with little work **out of print** – book no longer available from publisher **read the fine print** – read the legal terms of a contract

prison /**pri** zʌn/ [prisons] *noun* jail, place to lock up criminals *He was in prison for 20 years for murder.*

quick /**kwik**/ [quicker, quickest] *adj* 1 fast *She was quick to answer the phone.* 2 smart *He was a quick learner.* `Col:` **a quick one** – one alcoholic drink   **a quick study** – learns fast   **quick and dirty** – careless   **quick as a bunny** – encourage children to hurry   **quick as a wink** – very fast   **quick fix** – temporary solution   **quick on the draw** – react fast   **quick on the uptake** – grasps essential information fast   **quick-tempered** – easily angry   **quick-witted** – intelligent, funny

religion /ru **li** jun/ [religions] *noun* structured belief in a supreme being *In our community all religions are welcome.*

rhythm /**ri** Thum/ [rhythms] *noun* 1 musical beat *The drum beats maintained the rhythm of the music.* 2 a pattern or flow of sounds *English has a rhythm of stressed and unstressed sounds.* `Col:` **rhythm and blues** – type of music   **rhythm method** – natural birth control based on the woman's menstrual cycle

rib /**rib**/ [ribs] *noun* 1 curved bone structure that protects the lungs and heart in a mammal *He broke three ribs in the car accident.* 2 type of roast or barbecued meat *Barbecued ribs is our favorite meal.* `Col:` **stick to your ribs** – food that is satisfying and filling   **to rib someone** – tease

ring /**riNg**/ [rings, rang, ringing] *noun* 1 jewelry worn on a finger *He bought her a ring for their tenth anniversary.* 2 sound of the telephone *The ring was set so low we couldn't hear it.* 3 to call on the phone *Give me a ring when you want to come over.* 4 circle around *Raccoons have rings around their tails.* • *verb* sound from a bell or telephone *Their phone rings inside their house and outside in their garage.* `Col:` **ears are ringing** – too much loud noise or someone is gossiping about them   **familiar ring** – heard before   **ring around the rosy** – children's outdoor circle song/game   **ring hollow** – not true   **ring in the new year** – welcome   **ring off the hook** – many calls   **ring true** – sounds right   **run rings around** – out run   **the brass ring** – success   **three-ring circus** – busy, lots of activity   **toss one's hat into the ring** – run for elected office

river /**ri** vɛr/ [rivers] *noun* long body of fresh water that flows from high ground to lower ground *We often go fishing in the river on Saturday mornings.* `Col:` **sold down the river** – betrayed

scissors /**si** zɛrz/ *noun* double-bladed pinching tool used to cut fabric or paper. ✂ *It is dangerous to run with scissors.* `Col:` **rock paper scissors** – decision making hand game for two or more people

serendipity /se run **di** pu dɛy/ *noun* something good happens by accident *Serendipity is meeting your future husband at a car accident.*

shift /**shift**/ [shifts, shifted, shifting] *noun* 1 change *A small shift in direction can make a big difference in destination.* 2 set period of working hours *He liked working the night shift because it was quiet.* • *verb* change of position *Shift over and make room for me to sit on the bench too.* `Col:` **graveyard shift** – work period at night   **shift for oneself** – on your own   **shift gears** – change of approach or attitude   **make shift** – temporary with materials at hand   **split shift** – half of the working hours in the morning and half in the evening of the same day   **stick shift** – manual transmission control

ship /**ship**/ [ships, shipped, shipping] *noun* large vessel that travels over water *Ships are bigger than boats.* • *verb* send large items *We ship books all over the world.* `Col:` **abandon ship** – leave   **desert a sinking ship** – leave a situation that becomes unpleasant   **jump ship** – abandon during difficult times   **like

rats leaving a sinking ship – scrambling to get away   **runs a tight ship** – organized authoritarian in control   **shape up or ship out** – do better or leave   **ship shape** – tidy, clean and in good repair   **two ships passing in the night** – two people meeting for a short romantic time then moving on   **when one's ship comes in** – good things that will happen when fortune arrives

shit /shit/ [shits, shat, shitting, shittier, shittiest] *interj* a bad word, slang word of anger or dismay *Oh Shit!* • *adj, noun* and *verb* defecate   Col: **bullshit story** – a lie   **don't give a shit** – don't care   **happier than a pig in shit** – happy   **in deep shit** – in trouble   **shit happens** – bad things happen   **shit out of luck** – missed chance   **shit hit the fan** – anger when a serious mistake is discovered   **shit disturber** – trouble maker   **shoot the shit** – chat casually

sick /sik/ [sicker, sickest] *adj* 1 ill, unwell *She was sick with a fever and had to miss school.* 2 strange, deranged *He had a sick sense of humor.* 3 slang for great! *That's sick man!* Col: **heartsick** – disappointed   **sick** – really great   **sick and tired** – exhausted   **sick as a dog** – vomiting   **sick jokes** – inappropriate jokes at someone's expense   **sick to death** fed up or frustrated

silly /si lEy/ [sillier, silliest] *adj* foolish *Wearing your pajamas to school is a silly idea.* Col: **as silly as a goose** or **silly goose** – acting in a babyish way   **bored silly** – very bored   **the silly season** – slow news period where nonsense makes the headlines

silver /sil vEr/ [silvers] *noun* 1 type of valuable metal, sterling *She wore silver earrings.* 2 cutlery *Please set the table with the good silver.* • *adj* gray metallic color *The moonlight shone silver on the lake.* Col: **born with a silver spoon in one's mouth** – from wealth and privilege   **every cloud has a silver lining** – there is a good outcome from all misfortune   **served on a silver platter** – receive something special with all the trimmings   **silver screen** – Hollywood movies   **silver-haired** – gray haired person   **silver tongued** – smooth talker

simple /sim pul/ [simpler, simplest] *adj* straight forward uncomplicated *That math problem was simple.* Col: **a simpleton** – not very smart   **as simple as ABC** – basic, rudimentary, extremely easy   **pure and simple** or **plain and simple** – very clear and easy

sing /siNg/ [sings, sang, singing] *verb* vocally produce musical sounds *She sings like a bird.* Col: **it ain't over 'til the fat lady sings** – baseball term anything can happen even when it looks like the game is lost   **sing for one's supper** – entertain or work to pay for your meal   **sing like a canary** – turn criminal partners in to authorities   **sing one's praises** – compliment   **sing the blues** – whine and complain   **singing a different tune** – story has changed

single /siN gul/ [singles] *adj* unit of one *She had a single bed.* • *noun* unmarried person *He was single until he turned 30.* • *verb* choose or separate from a group *They were singled out of the crowd.* Col: **single file** – orderly line, one person behind the other   **single parent** – parent without a partner   **singlehanded** – unassisted   **single-minded** – focused, stubborn   **singles bar** – pick up club

sister /sis dEr/ [sisters] *noun* female sibling *I have three sisters.* 2 nun, member of religious order *The sisters grow their own vegetables behind the convent.* Col: **sisterhood** – relationship of support among sisters or women   **sister sounds** – eight pairs of consonant sounds where the mouth is in exactly the same position and air either moves in or out (p/b, t/d, k/g, s/z/,f/v...)   **soul sister** – a black woman or women friends who share a strong bond

sit /**sit**/ [sits, sat, sitting] *verb* rest, recline in seated position *Most people sit on the couch to watch TV.* `Col:` babysit – care for children   not sit well/right with me – something seems wrong   sit back – let it happen   sit idly by – do nothing while something bad is happening   sit this one out – take a rest   sit through – endure   sit tight – wait   sit up and take notice – pay attention to something   sit up with – not sleep in order to care for another   sit in judgment – condemn others   sit in – occupy space as a protest   sit on one's hands – do nothing or force oneself not to do something   sit on the fence – take neither side in discussion or can't decide   sit up and take notice – pay attention   sitting pretty – in a good position

six /**siks**/ [6, sixes] *noun* cardinal number, after five and before seven *Six is a half a dozen.* • *adj* six in number *I took a six-day course in teaching English.* `Col:` deep six that – get rid of   six feet under – dead and buried   six of one and half a dozen of another – no preference, both choices equal   six-figure income – earning $100,000 or more a year   six-pack – a set of six alcoholic beverages or the stomach muscles of the physically fit

skin /**skin**/ [skins, skinned, skinning] *noun* 1 covering organ of human body *My skin was dry in the winter.* 2 covering of an inanimate object *The case had a smooth plastic skin.* • *verb* remove the hide from an animal *He skinned the deer after he shot it.* `Col:` beauty is only skin-deep – personality is more important   by the skin of one's teeth – barely got away or away with   get under skin – affect emotionally deeply or annoy   it's no skin off nose – doesn't matter to me, negative tone   jump out of one's skin – startled, frightened   make skin crawl – creep out   save one's skin – rescue life or job   skin alive – punish severely   skin and bone – very thin   skin flick – pornographic movie   skin flint – cheap person   slip me some skin – slap hands as a gesture of friendship   soaked to the skin – very wet   there's more than one way to skin a cat – old saying about exploring alternatives   thick skin – resilient to cruelty

splint /**splint**/ [splints, splinted, splinting] *noun* hard material used to stabilize a broken limb *They were camping, and her husband cut tree branches for splints when she broke her leg.* • *verb* act of applying rigid support to a broken limb *She splinted his arm with a short pipe then drove him to the hospital.*

spring /**spriNg**/ [springs, sprang, springing] *noun* 1 season after winter *Flowers bloom in spring.* 2 source of water *Fresh water flowed from the underground spring.* • *verb* leap or jump *He springs from the diving board.* • *adj* youthful *She was no spring chicken.* `Col:` hope springs eternal – always hope even during bad times   springs to mind – suddenly remember   spring a leak - sudden seepage of liquid   spring into action – get very busy   spring on – surprise

sticky /**sti** kEy/ [stickier, stickiest] *adj* 1 tacky, gummy, gluey *She had sticky fingers after she ate the donut.* 2 humid *It was a hot sticky day in July.* `Col:` sticky business – dishonest   sticky fingers – tendency to steal   sticky wicket – in trouble because of bad decisions

still /**stil**/ [stiller, stillest] *adj* tranquil and calm *The summer night was quiet and still.* • *adv* nevertheless, all the same *And still we waited for him.* • *noun* apparatus to distill alcohol *They had a still in the forest where they made whiskey.* • *verb* make calm *The officers stilled the crowd after the outburst.* `Col:` be still my heart – old comment about romance, now sarcastic   better still – even better   hold still – stop moving   sit still – sit quietly   still waters run deep – sur-

/ i / is Pink

prising depth of thought in a shy person   **still-born** – baby born dead   **the jury is still out** – undecided

swim /swim/ [swims, swam, swimming] *verb* movement through water using arms and legs or fins and tails *We swam in the ocean on our summer holiday.* • *noun* activity of moving through the water *We went for a swim in the river.* • *adj* saturated in *The pancakes were swimming in syrup.* **Col: makes my head swim** – overwhelm   **sink or swim** – succeed or fail   **swim against the tide** – choose a different approach to the norm   **swimming in something** – to have too much of something

system /**sis** dum/ [systems] *noun* plan, organization or method *This is a good system for teaching people to speak English.* **Col: all systems go** – everything is ready to proceed   **buck the system** – stand up against tradition or authority   **get something out of one's system** – stop obsessing about something or someone

thick /THik/ [thicker, thickest] *adj* 1 deep *The board was six inches thick.* 2 dense liquid *The fog was as thick as pea soup.* 3 stupid person *He was a bit thick and couldn't understand simple mathematics.* **Col: lay on thick** – exaggerate   **thick as thieves** – spend most of the time with a close friend   **thick-skinned** – insensitive to criticism or insults   **through thick and thin** – together in good and bad times

thin /THin/ [thinner, thinnest] *adj* 1 slim, small, slender *She was as thin as a rail.* 2 watery consistency *The soup was as thin as dishwater.* • *verb* water down *Thin the gravy by adding water.* **Col: disappear into thin air** – magically vanish   **on thin ice** – precarious spot   **spread oneself too thin** – doing too much, something will give   **thinning on top** – loosing hair   **thin-skinned** – sensitive and upset by meanness and criticism   **wearing thin** – losing patience

thing /THiNg/ [things] *noun* 1 nonliving object *Get that thing out of here.* 2 a happening, event *We have a thing tonight at the theatre.* 3 a matter of concern *I have many important things on my mind.* **Col: a little knowledge is a dangerous thing** – *proverb* overconfidence people can make dangerous mistakes   **all things considered** – taken into account before deciding   **as things stand** – evaluation   **be on to a good thing** – good idea worth pursuing   **Best things in life are free.** – *proverb* about what is important   **better things to do** – stop wasting time or annoying others   **doing one's own thing** – pursue one's own interest   **first things first** – taking command to organizing   **Good things come in small packages.** – *proverb* not to misjudge value by size alone   **Good things come to him who waits.** – *proverb* about patience   **have a thing about** – special interest or dislike   **if a thing is worth doing, it's worth doing well** – do a good job   **if you want a thing done well, do it yourself** – others don't do things as well as you'd like   **It's one thing after another!** – run of bad luck or responsibilities   **just one of those things** – don't try to make sense of it   **keep things straight** – clearly communicate thoughts and plans   **knows a thing or two** – an expert   **let things slide** – got behind   **make a big thing of** – overreact   **seeing things** – imagining things   **the best thing since sliced bread** – something new and useful   **the real thing** – true love   **the funny thing is** – strange or coincidental, unexplained   **the in thing** – popular fad   **the shape of things to come** – what the future will look like   **there is no such thing** – doesn't exist   **thingamabob** – item whose name one can't remember   **thingamajig** – item whose name one can't remember   **things are looking up** – a situation is improving after a bad spell   things are seldom what they seem — first impressions are incomplete or deceiving   things will work out — reassurance   too much of a good thing — over indulgence   work things out — patch up an argument or relationship

think /**THiNgk**/ [thinks, thought, thinking] *verb* 1 consider, meditate, study *I think about my children all the time.* 2 suppose, believe, guess *I think that is correct.* Col: can't think straight — not clearly   come to think of it — revelation   don't even think about it — threat to prevent an action   great minds think alike — I had the same wonderful idea too   just thinking out loud — saying ideas as they are forming   not think twice about — no hesitation before acting   think better of it — change mind   think little of — don't like   think nothing of it — polite   think on feet — react quickly   think outside the box — creative   thinks he is God's gift to women — conceited man (humorous)   thinks the world of — adores   think twice about — reconsider   think big — dream without barriers   think over — reflect on   think tank — group working together to generate ideas   think up — invent

this /**This**/ [these] *pron* indicating something present, close by or recently referred to *This is important.* • *adj* person or thing talked about *This car will not start.* • *adv* extent *Is it always this hot here?* Col: at this point — now   at this rate — at this speed   at this stage of the game — now   come to this — deteriorated   from this day on — transitional   get the show on the road — get moving   I don't need this — annoyed   I have this feeling — intuition   I've had enough of this! — done   in this day and age — now   keep this to yourself — secret   let's do this again — get together   new to this — beginner   not long for this world — dying   Now hear this! — pay attention   out of this world — fantastic   this and that — miscellaneous items   this doesn't suit me — not look good on, don't want to do   this is it — anticipation   This is the life! — good times   Two can play this game — back stabbing, dirty fighting   What do you think of this weather? — ice breaker

ticket /**ti** kut/ [tickets] *noun* 1 pass or admission *I bought two tickets to the concert.* 2 fine or citation *My daughter got a speeding ticket for driving too fast.* Col: big ticket item — big and costly   hot ticket — currently popular   meal ticket — an adult who is financially responsible for another   round trip ticket — with return   that's the ticket — good solution   write one's own ticket — bright future on one's own terms

tin /**tin**/ [tins] *noun* 1 soft metal *The plate was made of tin.* 2 container or can *Do you have a couple of tins of beans to bring on the camping trip?* Col: like a cat on a hot tin roof — nervous person   tin ear — plays music out of tune   tin soldier — child's toy

tip /**tip**/ [tips, tipped, tipping] *noun* 1 small amount of extra money for good service *Give the waiter a good tip.* 2 pointed end *The dog has a white tip on the end of its tail.* 3 advice *I can give you a few tips on buying a car.* • *verb* angle off center of off balance *Airplane seats are more comfortable when tipped back.* Col: anonymous tip — information from an unknown source   hot tip - extra information with high value   on the tip of my tongue — can't quite remember something • the tip of the iceberg - there is much more to the story than appears   tip off — warning   tipping point - the final piece of action or information that transforms a series of small parts into a big change   tip toe — walking quietly with heels in the air   tip the scales — change the balance of a close situation

tip your hand – reveal secret information **tip your hat** – acknowledge or respect

trick /**trik**/ [tricks, tricked, tricking] *noun* 1 scheme to deceive, prank or joke *He tricked the pensioners out of their money.* 2 paid for sexual favors *The prostitute turned tricks on Saturday night.* • *verb* deception or prank *He tricked me.* `Col:` **doesn't miss a trick** – smart **How's tricks?** – How are you? **play a trick on** – deceive for fun **take a trick** – point in card game **trick or treat** – Halloween saying **turn a trick** – sex for money **up to one's old tricks** – follows a regular pattern of bad behavior

twist /**twist**/ [twists, twisted, twisting] *verb* 1 perform a turning motion *She twisted the cap off the bottle.* 2 to injure one's body *He twisted his leg in the fall.* • *noun* type of dance from the 1960's *Let's do the twist.* `Col:` **twist of fate** – life changes radically, with ironic elements **twist off** – screw-off bottle cap **twist one's arm** – persuade someone with force **twist one's words** – viciously change another's intention **twisted around one's little finger** – controls one who loves them

until /un **til**/ *prep* 1 up to the time of *She danced until midnight.* 2 before a given time *You can't visit until I am finished.* `Col:` **talk until blue in the face** – talk for a long time, listener is ignoring **until all hours** – very late **until death do us part** – part of marriage vows meaning forever **until the cows come home** – for a very long time

unwilling /un **wi** liNg/ *adj* not going to do something *He'll clean your house but he's unwilling to wash windows.*

which (witch) /**wiCh**/ *pron* Wh question, asking identity or clarification *Which one do you want?* • *adj* one of a number of choices *At which point did you fall asleep in the movie?* `Col:` **which is which** – be specific **which witch is which** – word play

whistle /**wi** sul/ [whistles, whistled, whistling] *noun* blow air into a device to produce a shrill sound *The lifeguard blew the whistle when he saw the struggling swimmer.* • *verb* make a sound of air forced between lips or teeth *He whistled and the dog came.* `Col:` **bells and whistles** – extra gadgets **blow the whistle on** – draw attention to wrong doing **clean as a whistle** – spotless **just whistle** – help is near **wet one's whistle** – have a drink **whistle stop** – small or unimportant place en route **whistling in the dark** – guessing

will /**will**/ [wills, willed, willing] *noun* 1 legal document outlining one's final wishes *The family read the will after the funeral.* 2 focus and determination to complete a goal *She had an iron will.* • *helping verb* indicating future tense *I will come over after dinner.* `Col:` **at will** – whenever one pleases **God willing** – if it is meant to be **ready willing and able** – prepared, inclined and capable, let's start **the spirit is willing but the flesh is weak** – desire but not capable **where there's a will, there's a way** – if you want something badly, you'll find a way to get it

wind /**wind**/ [winds] *noun* 1 natural air movement such as breeze *The ship's sails caught the wind.* 2 gas in bowels *He passed wind after a big meal.* `Col:` **break wind** – pass gas/fart **get wind of something** – hear **gone with the wind** – gone **ill wind** – bad news is coming **run like the wind** – run fast **second wind** – have burst of energy after tiring once **spit into the wind** – bad idea **take the wind out of one's sails** – discourage one who is excited about an idea or project **three sheets to the wind** – drunk **throw caution to the wind** – impulsive in a good way

windbreaker /**win** brAy kEr/ [windbreakers] *noun* light jacket with a closing neck and cuffs *We always take windbreakers when we go sailing.*

window /**win** dOw/ [windows] *noun* opening allowing in air or light *Please close the window, I'm cold.* `Col:` **throw out the window** – reject **window of opportunity** – brief moment of opportunity **window dressing** – appears better than it really is **window shopping** – go shopping to look but not buy

wing /**wiNg**/ [wings] *noun* 1 structures on birds, insects or airplanes that make flight possible *The eagle has long wings.* 2 an addition or annex on a building *They built a pediatric wing on the hospital.* • *verb* fly *The jet winged its way over the Atlantic to Europe.* `Col:` **clip one's wings** – limit freedom and power **on a wing and a prayer** – hopeful with a small chance of success **spread one's wings** – grow by trying new things and new places **to take someone under one's wing** – to mentor/help **try one's wings** – independence **waiting in the wings** – theater term, waiting for a chance to star **wing it** – do a new activity (often successfully) without preparation

winter /**win** tEr/ [winters, wintered, wintering] *noun* season after autumn *It snowed a lot last winter.* • *verb* spend the winter *They wintered in Florida once they retired.* `Col:` **in the dead of winter** – in the middle of winter

wish /**wish**/ [wishes, wished, wishing] *noun* hope or desire *She gave her wish away.* • *verb* hope or desire *I wish it would stop raining.* `Col:` **death wish** – dangerously reckless **grant three wishes** – standard fairy tale ingredient **Make a Wish** – foundation that grants wishes to terminally ill children and their families **wish list** – list of goals and desires **wish upon a star** – make a wish **you were here** – line from a holiday to a loved one wish **wishy-washy** – weak or indecisive **wouldn't wish that on my worst enemy** – vary bad situation

witch (which) /**wiCh**/ [witches] *noun* a woman with magical powers, usually bad *The old woman with all the cats who lives alone in the forest is a witch.* `Col:` **witch craft** – practice of sorcery **witch hunt** – persecute a victim in order to relieve social pressure **Which witch is which?** – word play

with /**wiTH**/ *prep* accompany *Come with me.* `Col:` **with child** – pregnant **with it** – in vogue or cool **I'm with him.** – a couple or support their position

women /**wi** mun/ *noun* plural of woman *The women worked together to prepare the Thanksgiving meal.* `Col:` **Men make houses, women make homes** – men build, women nurture **thinks he is God's gift to women** – conceited man (humorous) **women's movement** – raise social awareness for equal rights

wrist /**rist**/ [wrists] *noun* joint connecting hand to arm *He twisted his wrist when he fell.* `Col:` **limp wristed** – nasty remark about a man who appears effeminate **slap on the wrist** – mild rebuke

zipper /**zi** pEr/ [zippers, zippered, zippering] *noun* closing device connecting two pieces of fabric *Your zipper is open.* • *verb* close with a zipper. *He zippered his jacket to keep out the wind.*

Chapter 7
/ow/ is Gold

Chapter 7
/ow/ is Gold

although /al ThOw/

below /bu lOw/
boat /bOwt/
baloney (bologna) /bu lOw nEy/
bologna (baloney) /bu lOw nEy/
bone /bOwn/
both /bOwTH/
bow /bOw/
broke /brOwk/
broken /brOw kun/

capote /ku pOw dEy/
chose /ChOwz/
close /klOwz/ /klOws/
clothes (close) /klOwz/
coal /kOwl/
coast /kOwst/
coat /kOwt/
cocoa /kOw kOw/
coconut /kOw ku nut/
coke /kOwk/
cold /kOwld/
cologne /ku lOwn/
colon /kOw lun/
comb /kOwm/
control /kun trOwl/

devote /du vOwt/
deodorant /dEy Ow du runt/
dome /dOwm/
donno /du nOw/
don't /dOwnt/
donut /dOw nut/
dougnut /dOw nut/

emotion /Ey mOw Shun/
emotional /Ey mOw Shu nul/

fold /fOwld/
froze /frOwz/
frozen /frOw zun/
focus /fOw kus/

globe /glOwb/
ghost /gOwst/
go /gOw/
goat /gOwt/
gold /gOwld/
golden /gOwl dun/
growth /grOwTH/

hello /hu lOw/
hold /hOwld/
hole (whole) /hOwl/
home /hOwm/
hope /hOwp/

know (no) /nOw/

load /lOw/
loan (lone) /lOwn/
lone (loan) /lOwn/
lonely (lOwn lEy)
lotion /lOw Shun/
low /lOw/

motion /mOw Shun/
motor /mOw dEr/

no (know) /nOw/
nose (knows) /nOwz/
note /nOwt/
notebook /nOwt b^k/

O (oh, owe) /Ow/
ocean /OwShun/
October /oktOwbEr/
oh (O, owe) /Ow/
ohm /Owm/
old /Owld/
only /Own lEy/
open /Ow pun/
over /Ow vEr/
owe (O, oh) /Ow/
own /Own/
owner /Ow nEr/

/ ow / is Gold

phone /fOwn/
photo /fOw dOw/
pneumonia /nu mOwn yu/
Polish /pOw liSh/
post /pOwst/
poster /pOw sdEr/
posting /pOw sdiNg/
program /prOw gram/
pros (prose) /prOwz/
prose (pros) /prOwz/
protest /prOw test/

road (rode, rowed) /rOwd/
roast /rOwst/
rode /rOwd/
romance /rOw mans/
rope /rOwp/
rose /rOwz/
row /rOw/

sew (so, sow) /sOw/
shoulder /ShOwl dEr/
show /ShOw/
slope /slOwp/
slow /slOw/

smoke /smOwk/
snow /snOw/
so (sew, sow) /sOw/
soap /sOwp/
soda /sOw du/
soldier /sOwl jEr/
sow (sew, so)
stone /stOwn/

toast /tOwst/
those /ThOwz/
though /Thow/
throat /THrOwt/
throw /THrOw/
toe (tow) /tOw/
tow (toe) /tOw/

vote /vOwt/

whole (hole) /hOwl/
wont /wOwnt/
wrote /rOwt/

yogurt /yOw gErt/

although /al ThOw/ *conj* in spite of the fact *Although we don't speak the same language, we still communicate well.*

below /bu lOw/ *prep* a lower place *It's cold, it's below zero.* Col: **Look out below!** – a warning

boat /bOwt/ [boats, boated, boating] *noun* a vehicle for transportation on water *They rented a boat on their holiday.* • *verb* to travel in a boat *We like to boat at the cottage.* Col: **in the same boat** – in a similar situation **Row, Row, Row Your Boat** – children's song sung as a 'round' **slow boat to China** – the long slow route to a destination

baloney (bologna) /bu lOw nEy/ *noun* inexpensive sandwich meat *Let's buy some baloney for sandwiches.* Col: **full of baloney** – not telling the truth, exaggerating **phoney baloney** – insincere

bologna (baloney) /bu lOw nEy/ *see above*

bone /bOwn/ [bones] *noun* 1 hard part inside structure of the body of humans and animals *Don't give the dog chicken bones.* Col: **I have a bone to pick with you.** – annoyed and need to talk about it **bone dry** – no water at all **like a dog with a bone** – won't let go of an issue **skin and bone** – very thin

both /bOwTH/ *adj* two together *They both got haircuts.* • *conj* with 'and' *Both cats and dogs make good pets.*

bow /bOw/ [bows] *noun* 1 pretty ribbon in a knot to decorate a present or a little girl's hair. *She had a bow in her hair for the party.* 2 old-fashioned weapon *I bought a bow and arrow when I joined the archery club.* Col: **bow and arrow** – old style weapon **ribbons and bows** – all the fancy trimmings

broke /brOwk/ *verb* irregular past tense of *break* damaged so it can't be used *The bike broke when it fell over.* • *noun* slang have no money: *I can't go to the movies, I'm broke.* Col: **flat broke** – absolutely no money **broke up with** – ended a love relationship

broken /brOw kun/ *verb* past participle of break *After they lost the business his spirit was broken.* • *adj* apart or destroyed *Don't sit on that chair it's broken.* Col: **broken down** – not in working order **broken heart** – disappointed in love **broken promise** – commitment made and not honored or kept

capote /ku pOw dEy/ [capotes] *noun* cape with a hood *Little Red Hiding Hood wears a red capote.*

chose /chOwz/ *verb* past tense of *choose* select *He chose trade school over Harvard.*

close /klOws/ *adj* physically or emotionally near: *The chair is close to the window. My son and I are close.* Col: **a close call** – an unpleasant event that almost happened **close friends** – an emotional bond, good friends who understand and accept one another **close to my heart** – feel strongly about

close (clothes) /klOwz/ [closes, closed, closing] *verb* shut *Close the door behind you.* • *adj* end *They close the show with a fireworks display. The subject is closed.* Col: **close the deal** – finish a business transaction **closed mind** – not interested in new ideas

clothes (close) /klOwz/ *noun pl* garments worn to cover the body: *Put your clothes on.* Col: **clothes horse** – owns or wears a lot of clothes **clothes make the man** – it is important to look your best, appearance matters

coal /kOwl/ *noun* black carbon found in the earth used to burn for heat and energy: *Coal is a dirty fuel.* **canary in a coal mine** – serves as a warning to others of possible danger **coal oil** – old time fuel for lamps and stoves

coast /kOwst/ [coasts, coasted, coasting] *noun* the shore, where land meets the sea *We spend our summer vacation at the coast.* • *verb* move easily without effort or energy: *He coasted*

/ ow / is Gold

through high school but found college more challenging. **Col: coast along** – move without effort **the coast is clear** – no danger in sight

coat /kOwt/ [coats, coated, coating] *noun* 1 a piece of body clothing worn over other clothes for warmth or rain protection *Put your coat on, it's cold.* 2 fur that covers animals *Mink have soft shiny coats.* 3 liquid covering that dries *The porch needs a coat of paint.* • *verb* cover with a liquid *The city workers coated the road with tar.* **Col: coat of armor** – design on a shield to protect and identify the warrior **coat of many colors** – bible story of Joseph and his special coat **coated tongue** – white surface on the tongue from stomach acid or ill health

cocoa /kOw kOw/ *noun* 1 powder made from chocolate *Add cocoa to make chocolate icing.* 2 hot chocolate drink *Have a cup of hot cocoa after playing hockey.* **Col: cocoa beans** – seeds from the cocoa tree **cocoa butter** – creamy fat from the cocoa bean used for cooking and making skin soft

coconut /kOw ku nut/ [coconuts] *noun* large hard brown hairy seed from a tropical palm tree *Coconut is a tasty ingredient in mixed drinks and desserts.* *adj* about the coconut *Coconut palms have no low branches.* **Col: coconut milk** – clear fluid drink from inside a fresh coconut **coconut oil** – skin softening oil pressed from coconuts

coke /kOwk/ [Cokes] *pr noun* 1 a soft drink or soda *noun* 1 illegal drug *Never use coke!* 2 carbon material from coal used for fuel *Coal is refined into coke for steel making.* **Col: things go better with Coke** – product slogan that became an expression

cold /kOwld/ [colds, colder, coldest] *noun* sick with a cough and a runny nose *I caught a cold in the doctor's waiting room.* • *adj* temperature without heat *Canada is cold in January.* **Col: blows hot and cold** – keeps changing one's mind **cold blooded** – amphibian or without feeling **cold cream** – night time beauty product **cold cuts** – sliced meats **cold hearted** – without feelings **cold shoulder** – reject, turn away from someone **cold storage** – refrigerated warehouse **cold sweat** – nervous perspiration **cold turkey** – quit a bad habit in an instant **common cold** – runny nose, cough, aches **head cold** – runny nose, sinuses, headache **in cold blood** – without warning or feeling **stone cold sober** – no alcohol at all **take a cold shower** – thinking too much about sex **trail is cold** – no recent clues to follow

cologne /ku lOwn/ [colognes] *noun* liquid perfume *My favorite cologne makes my husband sneeze.* **Col: eau de cologne** – scented body perfume

colon /kOw lun/ [:, colons] *noun* 1 largest part of the intestine *There was a block in his colon and he had to have an operation.* 2 punctuation mark that introduces a list, quotation, explanation or introduction *Put a colon after his name in the letter.*

comb /kOwm/ [combs, combed, combing] *noun* thin metal or plastic grooming tool for arranging hair *Keep a comb in your purse.* • *verb* arranging or taking knots and tangles out of hair *Comb your hair after your shower.* **Col: brush and comb** – tools for arranging hair **comb the forest** – search the woods carefully

control /kun trOwl/ [controls, controlled, controlling] *noun* hand-held mechanism for using electronic devices *Where is the control for the TV?* • *verb* turning on, off, managing, volume etc *Control your temper.* **Col: control panel** – set arrangement of buttons and switches to operate equipment **control yourself** – don't show emotion or behave badly **lose control** – become upset **remote control** – wireless control device

159

devote /du **vOwt**/ [devotes, devoted, devoting] verb commitment *He is devoted to his wife and his work.* Col: **devote time, attention or resources** – give

deodorant /dE **yOw** du runt/ [deodorants] noun personal hygiene product to cover up body odor *Put some deodorant on after your shower.*

dome /**dOwm**/ [domes] noun roof the shape of half a sphere. *The city is building a dome on the stadium.* Col: **chrome dome** – slang for bald   **Sky Dome** – Toronto's indoor stadium

donno (dunno) /du **nOw**/ contr don't know, spoken word only *English is Stupid Students are Not Chapter Four /I donno what time it is./*

don't /**dOwnt**/ verb auxiliary negative form of *do* perform an action *Don't touch the kettle you'll burn yourself.*

donut (doughnut) /**dOw** nut/ [donuts, doughnuts] noun 1 deep fried snack cake in the shape of a circle *I picked up a dozen donuts for the soccer team.* 2 small spare tire *He got a flat and drove around on the donut for a week* 3 tube shape *The baby likes to teethe on the toy donut.* Col: **coffee and donuts** – popular snack

dougnut /**dOw** nut/ *see above*

emotion /Ey **mOw** Shun/ [emotions] noun feeling *Love is a strong emotion.* Col: **tugs at emotions** – affects feelings

emotional /Ey **mOw** Shu nul/ [emotionally] adj about feelings *My grandparents renewing their vows was an emotional event.* • adv with feeling *It was an emotionally charged reunion.* Col: **emotional connection** – strong unexplained bond   **emotional decision** – not logical   **emotional disorder** – no physical cause for the disease or behavior   **emotional moment** – loaded with feelings

focus /**fOw** kus/ [focuses, focused, focusing] noun 1 the center of interest *The focus of this meeting is fund raising.* 2 clear image *The pictures didn't turn out, the camera was not in focus.* • verb 1 pay attention *Focus on the horizon and you won't get seasick.* 2 adapt or concentrate vision *Focusing on the computer for too long can give me a headache.*

fold /**fOwld**/ [folds, folded, folding] verb bend on itself *Fold your clothes and put them away.* 2 cooking term, turn ingredients gently towards the middle of the bowl *Fold the cream into the dry ingredients.* 3 end a business or a hand in poker *The company folded in 2008.* • noun enclosure for sheep *Return the lamb to the fold.* Col: **know when to fold** – when to quit (expression from poker)   **return to the fold** – come back to the group after an absence   **tenfold** – multiply by   **twofold** – two reasons

froze /**frOwz**/ verb irregular past tense of *freeze* – extreme loss of heat *We went skating and my toes froze.*

frozen /**frOw** zun/ verb past participle of *freeze* turn into a solid state from liquid or *The pond is frozen so we can go skating.* Col: **frozen in time** – person or thing who stuck in one moment in the past   **frozen tag** – children's playground game   **frozen treat** – popsicles, juice sticks from the freezer

globe /**glOwb**/ [globes] noun 1 sphere shape *Globe light fixtures are popular again.* 2 model of the earth *There is a globe on the desk in the library.* 3 the earth itself *News of the trapped miners flashed around the globe.*

ghost /**gOwst**/ [ghosts] noun spirit of a deceased person *The captain's ghost haunts the ship.* Col: **ghost of a chance** – smallest possibility   **ghost town** – abandoned community   **heavenly ghost** – spirit of humanity

go /**gOw**/ [goes, went, going] verb 1 leave *Go away!* 2 encouragement *Go get'm honey!* Col: **give and go** – sports term for a passing play   **go figure** – I didn't know that   **Go for it.** – try   **go-go girl** – style of dancer from the 60's   **Go team go!** – cheer at a sports event   **go to guy/girl** –

/ ow / is Gold

knowledgeable, helpful person in a specific topic or job   **Go west young man.** — a better future is somewhere else   **on the go** – busy   **touch and go** – urgency, life and death   **way to go** – congratulations   **you go girl** – congratulations, be strong and stand up for yourself

goat /gOwt/ [goats] *noun* small horned farm animal that gives milk *My uncle has three goats.* Col: **billy goat** – male goat   **get your goat** – bother or provoke   **goat cheese** – cheese made form goat's milk   **goat's milk** – drink from goats, available in grocery stores   **nanny goat** – female goat   **old goat** – mean old man   **separate the sheep from the goats** – task or challenge to identify the weaker members

gold /gOwld/ *noun* 1 yellow precious metal used for jewelry *Our wedding rings are 24 karat gold.* 2 denotes great value *He has a heart of gold.* • *adj* rich yellow color *Her hair shone gold in the sunlight.* Col: **All that glitters is not gold.** – *proverb* on values and what is really important   **go for the gold** – strive for the highest honor   **gold coin** – rare and valuable   **gold medal** – first place   **gold rush** – migration of hopeful people to an area where gold is discovered   **gold standard** – highest quality   **good as gold** – well behaved   **the gold watch** – retirement gift

golden /gOwl dun/ *adj* 1 shiny yellow color or made of gold *She saved a golden lock of his hair.* 2 special value *Receiving the award was a golden moment.* Col: **golden age of rock and roll** – 50's and 60's   **golden boy** – can do no wrong   **golden handshake** – forced retirement   **golden oldies** – music from past generations   **Golden Retriever** – popular, large, gentle breed of family dog   **golden rule** – Do unto others as you would have them do unto you.   **golden years** – old age

growth /grOwTH/ *noun* 1 the process of growing *The analysts are anticipating economic growth this year.* 2 unusual lump of extra skin *He had that growth removed from his neck.* Col: **growth factor** – why business is improving   **growth industry** – promising future

hello /hu lOw/ [hellos] *interj* greeting *Hello. How are you?*

hold /hOwld/ [holds, held, holding] *verb* 1 grasp or grip with one's hand. *Do you want me to hold your purse?* 2 contain *This bottle holds two litres.* 3 keep *I can hold onto your papers until you get back* 4 stop or wait *Hold the plane there is one more passenger.* • *noun* 1 storage part of a ship *Put the luggage in the hold.* 2 control *He has a hold on my heart.* Col: **hold hands** – clasp hands in affection   **hold on** – wait or endure   **hold out** – strategy for making a better deal   **hold up** - robbery   **Hold your horses.** – wait

hole (whole) /hOwl/ [holes] *noun* 1 opening or space where something is missing *Dig a hole in the ground.* 2 animal's home *The mouse lives in a hole under the hedge.* Col: **A hole** – swearing   **ace in the hole** – secret weapon   **hole in one** – perfect golf shot   **hole in the wall** – small, usually rundown and dirty place   **need like a hole in the head** – don't need   **Shut your cake hole.** – be quiet (not nice)   **square peg in a round hole** – doesn't fit or belong   **toad in a hole** – cooked sausage in pastry

home /hOwm/ [homes] *noun* 1 house, place where people live. *It's getting late, I have to go home.* 2 institution for people who need care *We finally had to put grandma in a home.* 3 destination in baseball *Run home!* Col: **Be it ever so humble there is no place like home.** – special warm attachment to where one lives   **eating me out of house and home** – exaggeration usually about guests or teenagers   **Home is where the heart is** – where you love to be or your loved ones are   **home plate** –

baseball – where the runners go **home run** – round all four bases to score in baseball or to succeed **home sick** – away and missing family and friends **home sweet home** – often a sign in homes **Home, Home on the Range** – old cowboy song

hope /hOwp/ [hopes, hoped, hoping] *noun* emotion about positive wishing *Hope is sometimes all we have.* • *verb* wishing well *I hope you feel better soon.* Col: **abandon hope** – give up **faith, hope and charity** – Christian virtues **get one's hopes up** – wishing against good the odds **hope chest** – where young women store household items for when she gets married **hope springs eternal in the human breast** – optimism in unlikely odds **not a hope in hell** – unlikely

know (no) /nOw/ [knows, knew knowing] *verb* understand *I know what you mean.* 2 have met *I know Bob he was my neighbor.* 3 have the skill *Don't tease him, he knows karate.* Col: **before you know it** – very soon **in the know** – access to private news **know your way around** – familiar territory **to know you is to love you** – a compliment *you should know better* – call out bad behaviour

load /lOw/ [loads, loaded, loading] *noun* 1 carried or contained. *The truck has a load of sand.* 2 emotional responsibility *Being a single parent is a heavy load.* • *verb* 1 add things in order to carry. *Load the car and let's go.* 2 put into a device *Load the dishwasher or software.* Col: **load off my mind** – relief **loaded remark** – hidden meaning **lock and load** – ready for action (military)

loan (lone) /lOwn/ [loans, lent/loaned, loaning] *noun* gave money to be returned later *I got a loan from the bank to start my business.* • *verb* give something with the understanding it will be returned *He loaned her his car for the weekend.* Col: **loan shark** – loans money at a high interest rate **call a loan** – demand immediate return of borrowed money **take out a loan** – arrange financing from an institution

lone (loan) /lOwn/ *adj* single, only one *A lone officer made the arrest.* Col: **the Lone Ranger** – old TV show hero with a horse named Silver

lonely (lOwn lEy) [lonelier, loneliest] *adj* sad being by oneself or feeling unconnected to others *I was lonely at the party I didn't know anyone there.* Col: **lonely and blue** – from an old song **lonely hearts club** – singles together **the Lonely Planet** – tour-guide books

lotion /lOw Shun/ [lotions] *noun* cream for softening or protecting skin *Put lotion on after a bath.* Col: **body lotion** – cream for dry skin **suntan lotion** – cream to prevent sunburn

low /lOw/ [lower, lowest] *adj* 1 down close to the ground *The low benches are for the kids.* 2 sad mood *He was feeling low.* 3 soft sound *Put the music on low.* 4 almost empty *The fuel tank is low.* • *adv* 1 close to the ground *The planes flew in low to stay under the radar.* 2 down near empty *The car is running low on fuel.* Col: **get the low down on** – updated information or gossip **highs and lows** – temperature or emotional ups and downs **low blow** – disappointment from an unexpected place **low brow** – vulgar or toilet humor

motion /mOw Shun/ [motions, motioned, motioning] *noun* 1 the act of moving *The rocking motion of the swing put the baby to sleep.* 2 suggestion at a formal meeting *There is a motion to adjourn the meeting.* • *verb* gesture *She motioned for him to come closer.* Col: **man in motion** – Rick Hansen global wheelchair icon **motion sickness** – nausea, stomach sickness from moving in a vehicle **second the motion** – formally support a suggestion at a meeting **slow motion**

/ ow / is Gold

– cut the speed of action for dramatic effect

motor /mOw dEr/ [motors, motored, motoring] noun engine that powers a car or equipment *The old tractor needs a new motor.* • verb slang for get moving *We better motor or we'll miss our plane.* `Col:` motor boat – water craft powered by an engine motor home – recreational vehicle motor hotel (motel) – inn by the highway were cars are parked outside the rooms motor skills – set of movements put together to make smooth actions for example walking

no (know) /nOw/ [no's] adv 1 negative response. *No, you can't have a sleep-over on a school night.* • noun 2 negative vote. *That was a big fat no to a new cell phone.* `Col:` makes no sense – illogical no kidding – I'm surprised no way or no way José – no possibility of an event happening

nose (knows) /nOwz/ [noses] noun facial feature for breathing and smelling. *The baby has a little button nose.* `Col:` brown nose – not a nice way to gain favor (ass kiss) patronizing authority cut off your nose to spite your face – hurt yourself more hoping to hurt another follow one's nose – go where your intuition leads you hard-nosed – practical and determined often in business keep one's nose clean – behave well and stay out of trouble look down one's nose at – snobby superior attitude over someone or something nose around – look around nose for value – good shopper nose out of joint – hurt feelings nose to the grindstone – back to work no skin off my nose – doesn't matter to me or affect me pay through the nose – overpay plain as the nose on your face – obvious to everyone powder my nose – polite excuse in order to go to the toilet win by a nose – win by a very small margin

note /nOwt/ [notes, noted] noun 1 written message. *Leave me a note to say where you'll be.* 2 single musical tone *He missed a note in the chorus.* 3 importance *The election poll is an item of note in the paper today.* `Col:` compare notes – share opinions duly noted – formal I heard you end on a high note – stop at a positive point love note – affectionate, often short written exchange mental note – intend to retain without writing down take note – pay attention take notes – write down the main points of this information

notebook /nOwt b^k/ [notebooks] noun book of blank pages for writing in *Students need a different notebook for each course.*

O (oh, owe) /Ow/ [O's] noun fifteenth letter of the Latin alphabet *Open starts with an O.* `Col:` OK or okay – 👌 everything is fine O Magazine – Oprah Winfrey's lifestyle magazine OWN – Oprah Winfrey Network

ocean /Ow Shun/ [oceans] noun huge body of salt water *I've always try to visit the ocean in summer.* `Col:` as deep as the ocean – extremely ocean bed – bottom of the ocean ocean going vessel – big ship

October /ok tOw bEr/ [Oct., Octobers] prop noun tenth month of the calendar year *Halloween is October 31st I need a ghost costume.*

oh (O, owe) /Ow/ [oh's] interj surprise or dismay *Oh no!* `Col:` Oh Henry – American candy bar with nuts, caramel and chocolate

ohm /Owm/ [ohms] noun unit of electrical resistance

old /Owld/ [older, oldest] adj 1 description about age *Never ask a woman how old she is.* 2 former *There goes the old mayor.* `Col:` old boyfriend – ex-boyfriend old boy network – closed circle of men who hold community power old fashioned – traditional or

163

out of date styles, words or behaviour   Old Glory – America flag   **old hand at** – pro, proficient or good at a specific task or skill   **old maid** – spinster, negative label for an unmarried woman   **old news** – everyone knows that   **old school** – traditional   **old timer** – old man   **old wives tale** – unscientific old story with some merit   **olden days** – a long time ago   **same old, same old** – no significant news to report   **the more things change the more they stay the same** – *proverb* about patterns of behaviour

only /**Own** lEy/ *adv* 1 single time *I only called him once.* 2 insignificant *There are only crumbs left.* • *adj* single or very few *The pilot and one passenger were the only survivors.* • *conj* but or except *I would walk over only it's raining.* Col: **one and only** – very special   **only child** – no brothers or sisters   **It's only money** – sarcastic way of saying money isn't important

open /**Ow** pun/ [opens, opened, opening] *adj* accessible *We are open for business.* 2 direct and honest *We had to be open about our fears.* 3 accepting of new ideas *The principal is open to student suggestions.* • *verb* not closed or shut *Open the window and let in some air.* 2 begin *We always open the meeting with a guest speaker.* Col: **open and closed case** – straight forward, didn't take any time   **open book** – unguarded nature   **open concept** – few interior walls   **open for business** – a business became operational   **open heart** – loving and caring   **open heart surgery** – serious medical operation   **open house** – public welcome   **open mike** – anyone can speak   **open mind** – willingly considers new ideas and information   **open up** – reveal private information   **open season** – hunting term, time of the year when it is legal to kill   **open your eyes** – look at the obvious, it speaks to denial   **opens doors** – provides access to more positive experiences   **wide open spaces** – no buildings

over /**Ow** vEr/ *prep* 1 above *The clock is over the refrigerator.* 2 across *The news was broadcast over the ocean.* 3 during *She is visiting over the holidays.* 4 about *They fought over money all the time.* • *adv* 1 to a place *I'm coming over to your house.* 2 to the side *Shove over.* 3 once again *Play it over I love that song.* • *adj* 1 excess of *My grandma is over 100.* 2 end *The relationship was over.* Col: **do over** – start again and pretend the first time didn't happen   **gloss over** – avoid including detail   **head over heels** – deeply in love   **over and above** – extra good effort   **over and over** – often repeated   **over board** – literally into the sea or just too much   **over compensate** – trying too hard   **over one's head** – didn't understand the joke or information   **over rated** – not as good as expected   **over the top** – excess, too much   **over with** – get to the end quickly   **over you** – broken heart healed

owe (O, oh) /**Ow**/ [owes, owed, owing] *verb* debt *I owe money to the bank for my car loan.*

own /**Own**/ [owns, owned, owing] *adj* belongs to *He wants his own room.* • *verb* 1 possess *I own a car.* 2 take responsibility *I own my share of the blame.* *noun* acronym for Oprah Winfrey Network *OWN is a fantastic resource for learning to live a healthy lifestyle.* Col: **on my own** – by myself, no help   **own little world** – private and separate from reality or others   **own up** – confess bad behaviour

owner /**Ow** nEr/ [owners] *noun* purchaser or keeper *Who is the owner of this dog?* Col: **home owner** – own not rent a house or condominium   **owner occupied** – person who bought the property lives in it   **part owner** – shares ownership with one or more others

phone /fOwn/ [phones, phoned, phoning] *noun* short form or telephone or cell phone – device for making calls *Is that a new phone?* • *verb* make a call *Phone me when you get home.* Col: **cell phone** – wireless call device **iPhone** – small computer that makes calls and accesses the net **pay phone** – public phone that needs coins or credit card payment **phone booth** – cubicle for public pay-phone services **phone call** – phone contact **phone plan** – payment contract for using phone services **phone service** – company that sends and monitors phone signals **speaker phone** – option for calls to be broadcast through a room **telephone** – long form of phone

photo /fOw dOw/ [photos] *noun* short form of photograph *Is that a photo of your family?* • *adj* about pictures *We stopped making photo albums when we started using a digital camera.* Col: **photo album** – special book for saving pictures and memories **photo finish** – close race finish **photo shop** – technology for changing pictures **photo shoot** – pictures taken by a professional **take a photo** – take a picture with a camera or phone

pneumonia /nu mOwn yu/ *noun* fluid in the lungs from infection *He was sick with a bad cold that turned into pneumonia.*

Polish /pOw liSh/ *prop noun* people from Poland *My husband is Polish.* Col: **polish sausage** – processed meat and spices in a long thin skin tube

post /pOwst/ [posts, posted, posting] *noun* 1 support pole fixed in the ground *Who is digging the holes for the fence posts?* 2 sign or notice for others to see *OMG I saw your post on Facebook.* • *verb* mail 1 *Did you post those wedding invitations?* 2 written comment on the internet *He posted on my LinkedIn page.* • *prefix* after *post graduate, postpartum* Col: **Canada Post** – federal institution for mail delivery **dumb as a post** – not nice (stupid) **fence post** – vertical part of wooden animal or yard enclosures **last post** – military tradition, trumpet tribute to fallen soldiers **movie poster** – advertises a movie **p.m.** – post meridian – afternoon **post a warning** – written alert to the public about danger **post and beam** – type of building construction that doesn't use nails **post and rail** – type of wood fence **post haste** – in a hurry **post office** – building that processes mail **postage paid** – sender prepaid for the letter's reply

poster /pOws dEr/ [posters] *noun* large notice or advertisement *My kids have posters of Lady Gaga on their bedroom walls.* Col: **poster child** – idea example representing an organization **wall poster** – large picture with an image or message

posting /pOw stiNg/ [postings] *noun* 1 military assignment. *He finished his posting in the Far East.* 2 notice for a specific purpose *I read the job posting on the internet.* Col: **job posting** – advertizing for an employment position

program (programme – British) /prOw gram/ [programs, programmed, programming] *noun,* 1 schedule of activities *Did you keep the program from the concert?* 2 show *What is your favorite radio program?* • *verb* scheduling activities *I program special activities for my students.* 2 enter instructions into a computer *Will you please program some accounting software into my office computer?* Col: **computer program** – coded instructions for electronic devices **exercise program** – series of regular physical activities **fitness program** – long-term schedule of activities for increasing physical fitness **radio program** – radio broadcast **television program** – show on tv

pro /prOw/ [pros (prose)] *noun* 1 support an idea or movement *The* mayor is pro equal opportunity. 2 short form of professional *She is a real pro at teaching pronunciation.* `Col:` **pro-active** – taking action towards an identified goal   **pro bono** – no charge for professional services   **pro-choice** – for the right to choose to have an abortion   **pros and cons** – list of reason for and against an idea

pros (prose) /**prOwz**/ *pl noun*

prose (pros) /**prOwz**/ *noun* written language *Jane Austen writes beautiful prose.*

protest /**prOw**test/ [protests, protested, protesting] *noun* objection or complain *Greenpeace staged a protest at the White House.* • *verb* the act of objecting or complaining. *The employee's protest ended in a three month strike.* `Col:` **lodge a protest** – formally file a complaint with an organization   **mount a protest** – organize others for support against something   **the lady doth protest too much** – excessive denial that seems like guilt (Shakespeare's Hamlet)

road (rode, rowed) /**rOwd**/ [roads] *noun* long wide flat surface for driving vehicles from place to place *Be careful crossing the road.* `Col:` **bump in the road** – small setback   **down the road** – in the future   **on the road** – travelling   **road map** – motor travel reference for a wide region   **side road** – smaller road off the main road, often unpaved   **up the road** – in the future

roast /**rOwst**/ [roasts, roasted, roasting] *noun* large cut of meat *Put the roast in the oven.* • *verb* method of cooking usually in the oven, over time *The turkey is roasting and the gravy is on the stove.* • *adj* describes something heated over time *Roast potatoes are my favourite.* `Col:` **ground roast** – process of preserving beans like coffee   **oven roasted** – describes a drying process for food   **pot roast** – large piece of meat cooked on the stove, in water   **roast beef** – large cut of meat from a cattle beast   **roasting marshmallows** – puffs of sugar toasted over an open fire

rode (road, rowed) /**rOwd**/ *verb* past tense of ride *We rode our bikes to school.* `Col:` **rode roughshod over** – treated harshly

romance /**rOw**mans/ [romances, romanced, romancing] *noun* a love affair or emotional attachment *Their romance lasted a lifetime.* • *verb* actively pursuing emotional love *After years of romancing his sweetheart, she agreed to marry him.* • *adj* 1 about feelings and emotions *What a romantic idea.* 2 Latin origin *Spanish is a romance language.* `Col:` **romance languages** – from Latin origins including French & Italian   **romance novel** – a long story about the pursuit of love   **romantic comedy** – light hearted movie about love

rope /**rOwp**/ [ropes, roped, roping] *noun* long cord of tightly woven fibres *He needs a rope to tie up the dog.* • *verb* to catch with a rope or lasso *The cowboys roped the calves and branded them.* `Col:` **at the end of one's rope** – at the emotional limit, stressed out   **learn the ropes** – learn how things are usually done at a new job   **on the ropes** – boxing term, in a bad position, about to lose   **roped and tied** – can't get away   **roped in** – manipulated, tricked and taken advantage of   **rope off** – separate an area with rope, for example a crime scene

rose /**rOwz**/ [roses, rosier, rosiest] *noun* beautiful flower with sharp thorns *Roses are my favorite flower.* • *adj* light pink *She wore a rose satin gown to the formal.* • *verb* past tense form of *rise* get up *The sun rose this morning at 7:53.* `Col:` **a rose by any other name...** (Romeo and Juliet) – names don't matter only what you are   **everything is coming up roses** – success after effort or struggle   **Roses are red violets are blue...** –

/ ow / is Gold

famous children's love poem **rose bush** – flowering rose shrub **rose-colored glasses** – too optimistic an outlook **rose garden** – spectacular garden with only rose plants **rose hip** – fruit of the rose plant **rosy cheeks** – healthy facial color

row /rOw/ [rows, rowed, rowing] *noun* things people arrange in a straight line *Corn is planted in rows.* • *verb* propel a small boat using oars *Row the lifeboats to shore.* `Col:` **in a row** – consecutively **Row row row your boat...** – famous children's song sung in a *round*, also useful for ESL **row house** – identical houses side by side, sharing a wall, town house **tough row to hoe** – long-term difficult life/situation

sew (so, sow) /sOw/ [sews, sewed, sewing] *verb* to stitch with a needle and thread *She sews her own clothes.* `Col:` **sew up** – finish

shoulder /shOwl dEr/ [shoulders, shouldered, shouldering] *noun* joint where the arm is attached to the body *He strained his shoulder lifting heavy bags of flour.* • *verb* carry weight or responsibility *She shouldered extra responsibility when her boss was away.* `Col:` **dislocated shoulder** – painful unlocking of the shoulder joint **off the shoulder** – hairstyle above or dress below the shoulder **shoulder bag** – purse with a long strap to carry on the shoulder **shoulder of the road** – unpaved edge on each side of the road **shoulder responsibility** – take on **shoulder the blame** – accept full responsibility for a bad outcome **shoulder to shoulder** – stand or work close together **shoulder to the wheel** – work physically hard at a task

show /shOw/ [shows, showed, showing] *noun* 1 exhibition, movie or live performance *Let's go to the show this weekend.* 2 outward appearances to impress others *The fancy car is just for show they don't really have any money.* • *verb* demonstrate *Show me how the program works.* 2 display or exhibit *Are you showing your dog this year?* `Col:` **car show, cat show, dog show, horse show...** – exhibitions of performance and appearance **let's get this show on the road** – motivate a group to get moving **no show** – someone expected didn't arrive **peep show** – old-fashioned coin operated sex video **show business** – film and live performance industry **show no mercy** – be severe with your conquered opponent **show of courage** – behave unexpectedly and courageously **show of hands** – informal vote by counting raised hands **show of strength** – demonstrate support, character or power **show off** – vain behaviour to impress others **show someone the door** – throw unwelcome people out **show stopper** – brilliant moment or entry in a performance **show up** – arrive

slope /slOwp/ [slopes, sloped, sloping] *noun* incline *What is the slope of that roof?* • *verb* on an angle or slant *The driveway slopes down to the street.* `Col:` **ski slope** – resort area for the winter sport of downhill skiing

slow /slOw/ [slower, slowest, slowly, slows, slowed, slowing] *adv* gentle pace or rate. *He drives so slowly everyone honks.* • *verb* reducing speed *Slow down!* • *adj* 1 little amount of activity. *It was a slow day at the store.* 2 mentally methodical or challenged *He is slow but he is pleasant, honest and a good worker.* `Col:` **slow and steady wins the race** – lesson taught in the Tortoise and the Hare fable **slow as molasses in January** – very slow, almost stopped **slow motion** – stilted action **slow pitch** – recreational baseball **slow poke** – slow moving person **slow up** – same as slow down

smoke /smOwk/ [smokes, smoked, smoking] *noun* 1 dirt particles that rise from burning material *I smell smoke.* 2

slang for cigarettes *Have you got any smokes?* • *verb* cigarette addiction *I used to smoke but I gave it up.* Col: **chain smoker** – smokes one cigarette after the other non-stop **quit smoking** – break the habit **smoke and mirrors** – intentional deception using distractions **smoke detector** – fire safety device for home and workplace **smoke house** – hut for drying meat **smoke inhalation** – serious or fatal breathing in smoke fumes **smoke screen** – obscure vision in order to escape or draw attention **smokestack** – metal chimney **smoking gun** – proof **smoking hot** – sexy **Where there's smoke there's fire** – evidence of a much bigger problem to be uncovered

snow /snOw/ [snows, snowed, snowing] *noun* frozen particles of water. *There is so much snow we have to shovel the sidewalk.* • *verb* cold weather activity *It snows in the mountains in winter.* Col: **snow blower** – machine for removing snow **snow cone** – handheld treat made of crushed ice and fruit syrup **snow job** – trick or con someone

so (sew) /sOw/ *conj* preceding a reason *I thought it was going to rain so I brought an umbrella.* Col: **so and so** – polite swearing **so so** – not good, not bad

soap /sOwp/ [soaps, soaped, soaping] *noun* 1 sudsy cleaning product *There is soap in the shower.* 2 TV drama *Watching a soap opera every day is a way to learn English.* Col: **bar of soap** – unit of hand-sized washing product **soap and water** – plain and simple cleaning suggestion **soap opera** – on-going regular (usually daily) TV drama **wash your mouth out with soap** – punish a child for swearing

soda /sOw du/ [sodas] *noun* carbonated soft drink *Can you grab me a soda from the fridge?*

soldier /sOwl jEr/ [soldiers, soldiered, soldiering] *noun* person who serves in the army *620,000 soldiers died in the American Civil War, more than all their other wars combined.* • *verb* serve or behave like a soldier *Soldiering is a way of life in America.* Col: **be a soldier** – don't cry or complain **dead soldier** – empty liquor bottle **soldier of fortune** - an independent who gains wealth or pleasure from conflict **soldier on** – continue regardless of adversity

sow (sew, so) /sOw/ [sows, sowed, sowing] *verb* plant crops *Farmers sow in the spring and harvest in the fall.* Col: **reap what you sow** – good or bad, How you behave is how you will be treated.

stone /stOwn/ [stones, stoned, stoning] *noun* 1 small rock *Put those stones back on the driveway.* 2 British unit of weight equal to 14 lbs. *He weighs 13 stone or 182 pounds.* • *verb* past tense slang for being drunk or on drugs *He was stoned when drove the car into a tree.* Col: **A rolling stone gathers no moss.** – *proverb* about keeping active out of trouble **cast the first stone** – be the first to criticize **headstone** – engraved cemetery identification marker **heart of stone** – cold, unfeeling **leave no stone unturned** – search or pursue thoroughly **People who live in glass houses shouldn't throw stones.** – *proverb* to be careful about accusing others of things you also do **stepping stone** – way to move forward to something better **Sticks and stones may break my bones but names will never hurt me** – *proverb* response to being taunted by name-calling **stone blind** – can't see anything **Stone Henge** – ancient site of large stones Salisbury, England **stone ware** – type of clay pottery **The Rolling Stones** – famous British 60's rock group

toast /tOwst/ [toasts, toasted, toasting] *noun* 1 roasted slice of bread *Do you*

/ ow / is Gold

want white or brown toast? 2 clink glasses and drink to honor an event or a person *Let's drink a toast to the bride and groom.* • verb to clink glasses, drink and honor *We toasted the couple, ate dinner and danced.* Col: **toast master** — introduces speakers and makes toasts

those /ThOwz/ [that] adj plural of that *Put those flowers in water.* Col: **those were the days** — fondly recalling the past, nostalgic

though /Thow/ conj despite *He went to Europe though he didn't have any money.* • adv however *He doesn't eat meat; he eats fish, though.*

throat /THrOwt/ [throats] noun inside the neck where the voice box is *The hot chocolate burned my throat.* Col: **ENT ear, nose and throat doctor** — specialist **froggy throat** — groggy unnatural morning voice **I have a frog in my throat** — my voice sounds strange from sickness or injury **sore throat** — difficulty swallowing due to infection and illness

throw /THrOw/ [throws, threw, throwing] verb toss *Throw me the ball.* 2 host a party *I threw a party for my daughter's 2st birthday.* 3 lose on purpose *He threw the match in order to make his boss feel superior.* Col: **a stone's throw** — nearby **don't throw the baby out with the bathwater** — keep the good parts **I wouldn't trust as far as I could throw** — don't trust at all **people who live in glass houses shouldn't throw stones** — *proverb* to be careful about accusing others of things you also do **throw a curveball** — unexpected **throw a game** — lose on purpose **throw a monkey wrench in the works** — a small new piece that ruins the whole **throw a party** — host a party **throw around** — casually discuss **throw back in face** — return a nasty remark **throw caution to the wind** — take a risk **throw cold water on** — douse an idea **throw down the gauntlet** — challenge **throw good money after bad** — continue to give money to a bad investment to try and recoup loss **throw hands up** — give up **throw hat in the ring** — run for office **throw in the towel** — boxing term for quit **throw into the bargain** — sweeten the deal **throw into the pot** — add **throw name around** — name drop **throw off balance** — disorient **throw off the scent** — trick the hunters **throw oneself at** — make a fool of oneself for a romantic interest **throw oneself at the mercy of some authority** — beg **throw oneself into** — focus and apply oneself **throw rug** — small loose carpet **throw the book at** — apply full extent of the law **throw to the wolves** — not support **throw together** — causally collect **throw up** — vomit **throw voice** — project **throw weight around** — intimidate **throw your weight behind** — support

toe (tow) /tOw/ [toes] noun one of five digits on each foot. *He stepped on my toe when we were dancing.* Col: **heel toe** — cowboy dance move **pigeon toed** — feet turn in at the toe **step on someone's toes** — upstage, aggressively or inappropriately move into someone's space **toe hold** — small ledge of support for future advantage **toe in the door** — start of a connection with good prospects

tow (toe) /tOw/ [tows, towed, towing] verb pull along behind *We towed the rusty old car to the dump.* Col: **kids in tow** — brought the children **tow truck** — vehicle designed for pulling cars or other trucks

vote /vOwt/ [votes, voted, voting] noun 1 poll a group *Let`s take a vote on what kind of pizza to order.* 2 single ballot *I cast my vote for Johnston.* • verb choice *I voted for Wilson.* Col: **cast a vote** — mark your choice **right to vote** — eligibility to participate in the selection **vote against** — select 'No' **vote for** —

169

select 'Yes' or Yes's win **vote in favor of** – 'Yes' **vote on** – topic or *motion on the floor* being decided **vote out** – someone loses power or position as a result of election

whole (hole) /**hOwl**/ *adj* all *The whole class went to the zoo.* Col: **whole heartedly** – with all your enthusiasm and energy

won't /**wOwnt**/ *aux verb* negative of will future *I won't eat onions.*

wrote /**rOwt**/ [writes, wrote, writing] *verb* irregular past tense of *write* scribe *I wrote the report and left it on your desk.*

yogurt /**yOw** gErt/ [yogurts] *noun* creamy dairy food often with fruit *There's yogurt in the fridge if you want a snack.* Col: **fat-free yogurt** – low calorie **probiotic yogurt** – with active cultures for health and digestion

Chapter 8
/o/ is Olive

Chapter 8
/o/ is Olive

across /u **kros**/
all (awl) /ol/
always /ol wuz/
apostrophe /u **po** stru fEy/
audio /o dE yOw/
author /o THEr/
auto /o dOw/
August /o gust/
awl (all) /ol/

ball /bol/
body /**bo** dEy/
bottle /**bo** dul/
bought /bot/
box /boks/
broccoli /**bro** ku lEy/

call /kol/
caught (cot) /kot/
cauliflower /**ko** lEy flA wEr/
chalk /Chok/
clock /klok/
cloth /kloTH/
coffee /**ko**fEy/
college /**ko** luj/
column /**ko** lum/
comedy /**ko** mu dEy/
comma /**ko** mu/
common /**ko** mun/
conscious /**kon** Shus/
contest /**kon** test/
continent /**kon** tu nunt/
copy /**ko** pEy/
cost /kost/
cot (caught) /kot/
cotton /**ko** tun/
cough /kof/

daughter /**do** dEr/
de**pos**it /du **po** zit/
doctor /**dok** dEr/
dog /dog/
dollar /**do** lEr/

draw /dro/
drop /drop/

e**col**ogy /Ey **ko** lu gEy/
e**con**omy /Ey **ko** nu mEy/

fall /fol/
false /fols/
father /**fo**ThEr/
floss /flos/
follow /**fo** lOw/
fox /foks/
frost /frost/

genre /**jon** ru/
God /god/
golf /golf/
got /got/
gotta /**go** du/

hobby /**ho** bEy/
honest /o nest/
hospital /**ho** spu dul/
hot /hot/
hy**poth**esis /hIy **po** THu sus/

jaw /jo/
job /job/
jog /jog/

knot (not) /not/
knowledge /**no** luj/
koala /ku wo lu/

laundry /**lon** drEy/
law /lo/
lock /lok/
long /loNg/
loss /los/
lost /lost/

monitor /**mo** nu dEr/

172

/ o / is Olive

nachos /**no** chOwz/
not (knot) /**not**/

off /**of**/
offer /**o** fEr/
office /**o** fis/
officer /**o** fi sEr/
olive /**o** luv/
on /**on**/
opera /**o** pru/
opposite /**o** pu sit/
opto**m**etrist /**op to** mu trust/
oxygen /**ok** su jun/

palm /**pom**/
paw /**po**/
pocket /**po** kut/
polish /**po** liSh/
positive /**po** zu div/
possible /**po** su bul/
pot /**pot**/
poverty /**po** vEr dEy/
probably /**pro** bu blEy/
profit /**pro** fut/
property /**pro** pEr dEy/
proverb /**pro** vErb/

raw /**ro**/
re**spon**sible /ru **spon** su bul/
rod /**rod**/
rotten /**ro** tun/

salami /su **lo** mEy/
saucer /**so** sEr/
sausage /**so** suj/
saw /**so**/
schwa /**Shwo**/
shock /**Shok**/
shop /**Shop**/
small /**smol**/
sock /**sok**/
soft /**soft**/
solid /**so** lud/
song /**soNg**/
stop /**stop**/
strawberry /**stro** be rEy/
strong /**stroNg**/

taco /**to** kOw/
talk /**tok**/
talker /**to** kEr/
taught (taut, tot) /**tot**/
taut (taught, tot) /**tot**/
thermo**m**eter /**THEr mo** mu dEr/
thought /**THot**/
top /**top**/
tot (taught, taut) /**tot**/

u**pon** /u **pon**/

walk /**wok**/
wall /**wol**/
wallet /**wo** lut/
wanna /**wo** nu/
want /**wont**/
wash /**woSh**/
watch /**woCh**/
water /**wo** dEr/
wrong /**roNg**/

yacht /**yot**/

across /u **kros**/ *prep* from one side to the other *He reached across the table for the salt.* `Col:` across the board – equally   come across – unplanned meeting or finding

all (awl) /**ol**/ *adj* 1 total, entire *All whales are mammals.* 2 any *The runner gave up all hope of finishing the race.* • *adv* each *The score for the match was two all.* • *noun* everything *All is well.* `Col:` all along – from the beginning   all in – exhausted or fully committed   all in all – considering the choices   all of – not more than   all of a sudden – unexpected   all or nothing – 100% or 0   all the same – of no difference   all there – fully able   at all – in any way   give it your all – extreme effort

always /**ol** wuz/ *adv* 100% of time *Old Joe always needs a nap in the afternoon.* `Col:` It's always darkest before the dawn. – *proverb* situation that seems terrible just before it improves   The first step is always the hardest. – *proverb* new efforts seem scary at the beginning   The grass is always greener on the other side of the fence. – *proverb* other people's lives seem better than one's own

apostrophe /u **po** stru fEy/ [apostrophes] *noun* 1 punctuation mark showing possession *Richard's mother is cold.* 2 a missing letter in a contraction *I'm cold.*

audio /**o** dE yOw/ *noun* sound *The audio was turned off so we couldn't hear the movie.*

author /**o** THEr/ [authors, authored, authoring] *noun* writer *Judy Thompson is the author of English is Stupid.* • *verb* create or write *Shakespeare authored many books and plays.*

auto /**o** dOw/ [autos] *noun* car *The new auto is faster than the old one.*

August /**o** gust/ [Aug., Augusts] *prop noun* the eighth month of year *August is the month between July and September.*

awl (all) /**ol**/ [awls] *noun* sharp pointed tool for punching holes in leather or wood *My dad punched a new hole in his belt with an awl.*

ball /**bol**/ [balls] *noun* 1 round object often used for play or sport *Throw the ball for the dog.* 2 formal dance party *She wore a beautiful designer dress to the New Year's Eve ball.* `Col:` ball and chain – burden   ball of your feet – thick pad below the toes   ball of fire – energetic person   ball is in your court – your turn to act   be on the ball – alert   behind the eight ball – difficult position   curveball – unexpected event   different ball of wax – completely different subject   drop the ball – let people down   get the ball rolling – initiate an action   great balls of fire! – interjection of surprise   have a ball – totally enjoy   have by the balls – vulnerable   in the ball park – in approximately the right place   keep an eye on the ball – focus   keep the ball rolling – continue on   slime-ball – sneaky underhanded individual   whole new ball game – other situation

body / **bo** dEy/ [bodies] *noun* 1 person or animal *Swimming is good exercise for the whole body.* 2 a large area of land or water *The Atlantic Ocean is a very large body of water.* `Col:` body and soul – completely   bodybuilder – person with large muscles   bodyshop – place that repairs cars   over my dead body – never

bottle /**bo** dul/ [bottles] *noun* glass or plastic container used to hold liquids *Water is sold in plastic bottles.* `Col:` bottle up – not talking about feelings   chief cook and bottle washer – one in charge usually of the home   hits the bottle – drinks a lot of alcohol

bought /**bot**/ [buys, bought, buying] *verb* past tense of *buy* purchased *She bought groceries at the store.*

box /**boks**/ [boxed, boxes boxing] *noun* 1 six sided container used for storage *My husband gave me a box of chocolates for Valentine's Day.* 2 four connected lines

/ o / is Olive

forming a square *The artist drew a box on the canvas.* • *verb* the sport of boxing – *Mohammed Ali didn't box in the Olympics.* `Col:` **boom box** – a portable music player **boxed in** – enclosed or trapped **boxer shorts** – men's underwear that fit like shorts **box office** -place to buy movie or concert tickets **box seat** – the best seats at a movie, play or concert **box spring** – part of a bed **checkbox** – place on computer screen showing options **jack-in-the-box** – a child's toy **jury box** – location of the jury in a courtroom **open Pandora's box** – uncover many unexpected problems

broccoli /**bro** ku lEy/ *noun* a green vegetable with dense florets *Broccoli is a rich source of vitamins.*

call /**kol**/ [calls, called, calling] *noun* 1 telephone conversation *There is a call for you.* 2 a chosen occupation *David heard the call then studied to become a minister.* 3 a sound made by a bird or animal *The blue jay makes loud calls during mating season.* • *verb* 1 telephone *The daughter called her mother every Sunday.* 2 to name *They called the baby Judy.* 3 visit *The son calls on his father at home daily.* 4 summon *Duty called him to serve his country.* `Col:` **call off** – cancel **call on** – choose or visit **call to arms** – ready for war **crank call** – a mean trick telephone call **last call** -final chance of the night to order food or drink **on call** -available for an emergency telephone call **person's calling** – destiny **prank call** – practical joke less vicious than a crank call **recall** – company asks customers to return defective items

caught (cot) /**kot**/ [catches, caught, catching] *verb* past tense of *catch* receive *His father threw him the ball and he caught it.*

cauliflower /**ko** lEy flA wEr/ *noun* a large white vegetable *Cauliflower tastes best with melted cheese and pepper.*

chalk /**Chok**/ [chalks, chalked, chalking] *noun* small round bars of white or colored limestone *We need more chalk for the blackboard.* • *verb* using chalk *Gymnasts chalk their hands to keep them from slipping.* `Col:` **chalk board** – dark slate for writing on with chalk **chalk it up to experience** – *keep the good lesson of experience from a bad event* **chalk off a list** - *know chalk from cheese* – be able to tell a difference

clock /**klok**/ [clocks] [clocks, clocked, clocking] *noun* 1 a device that displays time ☉ *The clock beside my bed has an alarm.* 2 time in general *He wants a sales job, off the clock.* • *verb* to time a person's activity *The Olympic runner clocked a new world record.* `Col:` **against the clock** – in a rush **around the clock** – 24 hours **beat the clock** – finish an activity before a deadline **clock in** – record arrival time **clock out** – record leaving time **face that could stop a clock** – un-attractive looking person **o'clock** – state the hour **punch a clock** – record work time **turn back the clock** – change time back to an earlier age

cloth /**kloTH**/ *noun* 1 fabric *I want cloth seats in my new car.* 2 a small square of material for cleaning *Please pass me a cloth to wipe the baby's face.* `Col:` **cut from the same cloth** – similar values and disposition **dishcloth** – cloth used for washing dishes **man of the cloth** – priest

coffee /**ko**fEy/ [coffees] *noun* a hot drink made from roasted coffee beans *Coffee is a popular morning drink.* `Col:` **coffee break** – short break from work **coffee table** – small table in the living room **wake up and smell the coffee** – notice what's happening

college /**ko** luj/ [colleges] *noun* education after high school *The student attended college to be a nurse.* `Col:` **old college try** – extra effort

HOW DO YOU SAY? PRONUNCIATION DICTIONARY

column /ko lum/ [columns] *noun* 1 a designated space for one writer in a newspaper *The ESL story is in the third column of the second page of today's newspaper.* 2 a space that goes from top to bottom *The Excel spreadsheet had 4 rows and 10 columns.* 3 a structure that stands tall *There are two big white columns in front of the White House entrance.*

comedy /ko mu dEy/ [comedies] *noun* 1 a funny show *'Modern Family' is a popular comedy show on tv.* 2 a genre or type of entertainment *I like comedies because they make me laugh.* `Col:` **sitcom** – comedy TV program

comma /ko mu/ [commas] *noun* punctuation mark – , – indicates a pause, list or separates large numbers *He paid $250,000 for his share of the business.*

common /ko mun/ *adj* 1 usual *Rice is a common food in Asia.* 2 public *Missionaries work for the common good.* `Col:` **a lot in common** – shared values and interests **common cold** – ordinary cough and runny nose **common ground** – areas or ideas where both parties agree **common sense** – practical **common thread** – idea chain **lowest common denominator** – math term in division or the common element across many situations **the common touch** – rich people who connect easily with the poor

conscious /kon Shus/ *noun* 1 awake *He just awoke from a coma so he is conscious now.* 2 aware of *Are you conscious of the fact that you spit when you talk?* • *adv* choose with awareness *Becoming a vegetarian was a conscious decision I made as a teenager.* `Col:` **gaining consciousness** – awaken from a sleep or coma **unconscious** – not aware of something or not awake after a head injury

contest /kon test/ [contests] *noun* a competition *The school ran an essay contest.* `Col:` **no contest** – win by a large margin **not going to win any beauty contests** – not attractive

continent /kon tu nunt/ [continents] *noun* one of seven main land masses on earth *Africa, Antarctica, Asia, Australia, Europe, North America, and South America are continents.*

copy /ko pEy/ [copies, copied, copying] *adj* similar appearance *Is that a copied text from the copy machine or the original page?* • *noun* exactly the same as *Leave a copy of the report on my desk before you go today.* • *verb* to duplicate *I copied the list on the back of an envelope and now I can't find it.* `Col:` **carbon copy** – an exact duplicate **copycat** – intentionally dresses or behaves the same as another **copier** – a machine that creates duplicate images **copyright** – legal ownership **make a copy** – duplicate **photocopy** – use the machine to duplicate a document or image

cost /kost/ [costs, cost, costing] *noun* the price *The cost of the house was more than they could afford.* • *verb* is valued at *Those shoes cost too much.* `Col:` **at all costs** – no matter the price **cost a fortune** – very expensive **cost a pretty penny** – expensive **cost and arm and a leg** – very expensive **cost one dearly** – emotional or monetary loss **cost out** – research the total expense of a project

cot (caught) /kot/ [cots] *noun* small bed *The hotel set up a cot in the room for their son.*

cotton /ko tun/ *noun* type of fabric *That summer dress is made from a light cotton.* `Col:` **cotton candy** – snack food commonly found at fairs **cotton onto** – become aware **wrap one in cotton wool** – overprotect

cough /kof/ [coughs, coughed, coughing] *noun* sound in throat from a cold *The sick girl had a loud cough* • *verb* expel from the lungs *She coughed for two weeks before her cold started to get better.* `Col:` **cough up** – pay amount owing **cough one's head off** – bad cough

/ o / is Olive

daughter /do dEr/ [daughters] *noun* relationship of female child to her parent *She is my only daughter.* Col: like mother like daughter – *proverb* to mean daughters tend to look and act like their mothers

de**po**sit /du **po** zit/ [deposits, deposited, depositing] *noun* 1 money put in the bank *He made a large bank deposit from yesterday's sale.* 2 partial payment *The landlord wanted a deposit of $100 to hold the apartment.* • *verb* give or return *He deposited all his money into the bank.*

doctor /dok dEr/ [doctors, doctored, doctoring] *noun* a trained medical professional or someone with a PhD *I sprained my ankle and had to go to the doctor.* • *verb* change or treat something *The chef doctored the recipe to make it spicy.* Col: an apple a day keeps the doctor away – *proverb* about eating nutritiously Dr. – short form for Doctor just what the doctor ordered -what is needed for good health You're the doctor. – in a position to give orders regarding health

dog /dog/ [dogs] *noun* a popular pet *We walk our dog in the park every day.* Col: a dog in the manger – hidden threat a dog's breakfast – done badly as sick as a dog -vomiting dirty dog – bad guy dog and pony show – sales tricks dog ate my homework – excuse dog eat dog – vicious competition dog-tired – exhausted Every dog has its day. – *proverb* everyone enjoys success at some point in their life fight like cats and dogs – incompatible pair because they fight all the time go to the dogs – decay hot dog – show-off If you lie down with dogs, you will get up with fleas. – *proverb* about the quality of your friends it's a dog's life – lazy/carefree it's raining cats and dogs – severe rain storm Let sleeping dogs lie. – *proverb* avoid possible trouble by not mentioning the past like a dog with a bone – won't let go of an issue or position Love me, love my dog. – deal breaker, accept me with all my baggage lucky dog – one experiencing good fortune meaner than a junkyard dog – vicious by nature see a man about a dog – man's excuse to go and pee the tail wagging the dog a minor player is running the business top dog – boss work like a dog – work hard You can't teach an old dog new tricks. – *proverb* people don't change underdog – not expected to win walk the dog – exercise the pet

dollar /do lEr/ [$, dollars] *noun* unit of money $ *Do you have a dollar to spare for a cup of coffee?* Col: bet one's bottom dollar – be sure enough to risk everything bet dollars to doughnuts – be sure of something dollar for dollar – compare all aspects dollar signs in one's eyes – see the economic possibilities look/feel like a million dollars – look or feel pay top dollar – pay the highest price phony as a three-dollar bill – insincere person, inauthentic sound as a dollar – works well and is in good condition the almighty dollar – capitalism

draw /dro/ [draws, drew, drawing] *verb* 1 sketch *She always draws pictures of horses.* 2 take from another source *He is drawing money out of his education fund for the new car.* Col: draw a blank – can't remember draw a conclusion – decide draw a line under – instructions for a classroom exercise draw alongside – pull up beside draw aside – speak to privately draw attention to – focus on draw blood – break the skin draw near – come close draw on – borrow from draw out – stretch out the time or encourage someone to speak draw people together – pull people emotionally closer draw straws for – each person blindly pulls various lengths of straws, who picks the shortest straw must do the task

177

HOW DO YOU SAY? PRONUNCIATION DICTIONARY

draw the line — set limits   draw the short straw — must do the undesirable task   draw to a close — end   draw up — write up or pull up in a car   luck of the draw — random good or bad luck   take a draw — receive partial payment

drop /**drop**/ [drops, dropped, dropping] *verb* 1 let go/fall to the ground *He dropped the glass and it broke.* 2 discontinue *Friday is the deadline to drop the course.* • *noun* very small amount *I take a drop of milk in my tea.* `Col:` a drop in the bucket — an insignificant amount   at the drop of a hat — ready at any moment   could hear a pin drop — total silence   drop a bomb — to deliver dramatic news   drop a bundle — to spend a lot of money   drop a hint — gave a clue   drop a line — send a letter or email   drop around — come and visit   drop behind — lag   Drop dead! — get out, go away   drop everything — stop what you are doing and come now   drop one's guard — trust momentarily   drop in — visit without giving notice   drop into one's lap — receiving good fortune without effort   drop like a hot potato — get rid of as quickly as possible   drop like flies — many quitting or dying at the same time   drop names — use names of important people in order to make yourself look important   drop out — to quit school   drop the ball — let someone down   drop the subject — change topics   drop-dead gorgeous — very beautiful   not to touch a drop — to not have even a very little, usually referring to alcohol   the bottom drops out of the market — stock market crashes   the penny drops — the moment of understanding   wait for the other shoe to drop — negative connotation, stand by for the inevitable

ecology /Ey **ko** lu jEy/ [ecologies] *noun* the science of the environment *People studying Ecology are concerned about pollution.*

economy /Ey **ko** nu mEy/ *noun* [economies] state's money structure *The U.S. economy is suffering because of a recession.* false economy — what looks like a good deal now will cost more later

fall /**fol**/ [falls, fell, falling] *noun* the season after summer also called autumn • *verb* 1 drop *Rain falls from the sky.* 2 go down *The temperature usually falls in the evening.* `Col:` fall guy — take the blame for the good of the team or cause   be heading for a fall — doomed   the bigger they are, the harder they fall — the more you have the more you have to lose   easy as falling off a log — easy   fall all over — treat someone as very special   fall apart — lose emotional control   fall by the wayside — forgotten   fall down on the job — do a bad job   fall flat on one's face — great failure   fall for — romantically attracted or duped   fall for hook, line and sinker — duped, conned or tricked   fall from grace — formally well thought of but now thought of poorly   fall heir to — inherit   fall ill — get sick   fall in love — romantic attraction   fall in on — collapse   fall in place — plans came together   fall into disfavor — once liked but now disliked   fall into the wrong hands — information or items go to the wrong people   fall off the wagon — drink alcohol after being sober for a long time   fall on deaf ears — don't listen   fall on hard times — no money   fall on one's knees — pray or beg   fall out with — fight or disagree   fall overboard — accidentally go off a boat into the water   fall prey to — be a victim   fall short of — not enough   fall through — plan didn't happen   fall to pieces — emotional breakdown   fall under spell — enamoured   Let the chips fall where they may. — *proverb* accept whatever happens   Pride goes before a fall. — *proverb* — big egos make big mistakes and fail   riding for a fall

/ o / is Olive

– take risks take the fall for – scapegoat the curtain falls – death, the end

false /fols/ *adj* 1 fake, the opposite of true *The teacher gave us a True or False quiz.* 2 artificial *Actresses often wear false eyelashes.* 3 mistake *The referee blew the whistle after the runner's false start.* Col: false hope – hope that probably won't become real false move – mistake

father /foThEr/ [fathers, fathered, fathering] *noun* relationship of male parent to a child *A father's father is a grandfather.* • *verb* sire *He fathered many children.* Col: father figure – a trusted person such as a religious advisor Father Time – history personified Father Christmas – Santa Claus like father like son – child resembles and behaves like dad

follow /fo low/ [follows, followed, following] *verb* come after *She went inside, and he followed her.* • *noun* a group united by a common belief *Education Reform is gaining quite a following.* Col: *follow in someone's footsteps* – do the same job or life path usually as a parent • *follow my lead* – take cues from how another person is behaving • *follow orders* – do exactly as your superior instructs, even if you don't agree with them • *follow suit* - act similarly (from card games like Bridge) • *follow the crowd* – is a negative comment about not making up one's own mind • Follow the leader – a children's copy cat game • *follow through* – see a project to the end • *follow to the ends of the Earth* – love and devotion • *follow up* – check in after the fact • *follow your nose* – trust your instincts and act on them

fox /foks/ [foxes] *noun* a wild animal related to the wolf and dog family *A red fox is small and cunning.* Col: outfox – trick sly as a fox – smart and sneaky

floss /flos/ [flosses, flossed, flossing] *noun* silky thread used for cleaning between teeth *The floss is in the bathroom cupboard.* • *verb* clean teeth with floss *I floss every morning and every night.* Col: dental floss – thin string for cleaning between teeth

frost /frost/ [frosts, frosted, frosting] *noun* thin coating of ice *A bad frost can damage plants.* • *verb* spread a thin layer *We frosted the birthday cake with chocolate icing.*

genre /Zhon ru/ [genres] *noun* type *My favorite genre of movie is romantic comedy.* * Genre is the only word in English that begins with the sound /Zh/.

God /god/ [Gods] *prop noun* supreme being *Egyptians worshipped many Gods.* Col: act of God – natural forces God bless you – wishing someone to have good fortune God-given right – deserving God forbid – I hope not God helps them that help themselves – opportunity and success comes to hard workers God only knows! – I don't know God rest her soul – bless the deceased man of God – religious professional Col: play God – make decisions for others without their permission thank God – express gratitude There but for the grace of God – appreciate good fortune think God's gift to women – man who thinks he is attractive to women

golf /golf/ [golfs, golfed, golfing] *noun* outdoor sport where small white balls are hit into small holes *Golf originated in Scotland.* • *verb* play the sport *She golfs on weekends while he cleans the house.* Col: golf cart – small car used on golf courses golf club – piece of equipment for playing golf golf course – special playing field

got /got/ [gets, got getting] *verb* past tense of *get* receive *I got paid for teaching children.* Col: A man's got to do what a man's got to do – *proverb* person's destiny Cat got your tongue? – speak up give it all you've got! – try one's best, enthusiastic support got game –

179

HOW DO YOU SAY? PRONUNCIATION DICTIONARY

excited about an activity and performing well   got it bad – in love   got to go – must leave   haven't got all day – hurry   If you've got it, flaunt it! – be proud of one's good qualities   one that got away – love or opportunity that was missed   You've got to be kidding! – disbelief

gotta /**go** du/ *contr* got to, spoken word only *English is Stupid Students are Not Chapter Four /I gotta go home now./*

hobby /**ho** bEy/ [hobbies] *noun* activity for pleasure *Her favorite hobby was riding horses.* Col: hobby horse – rocking horse

honest /**o** nest/ *adj* truthful *A nun is always honest.* Col: honest as the day is long – very honest   Honest Abe – Abraham Lincoln   make an honest woman of her – marry a woman

hospital /**ho** spu dul/ [hospitals] *noun* medical care center *She broke her leg so they rushed her to the hospital.*

hot /**hot**/ [hotter, hottest] *adj* 1 giving off or holding heat *Be careful! The plate is hot.* 2 slang for new and exciting *Tell me all the hot news.* Col: in hot water – in trouble   blow hot and cold – sometimes for and sometimes against   full of hot air – all talk no action   have the hots for – attracted to   hot and bothered – aroused   hot dog – sausage in a bun   Hot dog! – surprise   Hot enough for ya? – kidding about very hot weather   hot off the press – fresh news   hot spot – center of excitement   hot stuff – currently popular   hot ticket – desired, hard to get   in the hot seat – uncomfortable focus of the group or boss's attention   not so hot – just okay but not great   sell like hotcakes – sell quickly   Strike while the iron is hot. – *proverb* act now take the opportunity before it is gone

hy**po**thesis /hIy **po** THu sus/ *noun* idea or explanation without assuming it's true *Her hypothesis sounds good, now all she must do is prove it.*

jaw /**jo**/ [jaws] *noun* lower part of the mouth that can move *My jaw ached after my tooth was pulled.* Col: jaw dropped – surprised   snatch victory from the jaws of defeat – win at the last second

job /**job**/ [jobs] *noun* 1 paid work *My first job was in a grocery store.* 2 task *He did a good job putting in a garden.* Col: bang-up job – good work   Don't give up the day job! – have no talent for new activity   hatchet job – messy work   inside job – betray trust or position to bring harm to   lie down on the job – working with very little effort   nine-to-five job – office work from nine a.m. to five p.m.   snow job – lie   walk off the job – quit, strike

jog /**jog**/ [jogs, jogged, jogging] *verb* 1 slow steady run for exercise *They jog to the park every morning.* 2 tiny push *Music can jog one's memory about past times.* Col: jog in place – run for exercise without going forward

knot (not) /**not**/ [knots, knotted, knotting] *noun* 1 tie a rope *Make a knot so the dog stays tied to the tree.* 2 scar or mark in wood where a branch grew out *Pine has many beautiful distinctive knots.* 3 measure of speed for boats *We traveled at 30 knots for most of the afternoon.* • *verb* create or fasten a knot *She knotted her wool when she finished the mittens.* Col: knot a tie – tie a necktie   tie the knot – get married

knowledge /**no** lij/ *noun* education or information *I had no knowledge of his business.* Col: A little knowledge is a dangerous thing. – *proverb* too confident leads to mistakes   carnal knowledge – sex   Knowledge is power. – *proverb* – the more one knows, the more choices one has   to the best of one's knowledge – based on the information at hand

ko**a**la /ku **wo** lu/ [koalas] *noun* Australian mammal that looks like a teddy bear and carries its young in a pouch

/ o / is Olive

Koala bears live in the trees and eat eucalyptus leaves.

laundry /**lon** drEy/ *noun* 1 clothes and linens that are dirty or have just been washed *Put your laundry in the basket not on the floor.* 2 room or container where clothes are cleaned *Put your dirty clothes in the laundry.* Col: air your dirty laundry in public – tell private family problems   laundry detergent – special soap used to clean clothing   laundry list – list of tasks to complete

law /**lo**/ [laws] *noun* rules for society to follow *It is against the law to drive without a seatbelt.* Col: above the law – think one is exempt from the law   bend the law – ask for flexibility   break the law – commit a crime   in the eyes of the law – according to the society's rules   lay down the law – set rules   long arm of the law – there is no escaping the law   Possession is nine-tenths of the law – *proverb* one who has it keeps it   take the law into one's own hands – act illegally   on the wrong side of the law – criminal behavior   the law of averages – predict the possibility of a specific event   the law of the jungle – the strongest animals will survive   there's no law against – no official restriction   One's word is law. – verbal promise

lock /**lok**/ [locks, locked, locking] *noun* 1 mechanical device for keeping others from opening 🔒 *The locks on the windows and doors keep out the thieves.* 2 piece of hair *One tiny lock curled permanently on Elvis's brow.* • *verb* fasten with a key. *The door locks automatically when it closes.* Col: lock horns – argue   lock, stock and barrel – everything   lock up – arrest or secure away   pick a lock – open without a key   under lock and key – store safely

long /**loNg**/ [longer, longest] *adj* 1 length in distance or time *Have an apple, it is a long time until supper.* Col: a little will go a long way – use a little amount be long in the tooth – old   before long – soon   come a long way – improved a lot   in the long run – over time   it's a long story – explanation list as long as one's arm – long list   long arm of the law – lawbreakers can't hide and will be caught   long face – sad   long haul – far to travel   long shot – unlikely odds   long for – miss   long gone – dead or departed   long story short – in a few words   long time no see – haven't seen someone for a while   long-winded – boring speaker   not long for this world – dying   so long – good bye

loss /**los**/ [losses] *noun* 1 can't keep or continue *The loss of that job left him in deep trouble financially.* 2 defeat in a game or contest *The loss put our team at the bottom of the league.* Col: at a loss for words – speechless   cut one's losses – walk away from a losing investment before losing more   dead loss – nothing saved   one man's loss is another man's gain – *proverb* when one loses something another gets it

lost /**lost**/ [loses, lost, losing] *verb* past tense of verb *lose* failure to keep *I lost my gloves* 2 failure to win *We lost the game.* Col: get lost – go away   He who hesitates is lost. – *proverb* act quickly or the opportunity will be gone   lost cause – no chance of improvement or return   lost in thought – distracted   lost it – got angry   make up for lost time – hurry after a setback or separation to catch up   'Tis better to have loved and lost than never to have loved at all. – *proverb* meaning love is so great that it is worth the risk of sadness of loss

monitor /**mo** ni dEr/ [monitors, monitored, monitoring] *noun* 1 computer screen *I had to buy a new monitor.* 2 student classroom helper *Bobby is the attendance monitor this week.* • *verb* check, look at over time *The doctor monitored his patients carefully.*

nachos /**no** ChOwz/ *noun* Mexican food, tortilla chips covered in cheese and salsa *My son always orders nachos when we eat out.*

not (**knot**) /not/ *adv* negative *It is cloudy but it is not raining.* `Col:` **not a big deal** – not important   **not a chance** – no possibility   **not a clue** – no idea   **not a dry eye in the house** – all people are crying   **not a problem** – you're welcome

off /of/ *adj* opposite of on, not operating *The car engine is turned off.* • *adv* 1 away from job or duty; away from location *Teachers often take two months off during the summer.* 2 not supported or connected *The child fell off his bike.* `Col:` **a goof-off** – person who wastes time or should be working   **better off** – improved situation   **blow off steam** – release of frustration, anger or extra energy   **brush off** – rejected, ignored   **buy off** – money in exchange for silence or other 'bad' activity   **call off** – cancel   **chip off the old block** – similar to their father   **cool off** – calm down   **cut off one's nose to spite one's face** – revenge your enemy and accidentally hurt yourself   **fly off the handle** – suddenly display anger   **go off on a tangent** – change to unrelated topics while speaking   **goof off** – waste time   **lay off** – fire from job perhaps temporarily   **Mexican standoff** – argument neither party is trying to resolve   **mouth off** – rude backtalk   **off balance** – dizzy or a bit crazy   **off base** – wrong   **off center** – not in the middle   **off color** – rude joke or remark   **off the wall** – crazy   **sign off**- get off computer or say goodbye

offer /o fEr/ [offers, offered, offering] *noun* what is being presented *The house offer was too low so we didn't accept it.* • *verb* present an idea or thing to be accepted or refused *They offered a reasonable price for the house and it was accepted.* `Col:` **make an offer** – offer a price or solution   **offer you can't refuse** – a threat

office /o fis/ [offices] *noun* 1 place of professional business *He goes to the office to work every day at 8:30.* 2 position of trust *The office of mayor has a four year term.* `Col:` **corner office** – the best office in the building, given to a high level employee   **forced out of office** – dismissed with disgrace from an elected position   **home office** – space in the house dedicated to work   **take office** – start an elected position

officer /o fi sEr/ [officers] *noun* 1 person in a position of trust and authority either in government or business *As an officer of the law, he was called on to arrest the protesters.* 2 military ranking *He took command when his commanding officer was wounded.* `Col:` **customs officer** – officer whose job it is to protect a country's border by monitoring who and what enters   **officer and a gentleman** – very good man   **police officer** – enforces the law at the community level

olive /o luv/ [olives] *noun* 1 the small oval fruit from the Mediterranean evergreen tree *I like olives on my hotdog.* 2 a light yellowish green *Olive looks good on people with green eyes.* • *adj*, the color olive *Olive green is common in army clothes.* `Col:` **offer an olive branch** – gesture of peace

on /on/ *prep* 1 above and held by *The glass is on the table.* 2 near *Our cottage is on the river.* 3 time indicator *We got home on Tuesday.* 4 by way of *We talked on the phone.* `Col:` **and so on** – and there is more   **be on to** -be aware of   **big on** – likes   **brush up on** – review information or skills   **can bank on** – can depend on   **carry-on** – small bag taken on airplanes   **carry on** – continue what you were saying or doing   **chip on one's shoulder** – visible resentment in a person   **come on** – sexual invitation   **count on** – can rely on   **creep up on** – surprise

/ o / is Olive

quietly **get the show on the road** – get started **get up on the wrong side of the bed** – grumpy **go back on** – break a promise **go on record** – publically announce **have pity on** – feel sorry for **have one's head on a chopping block** – in serious immediate trouble **hit the nail on the head** – get it exactly **Johnny-on-the-spot** – portable toilet **keep an eye on** – watch carefully **keep your shirt on!** – be patient **know which side one's bread is buttered on** – respect provider **make your hair stand on end** – frightened **on account of** – because **on a dime** – quickly stop or turn **on an even keel** – evenly **on a roll** – momentum from many things going well **on a silver platter** – rich or spoiled **on edge** – nervous **on foot** – by walking **on hand**- ready, nearby **on loan** – given temporarily **on occasion** – sometimes **on one's toes** – ready **on pins and needles** – nervous **on principle** – according to values **on purpose** – with intention **on sale** – discounted price **on second thought** – reconsider the original decision **on-site** – at the location **on tap** – cheaper beer from a keg **on the coat-tails** – result of another's efforts **on your last legs** – tired **on your own** – alone **on the air** – on TV or radio live **on the ball** – quick mentally **on the blink** – broken **on the contrary** – of the opposite opinion **on the dot** – at the exact time given **on the double** – quickly and now **on the mend** – healing **on the nose** – exactly **on the off chance** – in the unlikely event that **on the q.t.** – keeping this information quiet **on the rebound** – in a new relationship too soon after another has ended **on the road** – travelling **on the rocks** – unstable relationship **on the shelf** – put aside **on the spot** – now **on the spur of the moment** -unplanned **on the take** – bribed **on the up and up** – honest and above board **on the wagon** – not drinking alcohol **on the warpath** – angry and looking for someone to blame **on the whole** – in general **on time** – not early or late **on tiptoe** – walk quietly on one's toes **one-on-one** – between two people **online** – connected to the internet **new lease on life** – invigorated, refreshed after a setback **Doesn't have a leg to stand on.** – no viable defense **out on a limb** – risky **pat one on the back** – to thank or congratulate them **pick on** – tease or bully **play on words** – using words to mean something else **put-on** – lie, deception, or trick **quick on the uptake** – understands quickly **rest on one's laurels** – stop trying after a success **roll-on** – continue forward or type of deodorant **slip-on** – type of shoe, dress, or skirt that is easy to put on **slow on the uptake** – takes a long time to understand **stand on ceremony** – act formally **step on one's toes** – interfere in someone's business **tattle on** – betray by reporting another's activity **turn-on** – sexual lure **turn the tables on** – switch **turn your back on** – pay no attention to **wait on** – serve customers in a restaurant

opera /o pru/ [operas] *noun* formal musical play *Operas are often sung in Italian.*

opposite /o pu sit/ [opposites] *adj* 1 across from *The door and the window are on opposite sides of the room.* 2 most different *Right is opposite of wrong.* • *prep* facing *My desk is opposite Jane's.* `Col:` **opposite sex** – other gender

optometrist /op to mu trust/ [optometrist] *noun* doctor who specializes in eyes *My optometrist told me I needed glasses.*

oxygen /ok su jun/ *noun* gas with no color or smell *Oxygen is part of the air we breathe.* `Col:` **oxygen mask** – mouth covering used to control the amount of oxygen a person inhales

palm /pom/ [palms] *noun* 1 tropical tree with large feathery leaves 🥥 *Coconuts grow on Coconut Palm trees.* 2 lower surface of the hand between the fingers and the wrist. *Your palm is in the middle of your hand.* `Col:` **grease palms** – bribe   **in the palm of one's hand** – control over or within reach   **itchy palms** – old wives tale indicating money is coming   **palm off** – trick into taking an unwanted task or item   **read palms** – fortune telling

paw /po/ [paws, pawed, pawing] *noun* animal's foot *The dog cut his paw on the ice.* • *verb* repeatedly tapping with a paw *We let the dog out when he paws at the door.*

pocket /po kut/ [pockets, pocketed, pocketing] *adj* small enough to fit into a pocket *He carries a pocket calculator at all times.* • *noun* patch of cloth, sewn on three sides for putting things in *I keep my keys in my pocket.* • *verb* put something in a pocket *He paid in cash and she pocketed the change.* `Col:` **deep pockets** – rich   **line your pocket** – keep money   **money burns a hole in one's pocket** – spends money instantly   **out-of-pocket expense** – company doesn't pay for purchase   **pick-pocket** – thief who steals wallets without one noticing

polish /po liSh/ [polishes, polished, polishing] *verb* shine by rubbing *She polished the silver ware every Monday.* `Col:` **polish off** – eat quickly   **spit and polish** – clean and orderly, from the military

positive /po zu duv/ [positively] *adv* absolutely *The economy was affected positively by low interest rates.* • *adj* 1 sure *There was a 100% positive reaction to the color chart in the industry.* 2 Yes *He gave a positive response to the party invitation.* 3 good or agreeable *The patient has a positive attitude even though she is sick.* 4 number or amount more than zero *My bank account has a positive balance.* `Col:` **think positively** – concentrate on good things

possible /po su bul/ *adj* 1 able *It is possible to stay warm if you dress properly.* 2 perhaps, maybe *It's possible he didn't answer you because he didn't hear you.* `Col:` **as soon as possible** – a.s.a.p.   **as far as possible** – limited   **do everything humanly possible** – try very hard

pot /pot/ [pots, potted, potting] *noun* 1 cooking container used on the stove top *Warm up the soup in a big pot.* 2 marijuana *Smoking pot is illegal in many countries.* 3 container for plants *Indoor plants grow in pots.* • *verb* plant *She potted the plants in rich soil and set them in the window.* `Col:` **doesn't have a pot to piss in** – poor   **gone to pot** – fell into decay   **melting pot** – multicultural place   **pot roast** – boiled roast beef   **pot calling the kettle black** – proverb – one who isn't perfect should not criticize others   **sweeten the pot** – money in the poker pot while playing poker   **a watched pot never boils** – much anticipated events seem to take a long time

poverty /po vEr dEy/ *noun* being poor *Poverty grows when people can't work and earn money.* `Col:` **poverty-stricken** – extremely poor

probably /pro bu blEy/ *adv* likely *Schools will probably close tomorrow due to the snowy weather.*

profit (prophet) /pro fut/ [profits, profited, profiting] *noun* positive difference between earnings and costs *Microsoft's first quarter profits were up by 50%.* • *verb* benefits *The plants in my garden profited from the rain this summer.* `Col:` **profit sharing** – net earnings are divided amongst employees   **turn a profit** – make money

property /pro pEr dEy/ [properties] *noun* 1 something owned *All my property is insured.* 2 piece of land *A property in New York City is worth more than a similar one in Atlanta.* 3 characteristic *Tasteless,* odorless and colorless are three properties of water. [Col:] private property – land owned and registered on title

proverb /**pro** vErb/ [proverbs] *noun* short saying that expresses a basic truth *Proverbs pass cultural wisdom from generation to generation.*

raw /**ro**/ [rawer, rawest] *adj* 1 not cooked *Raw vegetables are nutritious.* 2 unrefined *Raw silk is an expensive fabric.* 3 rough and sore *Cold weather can leave skin chapped and raw.*

respon**sible** /re **spon** su bul/ *adj* 1 dependable *I allow my teenage son to drive my car because he is a responsible young man.* 2 being the cause of *He is responsible for paying the bills.* 3 taking care of *The babysitter was responsible for the welfare of the children.*

rod /**rod**/ [rods] *noun* a long tube or stick *I bought a new curtain rod for my drapes.* [Col:] hot rod – modified racing car   lightning rod – draws the charge from a lightning hit to the ground

rotten /**ro** tun/ *adj* 1 past ripe *The rotten bananas sat on the counter for weeks.* 2 poorly behaved *That rotten dog chewed my new shoes.* [Col:] One rotten apple spoils the whole barrel. – badness spreads to those nearby   rotten luck – bad luck   rotten to the core – evil   spoiled rotten – child ruined by the kindness of parents

salami /su **lo** mEy/ [salamis] *noun* meat in a thin skin tube used in sandwiches *Salami, mustard and lettuce make a good sandwich.*

saucer /**so** sEr/ [saucers] *noun* 1 small plate that holds a cup *My dish set includes 12 cups and saucers.* [Col:] flying saucer – UFO (unidentified flying object) space ship   eyes like saucers – eyes wide open in surprise

sausage /**so** suj/ [sausages] *noun* ground meat encased in a thin skin tube *Sausages come in a wide variety of forms including beef, pork, and turkey.* [Col:] blood sausage – made with animal's blood

saw /**so**/ [saws, sawed, sawing] *noun* a tool used to cut wood • *We used a saw to cut wood in half.* ☐ *verb* past tense of to *see* look at *He saw the students improve every week*

schwa /**Shwo**/ [/u/, schwas] *noun* the vowel sound of unstressed vowels *Schwa is the tiniest sound the human voice can make.*

shock /**Shok**/ [shocks, shocked, shocking] *noun* 1 surprise *Winning the lottery was quite a shock.* 2 a jolt of electricity *A shock ran through his body when he put his finger in the light socket.* • *verb* to surprise or do something *She shocked the neighbors when she bought a pink car.* [Col:] culture shock – depression after the arrival in a new country because the cultures are so different   reverse culture shock – worse depression after returning home

small /**smol**/ [smaller, smallest] *adj* little in number or size *She has small hands.* [Col:] big fish in a small pond – good where there is no competition   Good things come in small packages. – *proverb* valuable things are often small   small change – coins   small print – important details of a contract printed so tiny they are hard to read   small talk – meaningless chit chat   Small things amuse small minds – *proverb* people who are not intelligent are concerned with silly things   Thank heaven for small mercies. – tiny good things can make a big difference in a crisis

shop /**Shop**/ [shops, shopped, shopping] *noun* place to purchase items or services *You can usually buy earrings and other jewellery at a dress shop.* • *verb* look for or purchase from a store *I shop for vegetables at the farmer's market.* [Col:] bull in a china shop – clumsy   set up shop – start a business   shop around – compare prices before buying   talk shop

— talk about work   window-shop — look with no intension of buying

sock /sok/ [socks] noun a cloth tube foot cover *Socks are necessary in winter to keep your feet warm.* • verb punch *The boys socked each other in a fight at school and both were suspended.* `Col:` **knock one's socks off** — hit hard or impress   **pull up one's socks** — improve performance   **put a sock in it!** — shut up   **sock money away** — save money

soft /soft/ [softer, softest] adj smooth *Cats have soft fur.*

solid /so lud/ adj dependable *The employee always did his work well. He was a solid performer.* • noun not liquid or gas *A solid will melt or burn when heated.* `Col:` **solid as a rock** — dependable

song /soNg/ [songs] noun musical story or poem for singing *Little children love to sing songs.* `Col:` **for a song** — cheaply   **song and dance** — long excuse   **swan song** — final performance   **theme song** — music identified with a person or TV show

stop /stop/ [stops, stopped, stopping] noun 1 don't move *The car stopped at the corner and turned right.* 2 place *There are bus stops all along the main street.* • verb discontinue moving *"Stop right there!," said the policeman.* `Col:` **pit stop** — brief stop while travelling   **bus stop** — place where the bus picks up and drops off passengers   **homely enough to stop a clock** - unattractive looking person   **make a stop** — pause during a journey   **nature stop** — break to use the bathroom   **put a stop to** — force an end   **stop at nothing** — committed to the task or success   **stop by** — visit causally   **stop dead in one's tracks** — stop suddenly   **stop from doing** — prevent   **stop in the name of the law** - police ask someone to halt their activity immediately   **stop on a dime** — accuracy   **stop short of** — almost all   **stop the music** — hold on   **stop up** — plug preventing fluid from draining   **stop, look, and listen** — safety advice about crossing the street   **The buck stops here.** — taking responsibility, no excuses

strawberry /stro be rEy/ [strawberries] noun a red ground fruit with seeds on the outside *Strawberries are available in markets almost all year around.* `Col:` **strawberry blond** — red-blond hair   **strawberry short cake** — dessert with strawberries, cake and whipped cream   **strawberry cheesecake** — sweet rich dairy dessert with fruit

strong /stroNg/ [stronger, strongest] adj 1 physical strength to lift or carry *You need a strong person to move furniture.* 2 made well; sturdy *The table was strong enough to stand on.* 3 extreme *Blue cheese has a strong smell.* `Col:` **A chain is only as strong as its weakest link.** — proverb a team's success is limited by the abilities of the weakest member   **come on strong** — be forceful   **going strong** — going well   **strong as an ox** — physically powerful   **strong language** — offensive, arrogant or belligerent words   **strong silent type** — cliché attractive qualities in a male   **strong stomach** — tolerates graphic violence or spicy food   **strong-arm** — threaten, push or influence   **strong-minded** — stubborn   **strong-willed** — stubborn

taco /to kOw/ [tacos] noun Mexican food made with meat in a corn shell *The kids love tacos so we make sure the ingredients are always on hand.*

talk /tok/ [talks, talked, talking] noun lecture or presentation *The teacher gave a talk on world poverty.* • verb speak *She talks in her sleep.* `Col:` **pep talk** — encouraging speech   **all talk** -a lot of talk but no action   **like talking to a brick wall** — talking to someone who does not listen   **the talk of the town** — the most interesting news   **can talk the hind leg off a horse** — talks too much   **double-talk** — deceit, sneaky   **fast-talking** — usually to cover up the truth

/ o / is Olive

know what one is talking about – a true expert in a field   Look who's talking! – you are guilty, too   money talks – cash will get what is wanted   pillow talk – lovers sharing info   straight talk – honest   sweet-talk – love words   talk a blue streak – fast and a lot   talk back – rude, mouthy   talk big – exaggerate   talk dirty – sex talk   talk down to – belittle   talk in circles – not make sense   talk into – convince someone to do something   talk is cheap – let's see action   talk out of – convince someone not to do something   talk over – share ideas   talk sense – be practical or logical   talk shop – talk about work   talks the talk and walks the walk – values and actions aligned   talk tough – threatening   talk until one is blue in the face – no one is listening   we need to talk – relationship is in jeopardy or over   Who do you think you're talking to? – response to rude remarks

talker /to kEr/ [talkers] noun someone who talks a lot or can't keep a secret Don't tell Bob about the surprise party, he's a talker. Col: *a fast talker* or *a smooth talker* - liar

taught (taut, tot) /tot/ [teaches, taught, teaching] verb past tense of *teach* instruct The teacher taught non-English speakers how to pronounce the sounds of English.

taut (taught, tot) /tot/ [tauter, tautest] adj pulled tight The rope holding the boat was taut.

thermometer /THEr **mo** mu dEr/ [thermometers] noun device used for measuring temperature The nurse used a thermometer to take the sick child's temperature.

thought /THot/ [thoughts, thinks, thought, thinking] noun idea Do you have any thoughts about the new school program? • verb past tense of *think* have ideas Judy thought she had the keys but they weren't in her purse. Col: penny for your thoughts – What are you thinking about?   train of thought – fluent line of thinking   collect one's thoughts – pause to organize ideas   food for thought – something new to consider   lost in thought – concentrating hard on an idea   don't give it another thought – You're welcome.   on second thought – reconsider   Perish the thought! – too horrible to consider   school of thought – theory   Who would have thought? – shock   well-thought-of – well liked

top /**top**/ [tops, topped, topping] adj highest position The big bowl is on the top shelf. • noun spinning toy The little boy spun his toy top all day. 2 clothing, shirt She changed her top and went out to the mall. 3 the highest point The US flag is at the top of the mountain. 4 the highest rating She is the top student in the class • verb perform better The student topped his last average by 3%. Col: at the top of one's game – peak   at the top of one's lungs – loud   at the top of the hour – o'clock   at the top of the ladder – corporate success   at the top of the agenda – first   be over the top – too much   be thin on top – balding   blow one's top – get angry   carrot-top – red hair   claw one's way to the top – fought for their business position   come out on top – win in the end   from top to bottom – all   get on top of – work has fallen behind   keep on top – maintain   off the top of one's head – without researching or checking   on top of the world – happy successful   pay top dollar – high price   take it from the top – start at the beginning   the top brass – military leaders   the top dog – boss   top flight – highest group   to top it all – final thought   top of the line – best quality   top off – finale   top secret – politically sensitive   top up – refill to the brim of the glass or cup   topless – without a shirt on   top-of-the-line – most expensive or best quality

tot (taught, taut) /**tot**/ [tots] noun young child *The tot was only two but she spoke very well.*

upon /u **pon**/ prep on *She placed the plate upon the table.* Col: once upon a time – beginning phrase found in many children's books

walk /**wok**/ [walks, walked, walking] noun travel on foot *He is taking the dog for a walk in the park.* • verb move by placing one foot in front of the other *She walked slowly and quietly.* Col: all walks of life – different backgrounds   can't walk and chew gum – can't do two simple things at once   If it looks like a duck and walks like a duck, it is a duck. – don't overanalyse   learn to walk before we can run – basics before success   Take a long walk off a short pier. – leave me alone • take a hike/walk – go away   talk the talk and walk the walk – values and actions align   walk all over – take someone for granted   walk away from – leave   walk off the job – quit   walk off with – steal   walk on air – happy   walk on eggshells – be careful not to upset someone   walk out – leave   walk out on – leave a spouse   walk softly and carry a big stick – proverb – don't invite trouble but be prepared for it   walk tall – be proud   walk the plank – certain death   walk-up – an building without an elevator   walkway – path such as a sidewalk   worship the ground someone walks on – adore, love unconditionally

wall /**wol**/ [walls] noun barrier dividing two spaces *A picture of her mother hung on her bedroom wall.* Col: a fly on the wall – listen to private conversations without being noticed   bouncing off the walls – too much energy   like talking to a brick wall – no response   up against a brick wall – no options   beat one's head against the wall – frustrated   climbing the walls – anxious   drive up the wall – annoy   hit a wall – abrupt stop   hole in the wall – small out of the way place   nail to the wall – make accountable   off the wall – crazy   put up a wall – reject emotionally   The writing is on the wall. – the message of future misfortune   wall in – protect from the outside   wall off – divide a section apart   wall up – close permanently   wall-to-wall – total floor coverage   walls have ears – be discrete

wallet /**wo** lut/ [wallets] noun small folder for money *He had $20 in his wallet.*

wanna /**wo** nu/ contr want to, spoken word only *English is Stupid Students are Not* Chapter Four /I wanna go home./

want /**wont**/ [wants, wanted, wanting] noun desire or wish *His wants are many but his needs are few.* • verb desire, wish or request *ESL students want to speak English.* Col: Do you want to make something of it? – threatening offer to fight   for want of a better word – not exactly what I mean but close   I don't want to wear out my welcome – don't stay too long   if you want a thing done well, do it yourself – no one does it as well as you like   know when one is not wanted – unwelcome   The more you get, the more you want. – proverb one never has enough   want a piece of me? – offer to fight   want ad – notice in the newspaper describing something wanted   want for nothing – has everything   want in – business opportunity   want out of – withdraw from   want so bad one can taste it – strong desire for a goal   want to bet – I think I'm right   want to curl up and die – embarrassed   waste not, want not – proverb – don't waste and there is enough

wash /**woSh**/ [washes, washed, washing] noun laundry *I do the wash in the laundry room.* • verb clean *Wash your face* and hands and come for dinner. Col: it will all come out in the wash – the truth will be revealed in time   wash away – remove   wash up -clean hands and face   wash your hands of it – stop being involved in something.   washed-out – pale and tired

watch /woCh/ [watches, watched, watching] noun 1 timepiece worn on the wrist. I got a watch for my birthday. 2 take responsibility for a fixed period of time *We have to take turns standing guard, I'll take the first watch.* • verb observe for a period of time *Do you want to watch the soccer game?* Col: A watched pot never boils – too much attention makes a wait seem longer   Big brother is watching you – actions you think are private are being monitored by the government (from George Orwell's 1984)   binge watch – view consecutive episodes or movies in a series for many, many hours   keep a close watch on – monitor very responsibly   like watching paint dry – boring   not on my watch – take great care that nothing bad happens when I'm in charge   stop watch – measures lapsed time   Watch it! – warning or threat   watch like a hawk – closely monitor suspicious behaviour   watch out – be cautious   watch the clock – boredom, check the time often anxious for the end   watch the time – be careful not to be late   watch the world go by – relax   watch this space – news updates will be posted here   watch your back – be mindful of enemies   watch your language – don't swear your step – be careful moving forward

water /wo dEr/ [waters] noun clear liquid that flows from the tap *Water is important for the survival of all animals.* • verb 1 make wet *She waters the plants every day.* 2 create saliva in the mouth *Her mouth watered when she saw the cake.* Col: a fish out of water – out of place, uncomfortable   dead in the water – in trouble   in deep water – in trouble   in hot water – in trouble   water under the bridge – happened in the past   Blood is thicker than water. – *proverb* family is more important than friends   blow out of the water – amaze   bread and water – bare basics   come hell or high water – no matter what   Come on in, the water's fine! – join me, you'll like it   doesn't hold water – illogical   Don't throw the baby out with the bath water. – *proverb* keep the good parts   dull as dishwate – boring   keep head above water – barely survive   like a duck to water – natural ability   muddy the water – obscure the facts   pour cold water on – reject an idea   spend money like water – no regard for the effort to earn it, entitlement   test the water – try first   tread water – stay in one place   water down – dilute   water off a duck's back – unaffected by adversity   waterfall – water running over a ledge   watering hole – usual bar   You can lead a horse to water, but you can't make it drink. – *proverb*, can't force someone to do anything

wrong /roNg/ [wrongs] adj 1 incorrect *He had the wrong answer.* 2 inappropriate *She said all the wrong things to her new mother-in-law.* 3 against the law or what is accepted *It is wrong for governments to tax the poor.* Col: barking up the wrong tree – looking in the wrong place   dead wrong – totally wrong   don't get me wrong – don't misunderstand my intention   fall into the wrong hands – information or items go to the wrong people   get on the wrong side of the law – caught breaking the law   get up on the wrong side of bed – crabby, nothing going right   get wrong – misunderstand   If anything can go wrong, it will. – Murphy's Law   in the wrong place at the wrong time – unfortunate coincidence   not put a foot wrong -perfect performance   off on the wrong foot – bad start   on the wrong track – not going where you want to go   rub the wrong way – annoy   take the wrong way – take offence when none was intended   the wrong side of 30 etc -old   Two wrongs don't make a right. – *proverb* not okay to do the wrong thing because someone else did   wrong number – misdial the phone.

yacht /**yot**/ [yachts, yachted, yachting] *noun* small private ship *Their yacht cost more than my house.* • *verb* travel by small private ship *The Royal Family yachted around the Mediterranean for the month of July.*

Chapter 9
/ʊw/ is Blue

Chapter 9
/Uw/ is Blue

aluminum /u lUw mu num/
amuse /u myUwz/
approve /u prUwv/

balloon /bu lUwn/
beautiful /bEyUw du ful/
blue /blUw/
boot /bUwt/
broom /brUwm/
bruise /brUwz/

cartoon /kAr tUwn/
choose /ChUwz/
clue /klUw/
computer /kum pyUw dEr/
cool /kUwl/
coupon /kUw pon/
cruel /krUwl/
cucumber /kyUw kum bEr/
Cuba /kyUw bu/
cube /kyUwb/
cue (Q, queue) /kUw/
cute /kyUwt/

dew (due, do) /dUw/
due (dew, do) /dUw/
duel /dU wul/
do (dew, due) /dUw/

ewe (U, you) /yUw/

few /fyUw/
flew (flu, flue) /flUw/
flu (flew, flue) /flUw/
flue (flew, flu) /flUw/
food /fUwd/
fool /fUwl/
fruit /frUwt/
fuel /fyU wul/
fuse /fyUwz/
future /fyUw ChEr/
glue /glUw/
goose /gUws/

goosebumps /gUws bumps/
group /grUwp/

hoof /hUwf/
humor /hyUw mEr/

jewelry /jUwl rEy/
Judy /jUw dEy/
juice /jUws/
June /jUwn/

kangaroo /kaNg gu rUw/

lieu /lUw/
loony /lUw nEy/
loose /lUws/

moon /mUwn/
moose /mUws/
move /mUwv/
music /myUw zik/

new /nUw/
news /nUwz/
noon /nUwn/

perfume /pEr fyUwm/
Peru /pu rUw/
pool /pUwl/
poor /pUwr/
prune /prUwn/
pure /pyUwr/

Q (cue, queue) /kyUw/
queue (cue, Q) /kyUw/

raccoon /ra kUwn/
roof /rUwf/
room /rUwm/
roommate /rUw mAyt/
rooster /rUws dEr/
root (route) /rUwt/
route (root) /rUwt/

/ Uw / is Blue

rule /rUwl/
ruler /rUw lEr/

school /skUwl/
screw /skrUw/
sewer /sU wEr/
shampoo /Sham pUw/
shoe /ShUw/
Sioux (sue) /sUw/
smooth /smUwTh/
soon /sUwn/
soup /sUwp/
spoon /spUwn/
stew /stUw/
student /stUw dunt/
sue (Sioux) /sUw/
suit /sUwt/

threw (through) /THrUw/
through (threw) /THrUw/
to (too, two) /tUw/
too (to, two) /tUw/
tool /tUwl/
tooth /tUwTH/
toothbrush /tUwTH bruSh/
tour /tUwr/
true /trUw/
Tuesday /tUwz dAy/
tuna /tUw nu/
tune /tUwn/
two (to, too) /tUw/

U (ewe, you) /yUw/
USA /yU we sAy/
unicorn /yUw nu kOrn/
uniform /yUw nu fOrm/
union /yUw nyun/
unit /yUw nut/
use /yUwz/

view /vyUw/
viewpoint /vUw pOynt/

W /du bul yUw/
who /hUw/
who's (whose) /hUwz/
whose (who's) /hUwz/
wound /wUwnd/

you (ewe, U) /yUw/

zoo /zUw/
zoom /zUwm/

amuse /u **myUwz**/ [amuses, amused, amusing] *verb* 1 entertain or interest *The kids amused themselves by playing a new computer game.*

aluminum /u **lUw** mu num/ *noun* strong, light silver-gray metal, chemical element of atomic number 13 *The little fishing boat is made of aluminum.* • *adj* content or qualities of aluminum *Aluminum boats are light and easy to steer.* `Col:` **aluminum foil** – thin metallic sheets for wrapping food

approve /u **prUwv**/ [approves, approved, approving] *verb* 1 accept as satisfactory *He definitely approved of the idea.* 2 agree officially *The council approved of the building plan.* `Col:` **seal of approval** – accepted

balloon /bu **lUwn**/ [balloons, ballooned, ballooning] *noun* a colourful, thin rubber bag filled with gas *The child wanted balloons at the amusement park.* • *verb* 1 travel somewhere in a basket attached to a large balloon *We ballooned over the desert on a special tour when we were in Arizona.* 2 puff up, to increase in size quickly *The costs for the repairs ballooned and we ended up paying more than we had planned.* `Col:` **go over like a lead balloon** – not a popular idea   **send up a trial balloon** – make a suggestion and see what people think about it

beautiful /**byUw** du ful/ *adj* 1 pretty *Megan Fox is a beautiful woman.* 2 morally good, excellent, enjoyable *We had a beautiful meal together.*

blue /**blUw**/ [blues, bluer, bluest] *adj* 1 the colour of a clear sky *Blond haired people often have blue eyes.* 2 feeling sad *After losing her dog, the little girl felt blue.* • *noun* the color *Blue is an eye color.* `Col:` **be blue** – sad   **blue blood** – noble family   **blue cheese** – string cheese with pieces of mold   **blue plate special** – low price dinner special   **blue light special** – featured sale item in a department store   **blue movie** – an indecent, pornographic film   **blue ribbon** – a prize for excellence   **blue-collar** – factory workers   **Blue-nose II** – a famous sailboat from Nova Scotia pictured on the Canadian dime   **into the wild blue yonder** – far away   **once in a blue moon** – rarely, from the frequently of two full moons in one month   **out of the blue** – unexpected   **room was blue** – the room was full of smoke or frequent bad language   **scream blue murder** – complain or shout loudly   **swear a blue streak** – a great deal of swearing   **the blues** – a style of jazz music   **true blue** – loyal

boot /**bUwt**/ [boots, booted, booting] *noun* rubber or leather covering the foot and part of the leg *I wear boots when working on the farm.* • *verb* slang throw out *George was booted out of the bar.* `Col:` **boot up** – starting the computer   **bootleg** – liquor made and sold illegally   **die with one's boots on** – die still active in one's work   **giving someone the boot** – firing an employee   **pull up by one's bootstraps** – success after extreme independent personal effort   **shaking in one's boots** – scared

broom /**brUwm**/ [brooms] *noun* bristles at the end of a long handle for sweeping *My old broom is made of straw and my new one of thin plastic fibres.* `Col:` **broom closet** – where one hides the practice of Wicca and other pagan beliefs

bruise /**brUwz**/ [bruises, bruised, bruising] *noun* an injury that leaves a purple mark on the skin without breaking it *I hit my head on the corner of the cupboard and it left a bruise.* • *verb* receive a purple or blue mark from an injury *I fell and bruised my knee.* `Col:` **big bruiser** – a large man   **bruised ego** – loss of pride   **cruisin' for a bruisin'** – provoking a spanking

cartoon /kAr **tUwn**/ [cartoons] *noun* 1 a drawing of characters with exaggerated features *Newspapers post political cartoons in the papers.* 2 an animated tv show or movie *My son loves watching Saturday morning cartoons.* `Col:` **cartoonist** – a cartoon artist **cartoonish** – silly **cartoon character** – funny drawn or animated people or animals **Loony Toons** – silly behavior that shouldn't be taken too seriously

choose /chUwz/ [chooses, chose, choosing] *verb* select *Chose a kind, loving marriage partner.* `Col:` **choose among** – select from many candidates or options **choose battles** – decide not to argue small matters and save time and energy for important issues **choose between** – select for two options **choose one's moment** – be mindful of the circumstances when making a big announcement or request **sides** – align with one or the other of two enemies **choose up sides** – divide a group into teams **choose the lesser of two evils** – both options are undesirable but you have to pick one **choose the path of least resistance** – the easiest way to achieve your goal **pick and choose** – select combinations as one likes

clue /klUw/ [clues] *noun* helps find answers *We are looking for clues on our treasure hunt.* `Col:` **clue in** – understand without a clue/**clueless** – unsure

computer /kum pyUw dEr/ [computers] *noun* an electronic tool that manages information 🖥 *I send emails, write essays, and play games on my computer.* `Col:` **computer geek/wizard** – spends too much time on computers

cool /kUwl/ [cooler, coolest, cools, cooled, cooling] *adj* 1 moderately cold *It's cool out this morning.* 2 calm, controlled *Be cool.* 3 fashionable, attractive *Cool boots you have there!* 4 slang for forgiven *No worries man, it's cool.* • *verb* to make cool *I left the pie on the windowsill to cool.* `Col:` **cool as a cucumber** – calm **cool heads** – remains calm **cool mil-**

lion – large amount of money **Cool!** – positive approval

coupon /kUw pon/ or /kyUw pon/ [coupons] *noun* small printed piece of paper that allows a discount *My grandma clips coupons out of the paper.*

cruel /krUwl/ [crueler, cruelest] *adj* desire to inflict pain *A cruel man hits his pets.* 2 emotionally painful *Alzheimer's is a cruel illness.* `Col:` **S.P.C.A.** – Society for the Prevention of Cruelty to Animals **You have to be cruel to be kind.** – hurting someone to help them in the long term

cucumber /kyUw kum bEr/ [cucumbers] *noun* a long dark green fruit that is grown in vegetable gardens *Cucumber sandwiches are nice in summer.* `Col:` **cool as a cucumber** – calm

Cuba /kyUw bu/ *prop noun* a Spanish-speaking island nation in the Caribbean. *We went to Cuba on holiday last winter.*

cube /kyUwb/ [cubes, cubed, cubing] *noun* 1 a three dimensional shape with six squares and four corners *A six sided die is in the shape if a cube.* • *verb* multiply any number by itself twice *two times two times two is two cubed.* $2 \times 2 \times 2 = 2^3$. `Col:` **cubic area** – measurement determined by length $\times$ width $\times$ height **cube root** – mathematical term **Rubik's cube** – a puzzle with many coloured squares on a cube

cue (Q, queue) /kUw/ [cue, cued, cuing] *noun* signal *Opening the curtain was his cue to go on stage.* • *verb* give a signal *The maestro cued the orchestra.*

cute /kyUwt/ [cuter, cutest] *adj* 1 loving, charming *Puppies are cute.* 2 slang for clever, shrewd *That was a cute deal you made.* `Col:` **cutie, cutie pie** – a sweet little boy or girl **cute as a button** – adorable

dew (do, due) /dUw/ *noun* moisture on the grass *You can see the dew on the grass in the morning.*

due (dew, do) /dUw/ *adj* a deadline *This bill is due on Friday.* • *noun* 1 appropriate or deserved *You have to give him his due in this matter.* 2 fees, tolls *Members pay dues every year.* • *adv* because of *He was wearing a bandage due to a recent fall.* **Col: due north** — straight towards north **give the devil his due** — give credit to someone you don't like when they do a good job **in due time** — not rushing **paid his dues** — worked hard for what he got

duel /dU wul/ [duels, dueled, duelling] *noun* a formal fight where rival s face each other *The duel took place outside the saloon.* • *verb* fight in facing pairs *The officer said he would duel to the death in order to defend the lady's honor.*

do (dew, due) /dUw/ [does, did, doing] *verb* 1 perform or carry out *Could you do me a favor?* 2 make or provide *Another piece of pie will do me just fine.* **Col: a big to-do** — big fuss **do away with** — get rid of **do her in** — finish or kill **do out of** — steal or trick what is rightfully another's **done for** — failure or death **I do** — marriage vows **It's doable.** — possible to accomplish **make do** — work with what is available although it's not ideal **nice do** — sarcastic comment on a new hairstyle **That will do.** — stop now **well-to-do** — rich **When in Rome, do as the Romans do.** — *proverb* to accept and participate in foreign culture

ewe (U, you) /yUw/ [ewes] *noun* adult female sheep *The ewe had twin lambs this spring.*

few /fyUw/ [fewer, fewest] *adj* some, but not many *There were only a few strawberries in the yoghurt.* **Col: a few choice words** — curse words to express anger **few and far between** — rare **man of few words** — a quiet man

flew (flu) /flUw/ [flies, flew, flying] *verb* past tense of *fly* travel through the air *We flew home from Europe in August.*

flu (flew) /flUw/ [flues] *noun* common sickness with a cough and fever *I had a bad flu last winter.*

flue (flew, flu) /flUw/ [flues] *noun* hollow pipe in the middle of a chimney *Open the flue or the smoke will fill the house.*

food /fUwd/ *noun* living things eat *We buy food at the grocery store to cook at home.* **Col: food for thought** — considering something

fool /fUwl/ [fools, fooled, fooling] *noun* 1 unwise *She thinks her boss is a fool.* 2 employed by a nobleman for entertainment *The fool in medieval times was also known as the court jester.* • *verb* trick or deceive *You can't fool me.* **Col: fool about** — being silly **fool's gold** — bright yellow metal in rock that looks like gold **fool's paradise** — false happiness **foolhardy** — irresponsible **foolproof** — works every time for everyone **make a fool of** — embarrass intentionally **play the fool** — deceive by pretending to be stupid **sent on a fool's errand** — unnecessary chore meant to occupy someone's time **tom-foolery** — silliness

fruit /frUwt/ *noun* edible seeds from a plant *Apples are my favourite fruit.* **Col: Be fruitful and multiply** — have many children **bear fruit** — a plant with fresh fruit **fruitless efforts** — no reward for hard work **fruits of labour** — benefits of working **He is a fruit.** — slang for homosexual

fuel /fyU wul/ [fuels, fueled, fuelling] *noun* any resource used to create energy *Fossil fuels are being replaced by renewable energy sources.* • *verb* 1 burning materials to make heat *The wood chips fuel our fire.* 2 create excitement *The protest was fueled by the anger of the workers.* **Col: fuel one's passions** — add more energy to an area of high interest **fossil fuels** — natural resources such as coal

fuse /fyUwz/ [fuses] *noun* a trigger for an explosion *We lit the fuse to set off the dynamite.* • *verb* joining objects *A blowtorch is used to fuse metals together.* **Col:**

/ uw / is Blue

short fuse – easily angered   **blow a fuse** – get angry

future /**fyUw** ChEr/ *noun* what will come *Everyone will have access to the internet in the future.* • Col: **in future** – from now on   **in the future** – distant time ahead   **future shock** – surprisingly rapid change

glue /**glUw**/ [glues, glued, gluing] *noun* sticky substance for attaching things together *I need glue to make a scrapbook.* • *verb* stick things together *The children are gluing macaroni on construction paper in art class.* Col: **eyes glued on** – focused   **stuck like glue** – loyal

goose /**gUws**/ [geese] *noun* 1 a large water bird *We often see geese in our pond.* 2 the female of this kind of bird *The female is called a goose while the male is a gander.* Col: **his goose is cooked** – no escape   **kill the goose that lays the golden eggs** – sacrifice possible future benefit   **led on a wild goose chase** – wasted energy following misinformation   **Mother Goose** – collection of old British nursery rhymes   **silly goose** – foolish   **What's good for the goose is good for the gander.** – *proverb*, what is good for men is also good for women

goosebumps /**gUws** bumps/ [goosebumps] *noun* 1 small bumps on the skin raised from cold or strong emotion *Listening to the child singing opera so beautifully gave me goosebumps.* 2 series of children's mystery stories *My granddaughter loves Goosebumps.*

group /**grUwp**/ [groups, grouped, grouping] *noun* people or things together *The teacher organized the class into three groups.* • *verb* put things together *She grouped five students together.*

hoof /**hUwf**/ [hooves] {also said /h^f/ see Wood} *noun* hard part of the foot of certain mammals *The blacksmith nailed a horseshoe on the horse's hoof.* Col: **hoof it** – walking

humor /**hyUw** mEr/ [humors, humored, humoring] *noun* funny *My brother has an odd sense of humor.* • *verb* endure *We humored grandpa by listening to his stories.* Col: **sense of humor** – laughs easily and often, rarely offended

jewelry /**jUwl** rEy/ *noun* pretty accessories *My mother let me try on her jewelry when I was a little girl.* Col: **costume jewelry** – cheap accessories that look expensive

Judy /**jUw** dEy/ *prop noun* female's name *Judy Thompson is the author of English is Stupid.* Col: **Punch and Judy** – British puppet show   **Teacher Judy** – wrote *English is Stupid Students are Not*

juice /**jUws**/ [juces] *noun* 1 liquid from fruits or vegetables *There is nothing like a fresh glass of orange juice.* 2 slang for electrical power *The printer isn't working because it isn't getting any juice!* Col: **juicy gossip** – rumors

June /**jUwn**/ [Junes] *prop noun* 1 the sixth month in a year *Father's Day is in June.* 2 woman's name *My mother-in-law's name is June.* Col: **June bride** – woman married in the month of June   **June bug** – a large brown clumsy beetle

kangaroo /**kaNg gu rUw**/ [kangaroos] *noun* a large animal from Australia that carries its babies in a pouch *We saw a kangaroo at the zoo.* Col: **kangaroo court** – unfair and unofficial court of law

lieu /**lUw**/ *noun* replace *The waiter gave us toast in lieu of crackers with our soup.*

loony /**lUw** nEy/ *adj* 1 crazy or foolish, short for lunatic *Don't trust him; he's a real loony.* Col: **Loony Tunes** – cartoon series on television.

loose /**lUws**/ [looser, loosest] *adj.* not well attached *The dog was running loose on the street.* • *verb* release *Make loose the sail!* Col: **at loose ends** – bored   **loose cannon** – reckless   **Loose lips sink ships.** – *proverb* cautioning against gossip   **loose woman** – flirty women   **loose-end** – small detail that relates back to a larger mystery   **loose-leaf** – a binder with unattached papers **loosen up** – relax **play fast and loose** – careless and irresponsible

moon /mUwn/ [moons, mooned, mooning] *noun* a satellite that orbits a planet ☾*There is usually one full moon a month.* • *verb slang for* showing a bare bottom as an insult or joke *The protesters mooned the politician.* Col: **ask for the moon** – make extreme requests for money and special treatment **moonlight** – work at another job during the night without paying taxes **moonshine** – illegally made whiskey **moonstruck** –a bit crazy **once in a blue moon** – rarely from the infrequency of two full moons in one month **promise the moon** – extravagant promises

moose /mUws/ *noun* a large North American mammal related to deer *The antlers of the moose are prized by hunters.*

move /mUwv/ [moves, moved, moving] *verb* 1 to change position *Could you please move over?* 2 go in one direction *I moved to the left so the people behind me could see.* 3 change your home *We are moving to Chicago.* 4 suggestion at a formal meeting *I move that we continue this meeting tomorrow.* 5 affect someone emotionally *She was so moved by watching the film that she cried.* • *noun* the act of moving *The move to New York last July was more expensive than we thought.* Col: **get a move on** – hurry up **be on the move** – active **make a move** – romantically flirt

music /myUw zik/ *noun* sounds of voices and instruments • *There was music playing on the radio.* Col: **face the music** – take criticism – or consequences

new /nUw/ *adj* recently made or purchased *I just got some great new shoes.* Col: **newborn** – a baby that has just been born **new age** – society changes its morals or beliefs

news /nUwz/ *noun* information about recent events *We watched the news on the television.*

noon /nUwn/ [noons] *noun* twelve o'clock in the day; midday *It's noon and we're going for lunch.* Col: **high noon** – middle of the day **morning noon and night** – all of the time

perfume /pEr fUwm/ [perfumes] {also said /pEr fyUwm/ see Purple} *noun* a liquid created to make a pleasant smell worn by women *Her husband bought her perfume from the boutique.*

Peru /pu rUw/ *prop noun* a country in South America *We took a vacation to Peru during the winter.*

pool /pUwl/ [pools, pooled, pooling] *noun* 1 a man-made body of water *We have an in-ground pool in our backyard.* 2 billiards *Some people play pool for money.* • *verb* combine resources, efforts *We pooled our resources and came up with a more efficient budget.* Col: **pool resources** – put assets together to go further **pool table** – game equipment for billiards **shoot some pool** – billiards

poor /pUwr/ [poorer, poorest] *adj* 1 not a lot of money *Our family was very poor when I was young.* 2 not good *Don't bring me any poor excuses for being late.* 3 feeling sorry for *Poor Reginald lost both his wife and son in the accident.* • *noun* people without wealth *Our family donates clothes we don't use to the poor.* Col: **dirt poor** – no money **poor as a church mouse** – poorest of the poor **poor cousin** –relative without money whom others feel obliged to help

prune /prUwn/ [prunes, pruned, pruning] *noun* a dried plum *My fingers looked like prunes after getting out of the pool.* • *verb* cut away *Our shrubs need pruning.*

pure /pyUwr/ [purer, purest] *adj* 1 not mixed with anything *It is hard to find pure juice that isn't diluted with water.* 2 free from anything that ruins, spoils, or contaminates *The maple syrup had been* boiled many times to make it pure. 3 innocent *My sister is a kind pure soul.* `Col:` **pure and simple** – no fuss or complications **pure nonsense** – doesn't make sense

Q (cue, queue) /kyUw/ [Q's] *noun* the seventeenth letter of the alphabet *Queen starts with a Q.* `Col:` **Q&A** – question and answer **FAQ** – frequently asked questions **mind your P's and Q's** – be polite **on the QT** – confidential **PDQ** – pretty damn quick

queue (cue, Q) /kyUw/ [queues, queued, queuing] *noun* line up *There is always a queue at the movie theater.* • *verb* line up *Everyone is queuing up in front of the movie theater.*

racoon /ra kUwn/ [raccoons] *noun* large rodent with ringed patterns on its tail *The racoons got into our garbage again.* `Col:` **coon-skin cap** – an old fashioned hat made of raccoon fur with the tail hanging down the back

roof /rUwf/ [roofs] *noun* the covering on top of a building *We need to put a new roof on the house this summer.* `Col:` **hit the roof** – become very angry **roof over one's head** – place to live out of the elements **through the roof** – rise sharply

room /rUwm/ [rooms, roomed, rooming] *noun* 1 part of a house separated by walls *You can't go in my brother's room.* 2 an amount of space *That desk is taking up too much room.* • *verb* stay or live somewhere *We will be rooming together for the night.* `Col:` **need some elbow room** – need more space **Not enough room to swing a cat** – small place **powder room** – women's washroom **room and board** – rent a bedroom with meals included **rooming house** – a house with bedrooms to rent out **room for improvement** – not perfect yet

roommate /rUw mAyt/ [roommates] *noun* shares accommodation and costs *My roommate loves to cook.*

rooster /rUw sdEr/ [roosters] *noun* a male chicken *The rooster crowed early in the morning.*

root (route) /rUwt/ [roots, rooted, rooting] *noun* 1 part of a plant that absorbs nutrients from the ground *The tree roots grew deep into the ground.* 2 the base of certain parts of the body *My teeth were pulled out from their roots.* 3 underlying cause *We need to get to the root of the problem.* 4 where a family history comes from *His roots are in Alabama.* • *verb* 1 originate *Her music was rooted in the African American experience.* 2 physically search *The pig rooted around with his snout to find food under the ground.* 3 loud supporting cheers *We rooted for the home team at the baseball game.* `Col:` **grass roots** – common citizens **put roots down** – staying in one place where one would raise a family **Money is the root of all evil.** – *proverb* commenting on the bad things people do for money **root out** – search intently **square root** – mathematical term **take root** – get established

route (root) /rUwt/ [routes, routed, routing] *noun* a plan to get somewhere *The back roads made for a scenic route back home.* • *verb* instructions for traveling to a destination *Road construction detour routed us to go past the old church yard.*

rule /rUwl/ [rules, ruled, ruling] *noun* 1 standard to be obeyed *Drivers obey traffic rules.* 2 good advice *As a general rule, it is best not to go swimming right after a big meal.* 3 a time during which a ruler has authority *The rule of Queen Victoria lasted almost 64 years.* • *verb* authority by law over a people *Stalin ruled over Russian with an iron fist.* `Col:` **rule out** – exclude as a possibility **rule of thumb** – informally accepted procedure **bending the rules** – making slight exceptions **the golden rule** – Do unto others as you would have them do unto you.

ruler /rUw lEr/ [rulers] *noun* 1 a person who has authority to rule *Queen Elizabeth was Great Britain's first female ruler.* 2

a straight measuring tool *He has a ruler in his pencil case.*

school /skUwl/ [schools] noun 1 a building of education *Our kids attended a public school.* 2 a faculty within a university *Laurier University is a school of Business.* 3 a group of artists, and philosophers that share the same approach *In the late 1800s, the school of impressionism had a big influence world-wide.* Col: **old school** – classic **school his temper** – control his temper **schoolmarm** – old-fashioned woman teacher **school of fish** – collective noun for a group of fish **school of hard knocks** – experience vs. formal education

screw /skrUw/ [screws, screwed, screwing] noun metal pin with a spiral thread *I'm looking for a screw small enough to fix my glasses.* • verb 1 fasten together two objects *She screwed the cabinet to the wall.* 2 slang for sex *They screwed everyday on their honeymoon.* Col: **a screw up** – mistake **have a screw loose** – acting strange **put the screws to him** – pressure someone **screw you** – go to hell **screwball** – silly, crazy **screwing with me** – trick or cheat

sewer /sU wEr/ [sewers] noun underground pipes that carry away human waste. *Alligator are a problem in big city sewers.*

shampoo /Sham pUw/ [shampoos] noun a liquid soap *We washed the dog with a special shampoo.*

shoe /ShUw/ [shoes] noun covering for the foot *She has a pair of shoes for every outfit.* Col: **a shoe-in** – will win uncontested **fill someone's shoes** – take on the responsibilities of a person no longer there **If the shoe fits, wear it.** – accept criticism that is proverb true **on a shoestring** – manage without much money **shoe a horse** – nail metal horseshoes on a horse **the shoe is on the other foot** – experience a situation from one's opponent's perspective **waiting for the other shoe to drop** – anticipating an unpleasant event

Sioux (sue) /sUw/ prop noun a native American Indian tribe *The Sioux live on the plains in North America.*

smooth /smUwTh/ [smoother, smoothest, smoothes, smoothed, smoothing] adj 1 no bumps *The cake batter must be smooth before it's poured into the baking pan.* 2 well practiced *The skier had a smooth run.* 3 a flavour that is not harsh *This coffee tastes smooth.* • verb press out flat *She smoothed the wrinkles out of her dress.* Col: **nothing but smooth sailing** – it will be easy **smooth-talking** – persuasive **smooth things over** – overcome difficulties

soon /sUwn/ [sooner, soonest] adv a short time *We'll be going home soon kids.*

soup /sUwp/ [soups] noun a liquid food eaten with a spoon from a bowl *My mother gives me chicken noodle soup when I'm sick.* Col: **in duck soup** – in trouble **soup-kitchen** – a charitable organization that gives free meals to the poor **souped-up** – made an engine more powerful

spoon /spUwn/ [spoons] noun a tool for eating or serving food *I prefer using a spoon over chopsticks.* Col: **born with a silver spoon in one's mouth** – born into a rich family **greasy spoon** – a cheap restaurant **spoon-feed** – given information in small measured amounts **spooning** – hugging from behind in bed **spoonerism** – mixing up the first letters in two different words (fool so feelish)

stew /stUw/ [stews, stewed, stewing] noun a thick soup cooked for a long time *Beef stew is a great dish to eat on a winter day.* • verb cook meat and vegetables together on the stove for a long time *There is always a pot of stew on the stove in the winter.* Col: **stew in one's own juices** – leave one to worry about the out-come of their bad decisions

/ Uw / is Blue

student /stUw dent/ [students] *noun* one who studies *My students love pronunciation class.*

sue (Sioux) /sUw/ [sued, suing] *verb* legal action against a person or business *I'm suing the manufacturer for not disclosing known side effects of a drug.* • *prop noun* female's name *Sue is short for Susan.* Col: **Sue the pants off of someone** – take to court for a lot of money

suit /sUwt/ [suit, suites, suited, suiting] *noun* 1 Clothing where the top and bottom part match *I bought a nice suit for my brother's wedding.* 2 one of four different symbols on playing cards • *Hearts and diamonds are red suits and spades and clubs are black.* • *verb* compliments *That pink color suits her perfectly.* Col: **birthday suit** – naked **follow suit** – following someone's example **play suit** – play cards that have the same symbol as were already played **suit of armor** – knight's protective outfit **suit yourself** – do as you wish **suits to a tee** – very well adapted to

threw (through) /THrUw/ [throws, threw, throwing] *verb* past tense of *throw* toss. *The boy threw the ball through the window.* Col: **threw in the towel** – quit **threw a hissy/fit** – tantrum

through (threw) /THrUw/ *prep* 1 in one end and out the other *You go through the tunnel to reach the other side.* 2 during a time period *He slept the whole night through.* Col: **she's through** – finished **through and through** – thoroughly

to (too, two) /tUw/ *prep* 1 a direction *We are going to the store.* 2 before an hour of time *It is ten to six.* 3 give *He gave the present to her.* 4 compare *The odds are ten to one that Lucky Boy will win.* 5 about *She told them about the baby to explain her absence.* Col: **go-to guy/girl** – expert in a specific topic or job **that's all there is to it** – no hidden meaning **true to life** – accurate

too (to, two) /tUw/ *adv* 1 more than needed *He drank too much beer.* 2 extremely *It's too good to be true.* 3. as well *Her brother wants to come too.* 4 negative *It's too expensive.* Col: **too good to be true** – unbelievably wonderful **too much information** – inappropriate often disgusting amount of detail

tool /tUwl/ [tools, tooled, tooling] *noun* 1 object used to help complete a project ✻ *Every toolbox needs a hammer and a wrench.* 2 a person who is used by someone else *The young boxer now felt he was just a tool for the mafia.* • *verb* modify equipment *The candy factory was re-tooled to make toothpaste.* Col: **tool and die** – manufacturing equipment **tools of the trade** – know-how and equipment useful in doing a specific job

tooth /tUwTH/ [teeth] *noun* 1 hard, white bony things in one's mouth for chewing *If you leave your tooth under your pillow the tooth fairy will bring you a dollar.* 2 points that stick out on a saw *Sharpen the teeth on the saw before you use it.* Col: **digging one's teeth into** – focusing **fight tooth and nail** – fight hard **get kicked in the teeth** – unexpectedly hurt **long in the tooth** – very old **search with a fine-tooth comb** – looking very carefully **the baby is teething** – the baby's teeth are growing

toothbrush /tUwTH brush/ [toothbrushes] *noun* bristles on the end of a short handle for scrubbing teeth. *Don't use my toothbrush.*

tour /tUwr/ [tours, toured, touring] *noun* 1 visiting several places for business or pleasure *I did a tour of France last year.* 2 visit to gather information *The government official had a tour of the new factory.* • *verb* go on a journey or visit *The actress toured with the new theater company.* Col: **go on tour** – perform in different places **tour de force** – clever/skillful performance

true /trUw/ [truer, truest] *adj* 1 reality or fact *It's true, I've never told a lie.* 2 ac-

HOW DO YOU SAY? PRONUNCIATION DICTIONARY

curate *He used a true to life scale.* 3 what one had hoped *Getting a horse was a dream come true for her.* 4 trusted *He was a true friend.* **Col:** show one's true colors – reveal qualities usually hidden   true to life – accurate   true to form – expected   true-blue – loyal

Tuesday /tUwz dAy/ [Tues., Tuesdays] *prop noun* the third day of the week following Mondays *I work every Tuesday evening.*

tuna /tUw nu/ [tunas] *noun* a large fish found in warm seas *Tuna is good for making healthy, delicious sandwiches.*

tune /tUwn/ [tunes, tuned, tuning] *noun* a key, or pitch *My brother is always out of tune.* • *verb* changing the pitch of an instrument *I already know how to tune my guitar.* **Col:** change one's tune – changing one's attitude   in tune – understand   to the tune of – price   tune out – ignore   tune-up – fixing an engine

two (to, too) /tUw/ [2, twos] *noun* number between one and three *All pairs come in twos.* • *adj* two in number *An avenue is a two way street.* **Col:** it takes two to tango – a man and women to make a baby   put two and two together – realize logically   two wrongs don't make a right – not appropriate to do the wrong thing because someone else did   two-bit – cheap   two bits – 25¢ piece   two-faced – liar   two-timing – unfaithful

U (ewe, you) /yUw/ [U's] *noun* the twenty first letter of the Latin alphabet *Uniform starts with a U.* **Col:** i.u. – international units   U-turn – turn around and continue the way one came   U-boat – German WWII submarine   I.O.U. – literally 'I owe you', a debt

USA /yU we sAy/ (also U.S.A.) *prop noun* The United States of America *I was born in the USA.*

unicorn /yUw nu kOrn/ [unicorns] *noun* a mythical horse with a horn *There's something magical about a white unicorn.*

uniform /yUw nu fOrm/ [uniforms] *noun* special matching clothing as a sign of belonging, or profession *Every soldier wears a uniform.* **Col:** make uniform – make each object in the group the same

union /yUw nyun/ [unions] *noun* 1 a group of people with a common purpose *The union of Great Britain and Ireland in 1801 was very important in Britain's history.* 2 political organization for a specific purpose *We formed a union at work because the workers were being treated unfairly.* **Col:** trade union – workers who are an important political force   credit union – provides financial services instead of a bank   student union – organization for students made up of students   the Union – political association of the northern states during the American Civil War in the 1860s that was opposed to the Confederacy of southern states

unit /yUw nut/ [units] *noun* independent piece of a whole *The army splits up into smaller units to be more effective on the field.* **Col:** C.P.U. – central processing unit of the computer   entertainment unit – furniture that holds electronics that work together

use (ewes) /yUwz/ [uses, used, using] *noun* doing something for a purpose *He put the computer to good use in taking notes.* • *verb* work with a tool *She used the toothbrush to clean her teeth.* **Col:** multi-use – more than one purpose   single-use – only one time   use somebody – take advantage of another's kindness   use up – none left   username – online identification

view /vUw/ [views, viewed, viewing] *verb* 1 see *We viewed the whole city from the top of the hill.* 2 having an opinion *She viewed her input as more important than her co-workers.* • *noun* 1 what you see *The view from the top of the hill was lovely.* 2 an opinion *His view was that we should all buy electric cars instead of gas powered cars.* **Col:** a dim view – negative opinion

/ Uw / is Blue

bird's eye view — overlooking point of view — an opinion room with a view — good lodgings

viewpoint /**vyUw** pOynt/ [viewpoints] *noun* opinion *I believe in global warming, what's your viewpoint?*

W /**du** bul **yUw**/ [W's] *noun* the twenty-third letter of the Latin alphabet *Woman starts with a W.* Col: Wh questions — What — object, When — time, Where — place, Who — person, Why — reason, How — manner

who /**hUw**/ [whose, whoever] *pron* Wh question, what person *Who left their dirty dishes in the sink?* Col: Abandon hope, all ye who enter here. — *proverb*, if you decide to come in, be prepared for the worst anyone who is anyone — everyone important God helps those who help themselves. — *proverb*, one also has to work for good things to happen, not just rely on providence Good things come to he who waits. — *proverb* patience is rewarded He gives twice who gives quickly. — *proverb*, it is more helpful to give a small amount sooner than more later He lives long who lives well. — *proverb* recommending one live virtuously He travels fastest who travels alone. — *proverb* without family responsibilities it is easier to get ahead He who fights and runs away, lives to fight another day. — *proverb*, discretion is the better part of valor He who hesitates is lost. — *proverb* act quickly before the opportunity is lost He who laughs last, laughs longest. — *proverb* about the sweetness of revenge He who pays the piper calls the tune. — *proverb* for the one who pays for the service, decides what is done He who would climb the ladder must begin at the bottom. — *proverb* for the value of starting at the bottom and working up Look who's talking! — accusing others of what one does People who live in glass houses shouldn't throw stones. — *proverb* about accusing others of things one does Says who? — What is your authority? show who's boss — dominate There's none so blind as those who will not see. — *proverb* you can't make someone understand something they don't want to know There's none so deaf as those who will not hear. — *proverb*, you can't make someone receive information they don't want to know Those who can, do; those who can't, teach. — *proverb*, those who do something well make a living at it, if you don't do anything well, become a teacher Who cares? — indifference Who knows? — I'm don't know either Who was it? — on the phone W.H.O. — World Health Organization Who would have thought?— imagine that Who's your daddy — slang for more powerful than you With friends like that, who needs enemies? — wronged by a so-called friend You and who else? — you aren't strong enough to defeat me by yourself who's who — important people

who's (whose) /**hUwz**/ *contr* who is *Who's going to the store?*

whose (who's) /**hUwz**/ *adj* belong to *Whose dog is it?* • *pron* that which belongs to *This is a sound dictionary whose purpose it to help English learners.*

wound /**wUwnd**/ [wounds, wounded, wounding] *noun* cut or injury *His wounds were mostly to his pride.* • *verb* tear the skin *He wounded the intruder but didn't kill him.* Col: lick one's wounds — sulk and feel badly after a defeat rub salt into the wound — intentionally make a bad situation worse for another wounded pride — ashamed, embarrassed or hurt feelings

you (ewe, U) /**yUw**/ *pron* 1 someone else *Could you help me?* 2 general people *You just never know.*

203

HOW DO YOU SAY? PRONUNCIATION DICTIONARY

zoo /zUw/ [zoos] *noun* a place to go see exotic animals *There are many lions at the zoo.* `Col:` *This place is a zoo!* – busy and unorganized   **zoo keeper** – someone who takes care of the animals at the zoo

zoom /zUwm/ [zooms, zoomed, zooming] *verb* move very quickly *He zoomed down the street on his motorcycle.* • *noun* a noise when something passes by quickly *We heard the zoom of the jet engine overhead.* `Col:` **zoom in/out** – get closer or further perspective   **zoom lens** – a type of camera lens

Chapter 10
/u/ is Mustard

HOW DO YOU SAY? PRONUNCIATION DICTIONARY

Chapter 10
/u/ is Mustard

above /u buv/
adjustment /u jus munt/
adult /u dult/
adulterant /u dul tu runt/
among /u muNg/

because /bEy kuz/
blood /blud/
blush /bluSh/
brother /bruThEr/
brush /bruSh/
bucket /bu kut/
buddy /bu dEy/
buffalo /bu fu lOw/
bulb /bulb/
bus /bus/
but (butt) /but/
butt (but) /but/
butter /bu dEr/
button /bu tun/

cha /Chu/
club /klub/
color /ku lEr/
come /kum/
comfort /kum fErt/
company /kum pu nEy/
construction /kun struk Shun/
country /kun trEy/
cousin /ku zun/
cover /ku vEr/
crush /kruSh/
culture /kul ChEr/
cup /kup/
cut /kut/

destruction /du struk Shun/
discovery /du sku vE rEy/
discussion /du sgu Shun/
disgust /du sgust/
does /duz/
done /dun/

double /du bul/
drum /drum/
duck /duk/
dust /dust/

enough /u nuf/

from /frum/
front /frunt/
fuck /fuk/
fudge /fuj/
fun /fun/
funny /fu nEy/

government /gu vEr munt/
gum /gum/
gun /gun/

honey /hu nEy/
hundred /hun drud/

ja /ju/
judge /juj/
juggle /ju gul/
jump /jump/
jungle /juN gul/
just /just/
justice /jus dus/

love /luv/
luck /luk/
lunch /lunCh/
lung /luNg/

Monday /mun dAy/
money /mu nEy/
monkey /muNg kEy/
month /munTH/
mother /muThEr/
much /muCh/
multiply /mul tu plIy/
muscle /mu sul/
must /must/

206

/ u / is Mustard

mustard /**mus** dɛrd/

nothing /**nu** THiNg/
number /**num** bɛr/
nut /**nut**/

of /**uv**/
once /**wuns**/
one (won) /**wun**/
other /**u** Thɛr/
oven /**u** vun/

plus /**plus**/
public /**pub** lik/
pump /**pump**/
punishment /**pu** nuSh munt/

rough /**ruf**/
rub /**rub**/
run /**run**/

scrub /**skrub**/
shut /**Shut**/
skull /**skul**/
skunk /**skuNgk**/
some (sum) /**sum**/
son (sun) /**sum**/
sponge /**spunj**/
stomach /**stu** muk/
structure /**struk** Chɛr/
substance /**sub** stuns/
subway /**sub** wAy/
such /**such**/
sudden /**su** dun/
sum (some) /**sum**/
summer /**su** mɛr/
sun (son) /**sun**/
sundae (Sunday) /**sun** dAy/
Sunday (sundae) /**sun** dAy/

the /**Thu**/
thumb /**THum**/
thunder /**THun** dɛr/
tongue /**tuNg**/
touch /**tuCh**/
trouble /**tru** bul/
truck /**truk**/
trust /**trust**/
tub /**tub**/

ugly /**ug** lEy/
uncle /**uNg** kul/
under /**un** dɛr/
up /**up**/
us /**us**/

W /**du** bul yUw/
was /**wuz**/
what /**wut**/
won (one) /**wun**/
wonder /**wun** dɛr/

young /**yuNg**/
yuk /**yuk**/

above /u **buv**/ prep 1 on top of *There is a picture above the desk.* 2 most importantly *Above all, be true to yourself.* `Col:` above average – better than most   above and beyond – extra effort   above and beyond the call of duty – gave or did much more than was expected   a cut above – superior quality   above reproach – no possibility one did the wrong thing   above suspicion – pure   above the law – laws don't apply to them   all of the above – previous selections inclusive   be above board – full disclosure   head and shoulders above – superior in every way   keep head above water – survive   marry above oneself – marry a higher class   none of the above – the answer is not included in the choices   rise above – overcome   tower above – much taller than

adjustment /u **jus** munt/ [adjustments] noun changing or fixing something *She made an adjustment to her budget after buying a car.*

adult /u **dult**/ adj describes fully grown *Testosterone levels for adult males decreases as they age.*

adulterant /u **dul** tu Runt/ noun an ingredient added that lessens purity *Chicory is an adulterant in coffee that reduces cost without affecting flavor.*

among /u **muNg**/ prep 1 in the middle of *They walked among the trees in the forest.* 2 together when talking about three or more people or things *Sue, Juanita and Josée shared the Chinese food among themselves.* 3 each person gets a part *The prize was shared among the team members.* 4 in the group *Reading and writing are among the skills students study when learning English.* `Col:` among friends – with friends

because /bEy **kuz**/ conj for the reason, answering the question Why? in the same sentence *John was happy because he won the race.* `Col:` because of – as a result

blood /**blud**/ noun 1 red liquid that pumps through the body of humans and many other animals *Jean gave blood at the blood donor clinic.* 2 relationship by being in the same family or race *The family was of French blood.* `Col:` bad blood – old problem and bad feelings between people   blood donor – gives blood for emergency medical use   blood type – a classification for human blood   bloodshot eyes – full of red lines   bloodstream – rivers of blood feeding every cell in the body   bloodthirsty – eager to kill   blood, sweat and tears – hard work, emotion and time   blue blood – aristocratic   flesh and blood – from the same family   in cold blood – without feeling   in one's blood – deep passion for   make one's blood boil – anger

blush /**bluSh**/ [blushes, blushed, blushing] verb become red in the face when embarrassed or ashamed *Joanne blushed when Abdul asked her to dance.* • noun when the face has turned red from embarrassment or shame *From the blush on his cheeks, his mother knew he was lying.* `Col:` at first blush – first look

brother /**bruThEr**/ [brothers] noun 1 two males having the same mother and/or father *My father has two brothers.* 2 men emotionally connected through shared interests or goals *They were brothers in spirit.* 3 member of a religious group *The brothers prayed together.* `Col:` Big Brother – all knowing   Big Brothers – mentors and volunteers to fatherless boys   brother-in-law – brother of a spouse or husband of a sister   brotherhood – group of men defined by a goal or purpose   brothers-in-arm – fight together   everybody and his uncle – many   Oh brother! – an expression of surprise or disgust

brush /**bruSh**/ [brushes, brushes, brushing] noun 1 a tool made of stiff hairs fastened to a handle used for grooming, painting or cleaning *The old* *brush was caked with dried paint.* 2 a thick group of small trees or bushes growing together *The dry brush caught fire quickly.* • *verb* 1 groom, paint or clean with a brush *José brushed the horses after the race.* 2 a light touch *He brushed up against her arm.* Col: **brush-off** – rejected or ignored **brush-up against** – touch lightly while passing by **brush off** – reject or dismiss **brush up on** – study again something learned before **tar with the same brush** – include a person in a group characterized by their faults

bucket /**bu** kut/ [buckets] *noun* 1 an open container with round sides, a flat bottom and a handle *They used the bucket to carry the water to the animals.* 2 a measure of amount *The room needed one bucket of paint* Col: **a drop in the bucket** – an insignificant contribution to solving a big problem **bucket list** – things ones intends to do before they die **kick the bucket** – die

buddy /**bu** dEy/ [buddies] *noun* 1 a good friend *He and his buddy liked to play computer games every Saturday.* 2 a partner or another person in a team *Swimming with a buddy is a good safety rule.* 3 generic name *Hey buddy!* Col: **bosom buddy** – a very close friend **buddy up** – to join with a person to form a team of two **buddy system** – people paired for safety or to help each other

Buffalo /**bu** fu lOw/ [buffalos] *prop noun* 1 a city in the USA *It is cheaper to fly from Buffalo, New York.* 2 *noun* a huge four-legged hairy animal with horns and a hump, closely related to cattle *The buffalo grazed on the open plains.* Col: **buffalo wings** – fried chicken wings with a hot sauce

bulb /**bulb**/ [bulbs] *noun* 1 underground stem or root that becomes a plant *Tulip bulbs are planted in the fall.* 2 light emitting device *The bulb burned out in the fridge.* 3 a rounded part *The bulb of the thermometer holds the mercury.*

bus /**bus**/ [buses, bused, busing] *noun* a large motorized people mover *I take the bus to school every day.* • *verb* 1 move people using a bus *The students bused to the school in the country.* Col: **busboy** – clears tables and cleans in a restaurant **miss the bus** – miss an opportunity

but (butt) /**but**/ *conj* 1 shows a difference *Paul tried to play but he couldn't.* 2 opposite to what is expected *She studied hard but still failed the test.* 3 except that *They wanted to buy ice cream, but the store was closed.* • *prep* except for *Everyone had cake but Joanne.* Col: **all but** – almost **but for** – if not for **but good** – thoroughly **but one (or more)** – except **close, but no cigar** – failed **everything but the kitchen sink** – almost everything **gone but not forgotten** – dead but still remembered fondly **in all but name** – together but not officially married **It never rains but it pours.** – *proverb* good or bad things happen in large numbers all at once **last but not least** – last in order, but not last in importance **no ifs, ands, or buts** – excuses **no buts about it** – no discussion **nothing but skin and bones** – thin **slow but sure** – steady progress **thanks, but no thanks** – not interested **The lights are on but nobody's home.** – stupid **You can lead a horse to water, but you can't make it drink.** – *proverb* can't force anyone to take an opportunity

butt (but) /**but**/ [butts, butted, butting] *noun* 1 rear end *I slipped on the ice and landed on my butt.* 2 the end *Cigarette butts stink.* 3 victim of cruel humor *He was the butt of mean jokes because his nose was so large.* • *verb* put out *Butt out your cigarette in the ash tray.* Col: **a kick in the butt** – motivation **be a pain in the butt** – annoying person or thing **butt up against** – press against **butt in** – to interrupt **butt of a joke** – target of a joke **butt out** – leave **get off one's butt (ass)** – quit sitting around **kick butt (ass)** – motivate **kick someone's butt (ass)** – punish or defeat convincingly   one's butt is on the line – critical to their future   work one's butt off – work hard

butter /**bu** dEr/ [butters, buttered, buttering] *noun* creamy fat spread for bread or cooking *She put butter on her muffin.* • *verb* spread butter *She buttered her toast.* `Col:` butter up – compliment   cut through like a hot knife through butter – fast and easy   know which side one's bread is buttered on – behave respectfully toward the bread winner/boss   bread and butter – job

button /**bu** tun/ [buttons, buttoned, buttoning] *noun* round flat disc that slips through a hole to fasten clothing *There is a button missing on your coat* • *verb* fasten with a button *Button your coat, it's cold.* `Col:` a hot button – emotional trigger   as bright as a button – smart   as cute as a button – adorable   button one's lip – stop talking   button down/up – close with buttons   hit the panic button – react without thinking in a crisis   push one's buttons – anger   push the right buttons – do what is needed to get the desired result   right on the button – exactly

cha /**Chu**/ *contr* t + you, spoken word only *English is Stupid Students are Not* Chapter One /*Wha cha doin'?*/

club /**klub**/ [clubs, clubbed, clubbing] *noun* 1 a heavy piece of wood used as a weapon *The club was an important tool for cavemen.* 2 organized group that shares a common interest *I belong to a tennis club.* 3 a suit in playing cards the shape of a clover *Clubs are trump.* • *verb* hitting with a blunt object *He clubbed the fish over the head after he caught it.* `Col:` club house – building where club members meet   golf club – one of a set of special sticks for hitting golf balls   join the club – share unfortunate circumstances   sports club – facility equipped to play multiple sports, often membership is required   welcome to the club – sarcastic saying for shared misfortune

color /**ku** lEr/ [colors, colored coloring] *noun* tints and hues of every shade, not black and white *A rainbow has many colors.* 2 look of health *There was good color in her cheeks after her holiday by the sea.* • *verb* give color too *The students colored the vowel charts together.* `Col:` a horse of a different color – something odd or a completely different subject   be off-color – vulgar remark   color barrier – discrimination   color-blind – unable to see color or the difference between colors   color-code – organize using color   come through with flying colors – spectacular recovery or effort   true colors – reveal true personality that is not good

come /**kum**/ [comes, came coming] *verb* 1 move toward *He comes over every Saturday night.* 2 enter *Come into the house.* 3 be from *She comes from India.* `Col:` come down on like a ton of bricks – to punish   come a long way – improvement   come about – occur   come across – find by chance   come across as/like – seem like   come again – come back sometime   Come again? – What did you say?   come along – accompany   come along for the ride – join for the adventure   Come and get it! – time to eat   come apart at the seams – emotional breakdown   come around – visit   come at a price – emotional cost   come away empty-handed – risk and return with nothing   come back – be popular again   come back to haunt you – un-resolved issues return   come by honestly – inherit or earn good fortune or ability   come clean – tell the truth `Col:` come close – near   come down in the world – lose status, importance or money   come down on someone – to negatively judge and berate   come down to earth – be realistic   come down with – get sick   come face to face with – deal with fears or past   **come forward** – offer help   **come from behind** – move ahead from a losing position in a race   **come from far and wide** – arrive from many distant places   **come from nowhere** – surprise   **come full circle** – returning to an original position or status   **come hell or high water** – no matter what   **come home to roost** – problems from the past returning   **come in** – order over the finish line of a race or enter   **come in handy** – useful   **come into effect** – become official   **come into some money** – unexpected wealth, usually inherited   **come into one's own** – hard fought independence   **come into sight** – begin to see from a distance   **come into the world** – born   **come Monday** – on Monday   **come of age** – legally responsible   **Come off it!** – skepticism   **Come on!** – support   **come on to someone** – sexual advance to show romantic interest   **come one, come all** – everyone   **come out** – declare homosexuality   **come out against** – opposition   **come out in the wash** – truth will be revealed in time   **come out of the blue** – suddenly   **come out of left field** – not expecting it   **come out on top** – win   **come out smelling like a rose** – unscathed after hardship   **come out swinging** – ready to fight   **come rain or shine** – unfailing   **come round** – finally agree   **come through** – survive   **come to** – regain consciousness   **come to a dead end** – no options   **come to a head** – critical point   **come to a standstill** – **come to a stop**   **come to an impasse** – can't move forward, stalemate   **come to blows** – fist fight   **come to grips with** – accept things that can't be changed   **come to light** – discovered   **come to no good** – end badly   **come to pass** – happen   **come to one's senses** – begin to think clearly   **come to terms with** – accept and move forward   **come to the table** – meet prepared to discuss and resolve   **come to this** – a situation finished with a negative, tragic result   **come under** – classified as   **come under fire** – criticized over   **come unglued** – breakdown   **come up against** – opposed by   **come up for air** – take a break   **come up with** – create or think of a solution   **come what may** – be peaceful about any outcome or situation   **come with the territory** – non-negotiable part of the package   **come within an inch of** – dangerously close   **comes naturally** – a skill that comes without effort   **Cross that bridge when we come to it.** – *proverb* don't worry too early   **easy come, easy go** – assets that appear and disappear randomly   **have it coming to one** – deserve   **How come?** – Why?   **if push comes to shove** – decision is forced as the situation worsens   **if worst comes to worst** – if the worst possible thing happens   **not know if one is coming or going** – so overwhelmed you cannot keep track of everyone   **oh, come on** – doubt the story   **take it as it comes** – accept   **until the cows come home** – not for a long, long time   **What goes around comes around.** – *proverb* one is treated the same way they treat others, good or bad   **where a person is coming from** – understand another point of view

comfort /**kum** fErt/ [comforts, comforted, comforting] *noun* physical and emotional care *She needed lots of comfort when her husband died.* • *verb* sense of well being *It comforts me to know you are well and happy.* Col: **cold comfort** – little or no comfort   **comfort food** – simply prepared and associated with home   **creature comforts** – luxuries   **too close for comfort** – event or accident dangerously close

company /**kum** pu nEy/ [companies] *noun* 1 business or organization *She prefers working for a small company.* 2 organized group with a common interest *The theater company puts on four performances a year.* 3 guests *Clean the house, company's coming.* 4 companionship *I enjoy your company.* Col: keep company – spend time with misery loves company – people love to complain part company – end a relationship present company excepted – exclude those nearby from negative generalizations *Two is company, three is a crowd.* – *proverb* ask a third party to leave so two can be alone

con**struc**tion /kun **struk** Shun/ *noun* build *My son works in construction.* • *adj* build *The construction site is dirty and noisy.*

country /**kun** trEy/ [countries] *noun* 1 a large area of land under one government *Canada is the second largest country in the worlds.* 2 open land between cities and towns *She lives on a horse farm in the country.* Col: a country mile – a great distance cross country – avoiding roads when traveling countrymen – same birth country countryside – outside urban area It is a free country! – right to freedom of speech old country – Europe to the immigrants who came from there

cousin /**ku** zun/ [cousins] *noun* aunt or uncle's child *Tom is uncle Al's son and my cousin.* Col: kissing cousins – distant relative kissed when greeted

cover /**ku** vEr/ [covers, covered, covering] *verb* 1 spread over top *The mother covered the sleeping child with a blanket.* 2 extend over *Frost covered the ground.* 3 distance *We covered about 50 km/day on our bike tour.* • *noun* something over to hide or protect *The book cover was torn but the book was fine.* Col: blow one's cover – reveal a person's true identity break cover – leave a hiding place cover all the bases – thorough cover up for – lie for cover a lot of ground – to deal with a lot of information cover tracks – hide evidence of past bad behavior cover something up – hide cover your ass – protect yourself against future blame *Don't judge a book by its cover.* – *proverb* can't know a person's value by looks alone read cover to cover – finish reading the entire book take cover – find shelter under cover – working as a spy

crush /kru**Sh**/ [crushes, crushed, crushing] *verb* flatten or defeat *Recycled material is crushed before it is transported.* • *noun* infatuation *I have a crush on Brad Pitt.* Col: crush on someone – in love with

culture /**kul** ChEr/ [cultures, cultured, culturing] *noun* 1 beliefs and behaviour of a community *Traditions vary across different cultures.* 2 the arts and celebration of intellectual achievement *The poor have limited access or appreciation of artistic culture.* 3 environment to grow bacteria or tissue *Dark damp places are perfect cultures for growing mushrooms.* Col: culture hero – perfectly embodies the values of a group • cultured pearls – pearls grown in artificial conditions • culture shock – an unpleasant feeling of confusion and surprise when immersed in a new environment • reverse culture shock – unpleasant feelings of displacement after returning home from a long period of living away

cup /kup/ [cups, cupped, cupping] *noun* 1 container used to hold liquids *I'll have a cup of tea.* 2 8 oz measure *The recipe calls for two cups of flour.* 3 trophy *The cup goes to the winner.* • *verb* form a cup with hands *She cupped two baby chicks in her hands.* Col: cup one's hands – form a bowl cup and saucer – tea cup with a tiny plate below my cup runneth over – fortunate one's cup of tea – preference

cut /kut/ [cuts, cut, cutting] *verb* 1 slice into separate parts *The bride and groom are cutting the cake.* 2 pierce *The baby is cutting a tooth.* 3 shorten *He cut his holiday short for an emergency at work.* • *noun* injury from a sharp object *The cut on his hand is from the carving knife took four stitches.* `Col:` **a cut above** – better than **can't cut the mustard** – the task is too difficult **clean-cut** – neat and tidy with short hair **cut a deal** – accept a bargain **cut a fine figure** – looks good **cut across** – take a shortcut or reach beyond a normal boundary **cut along** – follow a line **cut and dried** – simple and clear **cut and paste** – take a section of text and insert it elsewhere or simple and unoriginal **cut back** – reduce or reverse **cut both ways** – affects both sides **cut corners** – the fastest way may affect the quality of the work **cut a person down to size** – reprimand the overconfident **cut from the same cloth** – similar values and disposition **cut in** – interrupt or give a share of the profits **cut it out** – stop **cut loose** – relax or get fired **cut one's losses** – walk away from a bad venture before losing more **cut one's nose off to spite one's face** – hurt oneself more attempting to hurt another **cut one's teeth on** – begin with basics, first experience of many **cut one's own throat** – cause one's own failure, **not cut out for** – be unsuited to a job or activity **cut off without a penny** – exclude in a will; end allowance **cut out** – excluded **cut up** – criticize **cut short** – to end early **cut someone some slack** – show flexibility or generosity **cut the cheese** – fart or pass wind **Cut the comedy!** – Be serious! **cut the cord** – stop relying on mom for money and support **Cut the crap!** – stop saying things that aren't true or not important **cut through red tape** – cut short administrative procedures **cut to the bone** – radically reduce **cut to the chase** – get to the point without details **cut to the quick** – hurt someone emotionally deeply **cut up about** – upset **cuts like a hot knife through butter** – fast and easy **cutting it close** – barely acceptable or enough time **half-cut** – drunk **have one's work cut out for them** – have a difficult task ahead **make the cut** – selected **to cut long story short** – to be deliberately brief **You could cut the air with a knife.** – tension in the atmosphere

destruction /du **struk** Shun/ *noun* breaking apart or destroying *The tsunami caused immeasurable destruction to property and lives.*

discovery /du **sku** vE rEy/ [discoveries, discovered, discovering] *noun* what is found *The discovery of penicillin helped billions.* • *verb* find *Dawson City grew rapidly after they discovered gold.*

discussion /du **sgu** Shun/ [discussions] *noun* written or spoken exchange of ideas. *We had a discussion about giving children cell phones.*

disgust /du **sgust**/ [disgusts, disgusted, disgusting] *noun* strong dislike or offended *Stories of child abuse fill me with disgust.* • *verb* cause strong dislike or offence *Pornography disgusts me.*

does /**duz**/ [does, did, doing] *verb* third person singular of *do* act *He does the dishes every night.* `Col:` **easy does it** – move cautiously **Handsome is as handsome does.** – *proverb* behavior counts more than looks **How does that grab you?** – What do you think? **Man does not live by bread alone.** – *proverb* people need more than food to thrive **Money does not grow on trees.** – *proverb* warning not to spend much **That does it!** – finished a project or not tolerate any more **What difference does it make?** – doesn't really matter **What does that prove?** – So what?

done /**dun**/ *verb* past participle of *do* act *We are done talking.* `Col:` **done with** – finished **done for** – in serious trouble; dead or almost dead **done in** – physically exhausted

double /duˈbul/ [doubles, doubled, doubling] *adj* two times *Twins are double trouble* • *noun* 1 anything two times *Ten is double five.* 2 identical *Her sister could pass as her double.* • *verb* make twice as much *Double the cookie recipe and we'll freeze the extra.* Col: double back – reverse motion to put hunters off the trail look twice   double dip – getting paid twice one without integrity look twice   double double – two cream and two sugar in one's coffee look twice   double duty – two jobs at once   double entendre – word with two meanings one which is sexual   double over – bend in half at the waist   double take – look twice   double talk – way of speaking that confuses to avoid telling the truth   lead a double life – have a secret second life that is usually not socially acceptable   on the double – quickly

drum /drum/ [drums, drummed, drumming] *noun* musical instrument hit to keep a beat *He played the drums.* • *verb* tap a surface over and over *It drives me nuts when he drums his fingers on the desk.* Col: drum out – throw out   drum into – learn through repetition   drum up – to invent or create

duck /duk/ [ducks, ducked, ducking] *noun* a water bird with webbed feet and a flat bill *The ducks are nesting beside the pond.* • *verb* lower one's head and shoulders for protection *He ducked under the table when she threw the frying pan at him.* Col: get one's ducks in a row – tidy prepare, and organize affairs   like water off a duck's back – unaffected by adversity   sitting duck – exposed   take to something like a duck to water – adapt naturally and easily

dust /dust/ [dusts, dusted, dusting] *noun* tiny particles of dirt *Dust covered the shelves and the top of the refrigerator in the old man's house.* • *verb* clean the dust from *The maid dusts, cleans and does laundry.* Col: Ashes to ashes dust to dust... – traditional burial service words   bite the dust – die or fail   dust bunny – ball of dust and dirt under the bed   dust-up – a fight   leave one in the dust – best them in a race or contest   make the dust fly – work   when the dust settles – in time, when the situation quiets down

enough /uˈnuf/ *noun* amount needed, not too much and not too little *Did you get enough to eat?* • *adj* as much as required *Did you get enough food?* Col: Cold enough for you? – small talk about severely cold weather   enough is enough – stop now   enough said – be quiet now   enough to keep body and soul together – bare minimum   fair enough – agreed   get enough nerve up – find the confidence   Give him enough rope and he'll hang himself. – *proverb* in time the bad guy will destroy himself so you don't have to   good enough – passable   good enough for – social status   Hot enough for you? – small talk about severely hot weather   Man enough? – up to a challenge   not enough room to swing a cat – the area of a small room   not know enough to come in out of the rain – no common sense   old enough to be one's mother – age at least a generation apart   That's enough! – no more   There aren't enough hours in the day! – overwhelmed or too busy   Too many chiefs and not enough Indians. – *proverb* too many bosses and not enough workers

from /frum/ *prep* a starting point *Where are you from?* Col: from away – not originally from a certain place   from A to Z – complete set

front /frunt/ [fronts] *noun* forward positions *The buttons are on the front* • *adj* having to do with first position or the forward side *No one uses the front door.* Col: can't see one's hand in front of one's face – poor visibility   front and centre – the most prominent position

front runner – in the lead so far **front some money** – advance **go to the front of the line** – reward or special treatment **in front** – in the lead **one foot in front of the other** – take the next step, keep going **put up a brave front** – act bravely even if it isn't felt **up front** – fully disclose

fuck /**fuk**/ [fucks, fucked, fucking] *interj* vulgar slang to express anger *Fuck! I hit my thumb with the hammer.*

fudge /**fuj**/ [fudges, fudged, fudging] *noun* sweet creamy candy *Chocolate fudge is my favorite treat.* • *verb* deal with something in an inadequate way to hide the truth *He fudged the results of the experiment hoping to get a better mark in Science.*

fun /**fun**/ *noun* entertainment *It is important to have fun on holidays.* • *adj* providing amusement *Teaching ESL is a fun job.* Col: **for fun** – for a good time **fun and games** – sarcastic in a difficult or awkward situation **Getting there is half the fun.** – the journey is entertaining too **It was fun while it lasted.** – bittersweet end, no hard feelings **make fun of** – mock, tease, laugh at their expense **more fun than a barrel of monkeys** – loads of fun **not all fun and games** – there is work involved too **poke fun at** – humiliate or laugh at someone's expense or bully **Time flies when you are having fun.** – *proverb* time seems to go quickly when enjoying oneself

funny /**fu** nEy/ [funnier, funniest] *adj* 1 brings laughter *That was a funny joke.* 2 strange *This cheese tastes funny.* Col: **funny as a crutch** – not amusing **funny bone** – tingling in part of the elbow or a laugh trigger **the funny thing is** – odd thing

government /**gu** vEr munt/ [governments] *noun* political control of an area or nation *The government should be run like a business.*

gum /**gum**/ [gums] *noun* 1 skin at the base of the teeth *Dentists check gums as well as teeth.* 2 chewy candy *Peppermint gum before the interview will freshen your breath.* Col: **can't walk and chew gum** – can't do two simple things at once **flap one's gums** – talk endlessly about nothing important **gum up** – blocked or ruined

gun /**gun**/ [guns] *noun* weapon that fires bullets *Police officers are armed with hand guns.* Col: **go great guns** – proceed with great speed, skill or success **gun for** – hunt down in order to kill **gunned down** – hunted to kill **hold a gun to someone's head** – extreme pressure **jump the gun** – start too early **smoking gun** – strong evidence **son of a gun** – no kidding **stick to one's guns** – hold a position under attack **under the gun** – pressure

honey /**hu** nEy/ [honeys] *noun* 1 sweet sticky food made by bees *I take honey in my tea.* 2 term of endearment *Honey, can you make me a cup of tea?* Col: **the land of milk and honey** – a place where there is more than enough of everything **You catch more flies with honey than vinegar.** – *proverb* flattery works

hundred /**hun** drud/ [100, hundreds] *noun* the number that comes after 99 *There are one hundred years in a century.* • *adj* one hundred in number *A hundred years is a long time.* Col: **one hundred percent** – healthy

ja /**ju**/ *contr* d + you, spoken word only *English is Stupid Students are Not* Chapter One /*Could ja help me?*/

judge /**juj**/ [judges, judged, judging] *noun* a person trained to make decisions based on the law *The judge sent him to jail for two years.* • *verb* form an opinion *He judged the dog show at the county fair.* Col: **Don't judge a book by its cover.** – *proverb* can't know a person by appearances alone **Judge not lest ye be judged.** – *proverb* condemn others and you will also be condemned **sober as a judge** – not drunk

juggle /ju gul/ [juggles, juggled, juggling] *verb* 1 continuously keep objects in the air *He juggled balls first, then he juggled swords.* 2 manage numerous tasks simultaneously *If I juggle my schedule we can have lunch together nest week.*

jump /**jump**/ [jumps, jumped, jumping] *verb* 1 leap off the ground *The kids were jumping on the trampoline in the back yard.* 2 sudden movement *I jumped when I saw the snake.* • *noun* 1 increase suddenly *There was a jump in gas prices after the trouble in the middle east.* 2 obstacle *The horses leapt over a timed course of jumps.* Col: get the jump on – early start   jump in the lake – go away   jump at – accept enthusiastically   jump down one's throat – reply immediately and sharply   jump for joy – happy and excited   jump in – join in with enthusiasm   jump on – sudden attack   jump out at – grab attention   jump out of one's skin – startled   jump ship – leave or desert   jump someone's bones – sex   jump the gun – start too soon   jump the queue – join the line in the middle not the end   jump through hoops – extra effort   jump to conclusions – decide before facts are considered   jump to it – hurry up   jump rope – skipping over a cord

jungle /juN gul/ [jungles] *noun* tropical forest *Monkeys live in the jungle.* Col: It's a jungle out there. – outside the shelter of home the world is full of challenges   the law of the jungle – nature's justice system

just /**just**/ *adj* based on what is morally right *The punishment was appropriate and just.* • *adverb* 1 in the immediate past *I just saw this in the news yesterday.* 2 only *It's just 8:00, I thought it was later.* 3 exactly *This is just what I wanted for my birthday.* Col: I could just spit – I'm so angry   it just so happens – positive circumstances   Just a matter of time – it will happen   Just a minute – stop, maybe rethink it   just around the corner – almost there   just between you and me – our little secret   just desserts – deserve the bad outcome   just good friend – not a romantic couple   just for the heck of it – for fun   just for the record – get facts straight   just getting by – not enough money   just one oar in the water – not smart   just in case – prepare for the worst outcome   just in the nick of time – at the last possible minute   just looking – when a shopkeeper asks if you need help   just my luck – bad things always happen to me   Just the facts Ma'am – get to the point, quoted from Dragnet an old TV show   just the ticket – perfect solution   just what the doctor ordered – probably a much needed vacation   just wondering – maybe   just a pretty face – she's smart too   that's just it – identified the problem   You just don't get it! – you don't understand even after it is explained

justice /**jus** dus/ *noun* morally right *The legal system is about precedent not justice.* Col: bring to justice – prosecute for a crime   Col: do justice to – give a good effort   justice of the peace – low court authority   travesty of justice – mistake or abuse of legal authority

love /**luv**/ [loves, loved, loving] *noun* a bond stronger than like *Love is the greatest power on Earth.* • *verb* feelings of love *I love you.* Col: fall in love – develop a romantic interest or passion for another   for love – out of concern   for love or money – not under any circumstances   for the love of – the sake of   in love – passionately involved   make love – have sex   There's no love lost between them. – they dislike each other

luck /**luk**/ [lucky] *noun* turn of fortune either good or bad *Winning the lottery is good luck.* • *adj* more fortunate than most *She's lucky to have a job she can do from home.* Col: a run of bad luck – many misfortunes in a row   as luck would have it – by chance   down on one's luck – poor   Good luck! – wish good fortune   in luck – fortunate   No such luck! – unfortunately not   out of luck – no luck left   push one's luck – risk   try one's luck – attempt

lunch /**lun**Ch/ [lunches, lunched, lunching,] *noun* noonday meal *I usually bring a sandwich for lunch.* • *verb* eat at noon *We'll be lunching at the club.* • *adj* about the noon meal *Lunch meat is on sale at the grocery store this week.* [Col:] out to lunch – crazy

lung /**lu**Ng/ [lungs] *noun* part of the body used to breathe *Swimmers fill their lungs with air to swim underwater.* • *adj* about lungs *Smoking damages lung capacity.* [Col:] at the top of one's lungs – loudly

Monday /**mun** dAy/ [Mon., Mondays] *prop noun* first day of the work week *Thanksgiving Monday is a holiday.*

money /**mu** nEy/ [monies] *noun* currency, coins and bills 💰 *Dad, can I have some money?* [Col:] for my money – in my opinion   in the money – rich, have money   mad money – money for extra little luxuries   on the money – on target   put money on – bet on   put one's money where one's mouth is – invest or take action not just talk

monkey /**mu**Ng kEy/ [monkeys] *noun* long-tailed mammals that live in trees and look like humans *The monkeys are the most popular exhibit at the zoo.* [Col:] freeze the balls off a brass monkey – nautical term for cold   have a monkey on one's back – a small persistent problem   I'll be a monkey's uncle. – astonished   Monkey see monkey do. – *proverb* children imitate what others do   monkey suit – tuxedo

month /**mun**TH/ [months] *noun* one of twelve named sections of the year each about thirty days long *We go to the library once a month.* [Col:] month of Sundays – not for a long period of time

mother /**mu**ThEr/ [Mom, mothers, mothered, mothering] *noun* female parent who bares or nurtures offspring *Some mothers choose natural childbirth.* • *verb* behaving in a motherly way *The old cat mothered two litters of kittens at once.* • *adj* about motherhood *She has a mother's touch.* [Col:] MADD – Mothers Against Drunk Driving, advocacy group against driving under the influence of alcohol   Mother's Day – celebrate our mothers on the second Sunday in May   mother-country – the country where one was born   mother-in-law – mother of one's husband or wife   Mother Nature – force that contains all the natural world   mother-tongue – a person's native language   the mother of all – the greatest example of its kind

much /**mu**Ch/ *adj* degree or amount *How much is this pencil?* • *adv* to a degree *I don't care much for cucumbers.* [Col:] a bit much – quite excessive   be too much for – be too difficult for   as much – almost the same   make much of – make a big fuss over   much the same – similar   not much – nothing important   not up to much – doing nothing   so much for – that's all to be said   think too much of – to have too high opinion of   without so much as – without even

multiply /**mul** tu plIy/ [×, multiplies, multiplied, multiplying] *verb* 1 increase in number *Profits multiplied when we hired more sales people.* 2 mathematical operation $2 \times 4 = 8$

muscle /**mu** sul/ [muscles, muscled, muscling] *noun* bundles of fibers that move the body by tensing and relaxing *Lifting weights makes my arm muscles ache.* • *verb* physical force *The police officer muscled his way through the crowd.* [Col:] didn't move a muscle – did nothing   flex muscle – exert emotional pressure over a dependant   muscle in – force one's way in   pull a muscle – strain or injure

must /**must**/ *helping verb* 1 necessary *We must breath to live.* 2 the law *Everyone must wear a seatbelt.* 3 command or suggest *You must study if you want to do well.* Col: All good things must end. – *proverb* all things even good things will end   ears must be burning – we were just talking about you   He who would climb the ladder must begin at the bottom. – *proverb* work one's way up   I must be off – have to leave   If Mohammed will not go to the mountain, the mountain must come to Mohammed. – *proverb* don't wait too long, before do it oneself   the show must go on – even when things do not go as planned, continue   they must have seen you coming – naïve swindlers   What can't be cured must be endured. – *proverb* tolerate what can't be changed   What goes up must come down. – *proverb* the law of nature, what has risen eventually will fall   You must be joking! – disbelief

mustard /**mus** dErd/ [mustards] *noun* 1 tangy golden yellow spread for fast food *I like mustard on my hamburger.* 2 the color between tan and gold or dirty yellow *Mustard is a color that goes in and out of fashion.* • *adj* the color *She doesn't like her mustard jacket but it looks good on her.* Col: cut the mustard – deal with the problem, do what is expected

nothing /**nu** THiNg/ *noun* 1 not anything *There is nothing to do.* 2 zero *We won the soccer game two nothing.* Col: for nothing – for no reason or money   have nothing to do with – avoid   have nothing on – naked   in nothing flat – very quickly   next to nothing – almost zero   nothing but – only   Nothing doing! – No!   stop at nothing – committed   sweet nothings – love talk   there's nothing like – enjoy   there's nothing to it – easy   think nothing of it – you're welcome, my pleasure   to say nothing of – also

number /**num** bEr/ [numbers numbered, numbering] *noun* 1 ordered unit of math *One, two, three, four… are all numbers.* 2 identification *What is your phone number?* 3 musical piece *They practiced three numbers for the recital.* Col: any number of – many   do a number on – defeat or humiliate in a planned way   have someone's number – see their hidden motives or character   one's days are numbered – dying   one's number is up – dying soon

nut /**nut**/ [nuts] *noun* 1 dry seed covered in a hard shell *Acorns are nuts of oak trees.* 2 crazy *My aunt is the nut who lived in the pink house trailer and planted trees on the roof.* 3 slang for testicles *He passed out when he got kicked in the nuts.* Col: a tough nut to crack – a difficult person to understand   in a nutshell – tell briefly   off one's nut – be crazy

of /**uv**/ *prep* connects *The color of the sky is grey when it rains.* Col: coat of many colors – bible story   made of money – rich   speaks of love – romantic intentions   with an inch of his life – almost killed

once /**wuns**/ *adv* only one time *My son cuts his hair once a month.* • *noun* one time *Once is enough.* Col: all at once – together   at once – now or concurrently   for once – this time only   once and for all – never again   once in a while – occasionally   once upon a time – classic beginning to fairy tales

one (won) /**wun**/ [1, ones] *noun* first cardinal number between zero and two *One is the loneliest number.* • *adj* one in number *People have one nose and two eyes.* Col: at one – together in agreement   be one up on – an advantage   for one thing – a single thought   one and all – everyone   one by one – one at a time after another   one or two – a few   way or another – either way

other /**u** ThEr/ [others] *adj* different from or remaining *This is my seat and the other one is yours.* Col: a significant other – sexual or romantic partner   at each other's throats – arguing and fighting   bat for the other side – homosexual   every other – alternate   go from one extreme to the other – totally opposite direction   go in one ear and out the other – not listening   how the other half lives – how rich people live   in other words – reword   look the other way – deliberately avoid addressing bad situations   on the other hand – explore a different perspective   one after the other – in order   one way or the other – re-assurance of the outcome   other way around – the reverse   put one foot in front of the other – carefully and in order   six of one and half a dozen of the other – same either way   *The grass is always greener on the other side.* – *proverb* envy   the other day – recently   the wrong side of the tracks – the poor part of town   turn the other cheek – stay calm and ignore an insult   wait for the other shoe to drop – wait for expected bad news

oven /**u** vun/ [ovens] *noun* appliance for cooking food *Bake cookies and cakes in the oven.* Col: a bun in the oven – pregnant

plus /**plus**/ [pluses] *prep* more by adding *Two plus two equals four.* • *adj* having to do with addition *The plus sign is over the equal sign on the keyboard.* • *noun* advantage *Good hand-eye coordination is a plus for a carpenter.*

public /**pub** lik/ *noun* community as a whole *The public supports capital punishment.* • *adj* about or for the community *The public pool is closed for repair.* Col: air one's dirty linen in public – to fight about private matters in public   go public – announce to the public or sell shares in a privately owned company   in public – widely known   in the public eye – famous   public displays of affection (PDF) – inappropriate amount of affection shown in public   public enemy number one – many people love to hate   take public – to make information known to the public

pump /**pump**/ [pumps, pumped, pumping] *noun* 1 a machine used to move liquid or gas from one place to another *The pump brings water from the well.* 2 woman's shoe without laces *Most of the teachers wear pumps to work.* • *verb* 1 move liquid or gas with a machine *He pumps gas at the service station for a summer job.* 2 quick motions up and down *He pumped air into the tire at the garage.* Col: prime the pump – prepare the machine to do its job   pump iron – lift weights   pump someone for information – try to extract get information from a third party   pump up – ignite enthusiasm in another   pump one's stomach – draw contents out through the nose   pumped up – excited

punishment /**pu** nuSh munt/ [punishments] *noun* penalty for doing the wrong thing *Jail is not punishment enough for some crimes.* Col: a glutton for punishment – chooses to work brutally hard   *Let the punishment fit the crime.* – enforce penalties directly related to the offense

rough /**ruf**/ [rougher, roughest] *adj* 1 not smooth *The road into the bush is too rough for a car.* 2 difficult conditions *It was a rough summer with both parents in the hospital and a new baby.* 3 course or crude *A rough crowd hangs out by the beer store.* Col: a rough ride – a hard time   a diamond in the rough – great potential not easily seen   give a rough time – tease, bully or obstruct   have a rough time of it – not coping well   rough and ready – simple but effective   rough-and-tumble – aggressive   rough around the edges – not top quality but still functional   rough idea about –

general idea   rough going – difficult to advance   rough in – prepare for possible future development   rough it – without basic comforts   rough someone up – bully   rough something up – to rub to make it uneven, texture

rub /**rub**/ [rubs, rubbed, rubbing] *verb* apply pressure in a back and forth motion *Please rub my sore feet.* • *noun* the process of rubbing *I need a back rub.* Col: not have two cents to rub together – very poor   rub up against – gently brush   rub down – massage   rub elbows with – connect with at a social event   rub one's nose in it – hurting another by reminding them of their shortcomings   rub off – remove by erasing   rub off on – a trait transferred to another   rub salt in the wound – aggravate an already hurtful situation   rub something in – repeat an embarrassing fact   rub someone out – kill them   rub the wrong way – to irritate   there's the rub – the essence of a problem

run /**run**/ [runs, ran running] *verb* 1 go forward by moving legs quickly *The dog ran after the ball.* 2 cause to run *He ran the cranes down at the dock.* 3 fast trip *Run to the store and get some milk.* 4 seek office in an election *She ran for mayor.* Col: a dry run – practice preview   a run for one's money – a strong challenge   be on the run – sought by police   eat and run – not stay and talk   have a run-in – a conflict   have the run of – full access   I've got to run – I'm leaving   in the long/short run – in the distant or near future   make a run for it – escape   make one's blood run cold – shocked or frightened   Pick up the ball and run with it – take an idea and develop it   run a fever – have a high body temperature from an illness   run a red light – traffic violation failing to stop at a red light   run a risk – take a chance   run a tab – to put drinks on a bill and pay once before leaving   run a tight ship – organized efficient control of a household or business   run an errand – travel a short distance to accomplish a task   run across – find without looking   run after someone – pursue a romantic interest   run against – political rival   run along – leave   run away with someone – elope   run away with – win easily   run before you can walk – attempt before learning the basics   run counter to – be oppose   run deep – rooted in one's spirit   run down – wear out   run dry – nothing left   run into – crash into   run into the ground – overworked   run its course – continue until it finishes naturally   run like clockwork – run well   run like the wind – run very fast   run-of-the-mill – ordinary   run off one's feet – over worked   run on all cylinders – peak performance   run out of gas – not enough energy to continue   run out on – leave a partner   run over – knock down or crush with a vehicle   run up against – meet with a problem   run ragged – over worked   run rings around – show more skill than other people   run the gamut – try everything   run through – read something quickly or practice something   run wild – out of control   Still waters run deep. – quiet people have strong emotions

scrub /**skrub**/ [scrubs, scrubbed, scrubbing] *verb* clean by brushing or washing vigorously *I scrub the bathroom every Saturday morning.*

shut /**shut**/ [shuts, shut shutting] *verb* close *Shut the door.* Col: Keep your mouth shut. – be quiet   open and shut case – facts are clear and easy to make a decision   put up or shut up – act or be quiet   shut down – stop from working   shut off – turn off   shut somebody out – exclude   shut the barn door after the horse got out – act too late   shut up – rude for stop talking shut up about it – don't tell anyone about it   shut your face – rude be quiet   When one door shuts another opens. – *proverb* when one opportunity is lost, another often appears

skull /**skul**/ [skulls] *noun* bones of the head *Skulls protect brains.* Col: get through one's thick skull – struggle to make someone understand   pissed out of one's skull – drunk

skunk /**skuNgk**/ [skunks, skunked, skunking] *noun* a black and white mammal that defends itself by spraying a very bad smell *They had skunks living under their porch and had to call the exterminator.* • *verb* sprayed by a skunk *The dog got skunked and we had to bathe him in tomato juice.* Col: as drunk as a skunk – very drunk

some (sum) /**sum**/ *adj* an amount that is not clear *He gave some money to the poor.* • *pron* things not known *I don't eat peppers, some are hot and some are not.* Col: and then some – and lots more   catch some rays – suntan   catch some Zs – take a nap   for some reason – don't know why   give some sugar – loving   in some respects – partial agreement   kick some ass – fight back   open some doors – opportunities   raise some eyebrows – shock or get the attentions of people   take some doing – lots of effort   turn some heads – get noticed   You win some, you lose some. – *proverb* can't always be the winner

son (sun) /**sun**/ [sons] *noun* male child *My son looks like his dad.* Col: a favorite son – a famous person embraced by his place of origin   every mother's son – all of them   like father, like son – child resembles and behaves like dad   son of a bitch – nasty person   son of a gun – surprise

sponge /**spunj**/ [sponges, sponged, sponging] *noun* a tiny sea animal with many holes in its skeleton *Sponges live in colonies in the ocean.* 2 artificial material with many holes used as a cleaning tool *The dish sponge is beside the sink.* • *verb* soak up liquid with a sponge *Sponge up that milk on the floor.* Col: sponge someone down – bathe   sponge off – to live without contributing to the household   sponge something up – absorb with a sponge

stomach /**stu** muk/ [stomachs, stomached, stomaching] *noun* an organ in the body that digests food. *Cows have four stomachs.* • *verb* tolerate *I can't stomach violence on TV as entertainment.* Col: butterflies in one's stomach – nervous or excited feeling   cast-iron stomach – never gets sick from eating bad food   don't have the stomach for – can't watch   feel sick to one's stomach – nauseous, ready to vomit   have a strong stomach – unaffected by repulsive sights   not able to stomach – can't stand them   on an empty stomach – no food   one's eyes are bigger than one's stomach – taken too much food   pit of one's stomach – deep in one's emotional body   The way to a man's heart is through his stomach. – *proverb* to win a man's love, feed him well   turns one's stomach – rage

structure /**struk** ChEr/ [structures, structured, structuring] *noun* 1 many parts joined in a particular way *"English is Stupid" provides a structure for speaking English.* 2 anything already built *Many structures in the city are ugly and boring.* • *verb* custom formed *English lessons are structured around student needs.*

substance /**sub** stuns/ [substances] *noun* matter, what things are made of *There are substances in the back of the fridge that can't be identified.*

subway /**sub** wAy/ [subways] *noun* underground electric train in cities *Thousand of people in the city take the subway to work everyday.*

such /**such**/ *adj* that much *She takes such good care of her students.* Col: no such luck – didn't work out   such as – for example   such as it is – with its faults

such is life – it is what it is   **There is no such thing as a free lunch.** – *proverb* compensation is expected for kindness

sudden /**su** dun/ *adj* unexpected *There was a sudden change in the weather.* `Col:` **all of a sudden** – quick surprise

sum (some) /**sum**/ [sums] *noun* the amount from adding numbers *Four is the sum of two plus two.* `Col:` **sum up** – recap   **a zero sum game** – the winnings equal the cost of participating

summer /**su** mEr/ [summers, summered, summering] *noun* hot season between June and September *We like to take our holidays in the summer.* • *verb* spend the summer *My family summered at Cape Cod every year.* `Col:` **Indian summer** – a week of hot days in the fall, late in the season

sun (son) /**sun**/ [suns, sunned, sunning] *noun* 1 the center of our solar system ☼ *The planets rotate around the sun.* 2 the heat and light coming from the sun *Lying in the sun is relaxing.* • *verb* absorbing the sun's rays *The dog is sunning himself in front of the window.* `Col:` **catch the sun** – get a tan   **Make hay while the sun shines.** – *proverb* promoting action when opportunities arise   **place in the sun** – a positive position   **touch of the sun** – sunstroke   **under the sun** – everything

sundae (Sunday) /**sun** dAy/ [sundaes] *noun* ice cream dessert with flavored, sauce, whipped cream and a cherry on top 🍨 *It's hard to beat a chocolate sundae as a special treat.*

Sunday (sundae) /**sun** dAy/ [Sun., Sundays] *prop noun* last day of the weekend *On Sunday we usually take the dog for a long walk in the forest.* `Col:` **a month of Sundays** – a long time   **Sunday best** – good clothes and manners saved for special events   **Sunday driver** – too slow

the /**Thu**/ *definite article* 1 specific item *The glass is on the table.* 2 used before a noun already mentioned *Please pass me a pencil. The pencil you gave me isn't sharp.* 3 before proper names or special places *The Empire State building is a popular destination.*

thumb /**THum**/ [thumbs, thumbed, thumbing] *noun* short thick first finger separate from the other four *Thumbs are useful for holding, gripping and twisting.* • *verb* moving with the thumb *The patient thumbed through a magazine while waiting for her doctor.* `Col:` **all thumbs** – uncoordinated   **green thumb** – good gardener   **rule of thumb** – general guideline decided by experience not science   **sticks out like a sore thumb** – conspicuous, easy to see   **thumb one's nose** – disrespectful gesture, putting a thumb to the side of the nose   **thumbs down** – 👎 negative   **thumbs up** – 👍 positive or more   **thumb through** – look through casually not reading   **twiddle one's thumbs** – pass time by circling thumbs around   **under someone's thumb** – under the control of another

thunder /**THun** dEr/ [thunders, thundered, thundering] *noun* loud noise that is part of a rainstorm *The thunder woke us up and scared the dog.* • *verb* make the sound of thunder *The race horses came thundering around the track.* `Col:` **steal someone's thunder** – draw attention away from someone's big moment   **thunder past** – make a rumbling noise while moving along

tongue /**tuNg**/ [tongues] *noun* 1 the muscle organ at the bottom of the mouth for tasting. *I burned my tongue on my hot chocolate.* 2 language *People speak in thousands of tongues all over the world.* `Col:` **bite one's tongue** – self restraint   **Bite your tongue!** – be quiet   **Cat got your tongue?** – sarcastic taunt to a quiet person   **cause tongues to wag** – event people will want to talk about   **get one's tongue around** – difficulty pronouncing a tricky word or phrase   **have a sharp tongue** – critical   **Hold

/ u / is Mustard

your tongue! – be quiet   keep a civil tongue – avoid swearing and strong language   loosen your tongue – uninhibited usually after drinking alcohol   mother tongue – first language   on the tip of one's tongue – just about to be said or remembered   roll off the tongue – easy to say   silver-tongued – flatter people to get them to do what you want   slip of the tongue – reveal a secret by accident   speak with a forked tongue – lie   stick one's tongue out – rude gesture pushing the tongue straight out of the mouth   tongue-in-cheek – a joke with an element of truth in it   tongue-lashing – reprimand

touch /tuCh/ [touches, touched, touching] noun 1 one of the five senses, used to feel *A baby's skin is soft to the touch.* 2 a small amount *I take a touch of honey in my tea.* 3 contact *Stay in touch.* • verb 1 feel *He touched the kettle and burned his fingers.* 2 affect *Mother Teresa touched the lives of millions.* Col: a soft touch – easy to exploit   finishing touch – final details   keep in touch – stay in contact   lose one's touch – lose a rare, sensitive skill   lose touch with – lose contact   lose touch with reality – crazy   magic touch – a gift or special talent to make the ordinary better   not touch a drop – avoid alcohol   put in touch with – connect   soft touch – a gentle manner   the Midas touch – able to make a lot of money easily in any field   touch a nerve – evoke emotions   touch base – talk briefly   touch of – slight illness   touch off – cause to start, chain reaction   touch on – not dwell on a topic   touch wood – hope for good luck   touch-and-go – urgency   wouldn't touch it with a ten-foot pole – avoid at all costs

trouble /**tru** bul/ [troubles, troubled, troubling] verb 1 worry or problem *What is troubling you?* 2 bother or annoy *I don't want to trouble you but I need some help.* noun burdens *I wouldn't trade troubles with her.* Col: ask for trouble – tease or risk   borrow trouble – invite problems   drown one's troubles – drink in trouble – in danger   isn't worth the trouble – effort   make trouble – cause unhappiness   no trouble – you are welcome   trouble is brewing – building up

truck /**truk**/ [trucks, trucked, trucking] noun big vehicle for carrying heavy loads *You need a truck on a farm.* • verb move material using trucks *He trucks for a living.* Col: just fell off the turnip truck – unrefined   keep on trucking – continue doing well and enjoying what you do

trust /**trust**/ [trusts, trusted, trusting] noun believe in *We earned the orphan's trust but it took time.* 2 asset management for the benefit of another *He left his property to his grandchildren in trust.* • verb depend on *We trusted our agent and he didn't let us down.* Col: in trust – held by one person for the benefit of another   misplace one's trust – put trust in the wrong person   on trust – on credit   restore trust – rebuild   take on trust – one's word

tub /**tub**/ [tubs] noun large container for holding water *The big bathroom has a shower and a tub.* Col: tub of lard – overweight person

ugly /**ug** lEy/ [uglier, ugliest] adj not beautiful or attractive *That is the ugliest dog I have ever seen.* Col: an ugly duckling – late bloomer   rear its ugly head – reappear after being away for a while   ugly as sin – not attractive inside or out

uncle /**uNg** kul/ [uncles] mother or father's brother *John, is my favorite uncle.* Col: everybody and his uncle – lots of people   I'll be a monkey's uncle! – I'm surprised!   say uncle – give in, concede   Uncle Sam – United States of America government

under /**un** dEr/ prep below or less than *The garbage can is under the sink.* Col: out from under – resolved any problems   under the sun – anywhere in the world   under the weather – sick

up /**up**/ *adv* to, at or toward a higher place *We climbed up the stairs to go to bed.* 2 out of bed *We got up at 7:30.* `Col:` on the up and up – open, honest   something is up – unusual   up-and-coming – likely to do well   up and running – working   ups and downs – good and bad   Wha dup? – greeting

us /**us**/ *pron* first person plural object *Can you help us?*

W /**du** bul **yUw**/ [W's] *noun* twenty-third letter in the Latin alphabet *Women starts with a W.*

was /**wuz**/ *verb* past tense of the verb *to be* exist used in with I, he, she and it *It was raining.* `Col:` A good time was had by all. – everyone had fun   as I was saying – repeat myself   It was fun while it lasted. – bittersweet end, no hard feelings   like there's no tomorrow – eager   Rome was not built in a day. – *proverb* great things take a long time

what /**wut**/ *adv* Wh question, which one *What time is it?* • *pron* ask for information *What is your name?* • *adj* which one *What day is it?*

won (one) /**wun**/ [win, won, winning] *verb* past tense of *win* come first 🏅 *We won gold at the Olympics.*

wonder /**wun** dEr/ [wonders, wondered, wondering] *verb* question *I wonder what kind of parents my children will be?* • *noun* in awe *When people go to Niagara Falls, they are filled with wonder.* `Col:` a seven-day wonder – made perfect in seven days   a one-hit wonder – only one successful creation   no wonder – not surprising   wonder about – interest or doubt   Wonders never cease! – amazed   work wonders – great progress

young /**yuNg**/ [younger, youngest] *adj* an early stage in life *His younger sister is 5 years old.* • *noun* babies recently born *Kangaroos carry their young in a pouch.* `Col:` not as young as one used to be – feeling the restrictions of aging   young at heart – youthful spirit   young blood – new ideas and energy from young people

yuk /**yuk**/ *interj* repulsion *Yuk! The garbage stinks.*

Chapter 11
/^/ is Wood

HOW DO YOU SAY? PRONUNCIATION DICTIONARY

Chapter 11
/^/ is Wood

book /b^k/
bull /b^l/

cook /k^k/
cookie /k^ kEy/
could /k^d/
coulda /k^ du/
cushion /k^ Shun/

foot /f^t/
football /f^t bol/
footing /f^ diNg/
full /f^l/

good /g^d/
gonna /g^ nu/

hood /h^d/
hoof /h^f/
hook /h^k/
hooker /h^ kEr/

look /l^k/

nook /n^k/

pudding /p^ diNg/
pull /p^l/
push /p^Sh/
put /p^t/

shook /Sh^k/
should /Sh^d/
shoulda /Sh^ du/
stood /st^d/
sugar /Sh^ gEr/

took /t^k/

wolf /w^lf/
woman /w^ mun/
wood (would) /w^d/
wooded /w^ dud/
wooden /w^ dun/
woodpecker /w^d pekEr/
woodwinds /w^d winz/
woof /w^f/
wool /w^l/
would (wood) /w^d/
woulda /w^ du/

book /bʌk/ [books, booked, booking] *noun* paper bound together to record a story or facts 📖 *The dictionary is the biggest book in our classroom.* • *verb* reserve *We booked our flight to Mexico yesterday.* `Col:` **book it** – move quickly **by the book** – follow the rules **Don't judge a book by its cover.** – *Proverb* can't know a person by appearance alone **every trick in the book** – cunning **in the good books** – the person in authority is pleased **nose in a book** – to read a lot **off the books** – stealing in secret **open book** – accessible

bull /bʌl/ [bulls] *noun* male cow *There is one bull with a herd of cows.* `Col:` **a bull in a china shop** – clumsy **as strong as a bull** – very strong **bull pen** – baseball term where the pitcher warms up **bull's-eye** – centre of a target **bull-headed** – stubborn **cock and bull story** – nonsense **full of bull** – lie **like a red rag to a bull** – to draw attention **no bull** – the truth **take the bull by the horns** – openly confront a problem

cook /kʌk/ [cooks, cooked, cooking] *noun* prepare food *My mom is the best cook in the world.* • *verb* prepare food with heat *Who is cooking tonight?* `Col:` **chief cook and bottle washer** – one in charge of the home **cook one's goose** – damage one's business reputation **cook the books** – hide money **cook to perfection** – delicious **cook up** – plan or arrange **someone is cooked** – tired **too many cooks spoil the broth** – too many opinions ruins the project **What's cooking?** – What's happening?

cookie /kʌkEy/ [cookies] *noun* baked sweet dessert that fits in one's hand *May I please have a chocolate chip cookie?* `Col:` **smart cookie** – intelligent and sensible **That's the way the cookie crumbles.** – the way life goes **tough cookie** – emotionally strong, independent thinker

could /kʌd/ *helping verb* 1 action or state possible *There could be some rain today.* 2 able to *I could climb that tree if I wanted to.* `Col:` **could be better** – not perfect **could be worse** – bad but okay **could care less** – don't care **could do it in one's sleep** – so easy **could do with** – need **could do with one arm tied behind my back** – showing off **could have fooled me** – don't believe an explanation **could have heard a pin drop** – silent **Could I be excused?** – polite request to leave **Could I call you?** – date **Could I have a lift?** – ride **couldn't care less** – don't care **Could we continue this later?** – I have to go **could with eyes closed** – easy **Could you do me a favor?** – I need your help **face only a mother could love** – unattractive, not beautiful **How could you?** – shocked, hurt, angry, incredulous **I could eat a horse** – hungry **I could spit!** – angry **If looks could kill we'd all be dead.** – getting the evil eye **so clean one could eat off the floor** – spotless, sanitary **so mad I could scream** – angry **so still one could hear a pin drop** – quiet **would if I could** – can't help **one could cut the air with a knife** – tension **You could have knocked me down with a feather!** – shocked

coulda /kʌ du/ *contr* could have, spoken word only *English is Stupid Students are Not* Chapter Three and Four */You coulda told me he was married!/*

cushion /kʌ Shun/ [cushions, cushioned, cushioning] *noun* absorbing layer *She spilled her coffee on the couch and stained the cushion.* • *verb* soften *He fell off the garage roof but a big pile of* *leaves cushioned his fall.* Col: **cushion the blow** — reduce harm

foot /fʌt/ [feet] *noun* 1 part of the body below the ankle *The chair fell on my foot.* 2 unit of measurement equal to 12 inches *There are 12 inches in one foot.* Col: **foot the bill** — pay for   **get a foot in the door** — tiny opportunity as a start   **get off on the right foot** — a relationship starts well   **get off on the wrong foot** — a relationship starts badly   **lead foot** — fast driver   **on foot** — walk or run   **one foot in the grave** — very sick   **put best foot forward** — make a good impression   **put foot down** — assert oneself   **put one's foot in one's mouth** — regret stupid or hurtful words   **put one's foot in it** — accidently embarrass oneself or another   **shoe on the other foot** — experience bad treatment once caused for others   **shoot oneself in the foot** — cause oneself difficulty   **to not put a foot wrong** — perform perfectly   **wait on someone hand and foot** — attend to all a person's needs   **would not touch that with a ten-foot pole** — avoid a situation

football /fʌt bol/ [footballs] *noun* 1 in North America it's an oval pigskin ball that is kicked or thrown *He caught the football and ran it in for a touchdown.* 2 team game *Let's get the gang together and play football in the park.* 3 soccer *Outside of North America, football means soccer.* Col: **football jersey** — team shirt   **political football** — an issue that doesn't get solved just passed around

footing /fʌt diNg/ *noun* a firm base to stand on *The footing on the trail was rocky and steep.* Col: **lose one's footing** — slip

full /fʌl/ [fuller, fullest] *adj* containing all that can be held *The cup is full.* Col: **chock full of** — brimming with   **come full circle** — arrive back at the place or state one started   **cup half full or half empty?** — optimistic or pessimistic   **full alert** — ready for action   **full blast** — with as much force as possible   **full of crap** — false statements   **full of hot air** — talking nonsense   **full of it** — to exaggerate or lie   **full of oneself** — arrogant   **full of shit** — exaggerate the truth   **full plate** — many responsibilities   **full speed** — top speed, fast Col: **full speed ahead** — focus one's energy on the task at hand   **full steam ahead** — move forward with conviction   **full strength** — maximum power   **full swing** — peak of activity, moving forward quickly   **full tilt** — fast as possible   **have hands full** — busy   **playing with a full deck** — mentally sound   **the full monty** — as complete as possible

good /gʌd/ [good, better, best] *adj* 1 desirable qualities *He makes good soup.* 2 better than average *She is a good soccer player.* 3 pleasant *I had a good time at the festival.* Col: **a bill of goods** — cheated   **A good man is hard to find.** — *proverb* good men are all married   **a good Samaritan** — kind person who helps others in distress   **All good things must end.** — *proverb* all experiences, even good ones, end   **all in good time** — be patient   **as good as gold** — well behaved   **as good as new** — well repaired   **as good as one's word** — kept promises   **at a good clip** — quickly   **best defense is a good offense** — attack is the best protection   **come to no good** — a bad ending is likely   **deliver the goods** — did what he said he would   **do more harm than good** — more damaging than helpful   **do the world of good** — caused great improvement   **for good or for keeps** — forever   **for good measure** — extra effort   **for the good of** — benefit of   **get while the gettin's good** — take advantages of an opportunity before it passes **give as good as one gets** — can hold one's own in an argument or fight **good bet** — odds in favor of **Good Book** — Bible **good egg** — good person **Good enough** — not perfect but it will do **good-for-nothing** — useless **Good for you!** — congratulations **Good grief!** – Oh no! **Good luck!** — all the best **good old boy** — powerful business and political leader in a community **good old days** — yester years **good sport** — plays well, wins and loses gracefully **Good things come in small packages.** — *proverb* not to misjudge value by size alone **Good things come to he who waits.** — *proverb* about patience **good to go** — ready **Good-bye and good riddance** — bye and happy you are leaving **Good-bye for now** — see you again **goods and chattels** — part of private property **have a good arm** — throws a ball far **have a good command of** — solid ability **have a good head on one's shoulders** — sensible **have a good mind** — sharp and disciplined **have a good run** — success for a long period **have a good thing going** — healthy stable relationship **have it on good authority** — news from a credible source **If you can't be good, be careful.** — *proverb* about having fun but not getting hurt **in good company** — associated with good people **in good conscience** — do the right thing because it's the right thing to do **in good faith** — trust **in good graces** — well thought of **in good hands** — safe **in good repair** — working order **in good shape** — physically fit **in good spirits** — happy **look good on paper** — show sales but not all the costs of business **make good money** — earns a good salary **make good time** — no setbacks on the journey **No news is good news.** — *proverb* not to worry if there hasn't been news, bad news would have been reported **on good terms** — no bad feelings **put in a good word** — give me a reference **stand in good stead** — serve you well in the long run **take the bad with the good** — accept the whole person or job **the goods on** — gossip about **The road to hell is paved with good intentions.** — *proverb* it is not enough to mean well one has to produce results **throw good money after bad** — try to recover money from a bad investment by investing more money in it **too good to be true** — so wonderful there must be some bad hidden **too much of a good thing** — overindulgence in good becomes a vice or bad **up to no good** — trouble **when one is good and ready** — not when told or bossed into it **with good reason** — valid explanation **You can't keep a good man down.** — gets up and back to work after a setback **Your guess is as good as mine** — I don't know either

hood /h^d/ [hoods] *noun* 1 a head covering attached to clothes *The air is chilly, put up your hood.* 2 covers car engine *Pop the hood so I can check the oil.* 3 slang for poor neighborhood *The rapper sings about his life in the hood.* 4 slang for an uneducated bum from a bad neighborhood *A couple of hoods stole the old lady's purse.* `Col:` **check under the hood** — look at the car's engine **from the hood** — born and raised in a poor urban neighborhood **hoodwinked** — deceived **pop the hood** — open the car hood **Robin Hood** — fictitious character who stole from the rich and gave to the poor

gonna /g^ nu/ *contr* going to future, spoken word only *English is Stupid Students are Not* Chapter Four /It's gonna rain./

hoof /h^f/ [hooves] {also said /hUwf/ see Blue} *noun* hard part of the foot of certain mammals *The blacksmith nailed the horseshoe onto the horse's hoof.* Col: hoof in mouth — play on words for saying the wrong thing at the wrong time   hoof it — walking

hook /h^k/ [hooks, hooked, hooking] *noun* 1 a sharply bent barbed piece of steel used to catch fish *He changed his bait and his hook before he caught the big one.* • *verb* to catch something *We hooked a big fish.* Col: bait the hook — attach enticement   by hook or by crook — by any means possible   fell for it hook, line and sinker — duped, completely believed   get hooks into — persuade or control of another   hook it up — attach   hook one up — introduce one to a possible love or business interest   hook up — meet friends   hooked on — captivated or addicted to banned substances   off the hook — free from punishment, consequences   on the hook — responsible for   ringing off the hook — the telephone rings constantly

hooker /h^ kEr/ [hookers] *noun* prostitute *Hookers hang out behind the bar most nights of the week.*

look /l^k/ [looks, looked, looking] *noun* a style of fashion *The model has a great look.* • *verb* see or view *Look at the rainbow.* Col: a looker — an attractive person   dirty look — angry stare   Don't look a gift horse in the mouth. — *proverb* there is probably something wrong with it but be gracious   if looks could kill — vicious angry star, getting the evil eye   just looking — examining without the intention to buy   look alive — be attentive   look before you leap — don't be too impulsive   look down one's nose at — feel superior to someone else   look fit to kill — very angry   look forward to it — anticipate with pleasure   look into it — investigate   look me up — call me   look on the bright side — be optimistic   look the other way — ignore   look up to — admire   look what the cat dragged in — appear looking disheveled   look who's talking — criticizing for something they do themselves   not much to look at — unattractive   take a good look — analyze closely

nook /n^k/ [nooks] *noun* a small corner *She keeps her fine crystal figurines in the shelf in the nook beside the front door.* Col: breakfast nook — tiny eating area   every nook and cranny — look everywhere, even in tiny spaces

pudding /p^ diNg/ *noun* a soft custard-like sweet dessert *The restaurant offers homemade chocolate and vanilla pudding for dessert.* Col: The proof is in the pudding. — *proverb* for assessing success after the results have been evaluated

pull /p^l/ [pulls, pulled, pulling] *verb* move an object by bringing it near *Pull the drawer open.* Col: pull apart — separate into pieces, criticize   pull hair out — anxious, frustrated   pull in — drive in   pull it out of a hat — magic, make appear as if from nowhere or from nothing   pull one over on — deceive   pull oneself together — regain self control   pull out all the stops — do everything possible to achieve success   pull the wool over one's eyes — deceive, trick   pull through — survive serious injury or illness   pull up a chair — come, sit down   pull your leg — joke or kid around

push /p^sh/ [pushes, pushed, pushing] *verb* move an object away from *Push the door open.* Col: don't push — do not shove   don't push one's luck — luck is unlikely to continue endlessly   have to push off — need to leave   push aside a project — postpone   push over — easily swayed when push comes to shove – the situation becomes desperate

put /pʌt/ [puts, put, putting] *verb* place an object in a specific location *Put the book on the shelf.* Col: **put out** – have sex or be angry **puts his pants on one leg at a time** – *proverb* he is only human

shook /shʌk/ [shakes, shook, shaking] *verb* irregular past tense of *shake* move back and forth quickly *He shook his head no.* Col: **shook up** – scared

should /shʌd/ helping *verb* must or ought *People should get more sleep and eat more vegetables.* Col: **children should be seen and not heard** – remain quiet in the presence of adults **if anything should happen to me** – express a plan in case of death **should be going** – time to leave

shoulda /shʌ du/ *contr* should have, spoken word only *English is Stupid Students are Not* Chapter Three and Four /*You should told me you were married!*/

stood /stʌd/ [stands, stood, standing] *verb* irregular past tense of *stand* supporting oneself on two legs *They stood and clapped.* Col: **stood one's ground** – didn't back down when challenged **stood up** – didn't show up for a date and didn't notify the other party

sugar /shʌ gEr/ [sugars] *noun* sweetener *A regular coffee has one sugar and one milk.* Col: **A spoonful of sugar helps the medicine go down** – make the bad seem less unpleasant **give some sugar** – kiss **sugar and spice and everything nice** – what little girls are made of

took /tʌk/ [take, took, taking] *verb* past tense of *take* bring with or away *They took sleeping bags and tents on their camping trip.*

wolf /wʌlf/ [wolves, wolfed, wolfing] *noun* large wild dog-like animal *The wolf howls at the moon.* • *verb* eat hungrily *He wolfed down his dinner then went out with his friends.* Col: **cry wolf** – call for help when none is needed to manipulate **wolf in sheep's clothing** – bad person pretending to be good **wolfed down food** – to eat very quickly **wolves are at the door** – creditors want their money

woman /wʌ mun/ [women] *noun* adult female person *The woman dropped her purse.* Col: **a kept woman** – financially supported in exchange for sex *A woman's place is in the home.* – *proverb* about traditional role of homemaker *A woman's work is never done.* – *proverb* house work and raising children are endless responsibilities **be one's own woman** – true to herself, act independently *Hell hath no fury like a woman scorned.* – *proverb* nothing more frightening then an upset woman **make an honest woman of her** – marry one's sex partner **woman of one's dream** – ideal, preferred above any other **woman of the world** – well traveled and educated

wood (would) /wʌd/ [woods] *noun* hard material under the bark that makes up the trunk and branches of a tree *We need to cut some wood for the fire.* Col: **dead wood** – no longer useful **knock on wood** – hoping for a positive result **not out of the woods yet** – a negative outcome is still possible **touch wood** – for luck to continue

wooded /wʌdid/ *adj* an area covered with trees *Northern Ontario has many wooded areas.*

wooden /wʌ dun/ *adj* made of wood *Use a wooden spoon with butter on it to mix up marshmallow squares* Col: **Don't take any wooden nickels.** – *proverb* to be careful and take care of oneself

woodpecker /wʌd pe kEr/ [woodpeckers] *noun* bird with a long sharp bill that pecks holes into trees looking for insects *There's a red-headed woodpecker in the pine tree.*

woodwinds /wˆd winz/ *noun* group of musical instruments that air is blown through, originally made of wood *Clarinets, and oboes are woodwinds.*

woof /wˆf/ [woofs, woofed, woofing] *noun* the noise a dog makes *The big dog has a loud woof.* • *verb* barking *The dog woofs when someone comes to the door.*

wool /wˆl/ *noun* the thick, soft, and curly fleece of animals like sheep, goats and llamas *Sheep wool is very soft* .• *adjective* made of wool material *The sweater is made of wool.* Col: **pull the wool over their eyes** — to deceive

would (wood) /wˆd/ *helping verb* 1 an action that depends on something else *I would go with you if I had a car* 2 request *Would you help me with my homework?* Col: **How much wood would a woodchuck chuck if a woodchuck could chuck wood?** — tongue twister

woulda /wˆ du/ *contr* would have, spoken word only *English is Stupid Students are Not* Chapter Three and Four /*I woulda come over if I knew you were sick.*/

Chapter 12
/oy/ is Turquoise

Chapter 12
/Oy/ is Turquoise

boil /bO yul/
boiler /bOy lEr/
boisterous /bOy strus/
boy (buoy) /bOy/
broil /brO yul/
broiler /brOy lEr/
buoy (boy) /bOy/

coil /kO yul/
coin /kOyn/

destroy /du strOy/

employ /em plOy/
employment /em plOy munt/
enjoy /en jOy/

foil /fO yul/

groin /grOyn/

hoist /hOyst/

join /jOyn/
joint /jOynt/
joy /jOy/

lawyer /lO yEr/
loin /lOyn/
loiter /lOy dEr/
loyal /lO yul/

moist /mOyst/
moisture /mOys jEr/

noise /nOyz/
noisy /nOy zEy/

oil /O yul/
oily /Oy lEy/
ointment /Oynt munt/
oyster /Oys dEr/

point /pOynt/
poise /pOyz/
poison /pOy sun/

rejoice /ru jOys/
royal /rO yul/

soil /sO yul/

toilet /tOy lut/
toy /tOy/

/ oy / is Turquoise

boil /b**O** yul/ [boils, boiled, boiling] *noun* painful infected swelling filled with pus *The dog had a boil on his ear.* • *verb* heat a liquid until it bubbles and becomes a gas *Boil some water to cook the vegetables.* Col: I'm boiling – exaggeration for too warm

boiler /b**Oy** lEr/ [boilers] *noun* a contained system for providing heat to cook or heat a building *The boiler was broken and the school had to close until it was fixed.*

boisterous /b**Oy** strus/ *adj* loud and energetic *The birthday party was boisterous.*

boy /b**Oy**/ [boys] *noun* male child *The boys are playing soccer in the park.* • *interjection* expresses surprise *Boy it's cold today.* Col: atta boy – approval for a male, good job   boy oh boy – disbelief, excitement or anticipation   boys of summer – surfers   boys will be boys – dismissing bad behavior lightly   fly-boy – pilot   girly boy – sensitive or effeminate male

broil /br**O** yul/ [broils, broiled, broiling] *verb* method of cooking using the top element in the oven *He likes his steak broiled with garlic.*

broiler /br**Oy** lEr/ [broilers] *noun* 1 part of the oven that cooks food from the top *Leave the oven door open when the broiler is on.* 2 young chicken big enough to eat *Broilers were on sale so I bought three.*

buoy (boy) /b**Oy**/ [buoys, buoyed, buoying] *noun* a navigation marker that floats in a body of water *Steer to the left of the green buoy or you'll hit a rock.* • *verb* cause to float or rise up *Her spirits buoyed with the news there were survivors.*

coil /k**O** yul/ [coils, coiled, coiling] *noun* loops of long thin material *Bring a coil of telephone wire to the new house.* • *verb* to wind material in a circle either in the air or around a frame *Coil the garden hose and hang it in the garage.* Col: coiled to strike – ready to attack   shuffle off this mortal coil – die, from *Hamlet* in the *to be or not to be* speech

coin /k**Oyn**/ [coins, coined, coining] *noun* round metal unit of money *How many coins are in your pocket?* • *verb* invent *Shakespeare coined many new words and phrases.* Col: coin-operated – machine that needs money (change) to use   coin a phrase – originate, make up for the first time

destroy /du str**Oy**/ [destroys, destroyed, destroying] *verb* 1 break or damage beyond repair *The tornado destroyed the town.* 2 won a game by a large margin *The home team destroyed their opponents in baseball.* Col: seek and destroy – military order or expression

employ /um pl**Oy**/ [employs, employed, employing] *verb* 1 hire *Our company employs 1700 people.* 2 use *My father employs reverse psychology but it never works.*

employment /um pl**Oy** munt/ *noun* a job *He is out of work now but seeking employment.* Col: place of employment – where one works

enjoy /un j**Oy**/ [enjoys, enjoyed, enjoying] *verb* 1 like, give pleasure *I enjoy your company.* 2 get benefit from *My parents enjoy good health.*

foil /f**O** yul/ [foils, foiled, foiling] *noun* 1 very thin tin sheets for wrapping food *Wrap the potatoes in foil and put them on the barbecue.* 2 light-weight sword used in fencing *Grab that foil and we'll practice a duel.* • *verb* obstruct or ruin a plan *The rain foiled our picnic.* Col: aluminum foil – kitchen roll of food covering   dramatic foil – opposite minor character to highlight qualities in a main character   foiled again – tricked again

groin /gr**Oyn**/ [groins] *noun* area of the body where legs join the torso *He got kicked in the groin while playing basketball.* Col: groin injury – injured private parts

HOW DO YOU SAY? PRONUNCIATION DICTIONARY

hoist /hOyst/ [hoists, hoisted, hoisting] noun equipment for lifting *Put the car up on the hoist so we can look at the brakes.* • verb to lift up *He hoisted his daughter onto his shoulders.*

join /jOyn/ [joins, joined, joining] verb 1 attach together *The railway cars are joined to make a train.* 2 belong *He joined a gym to get in shape.* Col: **join hands** — hold hands   **join the club** — had a similar experience   **join the crowd** — had a similar experience   **join us** — an invitation   **joined at the hip** — always together

joint /jOynt/ [joints] noun 1 body part where limbs can bend *My joints ached when I finished the race.* 2 slang term for low–class bar *That joint closes at 2:00 a.m.* Col: **joint pain** — description of inflammation   **joint venture** — partnership

joy /jOy/ noun happy feeling *Find joy in the little things. It's the secret to happiness.* Col: **filled with joy** — expression of bliss   **Joy to the World** — Christmas carol   **Ode to Joy** — Beethoven's famous music   **tidings of great joy** — from the Christ story

lawyer /lO yEr/ [lawyers] noun professional in the practice of the law *Lawyers cost too much money.* Col: **He who represents himself has a fool for a lawyer** — representing oneself in court is likely to end badly

loin /lOyn/ [loins] noun 1 body part, lower back *Strong stomach muscles support the loin area in your back.* 2 cut of meat *I like a roast loin of pork with apple sauce and gravy.* **fruit of his loins** — children   **loin cloth** — simple, ancient Egyptian garment

loiter /lOy dEr/ [loiters, loitered, loitering] verb wait around for no reason *Students are not allowed to loiter in the halls.* Col: **charged with loitering** — criminal offense

loyal /lO yul/ adj faithful *A dog is a loyal and trusted friend.* Col: **brand loyalty** — keep buying a product   **loyal to the end** — steadfast, enduring

moist /mOyst/ [moister, moistest] adj 1 slightly damp, not dry *This cake is very moist.*

moisture /mOys jEr/ noun dampness *In the rainforest there is a lot of moisture in the air.*

noise /nOyz/ [noises] noun sound *What is that annoying noise?* Col: **Let's make some noise.** — complain or party   **noise violation** — criminal charge for too much racket

noisy /nOy zEy/ [noisier, noisiest] adj too much sound *The kids are too noisy, I can't study.*

oil /O yul/ [oils, oiled, oiling] noun thick lubricating, softening or cooking liquid *Put oil in your car's engine or it will cease.* • verb the action of lubricating, softening or protecting with oil. *Oil your wood furniture so it doesn't dry out.* Col: **fried in oil** — stovetop cooking method   **motor oil** — engine lubricant   **oil and vinegar** — salad dressing   **oil and water** — don't mix, don't get along   **olive oil** — extracted from olives for cooking   **suntan oil** — applied before going in the sun to help tan   **vegetable oil** — extracted from corn or other plants for cooking

oily /Oy lEy/ [oilier, oiliest] adj 1 slippery or greasy *The hobo had oily hair.* 2 too much oil *These pancakes are oily.*

ointment /Oynt munt/ [ointments] noun cream for healing skin irritations *Put some ointment on that rash.* Col: **fly in the ointment** — small problem that ruins everything   **medicated ointment** — antibiotic or anti–inflammatory cream

oyster /Oys dEr/ [oysters] noun hard shelled seafood that can also grow pearls *When are oysters in season, we'll have a feast.* Col: **oyster bed** — where oysters grow   **oysters on the half shell** — restaurant presentation of the delicacy   **pearl in the oyster** — surprise value

/ oy / is Turquoise

point /p**oy**nt/ [points, pointed, pointing] *noun* 1 observation or opinion. *What is the point of this exercise?* 2 sharp tapered end *Sharpen that pencil, there is no point left on it.* 3 specific moment in time. *At what point did you realize you were in love?* 4 used for keeping score *One point for a goal.* • *verb* 1 indicate a direction with your finger ☞ *Don't point, it's rude.* 2 face a direction *The compass always points north.* 3 highlighting or identifying *Thank you for pointing that out.* `Col:` **case in point** – the example proves the argument   **good point** – I hadn't thought of it   **have a point** – valid idea   **make a point** – clarify an idea   **make points with** – endear one's self in some way   **not to put too fine a point on it** – recognizing the idea has been shared and continuing to explain anyway   **point a finger at** – blame   **point in the right direction** – start off right   **point of view** – way of looking at a situation   **point out** – show   **pointed remark** – nasty hidden message   **what is your point** – stop babbling

poise /p**oy**z/ [poises, poised] *noun* a state of calm elegance in any situation *Katherine has poise.* • *verb* readiness *His pen is poised over his notebook.*

poison /p**oy** zun/ [poisons, poisoned, poisoning] *noun* substance that can kill or cause harm to living things ☠ *The poison was in his drink.* • *verb* giving the harmful substance *I'll poison the rats in the shed.* • *adj* description *Sleeping Beauty ate a poison apple.* `Col:` **poison ivy** – wild plant that gives an itchy rash   **poison oak** – tree that gives an itchy rash   **choose your poison** – alcoholic drink

rejoice /ru j**oy**s/ [rejoices, rejoiced, rejoicing] *verb* take great pleasure in *The families rejoiced when the soldiers came home.*

royal /r**O** yul/ [royals] *noun* people of the monarchy or royal family. *The royals were in town for the big horse race.* • *adj* 1 about sovereignty *The royal family lives in Buckingham Palace.* 2 special or excellent *We got the royal treatment at the five star hotel.* `Col:` **royal pain** – extremely annoying or bothersome   **royal wave** – specific gesture the queen uses to greet crowds

soil /s**O** yul/ [soils, soiled, soiling] *noun* dirt, earth *Plant the seeds in the rich soil.* • *verb* making something dirty *Get up off the lawn, you are soiling your jeans.* 2 polite way of saying bowel movement *The patient soiled the sheets in the night and they had to be changed.* `Col:` **get one's hands in the soil** – plant a garden   **till the soil** – farm

toilet /t**Oy** lut/ [toilets] *noun* bathroom fixture for taking away human waste *Go to the toilet before you get in the car.* `Col:` **toilet paper** – tissue for wiping oneself after using the toilet

toy /t**Oy**/ [toys, toyed, toying] *noun* an object only for fun and enjoyment usually for children *Put your toys in the toy-box.* • *verb* tease *Don't toy with my feelings.* `Col:` **boys and their toys** – expensive unnecessary equipment   **toy box** – container for playthings   **toy poodle** – miniature type of dog   **toy with** – tease and fool around

Chapter 13
/Aw/ is Brown

Chapter 13
/Aw/ is Brown

about /u bAwt/
account /u kAwnt/
allow /u lAw/
amount /u mAwnt/
announce /u nAwns/
announcement /u nAwn smunt/
around /u rAwnd/

blouse /blAwz/ or / blAws/
bough (bow) /bAw/
bounce /bAwns/
boundary /bAwn drEy/
bow (bough) /bAw/
brown /brAwn/

cloud /klAwd/
clown /klAwn/
count /kAwnt/
countable /kAw tu bul/
counter /kAw tEr/
cow /kAw/

doubt /dAwt/
down /dAwn/
drought /drAwt/
drown /drAwn/
drowsy /drAw zEy/

flour (flowers) /flA wEr/
flower (flour) /flA wEr/
found /fAwnd/
fountain /fAwn tun/
foul (fowl) /fA wul/
fowl (foul) /fA wul/
frown /frAwn/

gown /gAwn/
ground /grAwnd/

hour (our) /A wEr/
house /hAws/
housing /hAw ziNg/
how /hAw/
loud /lAwd/

mountain /mAwn tun/
mouse /mAws/
mouth /mAwTH/

noun /nAwn/
now /nAw/

ounce /Awns/
our (hour) /A wEr/
out /Awt/
outer /Aw dEr/
outlet /Awt lut/
owl /A wul/

plough /plAw/
pound /pAwnd/
pout /pAwt/
powder /pAw dEr/
power /pA wEr/
pronounce /pru nAwns/

round /rAwnd/

shout /ShAwt/
shower /ShA wer/
sound /sAwnd/
south /sAwTH/

thousand /ThAw zund/
towel /tA wul/
town /tAwn/
trout /trAwt/

vowel /vA wul/
wound /wAwnd/
wow /wAw/

/ Aw / is Brown

about /u **bAwt**/ *adv* more or less, not exactly *The temperature is about 15 degrees today.* • *prep* on the subject of *I watched a TV program about the weather.* `Col:` **about time** — sarcastic for taking longer than expected   **go on about** — talk for a long time without changing the subject   **out and about** — socialize; spend leisure time out of the home   **what about/how about** — ask an opinion, introduce an additional idea

account /u **kAwnt**/ [accounts, accounted, accounting] *noun* a list of money received and paid out *The company keeps careful accounts of all its money.* • *verb* give a reason or explanation *How do you account for failing the test?* `Col:` **by all accounts** — everyone agrees

allow /u **lAw**/ [allows, allowed, allowing,] *verb* permission, *The teacher allowed the students to go home early.*

amount /u **mAwnt**/ [amounts, amounted, amounting] *noun* quantity *He is a growing boy, so he eats a large amount of food.* `Col:` **amount to** — become, grow up to be

announce /u **nAwns**/ [announces, announced, announcing] *verb* make known *They announced their engagement at dinner.*

announcement /u **nAwn** smunt/ [announcements] *noun* information or news presented in an official way *The prime minister made an official announcement.*

around /u **rAwnd**/ *adv* about, not exactly *We will arrive around 3 p.m.* • *prep* surround or envelop on all sides *There is a fence around the school.* `Col:` **beat around the bush** — talk without getting to the point   **he/she gets around** — has many sex partners   **what goes around comes around** — good or bad, one's own behavior dictates how one will be treated

blouse /u **blAwz**/or / **blAws**/ [blouses] *noun* woman's dressy shirt *Blouses are on sale at the boutique.* `Col:` **big girl's blouse** — (for men) weak character or easily afraid

bough (bow) /**bAw**/ [bows, bowed, bowing] *noun* branch of a tree *We hung the swing from the highest bow of the oak tree.*

bounce /**bAwns**/ [bounces, bounced, bouncing] *verb* 1 something moving up or away from a hard surface *The ball bounced off the wall and up and down on the floor.* 2 recover from illness *We thought he was going to die from his heart attack but he bounced back really well.* 3 raise a lower a child on one's knee *The baby laughed when she was bounced on her grandpa's knee.* 4 check returned for insufficient funds *There wasn't enough money in the account for the house insurance and the check bounced.* • *noun* movement up and down *A bounce in the real estate market increased house prices.* `Col:` **bounce an idea off someone** — suggest a new idea for feedback   **bounce in one's step** — a sign of happiness and self confidence   **bouncing off the walls** - too much energy   **follow the bouncing ball** — follow visual cues   **that's the way the ball bounces** — that's life a bit random, sometimes down

boundary /**bAwn** drEy/ [boundaries] *noun* a line that separates two areas or countries *The boundary between the U.S. and Canada is the longest unguarded border in the world.*

bow (bough) /**bAw**/ [bows, bowed, bowing] *noun* the front part of a boat *We dragged the bow of the boat up on the sand.* • *verb* lower the head, and often the upper half of the body, towards the floor to show respect *In Japan, people bow as a greeting.* `Col:` **bow and scrape** — subservient   **bow out** — quit or drop out   **take a bow** — stand and bend at the waist to receive praise

brown /**brAwn**/ [browns, browned, browning, browner, brownest] *adj* the color of chocolate and coffee *He bought a new pair of brown shoes.* • *noun* the color Brown is the color of dirt and chocolate bars.

• **verb** lightly fry food until it darkens color (usually meat or onions) *In a saucepan, brown the onions, and add salt and pepper.* Col: **brown cow** – sweet chocolaty alcoholic drink **browned off** – angry or annoyed **brown-noser** – tries too hard to get the attention of their boss or teacher **brown-out** – loss of electricity during an electrical storm or massively reduce electricity as in wartime

cloud /klAwd/ [clouds, clouded, clouding] noun 1 big puffy objects in the sky that hold rain *There was not a cloud in the sky.* 2 technology for electronic storage *My data is backed up onto a cloud in case my computer crashes.* • **verb** 1 make darker *His face clouded over when he heard the bad news.* 2 make less visible or clear *There were so many different stories that it clouded the truth.* Col: **cloud over** – go from sunny to overcast **every cloud has a silver lining** – there is a good outcome from all misfortune **have one's head in the clouds** – not pay attention and daydream **on cloud nine** – happily in love

clown /klAwn/ [clowns, clowned, clowning] noun 1 an entertainer who dresses up and paints their face *They hired a clown for the birthday party.* 2 a silly person who frequently jokes around *My brother is a real clown.* • **verb** joke around and be silly *My teacher clowns around all the time.* Col: **circus clown** – professional entertainer who paints his face and dresses in funny clothes **class clown** – a student who makes his classmates laugh **clown around** – joke and behave in a silly way **party clown** – professional who entertains at children's parties

count /kAwnt/ [counts, counted, counting] verb 1 determine how many *We counted 86 cars in the train.* 2 figure in or consider *This mark counts as 50% of the final grade.* 3 depend on *I'm counting on you to bring the drinks to the picnic.* • noun 1 a nobleman *The count invited the king to a hunting party.* 2 charge for illegal actions *He was charged with three counts of murder.* Col: **be out for the count** – asleep, from the sport of boxing **close only counts in horseshoes** – it happened or it didn't **count blessings** – appreciate all we do have **count down** – to say numbers backwards (usually from 10 to 1) to a big moment **count for** – add valuable **count heads** – number of people **count me in** – include **count me out** – don't include me **count the cost** – including money, time effort and resources **count up to** – 1, 2, 3, … **stand up and be counted** – show support in a protest **count against** – demerits that hurt one's reputation **count on** – depend on **Don't count your chickens before they hatch.** – *proverb* don't assume, wait until you are sure **every minute counts** – urgency

countable /kAwn tu bul/ adj can be counted *Chairs is a countable noun and furniture is non countable.*

counter /kAwn tEr/ [counters, countered, countering] noun 1 a high table used to prepare food or do business *The cook is chopping vegetables on the kitchen counter.* 2 place marker in a board game. *He moved his counter the last two spaces and won the game.* 3 a device that counts *The traffic counter reads 3,021 cars have crossed the bridge today.* • **verb** offer an argument against *He countered the woman's story with evidence to the contrary.* • **adj** opposite *The lawyer offered a counter argument.* • **adv** to go in an opposite direction *Criminals behave counter to the law.* Col: **bean counter** – impolite nickname for an accountant **counter clockwise** – opposite to the direction the hands move on a clock **counter intuitive** – against accepted understanding **over the counter** – drugs purchased without a doctor's prescription **under the counter** – illegal

cow /kAw/ [cows, cowed] *noun* a large farm animal that produces milk *The farmer milked the cows.* • *verb* intimidate *He cowed her into taking out the garbage and cutting the grass.* Col: brown cow – alcoholic drink   cash cow – business that brings in a lot of money   cow patty – disk of cow manure   don't have a cow – calm down   until the cows come home – long time usually with no success   Why buy a cow when you can get milk for free? – no reason to marry if the sex is available

doubt /dAwt/ [doubts, doubted, doubting] *noun* a feeling something is not true *I have my doubts about how much money they make.* • *verb* believe unlikely *I doubt that it will snow today; it is not cold enough.* Col: doubting Thomas – pessimist; who doesn't believe others easily   no doubt about it – for sure   benefit of the doubt – choosing to believe a questionable story   beyond a reasonable doubt – with almost no doubt   beyond a shadow of a doubt – absolutely sure

down /dAwn/ [downs, downed, downing] *prep* direction, the opposite of up *My house is down the street.* • *adv* from a higher to a lower *He tripped and fell down.* • *noun* the soft under feathers of a bird *I have a goose down duvet on my bed.* • *adj* 1 depressed *He's been feeling down since the accident.* 2 slang for agreement with a plan *He was down with his friend's party idea.* • *verb* quickly eat or drink *He downed his soda in ten seconds.* Col: downcast – sad demeanor   downer – someone or something depressing or making a situation worse   down and out – lost everything   down in the dumps – low energy   down on your luck – financial or other significant difficulties   down payment – deposit of money on a high-priced item   downfall – cause of failure   downhill – getting worse   downpour – heavy rainfall   downright – total, complete   downstairs – the floor below   down-to-earth – humble, friendly   downtown – at the city centre   get down and dirty – have sex   get down to – get busy, start   lead down the garden path – take advantage of an innocent person   turn that frown upside down – smile, cheer up   up and down – sometimes good and sometimes bad

drought /drAwt/ [droughts] *noun* no rain *In periods of drought, plants and animals die.*

drown /drAwn/ [drowns, drowned, drowning] *verb* 1 die from water in the lungs. *Almost 1500 people drowned when the Titanic sank.* 2 too much *I am drowning in paperwork* 3 to cover over with liquid *He drowned his French fries in ketchup.* Col: drown out – cover the sound of something with louder noises   drowning in debt – too many bills and financial responsibilities   look like a drowned rat – soaking wet

drowsy /drAw zEy/ *adj* sleepy *Don't drive when you are drowsy, pull over and rest.*

flour (flowers) /flA wEr/ [flours] *noun* powder from ground grain used to make bread *Whole wheat flour is better for you.*

flower (flour) /flA wEr/ [flowers, flowered, flowering] *noun* a colorful plant *A rose is a beautiful flower.* • *verb* open up or bloom *The tulips flowered last week. adj* about flowers *Flower pots are on sale at the nursery.* Col: April showers bring May flowers. – *proverb*, after annoying (bad) rain flowers (good) come everything   flower arrangement – an artful presentation of flowers   flower arranging – the art of decorating using flowers   flower children – people who were part of the peace movement of the 1960's and 1970's   flower garden – a small area of land for growing flowers   flower girl – a young girl who carries flowers in a wedding   flower power – phrase from the peace movement   **flowery language** – write or speak using big descriptive words

found /fAwnd/ [finds, found finding] *verb* 1 past and past participle of *find* discover *He found his keys under the bed.* 2 start an organization or business *His dream is to found a newspaper company.* • *adj* to come upon unexpectedly *He has a museum of found art.* Col: **lost and found** – a place where left items left in public places are stored until the owner picks them up   **found guilty** – verdict, court decided a person had committed a crime   **found not guilty** – court decided a person is innocent

fountain /fAwn tun/ [fountains] *noun* 1 a place where water comes up and then falls again *There is a beautiful fountain in the centre of the city.* 2 source *The Internet is a fountain of information.* Col: **fountain of youth** – a product that is believed to make a person young again   **drinking fountain** – a small sink in a public place that provides fresh drinking water   **soda fountain** – a machine that produces soda or soft drinks in a restaurant   **chocolate fountain** – a machine that melts chocolate for fruit and cookies to be dipped in

foul (fowl) /fA wul/ [fouls, fouled, fouling, fouler, foulest] *noun* failure to follow the rules *The referee called the foul.* • *adj* 1 rotten or smelly *The meat smells foul.* 2 dirty or polluted *The air in cities is foul.* 3 evil or morally bad *They suspected foul play in the police investigation.* • *verb* make an illegal play in a sport *The batter fouled out.* • Col: **foul ball** – hit out of a specific area   **foul deeds** – dishonest   **foul language** – swearing, course offensive language   **foul play** – dishonesty   **foul smell** – a terrible smell   **foul up** – make a mistake

fowl (foul) /fA wul/ *noun* a large bird, (duck, goose or chicken) often hunted, cooked and eaten *He went hunting for fowl.* 2 the meat of birds that is sold for food *White wine is traditionally served with fowl.*

frown /frAwn/ [frowns, frowned, frowning] *noun* concerned or unhappy facial expression *He has a frown on his face most of the time.* • *verb* unhappy facial expression *He is frowning because he is thinking about the problem.* Col: **turn that frown upside down** – smile, cheer up   **it takes fewer muscles to smile than to frown** – gentle tease to encourage an unhappy person to smile   **to frown upon** – disapprove of

gown /gAwn/ [gowns] *noun* long formal dress or a dress to sleep in *She bought a new gown for the opening gala.* Col: **ball gown** – long formal dress   **bridal gown** – dress worn by the bride at her wedding   **hospital gown** – a thin piece of cotton open in the back, worn by hospital patients   **nightgown** – a sleeping dress   **wedding gown** – bridal dress

ground /grAwnd/ [grounds, grounded, grounding] *noun* 1 the land, the part of the earth that people walk on outside *The ground is frozen in winter.* • *verb* restrict the freedom of teens as punishment *I can't go to the movies because I'm grounded.* Col: **burial ground** – a place where the dead are laid in plots   **find higher ground** – find safety   **ground zero** – the starting point or site of a disaster   **on dangerous ground** – in an unsafe place or situation   **on familiar ground** – a situation or place one has been before   **on unfamiliar ground** – a situation or place that is new or strange   **sacred ground** – a spiritually important or holy place   **stomping ground** – where a person grew up or a favorite place to meet friends

hour (our) /A wEr/ [hours] *noun* an amount of time, 60 minutes. *There are 24 hours in a day.* Col: **rush hour** – time when city traffic is busiest, from 8 to 10 a.m. and 4 to 6 p.m.   **happy hour** – cheap drinks in a bar from about 5-

/ Aw / is Brown

7pm   hourly rate – the amount for a service for an hour of time   paid by the hour – not a salary

house /hAws/ [houses, housed, housing] noun a building where people live *She lives in a beautiful house.* • verb provide a place to live *The refugees were housed in the school gym until other arrangements were made.* Col: a full house – many visitors or a high-point hand in poker   eat out of house and home – joking about the amount a young person eats   household – living space   household appliances – work items in the home   People who live in glass houses shouldn't throw stones. – proverb to be careful about accusing others of things you also do

housing /hAw ziNg/ noun shelter or lodging *Our school doesn't provide student housing.*

how /hAw/ adv Wh question 1 in what way *How did you come to school, today?* 2 in what condition *How are you today?* Col: And how! – agree emphatically   How about that! – surprise   How come? – Why?   How so? – What do you mean?   How time flies – surprise that time passed quickly, usually during an enjoyable activity   How's it going? – How are you?   know how – expertise   That's a fine how do you do! – sarcastic expression of anger

loud /lAwd/ [louder, loudest, loudly] adj 1 big sound *The little girl was frightened by the loud thunder.* • noun the quality of a sound *Loud is the only setting on his stereo.* • adv quality of sound *He cleared his throat loudly.* Col: For crying out loud! – shock, anger or impatience   I read you loud and clear – I really understand   loudmouth – an outspoken or often rude person   say out loud – speak so others can hear, or to say something that many people are thinking, but not saying

mountain /mAwn tun/ [mountains] noun a very high, rocky hill, sometimes topped with snow *He wants to climb the mountain.* • adj reference to mountains *The Andes is a very high mountain range.* Col: Faith can move mountains. – proverb on the power of believing   If the mountain will not come to Mohammed, Mohammed must go to the mountain. – proverb a person must change if the situations won't   make a mountain out of a molehill – over-dramatize and make a small situation seem very serious   mountain to climb – a very difficult situation to overcome   move mountains for him/her – show devotion with unlimited acts of love

mouse /mAws/ [mice] noun 1 a small animal with a long tail that likes cheese *The mouse ran under the sofa.* 2 a device used with a computer to point and click on objects on the screen *I found the webpage with a click of the mouse.* • adj dull grayish brown color *She had mouse brown hair.* Col: poor as a church mouse – poorest of the poor   quiet as a church mouse – quietest of the quiet   cat and mouse – hurts another for fun because one can   Are you a man or a mouse? – an insult or encouragement for a person to be brave   Mickey Mouse – Disney character or a slang comment on unprofessional disorganization

mouth /mAwTH/ [mouths, mouthed, mouthing] noun 1 part of a person's face that is used to speak and eat *She put a cookie in her mouth.* 2 opening of a river *The boat was anchored near the mouth of the river.* • verb form words soundlessly *The teacher mouthed the words as the children sang.* • adj a loud, disrespectful person *He's a really mouthy kid.* Col: a big mouth- a person who tells others' secrets   a loud mouth – a person who says stupid things loudly   bad-mouth – say unkind things about someone behind their back   Don't look a gift horse in the mouth. – proverb there is probably something wrong with it but

245

be gracious Don't put words in my mouth. — say I said things I didn't say down in the mouth — discouraged foam at the mouth — enraged foul-mouthed — a person who swears or speaks offensively have your heart in your mouth — filled with fear or excitement mouth off — to talk loudly and disrespectfully, often to a person in authority put one's money where one's mouth is — support what you believe with cash straight from the horse's mouth — information from the source take the words out of a person's mouth — say the idea another was thinking Watch your mouth! — warn a person who has spoken rudely You eat with that mouth? — reprimand a person for using foul language

noun /**nAwn**/ [nouns] *noun* person, place, thing or idea *Proper nouns take capitals.*

now /**nAw**/ *adv* 1 at this time *We have to leave now so we won't be late.* Col: by now — before this time bye for now — Goodbye, but I'll see you again every now and then — sometimes not now — later now and then — occasionally now or never —only chance; at this time and no other Now you're talking! — enthusiasm about what one is saying Now. Now. — calming phrase nowadays — at the present time What now? — frustration during a series of problems

ounce /**Awns**/ [ounces] *noun* a small amount of weight (1 ounce = 28 grams) *A panda weights 3½ ounces at birth.* Col: An ounce of prevention is worth a pound of cure. — *proverb* it is better to prevent a problem than fix it

our (hour) /**A wEr**/ [ours] *adj* possessive form of we *Our class has students from many countries.*

out /**Awt**/ *prep* away from a place (home, work, school) *We are going out for lunch.* Col: down and out — lost everything ins and outs of — details needed to do a task correctly out and about — away from home or work and running errands out cold — unconscious out for blood — revenge out front — leading, as in a competition out in force — in great numbers out in left field — strange and unusual, kind of crazy passed out — unconscious

outer /**Aw** dEr/ *adj* closer to the outside *Neptune is found in the outer part of our solar system* Col: outer circle — not part of the popular group

outlet /**Awt** lut/ [outlets] *noun* 1 source *Is there an outlet for appliances in town?* 2 electric power source *I need an outlet to charge my computer.* • *adj* description *We went shopping at the outlet mall*

owl /**A wul**/ [owls] *noun* a nighttime bird of prey with large eyes *We heard the owl hoot last night.* Col: night owl — stays up late and performs best at night wise as an owl — intelligent and rich in life experiences

plough /**plAw**/ [ploughs, ploughed, ploughing] *noun* a farm implement used to prepare the land for planting *The farmer stores his plough behind the barn.* • *verb* 1 break up ground for planting *They ploughed last week.* 2 hit someone forcefully *He ploughed him in the nose.* Col: plough through — continue through a difficult exercise or stage

pound /**pAwnd**/ [pounds, pounded, pounding] *noun* 1 a measurement of weight (1kg=2.2 pounds) *The dog weighs 60 pounds.* 2 a shelter/place for homeless cats and dogs *I got my dog at the pound.* • *verb* hit heavily with a heavy object *My dad let me pound the nails into our new fence.* Col: 25 pounder — the size of food bought, or caught, such as a turkey or a fish pound of flesh — a price involving great suffering pound into — learn by merciless repetition

pout /**pAwt**/ [pouts, pouted, pouting] *noun* a facial expression where the lower lip juts out *She pouts when she doesn't* get her way. Col: **pouty face** — sad face **sexy pout** — lip sticking out meant to attract the opposite sex

powder /**pAw** dEr/ [powders, powdered, powdering] *noun* dry substance containing tiny particles *The lady put powder on her face.* • *verb* to put powder on a surface *She powdered her nose and cheeks.* Col: **powder-room** — toilet/washroom

power /**pA** wEr/ [powers, powered, powering] *noun* 1 energy or strength *A large hydroelectric dam produces enough power for an entire city.* 2 control over others *The government has power it often uses unwisely.* • *verb* supply with power *Electricity powers household appliances.* Col: **Absolute power corrupts absolutely.** — *proverb* one with total authority will abuse their position **girl power** — strength of women **in power** — current government **Knowledge is power.** — *proverb* the more one knows the more advantage they have **Money is power.** — *proverb* if one has money they can do more **More power to you!** — well done, shows support and encouragement **on a power trip** — ego exercising authority over others **power play** — an attempt to gain control in a situation, or a hockey team with a man advantage due to an opponent's penalty **power through** — continue through a long, difficult process **power to the people** — democracy **the power behind the throne** — the one who really controls the person in charge

pronounce /pru **nAwns**/ [pronounces, pronounced, pronouncing] *verb* the way a words are spoken *How do you pronounce this word?*

round /r**Awnd**/ [rounds, rounded, rounding. rounder, roundest] *adj* in the shape of a circle *The earth is round.* Col: **a square peg in a round hole** — not a good fit, out of place **all year round** — 365 days year, all seasons **buy a round** — buy a drink for everyone at the table **Love makes the world go round.** — *proverb* life is better when people treat each other with kindness **to do rounds** — doctors visit all their patients in the hospital **to round a number off** — change a fraction to the next closest whole number

shout /**ShAwt**/ [shouts, shouted, shouting] *verb* yell in a loud voice *We'll continue this conversation when you stop shouting.* Col: **shout over** — loud enough to be heard above other noise

shower /**ShA wEr**/ [showers, showered, showering] *noun* 1 the fixture in the bathroom for washing the entire body *He takes a shower every night.* 2 light rain *We saw a rainbow after the shower.* 3 cultural support for a big event *Her sisters had a shower for her when she got married.* • *verb* pour down in a spray *The guests showered the bridal couple with confetti.* Col: **bridal or baby shower** — party to support a life changing event with gifts **take a shower** — standing wash **take a cold shower** — thinking too much about sex **April Showers bring May flowers.** — *proverb,* after annoying rain (bad) flowers come (good)

sound /s**Awnd**/ [sounds, sounded, sounding, sounder, soundest] *noun* noise *I love the sound of birds in the morning.* • *verb* healthy *The horse at the auction was sound so we bought him.* • *adj* logical *Investing in gold is a sound idea.* • Col: **of sound mind and body** — mentally and physically fit **safe and sound** — home and well after being lost or delayed **sound asleep** — sleeping deeply **sound off** — voice opinions **sound out** — pronounce words by focusing on individual letters and syllables **sound someone out** — try to find out what one is thinking **sound hollow** — the listener does not believe in the speaker's words

south /s**AwTH**/ *noun* direction the opposite of north *The weather is warmer in the south.* Col: **down south** — southern region of the area or country **south seas** – Pacific Ocean south of the equator

thousand /**THAw** zund/ [thousands] *noun* a number, written as 1,000 *There are thousands of expressions in the English language.* Col: A thousand times, no! – clear definite no **not in a thousand years** – will never happen **A picture is worth a thousand words.** – *proverb*, images deliver messages better than words **batting a thousand** – baseball term for perfect **If I've told you once, I've told you a thousand times!** – exaggeration/frustration from repeating oneself **Thousand Islands** - salad dressing or the name of a large group of islands in the St Laurence River

towel /**tA w**ul/ [towels, toweled toweling] *noun* large soft cloth for drying *Bring a towel with you to the beach.* • *verb* dry *Towel off that wet dog before you bring it into the house.* Col: **towel dry** – rub hair with a towel until it is dry **throw in the towel** – quit

town /**tAwn**/ [towns] *noun* a group of houses and other buildings *A town is larger than a village, but smaller than a city.* Col: **downtown** – the city center **all over town** – gossip, everyone in town has heard the news **Get out of town!** – disbelief or tell a person to leave **go to town** – enthusiasm about a big budget to do first rate project **night on the town** – evening fun out of the house **paint the town red** – celebrate enthusiastically, often drinking

trout /**trAwt**/ *noun* a type of fish *I like to fish for rainbow trout.*

vowel /**vA w**ul/ [vowels] *noun* 1 the letters a, e, i, o, u in the Latin alphabet *Every word has at least one vowel.* 2 sound that stretches unlike consonant sounds which stop *The elastic quality of vowels is what allows humans to convey accents, emotions and singing occur because of vowels.* • *adj* about vowels *There are 16 vowel sounds in English.* Col: **long vowels** – include a consonant sound which makes the duration of the sound longer: Gray /Ay/, Green Ey/, White /Iy/, Yellow /Ow/, Blue /Uw/, /Turquoise /Oy/, Brown /Aw/, **short vowels** – short in duration and do not include a consonant: Black /a/, Red /e/, Pink /i/, Olive /o/, Mustard /u/, wood /^/ **R vowels** – vowel sounds created because of their close relationship to the letter: R Purple /Er/, Charcoal /Ar/, Orange, /Or/

wound /**wAwnd**/ [wind, wound, winding] *verb* the past tense of *wind* turn *The road wound through the mountain.* Col: **have someone wound around one's little finger** – unusual ability to control another **tightly wound** – nervous person easily upset **wound up** – the end result **wound one up** – intentionally upset or excited another **wound up** – turned a knob to store energy in order to run a machine

wow /**wAw**/ [wows, wowed, wowing] *interj* shows surprise and printed with an exclamation mark. *Wow! I didn't expect to see you here.* • *verb* dazzle *She wowed the board with her presentation.*

Chapter 14
/Er/ is Purple

Chapter 14
/Er/ is Purple

alert /u lErt/
allergic /u lEr jik/

bird /bErd/
birth (berth) /bErTH/
birthday /bErTH dAy/
berth (birth) /bErTH/
burglar /bEr glEr/
burn /bErn/
burst /bErst/

certain /sEr tun/
certainly /sEr tun lEy/
certify /sEr du fIy/
chauffeur /shOw fEr/
cher /ChEr/
church /ChErCh/
circle /sEr kul/
circus /sEr kus/
colonel (kernel) /kEr nul/
concern /kun sErn/
convert /kun vErt/
curl /kErl/
current /kE runt/
curse /kErs/
cursor /kEr sEr/
curtain /kEr tun/
curve /kErv/
curvy /kEr vEy/

deserter /du zEr dEr/
dessert /du zErt/
detergent /du tEr junt/
dirt /dErt/
dirty /dErd Ey/

early /Er lEy/
earn (urn) /Ern/
earth /ErTH/
Europe /yE rup/

fertile /fEr dul/
first /fErst/
furniture /fEr nu ChEr/
further /fEr ThEr/

girl /gErl/

heard (herd) /hErd/
her /hEr/
herd (heard) /hErd/
hurt /hErt/

insert /in sErt/
insurance /in ShE runs/

jer /jEr/
jerk /jErk/
journey /jEr nEy/
jury /jEry/

kernel (colonel) /kEr nul/

learn /lErn/

murder /mEr dEr/

nerve /nErv/
nervous /nEr vus/
nurse /nErs/

/ Er / is Purple

pearl /pErl/
perfume /pEr fyUwm/
person /pEr sun/
purple /pEr pul/
purpose /pEr pus/
purse /pErs/

refer /ru fEr/
return /ru tErn/

servant /sEr vunt/
serve /sErv/
shirt /shErt/
sir /sEr/
skirt /skErt/
slur /slEr/
squirrel /skwErl/
stern /stErn/
sure /shEr/
surf /sErf/
surfer /sEr fEr/
surgery /sEr ju rEy/

third /THErd/
thirsty /THErs dEy/
thirty /THEr dEy/
Thursday /THErz dAy/
turkey /tEr kEy/
turn /tErn/
turnip /tEr nup/
turquoise /tEr kOyz/
turtle /tEr dul/

urgent /Er junt/
urn (earn) /Ern/

verse /vErs/
virtue /vEr ChUw/

were /wEr/
word /wErd/
work /wErk/
world /wErld/
worm /wErm/
worst /wErst/
worth /wErTH/

your /yEr/

HOW DO YOU SAY? PRONUNCIATION DICTIONARY

alert /u lErt/ [alerts, alerted, alerting] *noun* warning *They heard the hurricane alert outside their hotel.* • *verb* warn *The police alerted the townspeople that a bear had been spotted.* • *adj* wide awake and quick to notice *After drinking two cups of coffee, he was alert and ready for work.* `Col:` **on the alert** — ready for action   **red alert** — prepared for danger

allergic /u lEr jik/ *adj* body reactions to the environment with sneezing and itchy eyes *She can't have a cat because her son is allergic to them.* `Col:` **allergic reaction** — adverse response

bird /bErd/ [birds] *noun* a two-legged, egg-laying animal with feathers and wings that can usually fly 🎵 *Birds fly south for the winter.* `Col:` **A little bird told me.** — gossip   **bird brain** — not smart   **Birds of a feather flock together.** — *proverb* like-minded people stay close   **bird of paradise** — tropical flower   **flip the bird** — a rude hand gesture raising only the middle finger   **have a bird** — get upset   **Kill two birds with one stone.** — *proverb* opportunity for efficiency   **The early bird catches the worm.** — *proverb* about becoming a success

birth (berth) /bErTH/ [births] *noun* being born *She gave birth to eight children.* `Col:` **birth certificate** — official document when and where someone was born   **birth control** — contraception   **birth date** — the date of birth   **birth defect** — a rare physical imperfection in a new baby   **birth mark** — skin discoloration   **birth rate** — babies born in a year divided by average population   **birthstone** — one of twelve precious stones designated by month

birthday /bErTH dAy/ [birthdays] *noun* the day a person was born *When is your birthday?* `Col:` **birthday boy/girl** — reference to the person whose birthday it is   **birthday suit** — naked   **Happy Birthday** — good wishes people say to someone on their birth day   🎵 **Happy Birthday to you** 🎵 ... — traditional song sung to celebrate usually with candles on a cake

berth (birth) /bErTH/ [berths] *noun* 1 a bed in a boat or a train *I slept in the upper berth and the woman below me snored all night.* 2 space at a dock for a boat to park *The ship was moored in its berth.* `Col:` **give a wide berth** — make lots of space in order to avoid contact

burglar /bEr glEr/ [burglars] *noun* thief who enters a building illegally and steals private property `Col:` **burglar alarm** — home protection device that makes a loud sound   **cat burglar** — a professional thief

burn /bErn/ [burns, burned/ burnt, burning] *noun* injury caused by heat `Col:` *The red mark on his arm is a burn from the stove.* • *verb* 1 hot stinging sensation *The hot chocolate burnt his tongue.* 2 overcooked *She was talking on the phone and burned dinner.* `Col:` **burn at the stake** — reference to centuries old killings   **burn out** — emotional and physical exhaustion from a demanding job   **burn someone** — cheat or do better than another   **burn the candle at both ends** — not rest enough during the day or night   **burn the midnight oil** — stay up late   **crash and burn** — financially or emotionally destroyed   **don't burn your bridges** — *proverb* advising against destroying the chance of a future relationship   **money to burn** — very wealthy   **Play with fire and you'll get burned.** — *proverb* caution against personal harm from choosing dangerous activities

burst /bErst/ [bursts, bursting] *verb* break open suddenly *He put too much air in the balloon and it burst.* `Col:` **burst at the seams** — full to capacity   **burst into song** — sing suddenly   **burst into tears** — cry suddenly   **burst onto the scene** — become widely know suddenly   **burst one's bubble** — share truth that brings disappointment   **burst with**

joy or **excitement** – overflow with emotion   **money burning a hole in one's pocket** – anxious to spend

certain /sEr tun/ *adj* 1 sure *I am certain I locked the door.* 2 particular *They asked certain children to sing.* 3 set *He will pay a certain amount each month.* Col: **certain circumstance** – particular, specific conditions are present or met   **dead certain** – absolutely sure   **make certain** – check to be sure   **Nothing is certain but death and taxes.** – *proverb* caution against being over confident

certainly /sEr tun lEy/ *adv* no question or doubt *Certainly you are invited to the party.* Col: **certainly not** – definitely not

certify /sEr du fIy/ [certifies, certified, certifying] *verb* 1 guarantee or confirm *The doctor certified the results of the blood test.* 2 license *She is a certified ESL teacher.* Col: **certify a will** – legally validate   **certified check** – bank guaranteed

chauffeur /shOw fEr/ [chauffeurs, chauffeured, chauffeuring] *noun* drives a car for a living *The chauffeur has an apartment beside the garage.* • *verb* drive people in a vehicle *Parents chauffeur children all over the place.*

cher /ChEr/ *contr* t + your, spoken word only *English is Stupid Students are Not Chapter One* /Wha cher name?/

church /ChErCh/ [churches] *noun* 1 a building where people worship ✝ *Many Christians go to church on Sundays.* 2 spiritual service *Church is at 10:00.* Col: **church key** – beer bottle opener   **poor as a church mouse** – very poor   **The nearer the church, the further from God.** – *proverb* corruption and lack of piety in religious officials and organizations

circle /sEr kul/ [circles, circled, circling] *noun* round shape O *The children sat in a circle to listen to the story.* • *verb* make or move in a circle *Circle the correct answer.* Col: **circle of friends** – social group   **circle the wagons** – prepare for attack   **come full circle** – arrive back at the place or state one started   **go in circles** – cover the same ground over and over not moving forward   **social circles** – economic groups   **talk in circles** – talking a lot but not offer any meaningful information   **vicious circle** – try and try to get ahead with no possibility of success

circus /sEr kus/ [circuses] *noun* 1 a traveling show with clowns, trained animals and performers *The kids loved going to the circus.* 2 when people's behavior is out of control *The store was a circus the day of the big sale.* Col: **three-ring circus** – lots of activity

colonel (kernel) /kEr nul/ [colonels] *noun* an officer in the American armed services *Colonel ranks above lieutenant and below general.*

concern /kun sErn/ [concerns, concerned, concerning] *noun* topic of interest or worry *A concern for immigrants is learning to speak English.* • *verb* focus of interest or worry *I am concerned about not having enough money.* Col: **concern oneself** – personal interest   **To whom it may concern** – start of a letter to an unknown recipient

convert /kun vErt/ [converts, converted, converting] *verb* 1 change something into another use or state *I'd like to convert the old factory into apartments.* 2 change ethical or religious beliefs *She converted to Buddhism after university.* Col: **preaching to the converted** – talk to people who already agree

currant (current) /kE runt/ [currants] *noun* small red berry *Red currant jelly is good on crackers and cheese.*

current (currant) /kE runt/ [currents] *noun* a steady flow *The tiny boat was swept down river by the current.* • *adv* up to date *The current list of students is on my desk.* Col: **current events** – news   **current trend** – at the present time   **electrical current** – flow of electricity   **swim against the current** – opinion or position against popular belief

curse /kErs/ [curses, cursed, cursing] *noun* 1 evil spell or bad luck *Sleeping Beauty slept for 100 years under an evil curse.* 2 swear or use rude language *Don't curse in front of the children!* • *verb* mindfully wish bad events *The car stops running for no reason – I think it's cursed.* **Col:** curse under one's breath – swear but not loudly enough for others to hear   Curse you Red Baron! – general oath popular in the 1980's from Snoopy against the WWII German flying ace   It's a curse. – good-natured saying to accept a compliment   the curse of the ... – cliché

cursor /kEr sEr/ [cursors] *noun* moving arrow on the computer screen *Move your cursor over the print icon and click, to copy this page.*

curtain /kEr tun/ [curtains] *noun* cloth covering a window *Close the curtains at night so the neighbors can't in.* **Col:** curtain call – performers appear for the applause at the end of a play   curtain down or final curtain – theatre term for the end of a run of shows   it's curtains – it's the end   shower curtain – keeps the water inside the shower area

curve /kErv/ [curves, curved, curving] *noun* a rounded line *There is a curve in the road ahead.* • *verb* bend *The road curves ahead.* • *adj* bend *It's a curved line not a straight line.* **Col:** put a curve on it – distorted   thrown a curve – term from baseball for a bad surprise

curvy /kEr vEy/ [curvier, curviest] *adj* extreme bends in the line or silhouette *Marilyn Monroe had a very curvy figure.*

desert (dessert) /du zErt/ [deserts, deserted, deserting] *verb* abandon or leave *The jerk deserted his wife before the baby was born.* **Col:** desert a sinking ship – leave a situation that becomes unpleasant   get one's just deserts – receive the deserved punishment

deserter /du zEr dEr/ [deserters] *noun* leaves official responsibilities *The deserter was hunted down by the army and punished.*

dessert (desert) /du zErt/ [desserts] *noun* sweet food eaten after a meal *No dessert if you don't eat your vegetables!*

detergent /du tEr junt/ [detergents] *noun* soap *I can't do the dishes, we are out of detergent.*

dirt /dErt/ *noun* 1 soil *Brush the dirt off the knees of your jeans.* 2 gossip *What is the dirt on the town hall burning down?* **Col:** common as dirt – low class   dirt cheap – very inexpensive   dirt-poor – no income   get the dirt on ___ – gossip   hit pay dirt – get rich   treat someone like dirt – no respect

dirty /dEr dEy/ [dirtier, dirtiest] *adj* 1 not clean *Her hands were dirty after working in the garden.* 2 unfair or underhanded *Win with honor or not at all but don't play dirty.* **Col:** a dirty weekend – sex get-a-way   a dirty word – swearing   air dirty linen in public – argue in public   dirty dog – sly and underhanded   dirty hands – illegal activity   dirty look – angry stare   dirty joke – rude or vulgar humor   dirty old man – pervert   dirty politics – unfair politics   dirty pool – cheating   dirty trick – taking unfair advantage   down and dirty – careless work   get him to do one's dirty work – most unpleasant part of a job   talk dirty – sex talk

early /Er lEy/ [earlier, earliest] *adj* 1 before schedule, not late *Come to the show early so you can get a good seat.* 2 first part of a time period *She goes to work in the early morning.* **Col:** at your earliest convenience – call me as soon as possible   bright and early – very early morning   early days – just the beginning, anything could happen   Early to bed early to rise makes a man healthy, wealthy and wise. – *proverb* a formula for success   The early bird catches the worm. – *proverb* habit for becoming successful

earn (urn) /Ern/ [earns, earned, earning] noun anyone who makes money *The man is typically the primary income earner.* • verb make money *People have to earn money in order to pay their bills.* Col: *A penny saved is a penny earned.* – proverb it is good to save money   **earn one's keep** – work in exchange for a place to live   **earn your stripes** – show you deserve a rank or position

earth /ErTH/ [earths] noun the planet we live on 🌍 *The earth is made up of water and dirt.* Col: **come back to earth** – be more realistic   **disappear off the face of the earth** – vanished without explanation   **down-to-earth** – practical people   **earth shattering** – devastating news   **go to the ends of the earth** – do anything to achieve   **heaven on earth** – something so good it should only be available in heaven   **hell on earth** – something so horrible one thinks they are in hell   **like nothing on earth** – new and really exciting   **earth mother** – natural woman   **move heaven and earth** – to do anything to succeed   **salt of the earth** – honest hard working person   **scum of the earth** – lowlife   **wipe off the face of the earth** – completely gone

Europe /yE rup/ prop noun continent north of the Mediterranean Sea *We'll take a trip to Europe after we retire.* Col: **European Union** – union of 27 democratic countries in 1993

fertile /fEr dul/ adj ability to reproduce *Both partners have to be fertile to make a baby.* Col: **fertile imagination** – creative

first /fErst/ [1st, firsts] noun 1 ordinal number one 🏆 *The Canadian runner is in first place.* • adj number one in an order *The school is at the first street light.* Col: **at first** – order of ideas   **at first blush** – initial thoughts   **at first glance** – superficial look   **at first hand** – personal experience   **at first light** – dawn   **at first sight** – initial experience   **be carried out feet first** – dead   **be first past the post** – win   **cast the first stone** – be first to criticize   **first aid** – medical care   **first and foremost** – important fact   **first come, first served** – not waiting   **first crack at** – attempt   **first hand** – personal experience   **First hundred years are the hardest.** – proverb life gets easier with time   **first of all** – before anything else   **first thing** – priority   **First things first** – order matters   **get to first base** – kiss   **give first refusal** – condition of sale   **If at first you don't succeed, try, try again** – persevere to succeed   **ladies first** – good manners   **love at first sight** – instant love   **Not if I see you first** – threat   **on a first name basis** – friends   **one chance to make a good first impression** – behave at introductions   **Self-preservation is the first law of nature.** – proverb on survival   **shoot first, ask questions later** – react without thinking   **The first step is always the hardest.** – proverb beginning is the most difficult part   **the first string** – best players   **you first** – if you live I'll try it

furniture /fEr nu ChEr/ noun household items for comfortable daily living *We bought new furniture for our bedroom.* Col: **be part of the furniture** – someone who has been around for a long time

further /fEr ThEr/ [furthers, furthered, furthering, furthest] adj compare by distant *The fire station is further down the street than the school.* • verb advance *He furthered his career by taking extra courses.* Col: **don't let it go any further** – secret   **without further ado** – without delay

girl /gErl/ [girls] noun female person *They had a baby girl this morning.* Col: **a golden girl** – talented and popular   **big girl's blouse** – (for men) show weak character or easily afraid   **call girl** – prostitute   **daddy's girl** – spoiled by father   **girl Friday** – variety of roles   **girl next door** – typical   **glamour girl** – likes to dress up   **that's my girl** –

address a female with affection and pride

heard (herd) /**hErd**/ [hears, heard, hearing] *verb* pass tense of *hear* use ears *He heard his mother calling him from down the street.* `Col:` **Children should be seen and not heard.** – *proverb* suggesting children be quiet around adults   **I've heard so much about you.** – polite greeting for a friend of a friend   **have heard the last of** – bad person gone away forever   **Have you heard?** – juicy gossip   **heard through the grapevine** – informal sources, gossip   **Never heard of such a thing!** – can't believe, shock

her /**hEr**/ *pron* female person or animal *Her favorite place is Paris.* `Col:` **Let 'er rip** – go without restraint   **what's her face?** – forgot her name

herd (heard) /**hErd**/ [herds, herded, herding] *noun* group of the same animal that live and travel together Only a few herds of wild horses are left in the world. • *verb* encourage a group to move together *Herd the cattle into the barn.* `Col:` **like herding cats** – a difficult task

hurt /**hErt**/ [hurts, hurt, hurting] *verb* cause physical or emotional pain *The sharp criticism hurt his feelings.* `Col:` **don't cry before you are hurt** – have a real problem before complaining   **hurt someone's feelings** – ridicule and teasing cause emotional pain   **it doesn't hurt to ask** – the answer might be yes, but you have to ask   **little hard work never hurt anyone** – sarcastic, don't be lazy   **never hurt a fly** – gentle   **Sticks and stone will break my bones but names will never hurt me.** – *proverb* it's one's choice not to be affected by mean words   **What you don't know wont hurt you.** – *proverb* about ignorance and bliss

insert /in **sErt**/ [inserts, inserted, inserting] *verb* put into *Insert the key into lock and open the door.*

insurance /in **ShEr** uns/ [insurances] *noun* money paid for protection against accident or loss *I need insurance for the new car.* `Col:` **car insurance** – policy on a vehicle   **house insurance** – policy for fire, theft and liability   **live insurance** – policy in case of death

jer /**jEr**/ *contr* d + your, spoken word only *English is Stupid Students are Not Chapter One* /*Could jer sister help too?*/

jerk /**jErk**/ [jerks, jerked, jerking] *adj* mean selfish person *That jerk just stole my parking space.* • *verb* sudden pull *He jerked my arm so hard it hurt.* `Col:` **jerk someone around** – intentionally not cooperate   **jerk something away** – take quickly   **knee-jerk reaction** – automatic reflex

journey /**jEr** nEy/ [journeys, journeyed, journeying] *noun* long trip *The journey from China took two weeks by ship.* • *verb* physical or emotional voyage. *Recovering from her mother's death was a long and painful journey.* `Col:` **have a safe journey** – good bye   **It's about the journey not the destination.** – *proverb* how you get there is more important than where you are going

jury /**jE rEy**/ [juries] *noun* group of selected citizens formed to make important decisions *The jury's decision was final and the pedophile was convicted.* `Col:` **The jury is still out.** – undecided

kernel (colonel) /**kEr** nul/ [kernels] *noun* seed of grain or inside a nut *Creamed corn uses only the kernels of the corn plant.* `Col:` **kernel of truth** – small true bit surrounded by lies

learn /**lErn**/ [learns learned/ learnt, learning] *verb* acquire new information *He learned the English Phonetic Alphabet in less than an hour.* `Col:` **It's never too late to learn.** – *proverb* to inspire life-long learning   **learn by doing** – understand the world through physical experience   **learn by heart** – memorize   **learn the hard way** – took longer to gain knowledge due to stubbornness or poor choices **learn the ropes** – similar to 'tricks of the trade' indicating hands on participation at a new job **learn the ticks of the trade** – acquired short cuts and best practices through on the job experience **learn to live with** – tolerate difficult circumstances that can't be changed **learned one's lesson** – closely tied to the 'learned the hard' way, where misadventure is finally overcome **live and learn** – valuable lessons gained from life experience

murder /**mEr** dEr/ [murders, murdered, murdering] *noun* kill a person *There were seven murders in the city last year.* • *verb* kill someone *He murdered the tourists and was tried and punished by death.* `Col:` **get away with murder** – bad or illegal behavior unpunished **murder case** – legal file **murder trial** – legal proceedings **scream blue/bloody murder** – complain or shout loudly

nerve /**nErv**/ [nerves] *noun* 1 cell pathways that take messages from the brain to the rest of the body *He burned his hand and damaged the nerves in his fingertips.* 2 bold *The new employee had a lot of nerve asking for a raise.* `Col:` **bundle of nerves** – jumpy with anxiety **get up the nerve** – build enough courage to act **nerves of steel** – courageous **on one's nerves** – annoying

nervous /**nEr** vus/ *adj* state of fear or worry *I was nervous before my speech.* `Col:` **nervous breakdown** – complete emotional collapse **nervous energy** – excess energy **nervous system** – organization of sensation pathways to the brain

nurse /**nErs**/ [nurses, nursed, nursing] *noun* 1 professional medical support person *A nurse took care of my mother in her home.* 2 the medical care support profession *Nursing is a demanding career.* • *verb* 1 physically taking care of another's health *He nursed his family when they had chicken pox.* 2 feed from the breast *She nursed her son until he was two years old.* `Col:` **nursing a cold** – at home resting and taking medicine to treat influenza **nursing a grudge** – choose to be angry for an inappropriately long time **nurse back to health** – long term care until the patient was well again **nurse old wounds** – self pity or choosing not to forgive and move on **private nurse** – takes care of one person **registered nurse** – professional **wet nurse** – a woman who breast-feeds other people's babies

pearl /**pErl**/ [pearls] *noun* a round gem formed inside of an oyster *He bought her pearl earrings to wear with her pearl necklace.* `Col:` **Cast pearls before swine.** – *proverb* waste something valuable on one who doesn't appreciate it **cultured pearls** – artificially grown pearls **pearls of wisdom** – small pieces of good advice

perfume /**pEr** fyUwm/ [perfumes, perfumed, perfuming] {also said /**pEr fyUm** / see Blue} *noun* 1 a pleasant smell *Perfume from the rose garden filled the air.* 2 a liquid made of flowers or other pleasant smelling ingredients *He bought her a bottle of perfume for her birthday.* • *verb* spread a sweet or pleasant smell *Purple lilacs perfumed the valley.*

person /**pEr** sun/ [people] *noun* 1 individual human being *I have never seen that person before.* 2 personal pronoun indicator rating *First person (I and we) indicates the writer or speaker, second person (you) is for the reader or listener and third person (he, she, it or they) is for the thing being talked about.* `Col:` **be the last person to ___** – least likely to do a specific behavior **feel like a new person** – healthy and refreshed or dressed up **in person** – physically present **morning person** – most alert and productive early in the day **night person** – most alert and productive after dinner each day **one's own person** – independent **person of interest** – suspicious

HOW DO YOU SAY? PRONUNCIATION DICTIONARY

purple /**pEr** pul/ [purples, purple, purplest] *noun* the color from mixing red and blue *Purple is the color of some grape varieties.* • *adj* having the color purple *What a beautiful purple flower!* `Col:` **purple nurple** – made up rhyme to showcase the /Er/ sound from page 61 of *English is Stupid Students are Not* **purple prose** – writing that is more flowery than necessary

purpose /**pEr** pus/ [purposes] *noun* reason *What is the purpose of this meeting?* `Col:` **accidently on purpose** – deliberately but made to look like an accident **at cross purposes** – opposition, goals that don't support each other **for all intents and purposes** – looking as if, like he was going to **for all practical purposes** – the most important, essential or realistic **on purpose** – intentionally **serves a purpose** – is useful

purse /**pErs**/ [purses] *noun* 1 woman's carry-all bag *Her purse matches her dress.* 2 prize money *The horses are racing for a $200,000 purse.* • *verb* draw a tight line *When she is annoyed, she purses her lips.* `Col:` **controls the purse strings** – manages the money in a family **You can't make a silk purse out of a sow's ear.** – *proverb* can't make quality products with bad quality materials

refer /ru **fEr**/ [refers, referred, referring] *verb* 1 direct to a resource for help *My doctor referred me to a specialist for my stomach troubles.* 2 make mention of *She referred to "English is Stupid Students are Not" in her pronunciation presentation*

return /ru **tErn**/ [returns, returned, returning] *noun* items brought back *The store pays 10¢ for bottle returns.* • *verb* come back *The birds return to the same nesting grounds every year.* • *adj* the means for coming back *The return route was blocked by fallen trees.* `Col:` **in return for** – make an exchange **point of no return** – committed, impossible to go back **return the compliment** – say something nice back **return the favor** – do a good turn for one who was kind

servant /**sEr** vunt/ [servants] *noun* a domestic employee *When I am wealthy I will hire lots of servants.* `Col:` **Fire is a good servant but a bad master.** – *proverb* to use fire carefully or it can cause harm

serve /**sErv**/ [serves, served, serving] *verb* work to protect or take care of another *Soldiers choose to serve their country.* `Col:` **dinner is served** – on the table **first come first served** – not waiting **if memory serves me correctly** – not sure if I remember details accurately **serve under** – work for someone **serve yourself** – don't wait to be served

shirt /**ShErt**/ [shirts] *noun* piece of clothing that covers above the waist *Her shirt matches her pants.* `Col:` **give one's shirt off one's back** – give anything requested or required **keep one's shirt on** – be patient **to lose one's shirt** – lose all assets

sir /**sEr**/ [sirs] *noun* honorable title placed before a man's name *Yes sir, I would like that very much.*

skirt /**skErt**/ [skirts, skirted, skirting] *noun* piece of clothing worn below the waist where the legs are not separated by clothe *Her skirt is too short.* • *verb* go around *The man skirted the problem.* `Col:` **skirt around** – to avoid **skirt the issue** – avoid the problem

slur /**slEr**/ [slurs, slurred, slurring] *verb* run words together, so they are difficult to understand. *The drunk slurred so badly we couldn't understand what he said.* • *noun* insult *Racial slurs are not acceptable in this country.*

squirrel /**skwErl**/ [squirrels, squirreled, squirreling] *noun* a gray or black tree-dwelling rodent with a bushy tail *Squirrels can be a pests if they nest in your attic.* • *verb* hide things away *The old man squirreled his money away under his mattress.*

/ Er / is Purple

stern /stern/ [sterns, sterner, sternest, sternly] *noun* rear of a boat *The motor is mounted at the stern of the boat.* • *adj* uncompromising appearance *He had a stern look on his face.* • *adv* with firmness *He shook his head sternly.* Col: **from stem to stern** – from one end to the other end

sure /ShEr/ [surer, surest] *adj* have certainty *I am sure we turn right at the corner.* • *adv* confidence *Surly you are not wearing that outfit to church.* Col: **for sure** – unquestionably **make sure** – check again to confirm **sure enough** – as expected

surf /sErf/ [surfs, surfed, surfing] *noun* portion of a wave *The surf crashed against the rocks.* • *verb* ride waves *He surfs in California.* Col: **surf and turf** – lobster and beef **surf the net** – browse the internet

surfer /sEr fEr/ [surfers] *noun* one who surfs *Beach Boys music is about the world of surfers.*

surgery /sEr ju rEy/ [surgeries] *noun* medical term for diagnosing and treatment *His broken leg requires surgery.* Col: **in surgery** – in the operating room

third /THErd/ [3rd, thirds] *noun* one of three parts 1/3 *He ate one third of the pie.* • *adj* ordinal number after the second and before the fourth *I came third in the marathon.* Col: **the third degree** – questioned heavily **third time's a charm** – success may come on the third attempt

thirsty /THErs dEy/ [thirstier, thirstiest] *adj* desire for fluid *I am so thirsty I could drink a lake.* Col: **thirst for knowledge** – academic **thirsty for something** – a strong desire

thirty /THEr dEy/ [30, thirties, thirtieth] *noun* a whole number 30 *He dreaded turning thirty but it beats the alternative.*

Thursday /THErz dAy/ [Thurs., Thursdays] *prop noun* day of the week *Thursday is after Wednesday and before Friday.*

turkey /tEr kEy/ [turkeys] *noun* 1 large North American bird *We are cooking a turkey for Thanksgiving.* 2 *proper noun* Turkey a European country *My friend is from Turkey.* Col: **you turkey** – name calling **cold turkey** – quit an addiction in one instant and never partake again

turn /tErn/ [turns, turned, turning] *verb* twist *Walk two blocks and turn right.* Col: **in turn** – in order **spoke out of turn** – said something one should not have said **turn of phrase** – an expression **which way to turn** – do not know what to do **take a turn for the better** – improve **take a turn for the worse** – decline **take turns** – sharing back and forth **turn a blind eye** – pretend not to see **turn a deaf ear** – pretend not to hear **turn the place upside down** – look everywhere **turn a profit** – make money **turn around** – go back **turn belly up** – die or fail **turn down** – decline an offer **turn heads** – get attention **turn inside out** – make the inside be the outside **turn in** – go to sleep **turn into** – transform **turn loose** – release **turn nose up** – think less of **turn on** – power on **turn off** – power off **turn on a dime** – change direction sharply **turn over** – rotate such that what was on the bottom is now on the top **turn over a new leaf** – start fresh **turn over in one's mind** – analyze or ponder **turned a corner** – pass a critical point **turn the heat up** – increase pressure **turn the other cheek** – ignore **turn the tables** – power shifts

turnip /tEr nup/ [turnips] *noun* a large yellow bitter root vegetable *Turnip is not my favorite vegetable.* Col: **just fell off the turnip truck** – dummy from the countryside

turquoise /tEr kOyz/ [turquoises] *noun* 1 the color light blue green *Turquoise is the color of the water in the Caribbean* 2 blue-green mineral of aluminum and copper *First nations people believe turquoise has special healing powers.* • *adj* having the color turquoise *What a gorgeous turquoise necklace.*

turtle /tEr dul/ [turtles] *noun* four legged reptile with a shell on its back *A turtle carries it's home on its back.* Col: turn turtle — to flip upside down the turtle and the hare — fable about perseverance and over confidence

urgent /Er junt/ [urgently] *adj* required immediately, emergency *Call the police, it is urgent.*

urn (earn) /Ern/ [urns] *noun* large vase – like container *Her father's ashes are on the shelf in the urn.*

verse /vErs/ [verses] *noun* lines of poetry *What is your favorite verse or nursery rhyme?* • *adj* know a topic well *My professor is well-versed in 18th century French poetry.*

virtue /vEr ChUw/ [virtues] *noun* goodness *She is a woman of virtue.* Col: Patience is a virtue. — *proverb* the ability to wait is a good quality

were /wEr/ *verb* past tense of *to be* exist *Where were you yesterday?*

word /wErd/ [words, worded, wording] *noun* 1 basic unit of meaning in language *The first thing students need to learn are words.* 2 promise *He gave me his word.* • *verb* construction of writing *He worded his message so clearly everyone understood.* Col: a man of his word — a man who can be trusted   A picture is worth a thousand words. — *proverb* more can be expressed in an image then in words   a war of words — long verbal argument   a word to the wise — advice   Actions speak louder than words. — *proverb* it does not matter what one says actions are what matter   as good as word — a dependable person   beyond words — cannot be expressed using just words   buzz word — popular word used because it is thought to be important   by word of mouth — learn information through conversation   can't get a word in edgeways — someone talks so much that no one else can contribute   dirty word — disrespectful word   don't believe a word of it — it is false so do not believe it   don't breathe a word — be silent   eat your words — admit you were wrong   famous last words — one is proved wrong following a public declaration   for lack of a better word — not the exact word but it's the best one can think of in the moment   four-letter word — swearing (rude words often have four letters)   from the word go — from the beginning   go back on word — go back on a promise   hang on every word — listen very closely   have a way with words — can express themselves clearly using words   have a word — May I speak with you?   have the final word — make the last comment in an argument   have words stick in throat — to be so emotional that one cannot speak   have words with — have a serious or angry discussion   in a word — in brief   in other words — to say something another way   in so many words — the short version of the story   keep word — keep a promise   lost for words — so angry or emotional one cannot think of what to say   man of few words — very quiet   Mark my words. — I predict   Mum's the word — just tell me and I'll do it   not mince words — be clear even if it may hurt someone's feelings   play on words — a joke made with words or phrases that have two meanings   put in a good word for — speak positively about me   put words in one's mouth — to reword what a person said to fit what the listener's needs   spread the word — share this information with everyone   take my word for it — trust what I say   take the words out of mouth — someone says the same idea that you were thinking   take word for – trust me   the operative word – the word in a phrase that holds all the meaning   true to word – honest person   twist words – change the meaning of the words with ill intention   What's the magic word? Said to children to prompt them to say 'please' or 'thank you'   word for word – repeat exactly what someone said   word is good – honest person   Words fail me! – I do not know what to say   words to live by – important pieces of advice

work /wErk/ [works, worked, working] *noun* the location or organization where one goes to earn a living *I work at the library.* • *verb* put forth effort to accomplish a task *I work for the local college.* Col: a woman's work is never done – raising children and house work are endless tasks • all in a day's work – downplay a significant contribution   all work and no play – no time for fun   at work – someone is at their job   dirty work – unpleasant tasks • grunt work – requires much effort • I've got work to do – I must go • in the works – in the process • keep up the good work – continue the productivity and effort • little work never hurt anyone – sarcastic, don't be lazy • make light work of it – task was completed easily   Many hands make light work. – *proverb* a task is easier with the help of many   out of work – unemployed • pile the work on – over burden • put in a hard day's work – put in a lot of effort through the day   take off from work – a planned period away from work   the works – everything   things will work out – everything will be okay   work against the clock – finish the task before a certain time   work around – accommodate   work fingers to the bone – toil   work like a dog – toil   work of art – artistic creation   work off – exchange effort for debt   work oneself into a lather – sweat   work out – fitness exercise   work out for the best – a bad situation will be okay   work my tail off – work very hard   work together – join with other people to accomplish a task   worked up – excited or angry   works for me – agree   work through something – get through a difficult period or circumstance

world /wErld/ [worlds] *noun* the universe *The astronaut can see the whole world from space.* Col: a world of difference – big change   all the time in the world – in no hurry   armpit of the world – an ugly place   best of both worlds – great enjoyment form two different areas of life   carry the weight of the world on shoulders – under a lot of pressure   come into the world – born   do a world of good – make a big positive difference   dead to the world – asleep   from all corners of the world – from many different places   in a dream world – unrealistic ideas   it's a small world – run into an acquaintance in an unlikely place   Love makes the world go around. – *proverb* life is more pleasant when people treat each other nicely   make one's way in the world – to be successful without receiving help   move up in the world – to advance at work   not have a care in the world – carefree/relaxed   not long for this world – will die soon   not the end of the world – no serious long-term harm on top of the world – ecstatic, happy   out of this world – extremely excited   set the world on fire – to do exciting things   to have the world at your feet – many opportunities and choices   to not have a care in the world – happy or carefree   where in the world? – Where?   worlds apart – great separation in location or idea

worm /wErm/ [worms, wormed, worming] *noun* insect that lives in dirt *I use worms as bait to catch fish.* • *verb* work one's way into a place or situation *She* *wormed her way into the club.* Col: **book worm** – avid reader   **the early bird catches the worm** – *proverb* about becoming a success   **worm something out of someone** – convince someone to tell a secret

worst /wErst/ [worse] *adj* most unfavorable *Death is my worst fear.* Col: **hope for the best prepare for the worst** – *proverb* to be positive but ready in case of a bad turn   **in the worst way** – very much   **one's own worst enemy** – repeatedly causing one's self to fail   **worst-case scenario** – most horrible possible outcome   **wouldn't wish something on one's worst enemy** – conditions so bad no one should endure them

worth /wErTH/ [worthy] *adj* have value *A gold coin has much worth.* Col: **worthy of the name** – deserving of one's reputable family name

your /yEr/ {*also said* /yOr/ *see Orange*} [yours] *adj* possessive form of *you* reduced in conversation *What is your name?* /whats yer name/

Chapter 15
/Ar/ is Charcoal

Chapter 15
/Ar/ is Charcoal

apartment /u pArt munt/
arc /Ark/
arch /ArCh/
architect /Ar ku tekt/
Arctic /Ar dik/
are (R) /Ar/
argue /Ar gyUw/
arm /Arm/
army /Ar mEy/
art /Art/
artery /Ar du rEy/

bar /bAr/
barber /bAr bEr/
barbecue /bAr bu kyUw/
bark /bArk/
barn /bArn/
bazaar (bizarre) /bu zAr/
bizarre (bazaar) /bu zAr/

car /kAr/
card /kArd/
carnival /kAr nu vul/
carpenter /kAr pen tEr/
cart /kArt/
carton /kAr tun/
cartridge /kAr truj/
charcoal /ChAr kOwl/

dark /dArk/
darling /dAr liNg/
darn /dArn/

embark /em bArk/

far /fAr/
fart /fArt/
farm /fArm/
farmer /fAr mEr/

garbage /gAr buj/
garden /gAr dun/
garlic /gAr luk/
guard /gArd/

guitar /gu tAr/

harbor /hAr bEr/
hard /hArd/
hardware /hArd wAyr/
harm /hArm/
harmony /hAr mu nEy/
harvest /hAr vust/
heart /hArt/

jar /jAr/

lard /lArd/
large /lArj/
lark /lArk/

March /mArCh/
margarine /mAr ju run/
mark /mArk/
marker /mAr kEr/
market /mAr kut/
martial arts /mAr Shul Arts/

parcel /pAr sul/
pardon /pAr dun/
park /pArk/
parka /pAr ku/
part /pArt/
party /pAr dEy/
partner /pArt nEr/

R (are) /Ar/

sergeant /sAr junt/
sharpener /ShAr pu nEr/
star /stAr/
start /stArt/

tar /tAr/
target /tAr gut/
tart /tArt/

yard /yArd/
yarn /yArn/

apartment /u **pArt** munt/ [apartments] *noun* group of rooms in a building where people live *I need to rent a one-bedroom apartment.* **furnished apartment** – with bed, table, chair, stove, refrigerator **high rise apartment** – more than 10 floors high

arc /**Ark**/ [arcs, arced, arcing] *noun* part of a circle *The rainbow made a perfect arc across the sky.* • *verb* electricity moving from one point to another *An arc of electricity jumped between the poles of the battery.*

arch /**ArCh**/ [arches, arched, arching] *noun* an arc-shaped entranceway *Roses covered the arch into the garden.* • *verb* bend *The cat arched its back and dug its claws into the carpet.* Col: **arch enemy** – The Joker is Batman's arch enemy.

architect /**Ar** ku tekt/ [architects] *noun* person who designs buildings *The art gallery was designed by a renowned architect.* Col: **Every man is the architect of his own fortune.** – *proverb* one's decisions determine their future

Arctic /**Ar** dik/ *prop noun* area around the North Pole inside the Arctic Circle *Santa Claus lives in the Arctic at the North Pole.* *adj* about the arctic region *Caribou roam the arctic wilderness.*

are (r)/**Ar**/*verb* plural in the present tense of to *be* exist *They are happy.*

argue /**Ar** gyUw/ [argues, argued, arguing] *verb* express opposing opinions or reasons *My kids argue about what to watch on TV.* Col: **argue against** – disagree **argue in favor of** – agree and give reasons supporting an idea

arm /**Arm**/ [arms, armed, arming] *noun* 1 the part of the human body that joins the hand to the shoulder *The doctor gave the vaccination needle in his arm.* 2 part of an object that is like a human arm *The spaceship used its mechanical arm to repair its own flap.* 3 weapon *All countries agreed not to make any more nuclear arms.* • *verb* got weapons *The villagers armed themselves with sticks to fight off the wolf.* Col: **a list as long as arm** – extensive **armed and dangerous** – ready for conflict **armed to the teeth** – lots of gun-power and weaponry **babe in arms** – baby **be up in arms** – angry and excited **bear arms** – carry a gun **cost an arm and a leg** – pricey **could do with one arm tied behind back** – bragging that some task is so easy **at arm's length** – held away physically or metaphorically **crossed arms** – both arms folded across the chest **give right arm** – sacrifice **greet with open arms** – warmly **have a good arm** – good throw **keep at arm's length** – distance **lay down arms** – surrender **long arm of the law** – law breakers will be caught and punished **shot in the arm** – boost of energy **strong-arm tactics** – bully **take up arms** – get weapons **twist arm** – torture **walk arm in arm** – stroll together with arms linked

army /**Ar** mEy/ [armies] *noun* military group trained for combat *The army protects our country.* Col: **army base** – soldiers live and train **army boots** – soldiers' footwear **tough as army boots** – meat that can't be chewed easily **You and what army?** – tough talk. Is going to stop me?

art /**Art**/ [arts] *noun* creative expression using color, shape, or human movement to make something of beauty or meaning *The students put their art on the wall.* Col: **art gallery** – a place to show pictures and sculpture **Art is long and life is short** – *proverb* that art work lives longer than people **down to a fine art** – ability perfected from long practice **state of the art** – most modern **work of art** – beautiful creation

artery /**Ar** du rEy/ [arteries] *noun* 1 tube that carries blood from the heart to the rest of the body *His blocked artery causing a heart attack.* 2 major road that carries traffic through a city *The main artery into the city was blocked by the car* *accident*. Col: hardening of the arteries – a disease of the heart   major artery – blood vessel or large highway

bar /bɑr/ [bars, barred, barring] *noun* 1 a long, straight, stiff object *Hold onto the handle bars when riding your bike.* 2 a high long counter or table *Drinks and appetizers were served at the bar.* 3 place to drink alcohol *Let's meet at the bar after work on Friday.* • *verb* prevent *The bouncers barred more patrons from entering the pub.* Col: bar none – no exceptions   bar stool – a chair that is high to sit at the bar   bar the door – lock the door behind bars – in jail   breakfast bar – serve yourself a selection of breakfast foods   called to the bar – when a lawyer can practice law   chocolate bar – candy   raise the bar – high expectations

barber /bɑr bɛr/ [barbers] *noun* cuts people's hair *My husband went to the barber and got his head shaved.*

barbecue /bɑr bu kyUw/ [barbecues, barbecued, barbecuing] *noun* 1 open fire or grill for cooking *Let the barbecue heat up before you put your burgers on.* 2 event where meat is cooked over an open fire *Come to our barbecue on Saturday.* • *verb* cook on a barbecue *My son barbecues all year, even in winter!*

bark /bɑrk/ [barks, barked, barking] *verb* 1 noise made by a dog *Dogs bark at cats.* 2 a noise similar to the noise made by a dog *The boss barked out orders.* • *noun* 3 the outer skin of a tree *Birch bark is white and fine like paper.* Col: almond bark – chocolate and nuts   barking up the wrong tree – believes the wrong explanation   his bark is worse than his bite – noisy but harmless

barn /bɑrn/ [barns] *noun* large farm building for livestock *The cows are milked in the barn.* Col: barn dance – social event held in a barn with music and dancing   barn raising – community of volunteers to build a barn   can't hit the broad side of a barn door – bad aim   Were you raised in a barn? – you have bad manners

bazaar (bizarre) /bu zɑr/ [bazaars] *noun* outdoor street market *The church is having a bazaar to raise money.*

bizarre (bazaar) /bu zɑr/ *adj* unusual *The cat with six toes is a little bizarre.*

car /kɑr/ [cars] *noun* vehicle, an automobile *He sold his car and uses public transit or his bicycle.* Col: car lease – long term borrow   new car smell – fresh from the factory smell of new things   rental car – pay to use a car short term   used car – previously owned

card /kɑrd/ [cards] *noun* flat, rectangular piece of stiff paper with symbols or information *Do you want to play cards?* Col: birthday card – humorous or touching birthday wish   business card – small portable identification for clients   calling card – signature token credit or debit card – plastic used for banking   card-carrying member – official member of a group   cards are stacked against – odds are not in his favor   deck of cards – 52 playing cards   flash card – classroom tool greeting card – fancy note to wish a range of good things   have a card up sleeve – surprise asset   have all the cards – all the power   house of cards – unstable   Lucky at cards, unlucky in love – *proverb* lucky gamblers have bad love lives   my card – business card not in the cards – not going to happen play cards close to chest – private with personal information   play cards right – profit from making good decisions   playing cards – deck of 52 stiff paper rectangles with numbered ☐☐♦☐ printed on   put cards on the table – disclose   tarot cards – fortune telling deck   wild card – questionable person or random advantage

carnival /kɑr nu vul/ [carnivals] *noun* festive event with games, rides, and live shows *My favorite ride at the carnival is the roller coaster.*

carpenter /kAr pun tEr/ [carpenters] *noun* skilled tradesperson who builds structures with wood *The carpenter is here to hang the new doors.* Col: **carpenter ants** – eat wood

cart /kArt/ [carts, carted, carting] *noun* a vehicle with two or four wheels used to carry things *We have so much luggage we need a cart.* • *verb* carry around *She carts her children the grocery store and everywhere with her.* Col: **go cart** – children's wheeled box **golf cart** – small motorized vehicle to carry golfers **putting the cart before the horse** – illogical sequence **shopping cart** – used to carry groceries at the market

carton /kAr tun/ [cartons] *noun* container made of cardboard or plastic *Egg cartons can be recycled.*

cartridge /kAr truj/ [cartridges] *noun* container that holds powder or liquid *The ink cartridge in the copier is empty.*

charcoal /char kOwl/ *noun* 1 black carbon substance used as fuel *Change the charcoal water filter once a month.* 2 for drawing in the form of a pencil or crayon *her son's charcoal drawings are beautiful.*• *adj* dark gray in color *Charcoal mascara is softer looking than black.* Col: **charcoal briquettes** – small pieces of charcoal to fuel the barbecue

dark /dArk/ [darker, darkest] *noun* 1 very little or no light *It's dark in the closet.* 2 sundown *Be home before dark.* • *adj* 1 toward black in color *He wears dark socks with his dress suit.* 2 superstitious, gloomy, disturbing *I find dark stories and dark comedy too upsetting.* Col: **afraid of the dark** – needs some light on **dark comedy** – loss and gloom **dark horse** – know little about **dark side** – bad, often hidden aspects of a person or job **in the dark** – not knowing **It's always darkest before the dawn.** – *proverb* very bad situations usually improve shortly **pitch dark** – no light at all **shot in the dark** – guess **whistle in the dark** – hopeful

darling /dAr liNg/ [darlings] *noun* affectionate name *You look wonderful tonight darling.* • *adj* refer to with love *To my darling wife I leave my entire fortune.*

darn /dArn/ *interj* expression of dissatisfaction or annoyance *Darn I've locked my keys in the car!* • *verb* mend wool clothing *My grandma darns the holes in our socks.* Col: **Darn toot'n** – definitely yes

embark /em bArk/ [embarks, embarked, embarking] *verb* 1 go onto a boat *When will you embark on your boat cruise?* 2 start a journey *We embark for Africa today.*

far /fAr/ [farther, farthest] *adv* long distance away *Vancouver is far from Toronto.* • *adj* distant *Chinas is in the Far East.* Col: **as far as is concerned** – opinion **as far as it goes** – limitations **by far** – more so or most **far and away** – by a big margin **far and wide** – long distances **far be it from me** – not my place or responsibility **far cry from** – not similar **far from it** – not true at all **far from the madding crowd** – misquoted phrase about peace **far gone** – unreachable **far into the night** – late **far out** – 60's for interesting **faraway look** – not present **few and far between** – occasionally **from far and near** – everywhere **go so far as to say** – tentative **go too far** – push the limit **so far, so good** – fine up to now **so near and yet so far** – can see but can't have **thus far** – to date **wouldn't trust as far as one could throw** – don't trust at all

fart /fArt/ [farts, farted, farting] *noun* 1 air that escapes from the rectum *Farts stink.* • *verb* air escaping from the rectum *Who farted?* Col: **farting around** – not being serious **old fart** – old man

farm /fArm/ [farms, farmed, farming] *noun* land used to produce animals or plants for food or other purpose *We picked fruit at the apple farm.* • *verb* raise animals or plants for eating *Before tractors, people farmed with horses.* `Col:` **bet the farm** – sure thing   **buy the farm** – died   **farm out** – lend   **funny farm** – insane asylum   **hobby farm** – a small acreage   **sell the farm** – liquidated assets

farmer /fArm Er/ [farmers] *noun* one who works on or operates a farm *Farmers are the backbone of the nation.*

garbage /gAr buj/ *noun* waste, refuse, trash *Reduce garbage by recycling.* • *adj* having to do with waste *The garbage bins are full.*

garden /gAr dun/ [gardens, gardened, gardening] *noun* land used for growing flowers, fruit or vegetables *Can you please water the garden?* • *verb* grow things in a plot *Grandma likes to garden.* `Col:` **garden-variety** – ordinary   **herb garden** – grows   **lead down the garden path** – take advantage of an innocent person   **patio garden** – plants in pots

garlic /gAr luk/ *noun* onion-like root used to give flavor to food *I add garlic to my famous spaghetti sauce.* `Col:` **cloves of garlic** – parts of a bulb   **garlic breath** – bad breath that lingers after eating garlic

guard /gArd/ [guards, guarded, guarding] *noun* protects property and people or prevents prisoners from escaping *His first job was a guard at the bank.* • *verb* protect *Can you guard my suitcase for a minute?* `Col:` **catch someone off guard** – by surprise in a careless moment   **drop one's guard** – trust   **let one's guard down** – relax   **on one's guard** – defense mode

guitar /gu tAr/ [guitars] *noun* a musical instrument with strings, a long neck and a large flat sound box *She plays guitar in the rock band.* `Col:` **air guitar** – imaginary instrument

harbor /hAr bEr/ [harbors, harbored, harboring] *noun* 1 safe sheltered place for boats *The harbor was a calm place to anchor the boat.* 2 to shelter from harm *The church was a safe place to harbor the orphans.* • *verb* keep and protect *She harbored bad feelings for her husband long after the divorce.* `Col:` **harbor a fugitive** – hide a criminal from the law   **harbor a grudge** – hang onto negativity for too long

hard /hArd/ [harder, hardest] *adj* 1 tough, strong surface not easily damaged *Concrete is hard.* 2 strict *My teacher is a hard marker.* `Col:` **A good man is hard to find.** – *proverb* rare if they are single   **hard pressed** – too difficult   **as hard as a rock** – solid   **hard pressed** – too difficult   **between a rock and a hard place** – in a difficult situation   **cold, hard cash** – currency   **die hard** – doesn't give up   **do the hard way** – bad choices   **drive a hard bargain** – settle a deal without giving up too much.   **fall on hard times** – lost money   **give a hard time** – tease, bully   **hard act to follow** – excellent performance   **hard done-by** – feel persecuted   **hard of hearing** – deaf   **hard on the heels of** – almost caught up to   **hard to believe** – incredible   **hard to swallow** – don't want to believe   **hard to take** – disappointment   **hard-boiled** – stern and non emotional   **hard-nosed** – cold and businesslike   **have a hard time** – not manage   **hard nut to crack** – mentally tough   **hard pressed** – too difficult   **hard time** – not fun   **hard up** – no cash   **hard wood floors** – dense wood   **hit hard** – devastated   **learn the hard way** – took longer to gain knowledge due to stubbornness or poor choices   **no hard and fast rules** – unstructured process   **no hard feelings** – don't be mad   **old habits die hard** – people don't change   **play hard to get** – coy   **school of hard knocks** – education by experience   **take a hard line** – firm   **take a long, hard look at** – study   **The bigger they are, the harder they fall.** – *proverb* prominent people fall more dramatically and severely   The first hundred years are the hardest – *proverb* life gets easier with time   The first step is the hardest. – *proverb* beginning is the most difficult part   the hard sell – fear and trickery sells things people don't need   the hard stuff – alcohol   think long and hard – consider

hardware /hArd wAyr/ *noun* 1 metal products, tools, equipment *You can buy a hammer at the hardware store.* 2 equipment used in computers *The hardware in your computer needs to be defragged.*

harm /hArm/ [harms, harmed, harming] *verb* to do physical, mental or emotional damage *Doctors may do no harm.* Col: do more harm than good – more damaging than helpful   come to no harm – be okay   in harm's way – likely to be hurt   no harm done – no damage   wouldn't harm a fly – gentle

harmony /hAr mu nEy/ *noun* 1 agreement in opinions or feelings *There was harmony in their home.* 2 musical part *I'll sing the melody, you sing the harmony.* Col: live in harmony – compatible   four-part harmony – quartet

harvest /hArvust/ [harvests, harvested, harvesting] *noun* crops cut and brought in from the fields *The harvest was plentiful this year.* • *verb* the act of gathering in a crop *Extra workers were hired to harvest the ripe peaches.* Col: harvest moon – The moon that appears at the time of gathering in a crop

heart /hArt/ [hearts] *noun* 1 organ in the chest that pumps blood around the body *Unborn babies hear their mothers' heart beat.* 2 center or core of a vegetable *Artichoke hearts are the best part.* 3 a symbol on a playing card or valentine *Red hearts represent love.* Col: all heart – kindness and caring   a man after own heart – similar tastes, values and disposition   Absence makes the heart grow fonder. – *proverb* love someone more after some time apart   best interest at heart – taking care of, support   bleeding heart – too tender   break heart – disappointed   by heart – memorize   change of heart – change mind   close to heart – important to   cross my heart – promise   cry heart out – cry bitterly   do heart good – warm feeling   faint of heart – cowardly   find it in heart – beg   follow heart – true to self   from the bottom of heart – sincerely   half-hearted – poor effort   hard hearted – unfeeling   have a heart – beg   have one's heart in mouth – fearful   heart and soul – complete surrender to love or a project   heart attack – stops pumping   heart bleeds – compassion   heart-felt – sincere   heart goes out to – compassion   heart is in the right place – generous and kind   heart isn't in it – poor effort, don't want to   heart of gold – extremely kind   heart of stone – unfeeling   heart set against – don't want   heart set on – want badly   heart sinks – despair   heart skips a beat – excited   heart stand still – suspended animation, anticipation   heart to heart – intimate talk   home is where the heart is – *proverb* about belonging   in heart of hearts – deeply in one's soul   know by heart – memorized   learn by heart – memorizing   let heart rule head – emotional vs. intellectual decision   lose heart – give up   lose heart to – fall in love   not have the heart – can't do it   open heart – trusting or surgery   open heart to – confide in   out of the goodness of one's heart – for no financial reward   pour heart out – confide in   put hand on heart – swear to   put one's heart into – commit, work hard towards   sick at heart – disappointed   steal heart – fell in love   strike at the heart of – attacks or addresses core issues   take heart – encouraged   take to heart – receive, adopt   tear heart out – emotionally hurt   The way to a man's heart is through his stomach. – *proverb* to win a man's love, feed him well   to heart's content – unrestrained access to happiness   warm the cockles of heart – touch emotionally in a good way   wear one's heart on one's sleeve – all emotions are plainly seen   with a heavy heart – sadly   with all heart – completely   young at heart – youthful attitude and disposition

jar /jArˈ/ [jars, jarred, jarring] *noun* a wide mouthed cylinder shaped container *Can you open the pickle jar please.* • *verb* suddenly move *The subway jarred to a stop.*

lard /lArd/ [lards] *noun* white solid fat *Flakey pie crusts are made with lard.* Col: tub of lard – rude for fat person

large /lArj/ [larger, largest] *adj* big, greater than average amount, size or extent *I'll have a large coffee.* Col: at large – on the loose   by and large – mostly   extra large – bigger than large   loom large – ominous, foreboding

lark /lArk/ [larks] *noun* 1 species of bird with a pleasant song *Larks sing in the meadow.* 2 adventure for fun *We flew to Paris on a lark.* Col: for a lark – for fun

March /mArCh/ [Mar., marches, marched, marching] *prop noun* 1 the third month of the year *St Patrick's Day is in March.* 2 military progress *It was a long march to the front.* • *verb* walk formally *Soldiers march into battle.* Col: March break – a week off of school in March   March comes in like a lion, and goes out like a lamb. – *proverb* about the season change from winter to spring in March   march on – organized protest   march to a different drummer – behave differently that others

margarine /mAr ju run/ [margarines] *noun* vegetable spread in place of butter *Put margarine on your toast.* Col: margarine tube – container useful for storing things

mark /mArk/ [marks, marked, marking] *noun* 1 visible spot or symbol *Put a question mark at the end of these sentences.* 2 a grade or score *I get good marks in math.* • *verb* making visible spots *Who marked up my book?* Col: black mark – demerit against   check mark – shows correct   close to the mark – near   easy mark – gullible, vulnerable   exclamation mark – ! punctuation mark indicating strong feelings   leave mark on – shows forever   make mark – successful   mark down – discount   marked man – targeted   mark for life – emotional scar   mark my words – forecast event   mark time – wait   marks man – shooting accuracy   off the mark – wrong   on the mark – right   On your mark, get set, go. – start of a race   quick off the mark – smart   slow off the mark – not smart   wide of the mark – missed target   X marks the spot – destination

marker /mAr kEr/ [markers] *noun* 1 used to show a place *It is dangerous beyond the red marker.* 2 felt-tipped pen *Use a dry erase marker on the white board.* Col: grave marker – headstone cemetery

market /mAr kut/ [markets, marketer, marketing] *noun* 1 where food and other items are sold *I buy fresh fruits and vegetables at the markets.* 2 a group of people likely to buy a certain product *The market for organic food is growing.* • *verb* promote sales *Fat food chains market to children and teens.* Col: farmer's market – farmers bring their produce to town   stock market – people buy and sell interest in companies

martial arts /mAr Shul Arts/ *noun* sport of self defense or combat *Karate is an ancient Japanese martial art.*

parcel /pAr sul/ [parcels] *noun* package *The mail carrier will not deliver big parcels to your door.* Col: part and parcel – everything

pardon /pAr dun/ [pardons, pardoned, pardoning] *noun* release from punishment, excused *The criminal received a last-minute pardon from the king.* • verb forgive an offence or intrusion *Pardon me, where are the washrooms?* Col: I beg your pardon. – excuse me   pardon my French – swearing

park /pArk/ [parks, parked, parking] noun 1 space for the public to use for recreation *Take the children to the park to play.* • verb leave a vehicle *You can't park your car here.* Col: car park – place to park cars   in park – gears locked   parallel park – park on the side of the street between two other cars   parking lot – place to park cars

parka /pAr ku/ [parkas] noun a heavy coat with a hood *Everyone in Canada wears parkas in the winter.*

part /pArt/ [parts, parted, parting] noun 1 piece, portion, or fraction of a whole thing *He was a large part of the success of the business.* 2 role in a play *He played the part of Christopher Columbus in the school play.* • verb divide into parts *She parts her hair down the middle.* Col: a part to play – a role in   be part of the furniture – someone who has been around for a long time   best part of – greater fraction   Discretion is the better part of valor. – proverb on good judgment   do one's part – contribute to the whole, help others   for the most part – mostly   in large part – credit due to   in these parts – this area   look the part – dress for the role   part company – leave   part time – less than 35 hrs/week   part with – sell   play a big part – affected significantly   private parts – under underwear   take part – participate   two bit part – small role

party /pAr dEy/ [parties] noun 1 social gathering for fun *We had a party to celebrate his birthday* 2 political organization *Which party are you voting for?* Col: hen party – all women   life of the party – energetic focus of attention   party animal – gets carried away and goes to many parties   party is over – stop now   party pooper – blocks fun   responsible party – who is liable   surprise party – arranged in secret for the guest of honor

partner /pArt nEr/ [partners] noun linked to another in an official way *She is my business partner.* • verb work together officially *We partnered with a major university to develop the speaking program.* Col: Howdy partner! – old greeting   silent partner – invested money   marriage partner – spouse   life partner – same sex spouse   partner in crime – humorous reference to a business partner

R (are) /Ar/ [R's] noun the eighteenth letter of the Latin alphabet *Red starts with an R.* Col: how R U? – text for *How are you?*   R rated – restricted to adults

sergeant /sAr junt/ [sergeants] noun a rank in the armed forces or police services *A sergeant ranks below a captain or lieutenant.*

sharpener /shAr pu nEr/ [sharpeners, sharpened, sharpening] noun a blade for putting an edge or a point on a tool or a pencil. *There is a sharpener in my desk.*

star /stAr/ [stars, starred, starring] noun 1 distant flaming object in the night sky *The sun is a star.* 2 symbol or shape with five points ★ *The teacher put a gold star on his perfect paper.* 3 celebrity, famous person *All the stars attended the Oscar's.* • adj exceptional potential *That young actor has star quality.* Col: a star in the making – potential   five star quality – excellent   gold star – excellent work   hitch one's wagon to a star – become successful by associating with a successful person   see stars – knocked unconscious   shoot for the stars – aim high   starry eyed – impressed with a celebrity   written in the stars – destiny   star-crossed lovers – ill-fated romantic partners

thank one's lucky stars – be grateful for a blessing

start /stArt/ [starts, started, starting] *noun* beginning point *The start of the race will be soon.* • *verb* begin, turn-on *Gentleman, start your engines.* Col: **head start** – advantage   **false start** – had to start again   **fits and starts** – stop and start   **fresh start** – start anew   **from start to finish** – run through the whole project   **get started on** – begin   **off to a flying start** – good start   **start from scratch** – basic ingredients, built it oneself   **start out** – begin as a journey   **start out as** – started as one thing and changed along the way   **start over** – begin again   **start something** – conflict   **start up** – venture capital   **start with a bang** – exciting start   **start with a clean slate** – fresh with no history or bad feelings

tar /tAr/ [tars, tarred, tarring] *noun* thick, black, oily guck *The roof is leaking so we'll have to get some tar.* • *verb* apply tar *Look Mom! They are tarring the road!* Col: **tar and feather** – punishment and humiliate a criminal   **tarred with the same brush** – include in a group of bad guys who share some characteristics

target /tAr gut/ [targets, targeted, targeting] *noun* destination for a gunshot or archery arrow *Aim for the bulls eye in the center of the target.* 2 goal *Our target is to increase sales by 20%.* 3 victim *A fat child is a target for bullies.* • *verb* focus group *Let's target middle-class families with two working parents for our babysitting campaign.*

tart /tArt/ [tarts, tarter, tartest] *noun* 1 small pastry dessert usually filled with fruit *My grandmother made the best peach tarts.* 2 spiteful label for an attractive flirtatious woman *That woman in the mini skirt is such a tart.* • *adj* a little sour *Cranberries are tart.*

yard /yArd/ [yards] *noun* 1 unit of distance measurement that equals 36 inches *We learned yards but our children learn meters.* 2 small piece of land around a house that belongs to the property *The kids are playing in the yard.* Col: **back yard** – behind the house   **the whole nine yards** – continue a difficult task until it is complete   **yard sale** – selling pre-owned items privately from the yard

yarn /yArn/ [yarns] *noun* 1 long twisted thread of wool or nylon used for knitting or weaving *It takes ten balls of yarn to knit a sweater.* 2 long, complicated story that may or may not be true *Grandpa tells the best yarns about fishing in the ocean.*

Chapter 16
/or/ is Orange

Chapter 16
/Or/ is Orange

authority /u THOr u dEy/

before /bu fOr/
boar (bore) /bOr/
board (bored) /bOrd/
border /bOr dEr/
bore (boar) /bOr/
bored (board) /bOrd/
boring /bO riNg/
born /bOrn/
borrow /bO rOw/

chord (cord) /kOrd/
chorus /kO rus/
coarse (course) /kOrs/
cord (chord) /kOrd/
cork /kOrk/
corn /kOrn/
corner /kOr nEr/
course (coarse) /kOrs/
court /kOrt/

divorce /du vOrs/
door /dOr/
drawer /drOr/

export /eks pOrt/

floor /flOr/
florist /flO rust/
for (fore, four) /fOr/
force /fOrs/
fore (for, four) /fOr/
foreign /fO run/
fork /fOrk/
form /fOrm/
former /fOr mEr/
formula /fOrm yu lu/
fortune /fOr Chun/
forward /fOr wErd/
four (for, fore) /fOr/

gorgeous /gOr jus/

hoarse (horse) /hOrs/
horn /hOrn/
horror /hO rEr/
horse (hoarse) /hOrs/

important /im pOr tunt/

more /mOr/
morning (mourning) /mOr niNg/
mortgage /mOr guj/
mourning (morning) /mOr niNg/

normal /nOr mul/
north /nOrTH/

oar (or) /Or/
or (oar) /Or/
orange /O runj/
orchard /Or ChErd/
orchestra /Or ku stru/
order /Or dEr/
ordinary /Or du ne rEy/
organ /Or gun/
organize /Or gu nIyz/
orient /O rE yunt/
ornament /Or nu munt/

pork /pOrk/
porter /pOr dEr/
portion /pOr Shun/
pour /pOr/

quarter /kwOr dEr/

record /ru kOrd/
reform /ru fOrm/
reporter /ru pOr dEr/
resort /ru zOrt/
roar /rOr/

/ or / is Orange

score /skOr/
short /shOrt/
shorts /shOrts/
sore /sOr/
sort /sOrt/
sport /spOrt/
storage /stO ruj/
store /stOr/
storm /stOrm/
story /stO rEy/
support /su pOrt/
sword /sOrd/

torn /tOrn/
torture / tOr chEr/

war (wore) /wOr/
warm /wOrm/
wart /wOrt/
wharf /wOrf/
wore (war) /wOr/

your /yOr/

authority /u **THOr** u dEy/ [authorities] *noun* 1 the power to make decisions or give commands *The police have the authority to arrest lawbreakers.* 2 someone with power to enforce rules *Stealing will get you into trouble with the authorities.* 3 an expert *My biology professor is an authority on pine trees.* Col: **have it on good authority** – from a trusted source

before /bu **fOr**/ *adv* 1 previously in time *The flight took off before sunrise.* 2 a place in a sequence *A comes before B in the Latin alphabet.* • *prep* 1 earlier than *Come before 3pm.* 2 in front of *She was before me in the line.* • *conj* earlier than a time when *They got home before it rained.* Col: **before long** – soon **Look before you leap.** – *proverb* caution gets more information **the calm before the storm** – peace and quiet prior to activity or stress

boar (bore) /**bOr**/ [boars] *noun* a male pig *Boars are very aggressive in mating season.*

board (bored) /**bOrd**/ [boards, boarded, boarding] *noun* 1 a long flat piece of hard material *The lumber store sells nails and boards.* 2 a group of people who manage a company or organization *He was elected to the company's board of directors.* 3 food included with a place to live *The rental price includes room and board.* • *verb* 1 cover with a board *They boarded the windows before the hurricane arrived.* 2 a fee paid to live somewhere *She boarded a horse outside of town.* 3 to get on a mode of transportation *The plane will board at eight am.* Col: **across the board** – same consideration for all involved **back to the drawing board** – start over, need fresh ideas **blackboard** – class tool **board game** – family activity **board of directors** – group leading a company or organization **bulletin board** – post notices **flat as a board** – small breasts **motherboard** – main electronic circuit board in a computer **on board** – agree with a plan of action **school board** – supervises schools in an area **scoreboard** – shows points in a game **skateboard** – short flat toy for big kids to stand on and ride **snowboard** – winter sport **surfboard** – wave rider **switchboard** – electronic connection of telephone lines **whiteboard** – demonstration tool written on and erased

border /**bOr** dEr/ [borders, bordered, bordering] *noun* the edge of or for decoration *Leave a white border of 2cm around the page.* • *verb* shares and edge *The United States borders Canada along the 49th parallel.* • *adj* about a border *Buffalo is a border town.* Col: **to border on** – touch edges

bore (boar) /**bOr**/ [bores, bored, boring] *verb* 1 tire with dullness *Grammar is boring.* 2 drill a hole *The drill bit bore a hole into the wood.* 3 past tense of *bear* carry *The natives bore the water from the well in oak buckets.* 4 past tense of *bear* give birth to *She bore six children.*

bored (board) /**bOrd**/ [bore, bores, boring] *verb* 1 past tense of *bore* tire with dullness *The teacher bored the students with grammar rules.* 2 past tense of *bore* drill *The holes he bored into the wood were too big for the screws.* • *adj* uninterested *I'm bored stiff teaching grammar.* Col: **bored out of one's mind** – extremely uninterested **bored silly** – extremely uninterested **bored to death** /tears – extremely uninterested

born /**bOrn**/ *verb* past participle of *bear* brought into life *Her baby was born this morning.* Col: **born and raised** – lived and grew up in an area **born out of wedlock** – have an unmarried mother **born to** – destiny or natural ability or qualities **born with a silver spoon in one's mouth** – born rich **not born yesterday** – can't be easily tricked **Were you born in a barn?** – said to a messy person

borrow /bOrOw/ [borrows, borrowed, borrowing] verb that taken needs to be returned *Members borrow books from the library.* `Col:` **on borrowed time** – near death

chord (cord) /kOrd/ [chords, chorded, chording] noun musical term for three or more notes sounded together *He learned 3 or 4 chords on the guitar then he could play simple songs.* • verb play a chord *I can strum and chord on the guitar, but I can't do anything fancy.* `Col:` **strike a chord** – find familiarity with someone

chorus /kOrus/ [choruses] noun 1 repeated portion of a song *I don't remember the whole song, just the chorus.* 2 a group of people singing or harmony *The chorus sings back up for the diva.* 3 words or opinions a group of people say together *A chorus of cheers rose from the happy crowd after the soccer game.*

coarse (course) /kOrs/ [coarser, coarsest] adj 1 rough texture *Sand paper feels coarse.* 2 thick *Coarse hairs grew on the old man's head.* 3 rude or bad-mannered *Adults shouldn't repeat course jokes in front of children.* `Col:` **coarse language** – swearing

cord (chord) /kOrd/ [cords, corded, cording] noun 1 long skinny material used to connect or tie *An electrical cord delivers power to the TV.* 2 short form of corduroy, a heavy cotton fabric with raised long strips of thicker weave *His cords are in the wash.* `Col:` **cut the cord** – end support for a grown child

cork /kOrk/ [corks] noun 1 the stopper on a bottle *Put the cork back in the wine bottle.* 2 the porous lightweight wood bark often used to make bottle stoppers *Cork is a great material for hot plates.* • verb stop the flow of liquid *Cork the bottle.* `Col:` **blow/pop one's cork** – suddenly lose temper **put a cork in it** – be quiet

corn /kOrn/ noun 1 tall grain with rows of yellow and white, sweet, juicy seeds on a long round cob *Hot corn with butter is part of our Thanksgiving meal.* 2 a spot of hardened skin, usually on a foot *The doctor cut the corn off his toe.* `Col:` **an ear/cob of corn** – a unit that comes from the corn plant, one person's serving **corn on the cob** – yellow grain held in the hands to eat **pop corn** – healthy snack, kernels of corn heated until they explode

corner /kOrnEr/ [corners, cornered, cornering] noun 1 the point where two lines or edges meet to make an angle *A triangle has three corners.* 2 a location *We can meet at the corner by the school.* • adj near a corner *Pick up some milk at the corner store.* • verb navigate a turn *She cornered her sports car in third gear.* `Col:` **around the corner** – not far away **backed into a corner** – forced into a difficult position **cut corners** – the fastest way, which may affect the quality of the work **from all corners of the world** – from everywhere **have someone cornered** – control someone in a position that benefits you **have someone in your corner** – to have someone's support **kitty-corner** – the opposite corner of a square **turn the corner** – events get better following a time of difficulty

course (coarse) /kOrs/ [courses, coursed, coursing] noun 1 a route of continuous movement *The ship is traveling on a steady course.* 2 a unit of education discussing one subject *My favorite course is history.* • verb swift movement *The water coursed over Niagara Falls.* `Col:` **as a matter of course** – in natural progression **crash course** – to condense information in order to learn something quickly **in due course** – in proper time **of course** – yes **off course** – in the wrong direction **on course** – in the correct direction **par for the course** – typical, what was expected to happen **run its course** – allow a natural progression even if the probable outcome is negative

court /kOrt/ [courts, courted, courting] *noun* 1 building where justice is decided *I must meet my lawyer at court on Monday.* 2 type of surface the games of tennis and basketball are played on *A grass tennis court is preferred to an asphalt court.* • *verb* woo *He courted her for two years before they got married.* Col: **appear in court** – show up at a scheduled court hearing **have the ball in one's court** – in control of a situation **have the ball in one's court** – in control of a situation **have the ball in one's court** – in control of a situation **have the ball in one's court** – in control of a situation **have one's day in court** – an opportunity to tell one's story **have the ball in one's court** – in control of a situation **take to court** – sue

divorce /du vOrs/ [divorces, divorced, divorcing] *noun* legal dissolution of a marriage *Stephanie's parents got a divorce.* • *verb* process of getting a divorce *I cannot believe they are divorcing.*

door /dOr/ [doors] *noun* the entrance to a building *Keep the door closed, it is cold outside.* Col: **answer the door** – greet who is knocking at the door **at deaths door** – dying **beat a path to someone's door** – many people arriving at one time **behind closed doors** – in privacy **broad as a barn door** – fat or very wide **by the back door** – in a dishonest way **crack the door** – open the door a very small amount **door to door** – visit every house personally **doors open up** – opportunities arise **get a foot in the door** – start at a low position for the opportunity to move to a better position **live next door** – in the neighborhood **next-door neighbor** – lives in the house next to your house **revolving door** – people continuously arriving and leaving **shut the door on** – close the door quickly, in their face **slam the door in someone's face** – angrily shut the door while the other outside person is talking **the boy/girl next door** – an average boy or girl **when one door shuts another will open** – when one opportunity is lost, another will appear

drawer /drOr/ [drawers] *noun* storage compartment with in a piece of furniture *Under garments are often kept in the top drawer.* Col: **drop your drawers** – lower your pants

export /eks pOrt/ [exports, exported, exporting] *verb* to transport abroad *Cars are exported from China.*

floor /flOr/ [floors, floored, flooring] *noun* 1 the base of a room *Hardwood floors are a feature in fine houses.* 2 one level of a building *Her office is on the 30th floor.* • *verb* slang for impress *The performance floored the audience.* Col: **floor it** – press the gas pedal to the floor for a burst of speed **in on the ground floor** – have involvement in a business or project from the beginning **take the floor** – have the full attention of an audience **to floor someone** – impress **walk the floor** – pace back and forth nervously

florist /flO rust/ [florists] *noun* a professional who arranges and sells for flowers *My boyfriend ordered flowers from our favorite florist.*

for (fore, four) /fOr/ *prep* purpose of an action *I had a sandwich for lunch.*

force /fOrs/ [forces, forced, forcing] *noun* the ability to create power *The force of Niagara Falls drives turbines that create hydro electricity.* • *verb* push through with strength *I had to force the key into the lock.* Col: **a force to be reckoned with** – strong personality, powerful enemy or mother nature **force of habit** – behavior that becomes automatic after continuous repetition **in full force** – all members of a group working towards a goal **join forces** – two or more groups come together to work towards a common goal **the driving force** – a person or thing that motivates a group

/ or / is Orange

fore (for, four) /f**Or**/ *adj* located toward the front *Steve Jobs was at the fore-front of technology.* `Col:` **fore-check** – hockey term for hitting an opposing player

foreign /f**O r**un/ *adj* outside of one's native country *Foreign trade drives the national economy.*

fork /f**Ork**/ [forks, forked, forking] *noun* a tool used to assist in eating *A fork has three or four points.* • *verb* move with a fork *The farmer forked the hay to the animals.* `Col:` **fork it out** – serve **fork over** – pay **forked tongue** – liar

form /f**Orm**/ [forms, formed, forming] *noun* 1 shape or outline *The form of a building must consider its function.* 2 document with blank spaces *We filled out the forms to apply for a bank loan.* • *verb* make a shape *The children formed castles in the sand.* `Col:` **form an opinion** – decide one's position on an issue **in any way, shape or form** – by any means **in rare form** – at one's absolute best **true to form** – as expected

former /f**Or** mEr/ *adj* previous, before *Pierre Elliott Trudeau is a former Prime Minister of Canada.* `Col:` **a shadow of one's former self** – wasted away physically emotionally

formula /f**Orm** yu lu/ [formulae or formulas] *noun* 1 liquid milk substitute for babies *My baby is allergic to milk, he can only have formula.* 2 a mathematical structure used to solve problems *A famous formula is E=MC².*

fortune /f**Or** Chun/ [fortunes] *noun* luck and money *He made his fortune in Dawson City when he found gold.* `Col:` **a small fortune** – more than moderate amount of money

forward /f**Or** wErd/ *adj* moving toward the front *The car raced forward to the finish.* `Col:` **bend forward** – tip frontward at the waist **bring something forward** – bring a topic to the attention of others **face forward** – turn to look to the front **go forward with** – continue on **inch forward** – move forward slowly **leap forward** – jump forward quickly **lurch forward** – leap forward suddenly **one step forward, two steps back** – forward progress is not a smooth curve **pass forward** – move an object to the front of a group

four (for, fore) /f**Or**/ [4, fours] *noun* cardinal number between three and five *Four is the number of seasons in Canada.* • *adj* four in number *There are four sides to a square.* `Col:` **a four-letter word** – bad words, swearing, profanity **from the four corners of the world** – from everywhere on earth **on all fours** – on hands and knees **scattered to the four winds** – sent to different places far away from each other **sixty-four dollar question** – the critical answer that solves a big problem

gorgeous /g**Or** jus/ *adj* very attractive *Megan Fox is gorgeous.* `Col:` **drop-dead gorgeous** – extremely beautiful

hoarse (horse) /h**Ors**/ [hoarser, hoarsest] *adj* rough sounding voice *His voice was horse from a bad cold.* `Col:` **hoarse as a crow** – very hoarse

horn /h**Orn**/ [horns] *noun* 1 pointy bones that grow from the head of some animals *Cows, dear and goats have horns.* 2 musical instrument *Trombones and trumpets are horns.* `Col:` **horn in on something** – butt in uninvited **Take the bull by the horns.** – *proverb* confront a problem directly **toot one's own horn** – brat, pay oneself a compliment

horror /h**O r**Er/ [horrors] *noun* feeling of severe fear *I was paralyzed with horror watching the tsunami videos.* `Col:` **a little horror** – poorly behaved child

horse (hoarse) /h**Ors**/ [horses] *noun* mammal in the same family as the donkey and zebra. *Cowboys and Indians ride horses.* `Col:` **back the wrong horse** – trusted the wrong person **beat a dead horse** – wasting of time **charley horse** – painful muscle cramp **closing the barn door after the horse has bolted** – take steps to prevent a problem after the accident has happened   don't spare the horses – hurry   dark horse – unlikely hero   Don't change horses in the middle of the stream. – *proverb* about timing and life changing decisions   Don't look a gift horse in the mouth. – *proverb* there is probably something wrong with it but be gracious   Don't put the cart before the horse. – *proverb* to plan the most logical sequence   eat like a horse – eat a lot   For want of a nail the shoe was lost; for want of a shoe the horse… – *proverb* about fixing little problems before they get big   get off high horse – do not be arrogant   hold your horses – be patient   horse around – being silly   horse and buggy days – olden times   horse of a different color – unique person   horse sense – commons sense   I could eat a horse – very hungry   one-horse race – one entry is expected to win without a challenge   one-horse town – small town   put a horse out to pasture – retire   straight from the horse's mouth – directly from the primary source   Trojan horse – trouble disguised as a gift   You can lead a horse to water, but you can't make it drink. – *proverb*, can't force one to take a suggestion   wild horses couldn't drag away – committed

important /im **pOr** tunt/ *adj* significant value *Books hold a lot of important information.*

more /**mOr**/ *adj* greater in number or size *One hundred dollars is worth more than ten dollars.* Col: be more fun than a barrel of monkeys – a lot of fun   bite off more than one can chew – accepted too much work and can't complete it   couldn't ask for more – received more then you expected   didn't exchange more than three words with – spoke very little with someone   do more harm than good – more damaging than helpful   had more than fair share of – too much of one experience   I couldn't agree more – in complete agreement   less is more – simple is effective   more bang for buck – good deal   more often than not – usually   more or less – approximately   more power to you! – go for it   more than bargained for – overwhelmed   more than meets the eye – more than it appears   more than one can bear – beyond tolerability   more the merrier – everyone is welcome   need I say more? – is more information necessary?   say no more – I understand   that's more like it – that is a more satisfactory answer   there are plenty of fish in the sea – there are many (better) choices for love   there's more than one way to skin a cat – there are multiple ways to solve a problem   wear more than one hat – multi-skilled   you are more than welcome – very welcome

morning (mourning) /**mOr** niNg/ [mornings] *noun* part of the day from dawn to noon *I prefer to get up early and enjoy the morning.* Col: good morning – greeting used before noon   morning, noon and night – activity all the time   morning person – most effective early in the day

mortgage /**mOr** guj/ [mortgages, mortgaged, mortgaging] *noun* debt against a property *The bank approved us for a mortgage and we are buying a house.* • *adj* mortgage related *The mortgage broker gets a percent of the amount borrowed.* • *verb* borrow against property *We mortgaged the house to put the kids through university.*

mourning (morning) /**mOr** niNg/ [mourns, mourned, mourning] *verb* past tense of *mourn* feel great sadness *My mother mourned for years after my father died.* • *noun* period of great sadness *He was in mourning for years after his wife died.*

normal /**nOr** mul/ *noun* the standard *Temperatures below zero are normal in Canada in January.* Col: under normal circumstances – typically

north /**nOrTH**/ *noun* the cardinal point located at 0° *Canada is north of the United States.* **Col:** **up north** – northern area of a country, cottage country

oar (or) /**Or**/ [oars] *noun* a long pole with a wide flat end used to row boats *The oars are stored beside the rowboat.* **Col:** **just one oar in the water** – not thinking clearly

or /**Or**/ *conj* indicate the second of two alternatives *Do you prefer chocolate or vanilla?*

orange /**O** runj/ [oranges] *noun* round citrus fruit orange in color *Oranges grow in warm climates.* • *adj* color made by mixing yellow and red *Oranges are orange.* **Col:** **comparing apples and oranges** – items are too dissimilar for comparison

orchard /**Or** ChErd/ [orchards] *noun* farm with fruit or nut trees *We pick our own apples at the local orchard every fall.*

orchestra /**Or** ku stru/ [orchestras] *noun* formal group of *He plays the violin in the orchestra.*

order /**Or** dEr/ [orders, ordered, ordering] *noun* predictable sequence *The order of numbers is 1 2 3…* • *verb* an official request *Servers ask if they can take your order.* **Col:** **alphabetical order** – organized by the first letter of each word in the order of ABC… **back-order** – sold out items have been ordered from the manufacturer **build to order** – built specifically for each customer **call the meeting to order** – get everyone's attention **could I take your order?** – what can I get you to eat or drink? **follow orders** – do what has been requested **get one's house in order** – organize finances before death **give marching orders** – kick out **in order to do** – one event depends on another being completed **in short order** – quickly **just what the doctor ordered** – exactly what is required for health to improve **keep in order** – organized **numerical order** – starting from lowest to highest number **on order** – requested from the manufactures **out of order** – not functioning **pecking order** – most to least dominant **Ready to order?** – have you decided what you would like? **short order cook** – fast food **tall order** – a significant request

ordinary /**Or** du ne rEy/ *adj* typical or normal events *An ordinary lunch is a sandwich and juice.* **Col:** **out of the ordinary** – atypical

organ /**Or** gun/ [organs] *noun* 1 musical instrument *There is usually an organ at the front of a church.* 2 part of the body that performs a specific function *The stomach, liver and large intestine are separate organs that work together to digest food.* **Col:** **mouth organ** – harmonica, hand-held reed instrument **organ donor** – donates their organs for science or transplant after they die

organize /**Or** gu nIyz/ [organizes, organized, organizing] *verb* arrange *If those files are organized alphabetically it will be easier to find the ones needed later.* 2 coordinate *I'll organize a time and a place for all of us to meet.*

orient /**O** rE yunt/ [orients, oriented, orienting] *pr noun* the countries east and southeast of Europe *Beautiful silk comes from the Orient.* • *verb* become familiar with a new place *A tour of the school oriented the exchange students to their new surroundings.*

ornament /**Or** nu munt/ [ornaments] *noun* decoration *A Christmas tree is decorated with many colorful ornaments.*

pork /**pOrk**/ *noun* meat from a pig *Bacon is a popular cut of pork.* **Col:** **pork and beans** – tinned lunch favorite for children **pork out** – eat too much, too fast

porter /**pOr** dEr/ [porters] *noun* baggage carrier *Hotel porters open doors and carry suitcases.*

portion /**pOr** Shun/ [portions] *noun* a segment within a larger piece *I would* like one portion of lasagna, please. **Col:** **por-tion out something** – serve in measured amounts

pour /pOr/ [pours, poured, pouring] verb transfer a liquid out of a container *Every morning I pour milk on my cereal.* **Col:** **pour heart out** – emotionally vulnerable **pour it on** – add more **pour money down the drain** – waste money **pour on** – over apply **pour oneself into** – give full effort **pour out** – empty **pour out soul** – share intimate details of one's troubles **pour over** – examine in detail **pouring rain** – heavy rain **when it rains it pours** – bad thing happening one after the other

quarter /kwOr dEr/ [¼, quarters, quartered, quartering] noun North American 25¢ coin *There are four quarters in a dollar.* 2 living space *The officer's quarters are nicer than the cook's.* 3 section of a game *There is no time-out after the first quarter.* • verb cut into fourths *Quarter the rations so all four campers get something to eat.* **Col:** **close quarters** – small living space **draw and quarter** – punish severely **quarter of an hour** – 15 minutes **quarterback** – play maker on a football team

record /ru kOrd/ [records, recorded, recording] verb preserve information in writing or electronically *Celine Dion recorded 'My Heart Will Go On' from the Titanic.* **Col:** **in record time** – very quickly **on the record** – marked down and can be shared publicly **off the record** – unofficial **one for the record books** – an extraordinary event **set the record straight** – correct false information **sounds like a broken record** – repeats over and over **track record** – history of accomplishments

reform /ru fOrm/ [reforms, reformed, reforming] noun change something for the better *Education reforms are long overdue.* • verb change for the better *Our school reformed its attendance policy.*

reporter /ru pOr dEr/ [reporters] noun professional writer for a newspaper *News reporters travel all over the world to investigate news stories.*

resort /ru zOrt/ [resorts, resorted, resorting] noun a location designated for holidaying *This winter we are staying at a resort in Mexico.* **Col:** **all inclusive resort** – holiday where all food and activities are included in one price **as a last resort** – desperate, last option **resort to something** – opt for an unethical solution

roar /rOr/ [roars, roared, roaring] noun animal cry *The roar from the lion could be heard throughout the park.* • verb loud, deep noise from animal's throat *Lions roar to warn intruders.* **Col:** **roar at** – yell loudly at a person **roar away** – drive a car away quickly while revving the engine **roar out** – yell loudly

score /skOr/ [scores, scored, scoring] noun record kept in sport to determine a winner *The score was 10 to 3, Toronto won the game.* • verb gaining a point *The player ran down the court and scored the winning basket.* **Col:** **have a score to settle** – a dispute to resolve **know the score** – to understand the facts and implications of a situation **He shoots, he scores!** – hockey term to indicate a goal has been scored

short /shOrt/ [shorter, shortest, shortly] adj describes height *Children are shorter than adults.* • adv in the near future *The party will start shortly.* **Col:** **a day late and a dollar short** – late and inadequate **a few fries short of a Happy Meal** – not smart **a short fuse** – easily angered **Art is long and life is short** – art lasts longer than people **caught short** – not have enough money **draw the short straw** – randomly chosen to do an unpleasant job **Eat my shorts!** – go to hell **fall short** – inadequate **fall short of goal** – fail **few bricks short of a load** – not smart **for short** – an abbreviation **have on a**

/ or / is Orange

short leash – over-monitored by another   in short – abbreviated version   in short order – right away   in short supply – few remain   in the short run – soon future   in the short term – temporary   Life is too short – let go of negativity and be happy   long and the short of it – the important point only   make short work of – quickly   nothing short of – extremely   on short notice – with no advanced warning   one card short of a full deck – not smart   one sandwich short of a picnic – not smart   pull up short – suddenly stop   run short – not have enough   sell short – step over good qualities and dwell on the bad   short and sweet – quickly and simply   short for – abbreviation   short of – not enough   short on – not enough   short with – little patience   short-change – cheat out of money   stop short of – end before   take a long walk off a short pier – go to hell

shorts /shOrts/ [sports] *noun* pants that only go down to the knee *ear shorts in hot weather to keep cool.*

soar (sore) /sOr/ [soars, soared, soaring] *verb* to fly *The birds soar into the horizon.*

sore (soar) /sOr/ [sores, sorer, sorest] *adj* painful feeling *He has a sore foot from stepping on a nail.* • *noun* wound *The sores on her arms are from insect bites.* [Col:] a sore spot – sensitive topic   sight for sore eyes – longed for reunion finally occurs   stick out like a sore thumb – noticeable

sort /sOrt/ [sorts, sorted, sorting] *noun* a group sharing particular characteristics *What sort of pet are you looking for?* • *verb* arrange or organize *Children sort the coins from their piggy banks* [Col:] in bad sorts – angry   out of sorts – not feeling well   sort it out – resolve a problem   sort yourself out – resolve your problems

sport /spOrt/ [sports] *noun* an activity with rules played for pleasure *Basketball is my favorite sport to watch on TV.* [Col:] good sport – plays fair, wins and loses gracefully   sport of kings – horse racing

storage /stOruj/ [stored, storing] *noun* 1 a place to keep extra items *During the winter my boat is kept in storage.* • *verb* the act of storing *I store my books in the attic.* [Col:] cold storage – special cool spaces   in store for someone – ready and waiting for the future

store /stOr/ [stores, stored, storing] *noun* place where items are available for purchase *I need to go to the store for groceries.* • *verb* put away *We store milk in the refrigerator*

storm /stOrm/ [storms, stormed, storming] *noun* weather system with rain, wind or snow *The storm blew down a tree and flooded the basement.* • *verb* strong elements or emotions *She stormed out and slammed the door.* [Col:] dance up a storm – dance for a long time with energy and enthusiasm   eye of the storm – the centre of a hurricane   storm is brewing – coming   taken by storm – conquer swiftly   the calm after the storm – following periods of intensity are periods of peace   the calm before the storm – periods of relaxation occur just before periods of anxiety

story /stOrEy/ [stories] *noun* oral or written account of events (true or fiction) *My favorite story is Peter Pan.* [Col:] a cock-and-bull story – obviously untrue   a likely story – sarcastic for not believable   a sob story – sad story told to gain sympathy, pity party   a tall story – exaggerated   break a story – new story/information   but that's another story – different topic of conversation   end of story – no more discussion   fishy story – the details appear to be untrue   inside story – first hand details no one else knows   it's a long story – many twists and turns along the way   it's the same old story – nothing has changed   it's the story of my life – self pity   make a long story short – leave details out of the story   that's my story and I'm sticking to it – defending a weak statement   There are two sides to every story – *proverb* to consider all the information before making a judgment   top story – most interesting or important story

support /su pOrt/ [supports, supported, supporting] *verb* 1 contribution *Our family supports a child in Africa.* 2 bears or holds up *The walls of the house support the roof.* 3 agree with *The mayor supports environmental issues.* • *noun* being supported *She is a support to her husband.* Col: child support – payments to an ex-spouse

sword /sOrd/ [swords] *noun* weapon with a long pointed blade *The three musketeers carry swords.* Col: a double edged sword – cause benefits and problems   cross swords with someone – argued   fall one one's sword – commit suicide for honor   Live by the sword, die by the sword. – *proverb* one who uses violence can expect to die violently   The pen is mightier than the sword. – *proverb* writing can affect peace better than killing

torn /tOrn/ [tear, torn, tearing] *verb* past participle of *tear* rip *The shirt was torn down the centre.* • *adj* cut *The torn cushion cover was sent out for repair.* Col: torn between – trying to make a difficult choice   torn up – emotionally upset

torture /tOr ChEr/ [tortures, tortured, torturing] *noun* inflict pain until information is extracted *Torture is a cruel way to extract information.* • *verb* the act of torture *The soldiers tortured the prisoner.* Col: torture into doing – apply physical or emotional pain to control

war (wore) /wOr/ [wars] *noun* armed conflict between two groups *War is always taking place somewhere in the world.* Col: All is fair in love and war. – *proverb* do whatever is necessary to win   all-out war – total war   an act of war – hostile acts during war times   declare war – formal announcement from one country to another   war of words – verbal argument

warm /wOrm/ [warms, warmed, warming, warmer, warmest] *adj* temperature opposite to cold *The sun is warm in the spring but hot in the summer.* • *verb* becoming warm *My hands are cold so I am warming them over the fire.* Col: bench warmer – a player who doesn't often get to play   warm up – pre-lesson activities, stretch or apply heat   warm up to – start to like someone

wart /wOrt/ [warts] *noun* skin growth *My son had warts on his fingers but they went away.* Col: warts and all – accept all aspects of a person, the good and the bad

wharf /wOrf/ [wharfs] *noun* dock for ships *My husband likes to fish off the wharf.*

wore (war) /wOr/ [wears, wore, wearing] *verb* past tense of *wear* put on clothes *She wore the same jeans yesterday.* Col: wore me out – made me tired

your /yOr/ {also said /yEr/ see Purple} [yours] *adj* the possessive form of you *A dog can be your best friend.*

/ or / is Orange

THOMPSON LANGUAGE CENTRE
PRODUCT LIST

BOOKS

ENGLISH IS STUPID, STUDENTS ARE NOT — Comprehensive guide for English **pronunciation** and **conversation** skills. Instructors who have avoided teaching pronunciation, this book is for you. Its pattern-based approach is simple and effective. Start teaching **Speaking** immediately. (Amazon)

THE ENGLISH PHONETIC ALPHABET WORKBOOK — Companion to Chapter One of *English is Stupid, Students are Not* contains over 200 photocopiable, **individual sound exercises** to instill the 40 sounds of General American (GA). GA is learners' most preferred accent. (Amazon)

HOW DO YOU SAY? — Dictionary of **expressions** rooted in the 2,000 most common English words. English spelling is illogical. TLC connects writing to speaking using colors. The sound is in the color! *How Do You Say?* provides functional access to native-like pronunciation, spelling and fluency. (Amazon)

BACKPACKER'S GUIDE TO TEACHING ENGLISH — The Backpacker booklets on **Pronunciation, Conversation** and **Fluency** boil down the speaking program introduced in *English is Stupid, Students are Not* with more tools to empower casual instructors making a difference for English learners. (Amazon)

SPEAKING MADE SIMPLE — This stand alone, 360-page, step by step Speaking Course Curriculum is treasured by a wide range of English teaching facilities around the world. An institutional purchase $250 CAN available only as a printable, photocopiable PDF from info@thompsonlanguagecenter.com

CLASSROOM MATERIALS

POSTERS — If a picture says 1,000 words, seven posters say 7,000! Check out the *Roadmap to Fluency*, *EPA Periodic Table*, the *Thompson Vowel Chart*, *Vennglish* and more colorful wall poster **PDFs** that print up to 2'X 3. Poster PDFs $7.99 CAN each info@thompsonlanguagecenter.com

FLASHCARD PDFs

- Past Tense 'ed' – 24 illustrated verb cards with multiple samples of /d/, /t/ and /id/
- Third Person Singular S – 26 verb-picture cards showcasing the three s-endings pronunciations
- Plural S /s/, /z/, /iz/ – 26 noun-picture cards with a variety of plural s pronunciation endings
- English Phonetic Alphabet – 125 units feature multiple examples of crazy English spelling in all 16 pronunciation families.

Flashcards PDFs $9.99 CAN per set contact info@thompsonlanguagecenter.com

ONLINE COURSES

The **WizTango.com** education platform hosts *The Effective Communicator* and *Opinions Matter* TLC's facilitated, English-learning courses for businesspeople and educators. The Swedish study circle *learn by doing* model combined with Thompson Language Center content quickly produces confident, effective communicators ready and able to contribute to the global conversation. WizTango.com

www.ingramcontent.com/pod-product-compliance
Lightning Source LLC
Chambersburg PA
CBHW071659160426
43195CB00012B/1521